THE BRICS COALITION AND A NEW GLOBAL ORDER

THE BRICS COALITION AND A NEW GLOBAL ORDER

Akhilesh Chandra Prabhakar, PhD

First edition published 2026

Apple Academic Press Inc.
1265 Goldenrod Circle, NE,
Palm Bay, FL 32905 USA

760 Laurentian Drive, Unit 19,
Burlington, ON L7N 0A4, Canada

CRC Press
2385 NW Executive Center Drive,
Suite 320, Boca Raton FL 33431

4 Park Square, Milton Park,
Abingdon, Oxon, OX14 4RN, UK

Apple Academic Press exclusively co-publishes with CRC Press, an imprint of Taylor & Francis Group, LLC

Library and Archives Canada Cataloguing in Publication

CIP data on file with Canada Library and Archives

Library of Congress Cataloging-in-Publication Data

CIP data on file with US Library of Congress

ISBN: 978-1-779642-92-9 (hbk)
ISBN: 978-1-779642-93-6 (ebk)

DOI: 10.1201/9781779642936

About the Author

Dr. Akhilesh Chandra Prabhakar

Prof. (Dr.) Akhilesh Chandra Prabhakar is an eminent economist, author, and educator with over two decades of extensive international academic and research experience across Asia, Africa, and the Pacific. Currently, he holds the position of Professor of Economics at the University of Technology, Lae, Morobe, Papua New Guinea. Dr. Prabhakar completed his MPhil and PhD in Economics at Jawaharlal Nehru University (JNU), New Delhi—India's premier institution, specializing in development economics, international trade, and financial systems.

Throughout his distinguished career, he has held professorial appointments at prestigious institutions such as the University of Technology (Papua New Guinea), Universiti Utara Malaysia, Hankuk University of Foreign Studies (South Korea), and several leading Ethiopian universities including Addis Ababa University, University of Gondar, Debre Berhan University, and Debre Tabor University. In India, he has made significant contributions to academia as Professor at the University of Petroleum & Energy Studies and Lovely Professional University. He also served as Director of the Global South Social Networks (GSSN) and was formerly Editor-in-Chief of the *International Journal of Asian Social Sciences.*

Dr. Prabhakar's scholarly engagements extend to Kenya, Uganda, Tanzania, and Singapore, enriching his comparative research perspective. His research portfolio primarily addresses sustainable development, industrial economics, and global economic transformations. Leveraging his wide-ranging cross-continental experiences, Dr. Prabhakar provides valuable insights into pressing economic debates and is recognized as a distinguished voice in both academic and policy domains.

Contents

Acknowledgments

I extend my profound gratitude to Dr. Ora Renagi, OL, Vice-Chancellor of the Papua New Guinea University of Technology (Lae), and Mr. Mathew Ku'usa, Head of the Department of Business Studies at UoT, for granting me the privilege of serving the University of Technology. I deeply appreciate Prof. Dato' Wira Dr. Mohamed Mustafa bin Ishak, Vice-Chancellor of UUM, for giving e the opportunity to serve UUM.

My heartfelt gratitude goes to Prof. Dr. Yusnidah Bt Ibrahim, Dean of COB, whose encouragement inspired me to undertake the writing of this book. I am equally thankful to Dr. Siti Aznor Ahmad, Deputy Dean of SEFB, Dr. Noor Azam, Head of the Department of Economics, and all my colleagues and nonacademic staff, including the Assistant Registrar of SEFB, UUM, for their invaluable support.

I also owe special debt to distinguished scholars and thinkers such as Prof. Prabhat Patnaik (former member of the Planning Commission of India), Jayati Ghosh (JNU), Michael P. Todaro, Stephen C. Smith, David Korten, Samir Amin, and Stewart Francis, whose work profoundly shaped my understanding of poverty, income inequality, and colonial legacies. My sincere thanks go to many reviewers in Malaysia and abroad who provided insightful comments, constructive criticisms, and thoughtful suggestions that greatly enriched this book.

Furthermore, I wish to acknowledge my current and former colleagues and friends for their invaluable input, particularly Dr. Mohammad Azam (Pakistan), Dr. Rabiul Islam (Bangladesh), Prof. Ashish Saha (India), Dr. Ahmad Sahidah (Indonesia), Dr. B. Bakhtiyar (Iran), and Dr. Abdullah Sumrahadi (Indonesia). I am especially grateful to the several thousand students I have had the privilege of teaching. Their immediate reactions—whether of puzzlement or enlightenment—have taught me invaluable lessons about how to effectively teach economics.

Finally, I extend my deepest thanks to my mother, Laxmi Devi; my life partner, Julie Rani; and my beloved children, Raj and Neel. Without their unwavering support, patience, and encouragement, the completion of this book would not have been possible.

I warmly invite suggestions for improvement from fellow educators and readers, as your feedback will be invaluable in refining this work.

Akhilesh Chandra Prabhakar, PhD

Preface

As we advance through the 21st century, the architecture of global power and influence is undergoing transformative shifts. The BRICS coalition—comprising Brazil, Russia, India, China, and South Africa—has emerged as a formidable force, challenging entrenched paradigms and reshaping the contours of the international order. Each BRICS nation represents a distinct fusion of political, economic, and cultural ambitions, forming a bloc whose shared vision and cooperative endeavors extend far beyond regional interests to impact the broader global landscape.

This volume seeks to examine the ways in which BRICS nations are redefining their roles within the modern global framework through economic integration, political alignment, and cultural exchange. Each chapter explores how these countries navigate their individual and collective challenges while simultaneously contributing to a multipolar world order that resists singular hegemonic dominance. Our aim is to elucidate not only the intricate strategic interactions within BRICS but also to introduce the broader influence of this coalition on key global issues such as sustainable development, technological innovation, and geopolitical equilibrium.

The 21st century presents a spectrum of urgent global challenges, from climate change and economic inequality to evolving trade policies. BRICS nations address these complexities both as sovereign states and as a cohesive alliance, crafting innovative paths of cooperation that call into question conventional models of development and diplomacy. This book aspires to furnish readers with a nuanced analysis of BRICS' ambitions, strategic approaches, and its potential to forge a more equitable and inclusive global order.

The BRICS Coalition and a New Global Order is designed to provide essential insights for academics, policymakers, and students of international relations and development studies who seek a deeper understanding of this evolving geopolitical landscape. The perspectives shared herein not only reflect the challenges facing BRICS but also illuminate the transformative opportunities that lie ahead.

—Akhilesh Chandra Prabhakar
University of Technology

CHAPTER 1

BRICS: Toward a New Global Order in the 21st Century

ABSTRACT

This chapter critically examines the shifting contours of international economic relations in the context of an emerging tripolar world order, with BRICS positioned at the epicenter of this geopolitical reconfiguration. As the forces of deglobalization intensify, the global economy appears poised to splinter into three dominant trading blocs, respectively led by the United States, China, and the European Union. This fragmentation is emblematic of escalating geopolitical rivalries—most notably between Washington and Beijing—and marks a decisive departure from the post-Cold War liberal economic consensus. European Commission President Ursula von der Leyen's pronouncement that "The West as we knew it no longer exists" poignantly underscores the gravity of this transformation. Conceived as a counterweight to Western economic hegemony, the BRICS consortium is increasingly asserting itself as a pivotal architect in the remaking of global governance. The projected U.S.-led bloc is expected to encompass the majority of the Western Hemisphere alongside key allies in Asia and the Middle East. Meanwhile, the China-centric bloc is likely to draw in Russia, large swathes of Asia, major African economies, and segments of Latin America. The comparatively smaller EU bloc comprises European nations and strategic partners such as Turkey and Ukraine. Forecasts suggest this economic tri-polarization could exact a cumulative cost of up to $3.8 trillion between 2025 and 2029, owing to heightened tariffs, geopolitical friction, and disrupted supply chains. With the global economy potentially unable to regain its former trajectory, this nascent world order may well precipitate irreversible structural transformations in global trade and power dynamics.

The BRICS Coalition and a New Global Order: Akhilesh Chandra Prabhakar (Author)
2026 Apple Academic Press, Inc. Co-published with CRC Press (Taylor & Francis)

DOI: 10.1201/9781779642936-1

1.1 INTRODUCTION

The 21st century has heralded a transformative epoch in global politics and economics, with the BRICS nations—Brazil, Russia, India, China, and South Africa—emerging as pivotal actors in the reconfiguration of the global order (Prabhakar, 2020a).

Currently, the BRICS nations collectively account for approximately 50% of global GDP—compared to just 21% for the G7—when measured in terms of Purchasing Power Parity (PPP). With the admission of new members, this share is projected to increase to 55% by 2030. Notably, BRICS and its partner economies represented nearly 28% of China's total foreign trade during the first half of 2025. Within this framework, China and its economic allies have been actively exchanging a diverse range of industrial goods, including chemicals, metallurgical products, electronic components, petrochemical equipment, metalworking machinery, and other capital-intensive commodities. In the first six months of 2025 alone, China's trade with BRICS member states reached 6.11 trillion yuan (approximately USD 855 billion), while the country simultaneously registered a global trade surplus exceeding USD 1 trillion. Intra-bloc trade volumes between BRICS members and their partners grew by 3.9% year-on-year during this period, underscoring the accelerating pace of regional economic integration. This upward trend reflects a broader strategic trajectory in which China and its BRICS partners are deepening economic interdependence and expanding cross-border trade and settlement frameworks.

In the broader context of the 21st-century global economy, few developments rival the transformative impact of China's meteoric rise. Over the past four decades, China has transitioned from a rigid, centrally planned economy to a dynamic socialist market system, positioning itself as a dominant force in global trade, manufacturing, and industrial innovation. A landmark moment in this transformation is China's recent overtaking of the United States in terms of GDP measured at PPP.

According to World Bank estimates (2024), China's GDP (PPP) has reached USD 33.01 trillion, surpassing the U.S. figure of USD 26.95 trillion, despite the United States carrying a public debt burden exceeding USD 38 trillion. This is far more than a statistical milestone; it signifies a fundamental redistribution of global economic influence, compelling a reassessment of prevailing international financial architectures and governance models.

1.1.1 A TECTONIC SHIFT IN GLOBAL ECONOMIC DYNAMICS

China's emergence as the world's largest economy by PPP constitutes a seismic realignment in the global economic order. While the United States continues to lead in nominal GDP—with 2025 projections approaching USD 30.5 trillion—China's vast industrial capacity, coupled with relatively lower domestic price levels, elevates its PPP-adjusted GDP to an estimated USD 40.7 trillion. Leveraging this economic advantage, China is asserting greater influence in reforming global governance structures and has played a central role in expanding the BRICS New Development Bank, which now accounts for roughly 70% of the bloc's total GDP.

This chapter introduces the BRICS coalition, tracing its origins and critically analyzing its evolving role within a multipolar world. The power dynamics of the global system are increasingly shifting away from Western-dominated institutions, thereby creating opportunities for the emergence of more inclusive governance structures. With its diverse membership and ambitious objectives, BRICS stands as a formidable challenge to established international frameworks. Moreover, this chapter explores the group's potential to disrupt hegemonic structures, offering a fresh and compelling narrative for global political and economic engagement.

This chapter underscores the transformative potential of strategic collaboration among emerging powers in shaping a multipolar world. The coalition of Brazil, Russia, India, China, and South Africa represents not merely an alliance of nations, but a visionary pursuit of an equitable and inclusive global order aimed at addressing the multifaceted economic, political, and environmental challenges of our era. Through this coalition, BRICS envisions an international system that transcends traditional power asymmetries and seeks to create pathways for greater parity in global decision-making.

Employing a meticulous blend of historical context, incisive analysis, and forward-looking perspectives, this work elucidates the achievements, complexities, and aspirations of BRICS as it seeks to redefine global governance, advance sustainable development, and foster cooperation across diverse cultures and regions. In examining the trajectory of these nations, this chapter critically engages with the broader implications of BRICS' rise, probing both its successes and its limitations.

In an era marked by uncertainties and rapid transformations, BRICS' role in championing systemic reforms and elevating the voice of the Global

South assumes profound significance. The coalition's unwavering commitment to innovation, equality, and unity exemplifies that the construction of a new global order is not a distant aspiration but an unfolding reality. As these nations work in concert to address global challenges, their actions carry the potential to reshape the international landscape in ways that reflect a more inclusive vision for the future.

For policymakers, scholars, business leaders, and globally engaged citizens, this chapter serves as an indispensable guide to understand the forces reshaping international relations, global economics, and sustainable development. It inspires readers to not only comprehend the dynamic changes occurring but to actively engage with the unfolding transformations that are defining the trajectory of the 21st century (Prabhakar, 2020b). By charting the path of BRICS, this work encourages a deeper engagement with the profound shifts that are recalibrating the global order and calls on individuals to play a role in shaping the future of our interconnected world.

Currently, the BRICS nations collectively account for approximately 50% of global GDP when measured by Purchasing Power Parity (PPP), in contrast to just 21% for the G7 economies (World Bank, 2025b).

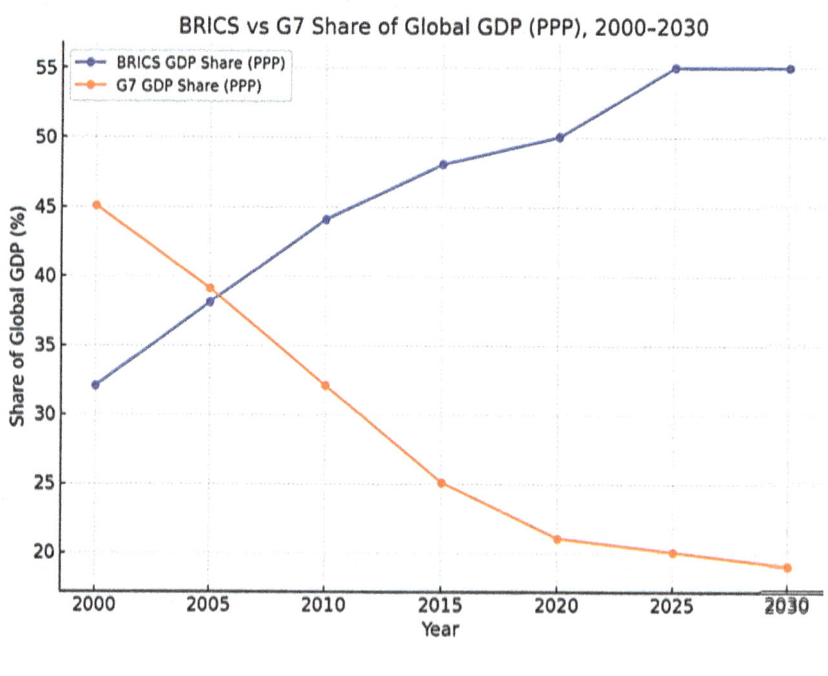

With the admission of new members, the BRICS share is projected to rise to 55% by 2030, signaling a profound shift in the global economic hierarchy (UNCTAD, 2025). In recent years, BRICS and its partner economies have expanded trade in a diverse spectrum of industrial goods, including chemicals, metallurgical products, electronic components, petrochemical equipment, and metalworking machinery—commodities that are both capital- and technology-intensive (OECD, 2025).

In the first half of 2025, China's trade with BRICS member states reached 6.11 trillion yuan (approximately USD 855 billion), constituting 28% of its total foreign trade (Administration, January-June 2025). Over the same period, China recorded a global trade surplus surpassing USD 1 trillion, while intra-BRICS trade volumes rose by 3.9% year-on-year, reflecting the bloc's accelerating economic integration (World Bank, 2025a). This expansion underscores a strategic trajectory of deepening economic interdependence, cross-border settlement mechanisms, and collective resistance to unilateral trade restrictions.

According to the latest World Bank estimates, China's GDP in PPP terms reached USD 33.01 trillion in June 2025, surpassing the United States' USD 26.95 trillion (Bank, 2025b). In contrast, the U.S. public debt has exceeded USD 38 trillion, while the European Union has experienced persistently weak GDP growth—averaging less than 1.2% annually since the 2008 global financial crisis (IMF, 2025). This divergence is more than a statistical anomaly; it represents a structural redistribution of global economic influence, necessitating a reassessment of prevailing international financial architectures and governance models (Stiglitz, 2023).

China's emergence as the world's largest economy by PPP constitutes a fundamental reconfiguration of the global economic order. Although the United States retains leadership in nominal GDP—with 2025 projections nearing USD 30.5 trillion—China's vast industrial capacity and relatively lower domestic price levels elevate its PPP-adjusted GDP to approximately USD 40.7 trillion (World Bank, 2025a). This economic advantage has empowered China to exert greater influence over global governance reforms, including the expansion of the BRICS New Development Bank, which now accounts for roughly 70% of the bloc's aggregate GDP (NDB, 2025).

BRICS is progressively moving toward local currency settlements in intra-bloc trade, reducing reliance on the U.S. dollar:

- In H1 2025, over 25% of bilateral trade between China and Russia was settled in yuan (Source: facilitated by energy transactions Wikipedia).
- India and Brazil have initiated limited rupee-real settlement arrangements.
- China's CIPS (Cross-Border Interbank Payment System) has expanded globally, linking over 1000 financial institutions as a yuan-based alternative to SWIFT.

TABLE 1.1 China and the United States (GDP in Trillion US$).

Latest Data Appendix				
Indicator	**Year**	**China**	**United States**	**Source**
GDP (PPP, USD trillion)	2024	38.19	29.18	World Bank
Nominal GDP (USD trillion)	2025 proj.	~27.4	~30.5	IMF
Global GDP share (PPP) – G7	2024	–	28%	IMF
Global GDP share (PPP) – BRICS+	2024	–	40–44%	IMF/BRICS portal
Gross national debt (USD trillion)	Aug 2025	–	37%	AP/Treasury
Arable land (% total)	Latest	11–13%	–	World Bank
Extreme poverty rate	2020	<1%	–	World Bank
UMIC poverty line rate	2021	17%	–	World Bank

Over the past four decades, China has transformed from a rigid, centrally planned economy into a dynamic, innovation-driven 'socialist market system' integrating technological, financial, and industrial modernization.

China successfully leads the "Fifth Industrial Revolution," which has global implications. First, it provides a replicable model for integrating advanced technologies, human-centric development, and sustainability at scale. Second, it raises critical questions about the resilience of state-led innovation models in a volatile global system. As nations worldwide seek to blend innovation with sustainability and inclusion, China's path may serve both as inspiration and as a test case for future industrial paradigms.

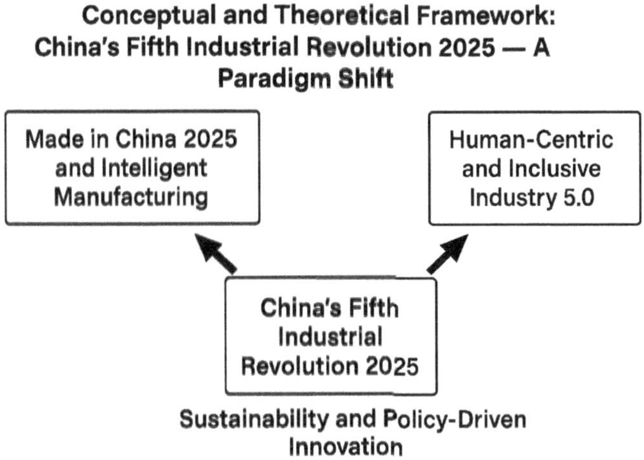

FIGURE 1.1 China's Fifth Industrial Revolution 2025.

The country's developmental trajectory is marked by its ability to mobilize the capacities of 1.4 billion people, despite possessing only 7% of the world's arable land. It has achieved a national poverty rate of less than 1%, implemented universal access to education and healthcare, maintained low inflation, and established itself as a central node in global supply chains—delivering affordable manufactured goods to markets worldwide (Huang, 2024).

China's success in leveraging trade, technology, and infrastructure to reshape international economic flows illustrates the transformative potential of strategic state-led development in the 21st century. As the BRICS bloc consolidates its economic weight, the shift in global economic governance away from G7 dominance appears not only probable but inevitable. The economic integration of BRICS spans strategic rearrangements:

- BRICS now functions as an institutional nucleus for the Global South, consolidating major portions of global GDP (PPP) and supply chains.
- It is leveraging collective influence in multilateral arenas—advocating for development finance equity, technology transfer, and global governance reforms.
- Expansion into energy-rich regions, such as Saudi Arabia and the UAE, enhances BRICS's geopolitical footprint and fiscal capacity through sovereign wealth influence.

- BRICS's growing prominence undermines the post–Cold War unipolar paradigm, paving the way for a multi-polar world in which competition and cooperation coexist across power centers.

1.2 ORIGINS AND EVOLUTION OF BRICS

The acronym BRICS, first coined by economist Jim O'Neill in 2001, initially underscored the burgeoning economic potential of Brazil, Russia, India, and China. These nations, distinguished by their substantial populations, abundant natural resources, and emerging market status, were perceived as the harbingers of future global economic expansion. The inclusion of South Africa in 2010 solidified the group's position as a coalition of preeminent emerging economies. This section explores the historical trajectory of BRICS, examining its formation, the underlying motivations behind its inception, and its gradual emergence as both a geopolitical and economic powerhouse. As these emerging nations—representing three distinct continents: Asia, Africa, and Latin America—endeavor to transition from their historically peripheral roles, having been colonized for centuries by Western imperial and colonial powers; have acquired significant technological and financial capacities. This transformation has positioned them as key global actors. The trajectory of BRICS' growth reflects the broader shift in the global balance of power, wherein influence is steadily moving from the West toward the Global South.

1.3 THE BRICS VISION

The vision of BRICS transcends mere cooperation in the realms of economy, technology, finance, trade, investment, security, health, education, agriculture, and infrastructure development. It embodies a strategic commitment to cultivate a more inclusive global economy, one that more accurately reflects the interests of emerging and developing nations. This section delves into the core objectives of BRICS: advocating for the reform of international financial institutions, such as the World Bank, the International Monetary Fund (IMF), the World Trade Organization (WTO), and the United Nations (UN) Security Council, while challenging the dominance of Western-led economic paradigms and striving to establish a more equitable system of global governance. The group's vision places a strong emphasis on promoting sustainable development, fostering peace, and encouraging multilateral cooperation among emerging economies, thereby positioning BRICS as a pivotal force in the pursuit of a more just and balanced world order. Through initiatives like the New Development Bank (NDB) and the Contingent Reserve Arrangement (CRA), BRICS endeavours to address critical global challenges, including poverty, inequality, and environmental sustainability.

1.4 HISTORICAL BACKGROUND OF WORLD ORDER

The concept of a "new world order" has long been a subject of profound contemplation and speculation, spanning decades of discourse within the realm of international relations. It encapsulates the evolving geopolitical landscape and the shifting dynamics that define contemporary global interactions. At the core of this notion lies the idea of a departure from the erstwhile dominance exerted by Western colonial and imperial powers—dominance that permeated military might, currency hegemony, trade supremacy, and technological leadership. In its place, a new narrative emerges, one that highlights the rise of novel global forces and interconnections.

The prevailing unipolar economic structure, which has been meticulously orchestrated by the United States since the conclusion of the Cold War, now finds itself navigating a period of transition. Historically, the global stage was divided into two distinct spheres: the erstwhile 'Soviet-led Socialist Bloc' (Prabhakar, 2015a) and the Capitalist-Imperialist Bloc, dominated by the United States in the aftermath of World War II.

The post-World War II 'world economy' was meticulously crafted by the United States, leveraging cutting-edge technologies and sophisticated financial mechanisms to catalyze investments and promote trade. This endeavor was underpinned by the establishment of three foundational frameworks: the IMF, the World Bank, and the General Agreement on Tariffs and Trade (GATT), which later evolved into the WTO. These institutions formed the bedrock of the global economic architecture that emerged in the wake of the Second World War, facilitating the steady rise of international trade and capital flows within a capitalist framework.

These frameworks served as conduits for the propagation of principles such as trade liberalization, privatization, marketization, corporatization, financialization, and the globalization of the economy, all under the pretext of enhancing economic efficiency and fostering global competitiveness. Through these mechanisms, a robust structure was meticulously laid out, fostering the expansion of global trade and the proliferation of capitalist ideals, shaping the trajectory of the world economy for decades.

Consequently, the United States has adroitly maintained its pre-eminence across various domains, exercising supremacy in military capabilities, technological innovation, currency dominance, energy control, trade, financial leadership, geopolitical influence, and cultural hegemony. This comprehensive hegemonic stance has played an instrumental role in shaping the global order, solidifying America's role as a central actor on the international stage.

The United States has actively cultivated the economic advancement of its allies through strategic initiatives, exemplified by the Marshall Plan, which sought to rebuild Western Europe after the devastation of World War II. Substantial financial assistance was also directed toward nations like Japan and South Korea during the Korean War, underscoring America's commitment to fostering the economic prosperity of its allies.

In essence, the hegemonic grip exerted by Western nations, including the United States and Europe, across domains such as politics, economics, trade, finance, technology, currency, military affairs, education, and culture stands as a testament to their enduring dominance over the past four centuries.

Western powers have historically wielded profound influence across a broad spectrum of global affairs, ranging from trade and finance to technology and military power. This hegemonic stature is underpinned by six pillars: trade, finance, technology, currency (primarily anchored by the US dollar), energy governance, and military dominance. This section seeks to meticulously examine each of these pillars to discern the scope and magnitude of Western ascendancy in the global arena.

1. **Trade:** Western nations have unequivocally dominated global trade. They have shaped international trade terms through the creation of agreements and institutions such as the WTO. Historically, these nations have been the primary exporters of goods and services, bestowing them with substantial influence in determining global trade policies. Moreover, leveraging their economic clout, Western powers have skillfully negotiated favorable trade agreements, further strengthening their economic positions.

2. **Finance:** Western nations, particularly the United States and its European counterparts, have long been at the forefront of global finance. By spearheading the establishment of international financial institutions such as the IMF and the World Bank, they have played pivotal roles in providing financial aid and stabilizing economies worldwide. Furthermore, with some of the largest and most influential banks and financial institutions, Western nations command an unparalleled position in the global financial ecosystem.

3. **Technology:** Western nations have been the vanguard of technological innovation, housing numerous esteemed corporations that have driven advancements in fields such as information technology, biotechnology, and telecommunications. Through substantial investments in research and development, these nations have maintained a competitive edge in the global technological arena.

4. **Currency (Dollar):** The US dollar has long reigned as the dominant global currency, securing its status as the world's reserve currency. Western nations, particularly the United States, have strategically exploited the dollar's preeminent position, allowing for easier borrowing and the financing of deficits. This has not only bolstered economic stability but also granted Western powers significant influence over global financial markets and international trade.

5. **Energy Governance:** Historically, Western countries have exerted considerable influence over global energy markets, both as major consumers and producers of energy resources. By leveraging control over energy reserves, they have secured favorable trade agreements and maintained dominance over energy markets. Additionally, Western nations have led the development of renewable energy technologies, positioning themselves strategically in the transition to sustainable energy systems.

6. **Military Supremacy:** Western powers, notably the United States, have meticulously maintained formidable military forces, enabling them to project power and influence across the globe. Their military prowess has been instrumental in shaping geopolitical landscapes, with NATO serving as a key instrument in maintaining global security and regional stability.

The hegemonic dominance of Western nations across these six pillars—trade, finance, technology, currency, energy governance, and military power—has solidified their preeminent role in shaping global affairs, marking them as the central actors in contemporary international dynamics.

However, the historical supremacy of Western nations is now undergoing a significant transformation, as emerging economies like China and India increasingly challenge the established hegemony of the West. The second decade of the 21st century has witnessed the emergence of a multipolar world order, underscored by shifting economic and geopolitical power.

Statistics from the World Bank underscore this transition, revealing a decline in the United States' share of global GDP from 30.6% in 2000 to 24.3% in 2015. Simultaneously, the United States' share of international trade and investment has diminished, signaling a waning of its global economic dominance.

Despite the resilience of the US dollar as the cornerstone of the global financial system, the United States is grappling with a host of economic challenges, including recessionary trends, rising inflation, and growing unemployment. These challenges have substantially diminished America's capacity to act as the principal engine driving global economic growth. In response, the United States has increasingly sought to externalize its domestic economic woes, endeavoring to preserve its competitiveness in the global economic arena.

In sum, the dawn of the 21st century has heralded a discernible recalibration of global power dynamics, signaling the decline of Western dominance and the rise of emerging economies. The narrative of the coming years will likely center around the evolving interplay between established and rising powers, charting the course of a new global order.

1.5 FOUR HISTORICAL EVENTS

Four seminal historical events have significantly reshaped the global economic architecture, precipitating a notable shift in the balance of power from the West to the East.

The first of these transformative moments was the collapse of the Bretton Woods system in 1973, a pivotal juncture in global economic history. Confronted with a trifecta of energy shortages, food crises, and foreign currency volatility, the United States was compelled to transition to a floating exchange rate system. This strategic pivot, essential to safeguarding the dollar's hegemonic position, required extensive coordination of macroeconomic policies among advanced economies to mitigate the ensuing instability.

The second event, the financial crisis that gripped the Four Asian Tigers during 1997–1998, catalyzed the implementation of the 'Washington Consensus' globalization framework. This initiative, adopted by the IMF and the World Bank, marked a paradigm shift toward economic liberalization, pushing for structural reforms, and market-driven policies in emerging economies.

Thirdly, China's meteoric rise as a global economic powerhouse has sparked the formation of regional economic and trade blocs spanning Asia, Latin America, and Africa. These alliances are vigorously committed to reshaping the global economic paradigm in favor of developing nations, marking a clear pivot from the Western-dominated order.

The fourth pivotal event, the 2007–2008 financial crisis, coupled with the subsequent sovereign debt crisis in Europe in 2010, profoundly challenged the invulnerability previously associated with developed economies. The fallout from these crises led to the reimagining of global governance structures, fostering the rise of regional economic governance frameworks such as the multilateralization of the Chiang Mai Initiative and the strengthening of the BRICS coalition. These developments have underscored the shifting locus of global economic influence, with Eastern powers asserting increasing control over economic and geopolitical affairs.

Collectively, these defining historical moments have precipitated a paradigmatic shift in the global economic landscape, recalibrating power dynamics and ushering in the ascendancy of Eastern influence on the global stage.

In 2022, the global order was further upended by a combination of geopolitical, technological, and societal transformations. This emergent paradigm reflected an adaptive response to the complexities of a highly interconnected and rapidly changing world.

Central to this new global order was a recalibration of power dynamics, wherein traditional economic and political giants—such as the United States, China, and the European Union (EU)—found themselves navigating a multipolar world. In this emerging environment, new powerhouses such as India, Brazil, and nations across Southeast Asia began to exert a discernible influence on global affairs, shaping a more diversified global landscape. This multipolarity fostered both collaboration and competition, creating a dynamic interplay of interests that defied the hegemonic dominance once enjoyed by the West.

Technology emerged as a crucial driver in the reshaping of this global order. The rapid proliferation of digital connectivity, artificial intelligence, and blockchain technology (Prabhakar, 2015b) spurred unprecedented innovation, challenging traditional industries and governance structures. Nations and corporations adept at leveraging these technologies gained a competitive edge, though they simultaneously confronted emerging ethical and security challenges in an increasingly digitized world.

The COVID-19 pandemic, an unforeseen disruptor, acted as a catalyst for profound reflection on global cooperation and resilience. The pandemic revealed the interconnectedness of nations and compelled a new level of international collaboration. From vaccine distribution to the revitalization of healthcare infrastructure and the stabilization of economic systems, multilateral institutions such as the World Health Organization (WHO) and the UN underwent significant reforms to address the complex challenges of the 21st century.

Environmental sustainability became another cornerstone of the evolving global order. Confronted with the urgency of climate change, nations are committed to ambitious targets for reducing carbon emissions and promoting renewable energy. The Paris Agreement, a vital component of global environmental governance, gained renewed momentum as nations rallied to mitigate the impacts of climate change and work toward a more sustainable future.

Concurrently, cultural and societal movements, advocating for social justice, gender equality, and human rights, gained significant traction. From the #MeToo movement to Black Lives Matter and youth-led climate activism, these grassroots efforts called for a reimagining of societal norms and compelled governments and institutions to address entrenched inequities. These movements were instrumental in reshaping the moral and ethical foundations of global governance.

In this emerging world order, the criteria for success extended beyond mere economic or military dominance. Instead, the ability to adapt to change, foster innovation, and engage in collaborative efforts to tackle shared global challenges became central metrics. Cooperation, resilience, and inclusivity emerged as guiding principles for navigating an uncertain future, as nations sought to build a world that embraced sustainability, peace, and equity for generations to come.

The United States finds itself at a crossroads in this evolving global context, struggling to maintain its preeminent role as the principal driver of the global economy. As Western hegemony continues to wane, the United States is increasingly confronted with the reality of a multipolar world. In its efforts to preserve its influence, the United States has resorted to strategies steeped in military engagement, arms trade, and the maintenance of currency supremacy, while simultaneously seeking to externalize domestic economic crises in an attempt to maintain its competitive edge. However, these strategies face substantial resistance from rising powers like China and Russia, who actively challenge U.S. dominance through initiatives such as de-dollarization and military counteractions.

Indeed, the U.S. GDP has seen a marked decline relative to China's accelerating economic might, accompanied by a diminishing share in global trade and investment. The enduring dominance of the U.S. dollar as the global reserve currency, while still significant, is increasingly threatened by the rise of alternative trade and payment systems championed by the BRICS coalition, which aims to undermine the dollar's central role in international finance.

At the same time, the United States is grappling with internal challenges, including rising debt, inflation, and unemployment, all of which further erode its superpower status.

The year 2022 marked a significant turning point in global politics and economics. The COVID19 pandemic served as both a catalyst for accelerating existing trends and a harbinger of new challenges and opportunities. Regional integration spearheaded by China and Russia emerged as a force capable of reshaping the global order, seeking to dismantle the entrenched hegemony of Western powers, particularly the United States and the United Kingdom, which have held sway over global affairs for the past four centuries.

This tectonic shift in the global order is unfolding through carefully orchestrated strategies aimed at de-dollarization and demilitarization across key regions such as Asia, Africa, Latin America, and Europe. De-dollarization, a concerted effort to reduce reliance on the U.S. dollar in global trade and finance, has become a cornerstone of this emerging order. Through diversifying currency reserves and establishing alternative payment systems, nations seek to circumvent the economic sanctions and coercion traditionally wielded by the United States.

China and Russia have emerged as leaders in these efforts, advocating for the use of their currencies in international transactions and promoting diplomatic resolutions to regional conflicts.

In Asia, China's Belt and Road Initiative (BRI) exemplifies its approach, fostering economic cooperation and infrastructure development across the continent. Meanwhile, in Africa and Latin America, China's economic influence is matched by Russia's growing engagement in energy and military cooperation. Both powers share a vision of mutual benefit and shared prosperity, offering an alternative to the historical dominance of the West.

In Europe, Russia promotes a vision of a 'common European home,' calling for the withdrawal of United States and NATO forces from Eastern Europe, while China seeks to solidify economic ties through strategic investments and cooperation frameworks.

China and Russia are spearheading a new, multipolar global order, dismantling the old Western hegemony while advocating for a world based on mutual cooperation and shared prosperity across continents.

1.6 REGIONAL INTEGRATION: RESHAPING THE NEW WORLD ORDER

Regional integration represents the collaborative efforts of nations within a defined geographical sphere to enhance economic, political, and social cohesion. This multifaceted endeavor spans a wide array of mechanisms, from trade agreements and economic unions to diplomatic alliances and military partnerships. The implications of regional integration extend far beyond the immediate confines of participating countries, profoundly influencing the global power equilibrium and fundamentally altering the dynamics of international relations.

According to estimates by the IMF, in 2001, the G7 nations accounted for approximately 43.4% of global GDP, measured in terms of purchasing power parity. However, by 2015, their share had markedly decreased to 31.5%, while the economic footprint of the BRICS nations surged from 19.3% to over 30.8% of the global total. This shift underscores the emergence of developing nations as formidable economic actors, assuming pivotal roles in global governance frameworks and asserting growing influence within key international institutions.

This paradigm shift is most strikingly evident in the rise of the Group of Twenty (G20), which includes both developed and developing economies. The G20 has become an essential platform for international economic cooperation, particularly in the domains of sustainable growth and climate change mitigation. For example, in September 2023, India, serving as the G20 chair, hosted the summit in New Delhi and introduced initiatives such as plans to integrate the African Union into the G20 and the formation of a novel biofuels alliance aimed at achieving zero net carbon emissions. By 2023, the G20 collectively represented 80% of global GDP, 75% of global exports, and encompassed 60% of the world's population, further solidifying its role as a cornerstone of global economic governance.

China's BRI, launched in 2013, stands as one of the most ambitious examples of regional integration. This initiative seeks to foster intercontinental connectivity across Asia, Europe, and Africa through a sprawling network of infrastructure projects. These projects, which include critical infrastructures such as roads, railways, ports, and energy pipelines, are poised not only to facilitate enhanced trade and connectivity but also to realign global trade routes. The BRI's transformative potential extends beyond mere infrastructural development; it seeks to deepen economic linkages between disparate regions, thereby reshaping the global economic landscape.

In parallel, Russia's Eurasian Economic Union (EAEU), established in 2015, represents a significant regional integration initiative. The EAEU strives to create a harmonized economic environment among its member states, facilitating the free movement of goods, services, and capital. Beyond its economic objectives, the EAEU also carries substantial geopolitical weight, enhancing Russia's influence within its immediate sphere while acting as a counterbalance to Western dominance in both economic and political domains.

Together, initiatives like the BRI and the EAEU epitomize the concerted efforts of nations to forge deeper regional ties and synergies. These undertakings are not only catalysts for economic prosperity and political stability within their respective regions but also resonate globally, driving shifts in the broader geopolitical framework and fostering a more interconnected and interdependent world order. As such, regional integration has become a pivotal force in reshaping the global landscape, laying the groundwork for a new, multipolar world order that increasingly reflects the power and agency of emerging economies.

1.7 IMPLICATIONS FOR A NEW WORLD ORDER

The rise of regional integration initiatives such as the BRI and the EAEU signals profound shifts in the global balance of power. These ventures present a direct challenge to the long-standing dominance of Western nations in the global arena, offering alternative models of economic and political collaboration. As such, they hold the potential to catalyze the formation of a new world order, defined by more diversified centers of influence.

One of the most significant implications of regional integration is the anticipated transformation in global economic dynamics. As countries across Asia, Africa, and Europe deepen their interconnections, they are poised to gradually reduce their reliance on Western markets and institutions. This trajectory suggests the emergence of a multipolar economic order, characterized by a growing number of distinct economic poles, each exerting influence over regional and global economic activities.

Moreover, regional integration initiatives have the capacity to reshape geopolitical alliances on the world stage. As nations from disparate regions forge deeper ties through economic and political integration, the formation of new alliances based on shared economic interests becomes increasingly feasible. This fluidity in geopolitical affiliations promises to usher in a dynamic and more unpredictable global political landscape, characterized by shifting alliances and recalibrated power structures.

The notion of a "new world order" encapsulates a broad array of political, economic, and social transformations, with regional integration efforts such as the BRI and EAEU playing a central role. These initiatives are poised to fundamentally alter the global power matrix, exerting a significant influence on international relations. As these developments unfold, it becomes crucial for global leaders and policymakers to remain attuned to their implications, as they have the potential to redefine the contours of the global political and economic system.

In 2022, regional economic integration, through the establishment of trade blocs and political alliances, assumes a pivotal role in shaping the emerging 'new world order.' Entities such as BRICS, the Shanghai Cooperation Organization (SCO), the East African Community (EAC), the Regional Comprehensive Economic Partnership (RCEP), the EU, and Mercosur exemplify the growing importance of integrated regions. These alliances have far-reaching implications, spanning global trade, political cooperation, security frameworks, cultural exchange, and technological innovation.

However, regional coalitions also face internal and external challenges that may impact their effectiveness and influence on the global stage.

One of the most striking effects of regional integration is its transformative impact on global trade dynamics. As integrated regions consolidate their collective influence, they gain the ability to shape global trade negotiations and agreements more effectively. The development of interconnected supply chains within these integrated regions further compels the reconfiguration of global trade routes, shifting the flow of goods and services across borders.

Political cooperation, an intrinsic facet of regional integration, fosters the formation of new alliances aimed at addressing shared challenges. This process enhances the ability of integrated regions to influence the delicate balance of power in international relations, forging a more equitable and collaborative global political order. Furthermore, security cooperation mechanisms within these regions, designed to mitigate common security concerns, may recalibrate the dynamics of global security structures.

In addition to these political and economic transformations, regional integration plays a critical role in facilitating cultural exchange across a myriad of domains, including education, tourism, and interpersonal connections. By nurturing cultural cohesion among member states, integration helps foster a deeper sense of social interconnectedness, contributing to global solidarity.

Despite its numerous benefits, regional integration is not without its challenges. Internal tensions arising from economic disparities, political discord, and uneven commitment among member states pose significant obstacles. External factors, such as global economic uncertainty, trade tensions, and geopolitical rivalries, further complicate the trajectory of these integration efforts.

The degree of integration in a given region is intricately linked to both bilateral and multilateral relationships, influencing the prioritization of partnerships between individual countries. These regional frameworks often intersect with global institutions, such as the UN, affecting the broader dynamics of multilateral diplomacy.

Moreover, integrated regions increasingly serve as hubs of technological innovation, driving global trends in science and technology. They also facilitate coordinated efforts to address pressing global challenges, such as climate change. These regions, by projecting diplomatic and soft power, can influence global governance structures and advocate for reforms within international institutions, thereby enhancing their global stature.

The experiences garnered from the COVID-19 pandemic have further underscored the importance of regional cooperation. In response to the health crisis, many integrated regions have intensified efforts to bolster health security and enhance pandemic preparedness, further reinforcing the significance of regional collaboration in addressing shared global challenges.

In sum, regional economic integration is a cornerstone of the evolving 'new world order.' As integrated regions shape global trade, political cooperation, security frameworks, cultural exchange, and technological advancement, they also confront a range of challenges that affect their effectiveness on the global stage. The continued metamorphosis of the geopolitical landscape demands close attention from global leaders, policymakers, and analysts, as these trends will inevitably shape the future of international relations.

1.7.1 TYPES OF ECONOMIC INTEGRATION

1. **Free Trade Area (FTA):**

   Objective: Elimination of tariffs and trade barriers among member countries for selected goods and services.

   Example: The African Continental Free Trade Area (AfCFTA) and the North American Free Trade Agreement (NAFTA), later transformed into the United States–Mexico–Canada Agreement (USMCA).

2. **Customs Union:**

   Objective: Establishment of a common external tariff against non-member countries, in addition to fostering free trade among member states.

   Example: Mercosur (Southern Common Market) in South America.

3. **Common Market:**

   Objective: Facilitates the free movement of goods, services, labor, and capital among member countries.

   Example: The European Single Market within the EU.

4. **Economic Union:**

   Objective: Involves a common market with a high level of coordination in economic policies, including the adoption of a common currency.

   Example: The Eurozone within the EU.

5. **Political and Economic Union:**

   Objective: Combines economic integration with substantial political cooperation.

   Example: The EU, characterized by political integration through shared institutions and decision-making processes.

1.7.2 KEY FEATURES OF ECONOMIC INTEGRATION

1. **Removal of Trade Barriers:**
   - *Tariff elimination:* Reduction or elimination of tariffs on imports among member countries.
   - *Non-tariff barriers:* Reduction of non-tariff barriers, such as quotas and technical regulations.
2. **Common External Policies:**
   - *Common trade policies:* Coordination of trade policies toward non-member countries, often implemented through a common external tariff in customs unions.
3. **Free Movement of Factors of Production:**
   - *Labor mobility:* Encourages the free movement of labor, enhancing employment opportunities.
   - *Capital mobility:* Facilitates unrestricted flow of capital, fostering investment.
4. **Harmonization of Regulations:**
   - *Technical standards:* Efforts to standardize technical regulations to ensure smooth movement of goods and services.

5. **Coordination of Economic Policies:**

   - *Macroeconomic coordination:* In economic and monetary unions, coordination of fiscal and monetary policies to ensure stability.

6. **Institutional Framework:**

   - *Supranational institutions:* Presence of supranational bodies, such as the European Commission (EC), with authority beyond individual member states.

1.7.3 ADVANTAGES OF ECONOMIC INTEGRATION

1. **Trade Creation:**

   Augmented trade and specialization among member countries catalyze economic growth.

2. **Economies of Scale:**

   Expanding market access allows businesses to benefit from economies of scale, improving efficiency.

3. **Increased Foreign Direct Investment (FDI):**

   Integrated regions attract higher levels of foreign investment due to larger market potential and reduced risks.

4. **Enhanced Competition:**

   Regional competition fosters innovation, improved product quality, and increased market efficiency.

5. **Job Opportunities:**

   Labor mobility provides greater job opportunities across borders.

6. **Political Stability:**

   Economic collaboration fosters political stability by aligning member nation's interests and reducing conflict.

1.7.4 CHALLENGES OF ECONOMIC INTEGRATION

1. **Trade Diversion:**

   A shift of trade from lower-cost non-member countries to higher-cost member countries potentially undermines integration efficiency.

2. **Loss of National Sovereignty:**

   Concerns regarding the erosion of national sovereignty, especially in political and economic unions.

3. **Regional Disparities:**

   Economic integration may exacerbate inequalities within member states, with some regions benefiting more than others.

4. **Policy Coordination Challenges:**

   Diverging economic conditions make harmonizing policies, particularly within monetary unions, difficult.

5. **Social and Labor Concerns:**

   Labor mobility may result in job displacement and social tensions, particularly in regions with significant wage disparities.

6. **Divergent Economic Cycles:**

   Differing economic cycles across member states complicate the implementation of uniform policies, particularly in monetary unions.

Economic integration is a complex process marked by both potential benefits and significant challenges. The rise of emerging powers, notably China, India, Russia, South Africa, and Brazil, has already begun to reshape the global economic order, and the establishment of the NDB reflects a growing shift away from reliance on the US dollar.

Since the advent of the twenty-first century, developing economies have exhibited sustained and robust growth, progressively consolidating their collective economic power to challenge the entrenched dominance of the Group of Seven Industrialized Countries (G-7). According to estimates by the IMF, in 2001, the G-7 nations commanded approximately 43.4% of the world's total GDP in terms of purchasing power parity. However, by 2015, their share had diminished to 31.5%, signaling a notable erosion in their economic influence. In contrast, during the same period, the combined economic footprint of the BRICS nations expanded markedly, rising from 19.3% to exceeding 30.8% of the global GDP share.

This shift underscores the growing prominence of emerging economies, particularly represented by the collective rise of BRICS nations, in reshaping the global economic landscape. As these nations assert their influence, the historical dominance of Western powers faces a formidable challenge, driving a profound realignment of global economic dynamics (Fan, 2022).

The global stage is currently undergoing a profound transformation, marked by a seismic shift in the balance of power, with the East and South emerging as formidable challengers in the realms of defence, finance, and technology. Led by nations such as China, Russia, North Korea, Iran, India, South Africa, and Brazil, this paradigm shift is fundamentally redefining the structure of the 21st-century global order. This chapter explores the multifaceted factors driving this transformation and the far-reaching implications for the future of the world which are as follows:

1. **Defence and Military:** The East and South have made remarkable advancements in strengthening their defence and military capabilities, thereby challenging the long-standing dominance of the West in this domain. Countries like China and Russia have undertaken ambitious modernization efforts, incorporating state-of-the-art weaponry and military technologies. This strategic investment has endowed these nations with the power to project influence globally, effectively contesting the military hegemony of Western powers that has prevailed for decades.

2. **Finance:** Simultaneously, the East and South have emerged as key players in the global financial sphere, with China and India assuming central roles as economic heavyweights. China, in particular, has solidified its position as a cornerstone of global finance, particularly with the rise of the Chinese yuan as a prominent reserve currency. Furthermore, countries such as Brazil and South Africa have gained significant standing within the international financial system, contributing to the diversification of economic power away from traditional Western strongholds.

3. **Technology:** Undoubtedly, the East and South have also become epicenters of technological innovation, with nations like China and India leading the charge in ground breaking advancements in fields such as artificial intelligence, biotechnology, and telecommunications. These countries have firmly established themselves as hubs of technological research and development, challenging the once-dominant technological hegemony of Western nations.

4. **Implications:** The shifting balance of power from the West to the East and South carries profound implications for the global order. It signals the emergence of a more multipolar world, where a

> variety of power centers compete for influence. This shift is likely to foster greater diversity and complexity in global politics; as disparate nations assert their interests and agendas on the world stage, ultimately reshaping the dynamics of international relations.

In essence, the recalibration of the global balance of power from the West to the East and South is irrevocably altering the fabric of the 21st-century global order. With nations such as China, Russia, North Korea, Iran, India, South Africa, and Brazil asserting their dominance in defence, finance, and technology, the once-unassailable power of Western nations is being vigorously contested. This transformative trajectory has profound implications for the future course of global affairs, heralding the dawn of a more multipolar, complex, and interdependent world order (Prabhakar, 2020a, b).

Tony Blair, the former Prime Minister of the United Kingdom, has astutely characterized the present historical juncture as akin to the epochal transition that transpired at the conclusion of World War II. During this critical period, major capitalist and imperialist powers united to forge new epicenters of affluence, epitomized by the creation of exclusive collectives such as the G-7, NAFTA (a formidable trade bloc), the EC, the EU, and NATO, a military coalition comprising 30 member states. Simultaneously, they engineered the establishment of international financial institutions like the World Bank and the IMF, which became the foundational pillars of the global banking and financial infrastructure, grounded in the principles of the Bretton Woods System. These initiatives were instrumental in consolidating their dominance over global economic affairs, most notably through the hegemonic status of their currency, the dollar.

In the mid-1990s, following the dissolution of the Soviet Union and the collapse of the Socialist Bloc, a pivotal shift occurred with the formation of the WTO. This continued dominance, which spanned over four centuries, initially orchestrated by British colonial powers before World War II and subsequently maintained by American imperialism well into the early 21st century, exemplifies a long-standing narrative in global affairs. However, the trajectory of the world economy is now undergoing a perceptible recalibration toward the East, symbolized by the rising influence of entities such as BRICS, EAC (East Asian Cooperation), the SCO, and the 15-nation RCEP, all buoyed by the growing power of China and Russia.

Presently, the dominance of the West is no longer unequivocal. We stand on the precipice of a monumental shift in global order, with Western political and economic hegemony facing a potential denouement. The evolving global landscape suggests an imminent transition toward a bi-polar, if not multi-polar, world order. The most significant geopolitical transformation of this century is expected to stem from China, rather than Russia. For a considerable segment of the Western populace, living standards have stagnated, with millions struggling to meet basic needs, exacerbated by inflationary pressures that threaten to erode real wages. This stark reality signals a profound recalibration of the global balance of power, heralding the dawn of a new era in international relations (Mayadeen, 2022).

In the mid-1990s, following the dissolution of the Soviet Union-led Socialist Bloc, a seminal development unfolded with the establishment of the WTO. This enduring continuum of dominance, which spanned over four centuries, was initially orchestrated by British colonial powers in the period preceding World War II and subsequently sustained by American imperialism into the early years of the 21st century, thereby encapsulating a profound and enduring narrative in global geopolitics. However, the trajectory of the global economy is presently undergoing a discernible shift toward the Eastern bloc, epitomized by the ascension of entities such as BRICS, EAC, the SCO, and the 15-nation RCEP, all underpinned by the formidable influence of China and Russia.

At present, the preeminence of the West is no longer unequivocally discernible. We stand on the cusp of an epochal denouement of Western political and economic hegemony, with clear indications pointing toward an impending transition to a global order that is, at the very least, bipolar, if not multi-polar. The most consequential geopolitical metamorphosis of the 21st century is expected to emanate from China, rather than Russia. For a substantial portion of the Western populace, living standards have stagnated, with millions struggling to meet basic necessities, exacerbated by the looming threat of inflation, which is poised to erode real wages.

China's economic transformation stands as a testament to its extraordinary trajectory. In 1977, China's economic stature was modest, significantly overshadowed by that of Italy. However, following the adoption of a new economic paradigm in 1978—pivoting toward globalization and embracing a socialist market model—China embarked on an unwavering mission to foster prosperity and alleviate poverty. Central to this endeavor was the redefinition of poverty itself, as the Chinese government instituted a new benchmark, classifying individuals earning less than $60 a day as impoverished. Three decades later, the Chinese government made the historic declaration of eradicating poverty within its borders, propelling the nation to the pinnacle of the global economic hierarchy as the second-largest economy. Projections suggest that China is poised to eclipse the United States within the next decade, buoyed by its pioneering advancements in 21st century technologies, such as artificial intelligence, regenerative medicine, and conductive polymers.

1.8 WORLD WAR III BEGINS

World War is a de facto reality. It appears to have commenced in earnest since early 2022. The direct intervention of NATO, led by the United States, in Ukraine's conflict with Russia, has escalated the situation far beyond the regional confines of Eastern Europe. North Korea and Iran have aligned themselves with Russia, thus creating a strategic front, while in parallel, a new theater of conflict has emerged in the Middle East, where Israel, a key ally of the United States, faces a formidable coalition of adversaries. The alliance between Russia, China, Iran, and select Arab Islamic nations stands in stark opposition to the United States, the United Kingdom, and France. This convergence of global power players signals that the conflict has long surpassed its initial scope, evolving into a complex, multi-dimensional geopolitical struggle.

Nuclear proliferation now represents an existential threat of far greater magnitude than climate change, especially given the escalating tensions between the superpowers, such as Russia and the U.S.-led NATO alliance, which includes pivotal players like the United Kingdom and France. Against this fraught backdrop, the recent BRICS summit, which took place in Russia and included Brazil, Russia, India, China, and South Africa, marked a significant geopolitical milestone. This summit fostered deeper cooperation not only among its core members but also with a growing coalition of non-Western nations, such as Iran, Egypt, and the United Arab Emirates. This alignment further underscores the shifting global order, presenting a challenge to Western hegemony while simultaneously raising concerns regarding strategic stability and the looming risks of nuclear brinkmanship.

1.8.1 WAR AGAINST THE IMPERIALIST COUNTRIES AND ENERGY CRISIS

The Energy Crisis of 2022 unfolded amid intensifying geopolitical tensions and global economic instability. Spearheaded by Russia, OPEC+ nations convened in Vienna on October 5, 2022, where they resolved to cut oil production by two million barrels per day. This decision is poised to have far-reaching consequences, driving up global oil and gas prices and inflating production and supply costs across industries.

A confluence of factors has exacerbated this crisis. Disruptions targeting the Russian Nord Stream 1 and 2 pipelines, coupled with Russia's seizure of Ukraine's Zaporizhzhia Nuclear Power Plant, have further strained energy supplies. Additionally, sanctions imposed by the United States and European nations on major energy suppliers such as Iran, Russia, and Venezuela have intensified the situation. These overlapping crises have given rise to a global dilemma encompassing energy, food, and financial systems. Advanced economies, heavily reliant on petroleum and gas imports, including North America, Western Europe, Japan, South Korea, Australia, India, Pakistan, Sri Lanka, and New Zealand, now find themselves contending with the severe repercussions. As a result, global food and energy prices have surged to unprecedented levels.

Forecasts from institutions such as the U.S. Federal Reserve, the Reserve Bank of India, and *The Economist* paint a grim picture of the global economic outlook. Projections indicate a looming economic downturn in 2022 that threatens to rival, if not surpass, the depths of the Great Depression of 1929–1933.

In the 1970s, the United States witnessed the first signs of its hegemonic decline, as numerous developing nations—emerging from the ashes of the post-war National Liberation Movement—championed the quest for a more equitable international economic system. Primarily represented by the non-aligned Third World countries, these nations fervently advocated for the creation of a New International Economic Order within the framework of the UN, a system designed to redound to their collective benefit.

1.9 GLOBALIZATION, PROTECTIONIST POLICIES, ECONOMIC SANCTIONS, AND THE GLOBAL RECESSION

Globalization, propelled by successive waves of liberalization, privatization, corporatization, financialization, and digitalization, has historically been championed as the cornerstone of global economic integration. This trajectory, however, underwent a profound transformation post-1990s, coinciding with the dissolution of the USSR and the disintegration of the socialist bloc, including Eastern European nations. Initially, globalization facilitated the unencumbered flow of goods, services, capital, and labor, catalyzing the expansion of global trade, fostering economic interdependence, and elevating emerging markets. However, this paradigm has encountered growing resistance, particularly from the United States and the EU, whose pivot toward protectionism, especially in the aftermath of the 2008 financial crisis, has challenged the ideals of unfettered market liberalization and free trade.

1.9.1 PROTECTIONIST POLICIES BY THE UNITED STATES AND THE EU

The United States, traditionally a proponent of liberalized trade, has progressively shifted toward protectionism. Under the Trump administration, this shift became conspicuous with the imposition of tariffs on Chinese goods, the withdrawal from multilateral trade agreements such as the Trans-Pacific Partnership, and the renegotiation of NAFTA into the USMCA. The Biden administration, while more multilateral in its approach, has retained elements of this protectionist stance, driven by domestic imperatives, including safeguarding jobs in manufacturing sectors, addressing deindustrialization, and mitigating widening socioeconomic disparities exacerbated by global competition.

Similarly, the EU, long an advocate of open markets, has recalibrated its economic strategy toward 'strategic autonomy.' This shift underscores efforts to reduce dependence on external players in critical sectors, particularly energy, agriculture, and advanced technology. The EU's aggressive regulation of foreign tech giants, its advocacy for digital sovereignty, and its imposition of trade restrictions on select Chinese firms exemplify a nuanced protectionist undertone. While the EU remains steadfast in its commitment to preserve the Single Market, its policies reflect heightened vigilance against geopolitical and economic vulnerabilities.

1.9.2 ECONOMIC SANCTIONS AND THEIR GLOBAL REPERCUSSIONS

The deployment of economic sanctions by Western powers, led by the United States and its allies, has emerged as a salient instrument of geopolitical strategy. These sanctions, ostensibly designed to address security threats, human rights violations, and territorial aggressions, have targeted nations such as Russia, China, India, Iran, North Korea, and Venezuela. However, their ramifications have reverberated beyond their immediate geopolitical objectives, reshaping global trade dynamics and exacerbating energy crises which are as follows:

1. **Russia:** Since the annexation of Crimea in 2014 and subsequent military interventions in Ukraine, Russia has been subjected to sweeping sanctions targeting its financial, defense, and energy sectors. These measures, compounded by declining oil prices and an overreliance on state-dominated industries, have strained the Russian economy, curtailing its growth trajectory and global trade linkages.

2. **China:** Trade wars and sanctions have escalated between the United States and China, with tariffs imposed on a plethora of Chinese goods and restrictions placed on access to advanced technologies. Allegations of intellectual property theft, alongside contentious issues in Xinjiang and Hong Kong, have intensified tensions. Despite these challenges, China's robust domestic market and expansive BRI have enabled it to partially offset the adverse impacts of these sanctions.

3. **India:** While India has not faced sanctions on the scale of other nations, sporadic measures linked to its defense partnership with Russia and its independent foreign policy have highlighted tensions with Western powers. India's efforts to diversify its economic ties, particularly with China and Russia, and its growing leadership in multilateral forums have bolstered its resilience.

4. **Iran:** U.S. sanctions on Iran, amplified, following its withdrawal from the Joint Comprehensive Plan of Action in 2018, have decimated the Iranian economy, targeting its energy sector and restricting financial transactions. Despite these setbacks, Iran's strategic alliances with Russia and China have underscored its defiance of economic isolation.

5. **North Korea:** Decades of stringent international sanctions, primarily imposed due to its nuclear weapons program and human rights violations, have entrenched North Korea's economic

isolation. Nevertheless, covert trade and strategic alliances with nations like China have allowed Pyongyang to navigate its prolonged economic hardship.

6. **Venezuela:** A combination of U.S. sanctions targeting Venezuela's oil industry and domestic economic mismanagement has plunged the nation into an unprecedented crisis. Hyperinflation, mass emigration, and systemic infrastructural collapse exemplify the socio-economic devastation wrought by sanctions and governance failures.

1.9.3 THE GLOBAL RECESSION

The intersection of protectionist policies, economic sanctions, and the lingering aftershocks of the COVID-19 pandemic has culminated in a global recession of considerable magnitude. This downturn is characterized by anemic economic growth, escalating inflation, and pervasive unemployment. While advanced economies such as the United States and the EU have sought to cushion their markets through aggressive fiscal and monetary interventions, developing nations face the compounded challenges of ballooning debt, depreciating currencies, and supply chain disruptions.

Sanctions, while isolating targeted nations, have disrupted global supply chains, driving up commodity prices and intensifying inflationary pressures worldwide. The energy crisis, exacerbated by geopolitical tensions and sanctions on Russian exports, has driven oil and gas prices to unprecedented levels, further straining economies dependent on energy imports. Concurrently, efforts by nations like China, Russia, and Iran to reduce reliance on the U.S. dollar in trade and investment transactions signal potential shifts in the global financial architecture.

1.9.4 ENERGY CRISIS AND INFLATIONARY PRESSURES

The energy crisis, accentuated by geopolitical upheavals and economic sanctions, has acted as a catalyst for inflation. Countries reliant on imported energy, such as Japan, South Korea, and European states, face soaring production costs, which have been passed on to consumers, constraining economic recovery efforts. Simultaneously, pandemic-induced supply chain vulnerabilities, compounded by protectionist barriers, have resulted in shortages of essential goods, dampening industrial output and exacerbating inflationary trends.

The interplay of globalization, protectionist policies, economic sanctions, and the looming global recession signals a critical juncture in the evolution of the global economic order. As nations pivot toward economic self-reliance, prioritizing domestic resilience over international interdependence, globalization's foundational principles face unprecedented challenges. Economic sanctions, while achieving short-term geopolitical objectives, have produced profound unintended consequences, disrupting trade flows and exacerbating global vulnerabilities. The ongoing recalibration of international alliances and financial systems underscores a period of profound transformation, where the balance between cooperation and competition will decisively shape the contours of the future global economy.

The necessity of adapting to shifting geopolitical fault lines—emphasizing resilience over efficiency, diversifying supply chains, and intensifying commitments to environmental sustainability—was emphatically affirmed by chief economists, achieving an overwhelming consensus of 94%. This imperative involves acknowledging the intensification of geoeconomic tensions (91%), the erosion of competitive markets (70%), and a troubling rise in sovereign debt levels (68%), each signaling profound challenges to global economic stability. Although labor markets demonstrate a measure of resilience, global economic growth remains lethargic, geopolitical tensions continue to intensify, and the cost of living crisis persists in numerous nations. This underscores an urgent imperative for immediate global policy coordination, complemented by sustained international collaboration, to establish a transformative growth framework that integrates inclusivity, sustainability, and resilience as central tenets of economic policy (Zahidi, 2023).

1.10 SUMMING UP

The BRICS coalition—encompassing Brazil, Russia, India, China, and South Africa —has ascended as a formidable catalyst in redefining the global geopolitical and economic paradigm. Its emergence represents a unified challenge to the entrenched Western-centric order, advocating for a multipolar framework that prioritizes equity, inclusivity, and sovereignty within international relations. Through initiatives such as the NDB, the promotion of intra-BRICS trade, and the cultivation of partnerships with emerging economies, BRICS underscores its unwavering commitment to foster sustainable development and rectify the systemic inequities that underpin the global economic architecture.

As the bloc consolidates its influence, the incorporation of new partners and its alignment with the aspirations of the Global South, enhances its potential to counterbalance traditional power centers like the G7. Nevertheless, the coalition's long-term efficacy will depend on its ability to reconcile internal divergences, ensure strategic coherence, and deliver substantive benefits to its member states and their constituencies. BRICS transcends being a mere economic or political alliance; it is an emblem of solidarity for a world increasingly interdependent yet yearning for equitable and just governance. Its evolution will indelibly shape the contours of a reimagined global order in the 21st century.

KEYWORDS

- **de-dollarization**
- **economic sanction**
- **global south**
- **hegemony**
- **multipolar world order**
- **renewable energy**
- **tariff**

REFERENCES

Administration. (January-June 2025). *China's trade statistics report*. Beijing: Government of China.

FAO. (2024). *World agriculture report 2024*. Rome: FAO.

Huang, Y. A. (2024). China's poverty alleviation and industrial transformation. *Journal of Asian Economic Studies*, *18*(3), 45–67.

IMF. (2025). *World economic outlook: Post-pandemic recovery and risks*. Washington, DC: IMF.

NDB. (2025). *Annual report 2025*. Shanghai: NDB.

OECD. (2025). *Global trade in industrial goods*. Paris: OECD.

Prabhakar, A. C. (2015a). A critical appraisal of comparative advantage theory under free market crony capitalism. *Investment Management and Financial Innovations*, *12*(3), 93–98.

Prabhakar, A. C. (2015b). Evaluation of technology, trade, and inclusive development: Chinese Experience. *Investment Management and Financial Innovations*, *12*(2), 180–188.

Prabhakar, A. C. (2020a). Globalization: Reshaping the world economy in the 21st century. In *Regional trade and development strategies in the era of globalization*. USA: IGI Global.

Prabhakar, A. C. (2020b). Trade and economic integration in BRICS: Towards multi-polarity. In *Foreign direct investments: Concepts, methodologies, tools, and applications*. USA: IGI Global.

Stiglitz, J. E. (2023). Globalization and its new discontents. New York, NY: Norton.

UNCTAD. (2025), *BRICS and the future of South-South trade*. Geneva: UNCTAD.

World Bank. (2025a). *China economic update 2025*. Washington, DC: World Bank.

World Bank. (2025b). *World development indicators*. Washington, DC: World Bank.

CHAPTER 2

BRICS: An Engine of Global South

ABSTRACT

This chapter critically investigates the evolving role of the BRICS consortium—comprising Brazil, Russia, India, China, and South Africa—in reconfiguring the global geopolitical and economic order from the vantage point of the Global South. As confidence in traditional Western-dominated institutions wanes and global power becomes increasingly diffused, BRICS has emerged as a strategic fulcrum for a more balanced and multipolar world order. This study interrogates the mechanisms through which BRICS nations harness their collective economic leverage, institutional innovations—such as the New Development Bank—and South–South cooperation to contest Western hegemony, elevate the voices of developing nations, and advocate for inclusive global governance. Through a rigorous analysis of trade patterns, diplomatic alignments, and developmental agendas, this chapter elucidates the bloc's potential not merely as a regional alliance, but as a catalytic force advancing the sovereignty, solidarity, and strategic ambitions of the Global South in the 21st century.

2.1 INTRODUCTION

BRICS—comprising Brazil, Russia, India, China, and South Africa—has ascended as an influential coalition, characterized by its members' shared aspirations for enhanced representation within global governance and a recalibration of power in the international economic order. This bloc represents a unified voice advocating for equity and inclusivity, challenging a world order historically dominated by Western powers.

The BRICS Coalition and a New Global Order: Akhilesh Chandra Prabhakar (Author)
2026 Apple Academic Press, Inc. Co-published with CRC Press (Taylor & Francis)

DOI: 10.1201/9781779642936-2

Collectively, BRICS accounts for over 40% of the global population and generates approximately 50% of the world's gross domestic product (GDP), underscoring its expanding influence within the global economic arena (Prabhakar, 2015). This chapter provides an incisive analysis of the economic profiles of each member state, examining their individual growth trajectories, trade interdependencies, and evolving economic strategies. The distinct yet interwoven characteristics of these economies—Brazil's agricultural richness, Russia's dominance in energy resources, China's unparalleled manufacturing prowess, India's burgeoning service-driven economy, and South Africa's mineral wealth and industrial base—demonstrate their collective capacity as formidable drivers of global economic advancement.

The diverse yet synergistic nature of BRICS economies facilitates their pivotal roles in fostering global growth, with significant contributions spanning trade, investment, technological innovation, and resource management. The bloc's ascendancy reflects a seismic shift in global power dynamics, heralding the transition from a Western-dominated economic paradigm to the rise of the Global South as a cornerstone of contemporary economic and geopolitical influence (Prabhakar, 2024).

2.2 SURVEY OF LITERATURES

The BRICS coalition, comprising Brazil, Russia, India, China, and South Africa, has attracted considerable scholarly interest as it evolves into a critical actor in the global political and economic landscape. Numerous studies have scrutinized its historical formation, the challenges it faces, and its potential to reshape global governance.

The inception of BRICS is frequently contextualized within the broader narrative of emerging economies striving to assert their influence in the face of Western hegemony. Stuenkel posits that the coalition emerged in response to the inadequacies of existing international institutions, which have historically failed to adequately represent the interests of developing nations. BRICS was conceived as a platform for fostering dialogue and cooperation among these nations, epitomizing a collective aspiration to amplify their voices in global discourse (Stuenkel, 2016). Furthermore, the bloc's emphasis on solidarity among its member states underscores a shared historical experience characterized by colonialism and economic exploitation (Gonzalez, 2020).

The literature identifies several formidable challenges that BRICS confronts, notably internal divergences and external geopolitical tensions. As Hill and Brant stated the coalition's diverse political systems and economic agendas can impede cohesive decision-making, often leading to conflicting priorities among its members (Hill, 2019). Moreover, the geopolitical rivalry between major powers—particularly between China and India—poses substantial risks to the bloc's unity and efficacy (Mishra, 2021). These tensions complicate the pursuit of a common agenda, as member states navigate their bilateral relations within the overarching framework of BRICS (Zhang, 2022).

Despite these challenges, scholars accentuate the latent potential of BRICS to engender significant global change. The bloc's vast demographic and economic resources uniquely position it to champion sustainable development and infrastructure investment, particularly within the Global South (Banga, 2020), The establishment of the New Development Bank (NDB) further exemplifies BRICS's commitment to financing projects that promote economic growth and development in member states and other developing nations (Chaudhuri, 2021).

The evolving geopolitical landscape presents strategic opportunities for BRICS to enhance its influence. Fardoust argues that the bloc is strategically positioned to lead the transition toward a multipolar world order characterized by equitable cooperation and diminished reliance on Western-centric institutions. The growing calls for reform in global governance structures further underscore the relevance of BRICS as a potential catalyst for transformative change (Fardoust, 2023). As the global balance of power shifts, BRICS can capitalize on emerging partnerships and fortify ties with other developing nations to amplify its collective voice (Chin, 2021).

2.3 THEORETICAL AND CONCEPTUAL FRAMEWORKS

This study is rigorously anchored in the theoretical constructs of **Neorealism** and **Multipolarity**, which together furnish a nuanced and sophisticated analytical lens to interrogate BRICS' evolving role within the contemporary international system. Neorealism, as articulated by Waltz (1979), posits that the anarchic nature of the international order inexorably compels states to pursue power as a means of securing their survival, thereby engendering persistent balance-of-power dynamics (Waltz, 1979).

Within this theoretical framework, the ascendance of BRICS can be construed as a deliberate and coordinated endeavor by pivotal emerging economies to counteract entrenched Western hegemony and to cultivate a more equitable and inclusive global order (Ikenberry, 2003).

Augmenting neorealist analysis is the theory of **Multipolarity**, which contends that the international system is undergoing a paradigmatic transformation from a predominantly unipolar or bipolar configuration toward a multipolar architecture, characterized by the diffusion of power among an increasingly diverse constellation of influential actors (Kupchan, 2012). The burgeoning economic prowess and intensifying geopolitical engagement of BRICS signify a potential inflection point in the evolution of the international order, one that challenges the preeminence of traditional Western-dominated institutions, such as the International Monetary Fund and the World Bank (Stuenkel, 2015).

Moreover, **Dependency Theory** (Prebisch, 1950; Cardoso, 1979) provides a critical interpretive framework to examine the deeply entrenched structural asymmetries that pervade the global economic system—inequities that BRICS explicitly seeks to redress (Cardoso, 1979). By advancing South–South cooperation and constructing alternative financial architectures, most notably through the establishment of the New Development Bank, BRICS endeavors to attenuate dependence on developed economies and to chart new trajectories for sustainable and autonomous development.

Taken collectively, these theoretical perspectives elucidate the intricate interplay of systemic constraints, collective agency, and transformative ambitions that underpin BRICS' concerted efforts to recalibrate the prevailing contours of global governance.

The **conceptual framework** guiding this inquiry situates BRICS at the nexus of three interrelated and mutually reinforcing dimensions:

1. **Complex challenges**
   (a) This dimension encapsulates a spectrum of geopolitical tensions, including Russia's adversarial relations with Western powers, pronounced internal asymmetries among BRICS members, and exogenous pressures emanating from established global actors (Wilson, 2015).

   (b) Such challenges are conceptualized as structural and systemic impediments that strain BRICS' internal cohesion and efficacy as a unified geopolitical bloc.

2. **Latent potential**

    (a) Latent potential refers to the vast, yet underutilized, economic, technological, and demographic endowments inherent within BRICS nations. Collectively, these countries encompass over 40% of the world's population and command substantial reserves of critical natural resources (BRICS Joint Publication, 2024).

    (b) Effectively mobilizing this latent potential highlights opportunities for deepening intra-BRICS cooperation, fostering innovation, and asserting leadership in articulating novel paradigms for sustainable development.

3. **Strategic opportunities**

    (a) Strategic opportunities encompass prospects for institutional innovation—exemplified by the prospective expansion and consolidation of the New Development Bank—agenda-setting within influential multilateral fora, such as the G20 and United Nations, and the advancement of initiatives designed to cultivate a more multipolar, equitable, and representative architecture of global governance (Hopewell, 2015).

2.4 THE POLITICAL CHARACTER OF THE BRICS AND STRATEGIC EXPANSION PROSPECTS

The political character of BRICS is deeply rooted in a longstanding tradition of non-alignment, with its intellectual and ideological lineage tracing back to the historic Bandung Conference of 1955. This seminal assembly—predominantly attended by recently decolonized nations and anti-colonial liberation movements—sought to articulate a collective stance against the hegemonic influence of the Cold War superpowers, namely the United States and the Soviet Union, while resolutely upholding the principles of sovereignty and self-determination. Over the ensuing decades, BRICS has increasingly been perceived as a counter-hegemonic coalition, contesting the global dominance of the United States and its allies, who are frequently criticized for intrusions into the sovereign affairs of other states.

In the contemporary geopolitical landscape, over forty countries from the Global South—many of which were previously aligned with the Group of 77's South–South cooperation framework—have expressed formal interest in BRICS membership. By May 2023, 13 nations had submitted official applications. While a shared political imperative to resist U.S. hegemony motivates many aspirants, a compelling economic rationale also underpins this interest: access to concessional financing and development support from the BRICS-led New Development Bank. This impetus has become particularly salient in the aftermath of the COVID-19 pandemic, as many emerging economies confront prolonged fiscal stress and structural recovery challenges.

Notable applicants include Saudi Arabia, Belarus, Ethiopia, Argentina, Algeria, Iran, Mexico, and Turkiye—each representing unique geopolitical leverage points across their respective regions

2.5 KEY FEATURES OF BRICS' ECONOMIC POWER

1. **Resource Abundance**

   The BRICS nations boast a wealth of natural resources, each making unique contributions to the global supply chain. Russia leads in energy exports, particularly oil and gas, and is a major supplier of wheat and defence technologies. Brazil's agricultural sector serves as a cornerstone for global raw material supplies, while South Africa's mineral wealth, including gold and platinum, underscores its strategic importance. Meanwhile, China dominates the market for cost-efficient manufactured goods, and India contributes significantly with its diverse agricultural output.

2. **Demographic Advantage**

   As the two most populous nations, India and China leverage their immense human resources to drive economic productivity. Their expanding labor forces fuel industrial growth, while vast consumer markets stimulate domestic and international demand, solidifying their positions as economic powerhouses.

3. **Technological and Industrial Growth**

   China's unparalleled manufacturing capacity and technological innovation, combined with India's burgeoning IT sector, position

BRICS as a global leader in industrialization and technological advancement. These strengths not only reinforce the domestic economies of the member states but also enhance the bloc's collective influence in global markets.

2.6 GLOBAL IMPACT

The BRICS bloc wields considerable influence in shaping global trade, financial systems, and developmental agendas. Institutions such as the New Development Bank (NDB) underscore its commitment to diminishing reliance on traditional, Western-dominated financial entities, such as the International Monetary Fund (IMF) and the World Bank. By financing infrastructure and sustainable development projects, the NDB bolsters economic sovereignty among member states while promoting growth throughout the Global South (Prabhakar, 2016b).

Moreover, BRICS has positioned itself as a leading advocate of South–South cooperation, emphasizing solidarity and mutual progress among developing nations. Its initiatives aim to foster a multipolar global order, directly countering the unipolar dominance of the United States and its allies (Prabhakar, 2011).

In tackling critical global challenges, including climate change, energy security, and economic inequality, BRICS assumes a pivotal role. Joint efforts in renewable energy investments and trade diversification underscore its capacity to drive sustainable and inclusive development, setting a benchmark for international collaboration.

As BRICS continues to expand its influence, it reshapes the contours of the global economic and geopolitical landscape. Beyond symbolizing the ascendancy of emerging economies, it serves as a clarion call for a more balanced, equitable, and inclusive global order.

2.7 BRICS: AN INSTRUMENT OF TRADE AND INVESTMENT FLOWS

BRICS has emerged as a transformative force in reconfiguring global trade and investment dynamics. By fostering initiatives that emphasize intra-group trade and investment, the bloc has carved pathways for enhanced economic collaboration and mutual growth. This section delves into the strategic economic policies adopted by BRICS nations, highlighting the pivotal role of infrastructure development, financial integration, and the establishment of novel financial institutions such as the NDB and the Contingent Reserve Arrangement (CRA).

Through these mechanisms, BRICS not only strengthens its internal economic linkages but also fosters regional cooperation, facilitating the creation of innovative economic paradigms that challenge traditional trade norms. The coalition's focus on self-reliance, resource optimization, and mutually beneficial trade relations positions it as a trailblazer in redefining global trade and investment flows.

2.8 BRICS AND THE GLOBAL FINANCIAL SYSTEM

BRICS has strategically positioned itself as a robust counterweight to the hegemony of traditional Western financial institutions, including the IMF, the World Bank, and the World Trade Organization (WTO). This section examines BRICS' concerted efforts to establish a parallel financial architecture that prioritizes the needs and interests of emerging economies, thereby addressing longstanding structural inequities in global economic governance.

Central to this endeavor are the NDB and the CRA, institutions designed to provide critical funding for infrastructure development, foster sustainable growth, and enhance financial stability in an increasingly volatile global economy. By leveraging these platforms, BRICS seeks to insulate its members from external economic shocks and promote greater financial autonomy.

Moreover, the bloc's advocacy for a more equitable allocation of global financial resources reflects its commitment to democratizing international economic governance. In challenging the status quo, BRICS not only amplifies the voice of the Global South but also lays the groundwork for a multipolar financial system that emphasizes inclusivity, fairness, and resilience.

2.9 EMERGENCE OF BRICS AS A PHYSICAL TEMPLATE

The BRICS coalition—comprising Brazil, Russia, India, China, and South Africa—together with the Shanghai Cooperation Organization (SCO), stands as a formidable force dedicated to restructuring a global order that has long been dominated by Western imperialist and colonial powers, particularly the United States, since the conclusion of the World War II. In the present context, the BRICS bloc confronts an intricate web of challenges, both internal and external, including intensifying geopolitical tensions, economic disparities among its members, and pervasive global uncertainties, all of which demand a coordinated and resolute response. Yet, amidst these challenges lies a profound opportunity for BRICS to unlock its latent potential and extend its influence on the global stage (Prabhakar, 2016a). The coalition's vast demographic, economic, and natural resource endowments uniquely position it to advocate for a transformative agenda that encompasses sustainable development, strategic infrastructure investment, and the reform of international financial institutions. In pursuing these goals, BRICS not only challenges the entrenched hegemony of the prevailing global paradigm but also presents a compelling alternative aimed at fostering a more equitable and inclusive world order (Prabhakar, 2020).

Moreover, as calls for a more multipolar and equitable international system grow stronger, BRICS is well positioned to capitalize on strategic opportunities that can enhance its geopolitical leverage and deepen its alliances, particularly with nations across the Global South (Prabhakar, 2016). At this pivotal moment, the ability of BRICS to reconcile its divergent interests, overcome inherent challenges, and harness its collective strengths will be crucial in determining whether it can fulfil its potential as a powerful catalyst for change in a reimagined global order (Prabhakar, 2020a). The path forward requires not only strategic foresight but also a unity of purpose and decisive action to navigate this transformative epoch effectively.

The literature on BRICS elucidates the intricate interplay of challenges, potential, and opportunities that delineate its current trajectory. As the coalition navigates both internal and external pressures, its capacity to harmonize diverse interests while seizing strategic opportunities will be pivotal in shaping a reimagined global order. Ongoing scholarly inquiry into BRICS's evolution is essential for comprehending its implications for international relations and global governance.

The BRICS coalition, comprising Brazil, Russia, India, China, and South Africa, has attracted considerable scholarly interest as it evolves into a critical actor in the global political and economic landscape. Numerous studies have scrutinized its historical formation, the challenges it faces, and its potential to reshape global governance.

Historical Context and Formation: The inception of BRICS is frequently contextualized within the broader narrative of emerging economies striving to assert their influence in the face of Western hegemony. The coalition emerged in response to the inadequacies of existing international institutions, which have historically failed to adequately represent the interests of developing nations. BRICS was conceived as a platform for fostering dialogue and cooperation among these nations, epitomizing a collective aspiration to amplify their voices in global discourse (Stuenkel, 2016). Furthermore, the bloc's emphasis on solidarity among its member states underscores a shared historical experience characterized by colonialism and economic exploitation (Gonzalez, 2020).

Challenges Facing BRICS: The literature identifies several formidable challenges that BRICS confront, notably internal divergences and external geopolitical tensions. As Hill and Brant stated, the coalition's diverse political systems and economic agendas can impede cohesive decision-making, often leading to conflicting priorities among its members (Hill, 2019). Moreover, the geopolitical rivalry between major powers—particularly between China and India—poses substantial risks to the bloc's unity and efficacy (Mishra, 2021). These tensions complicate the pursuit of a common agenda, as member states navigate their bilateral relations within the overarching framework of BRICS (Zhang, 2022).

Unlocking Potential and Opportunities: Despite these challenges, scholars accentuate the latent potential of BRICS to engender significant global change. The bloc's vast demographic and economic resources uniquely position it to champion sustainable development and infrastructure investment, particularly within the Global South (Banga, 2020), The establishment of the NDB further exemplifies BRICS's commitment to financing projects that promote economic growth and development in member states and other developing nations (Chaudhuri, 2021).

Strategic Opportunities for a New Global Order: The evolving geopolitical landscape presents strategic opportunities for BRICS to enhance its influence. Fardoust argues that the bloc is strategically positioned to lead the transition toward a multipolar world order characterized by equitable cooperation and diminished reliance on Western-centric institutions. The growing calls for reform in global governance structures further underscore the relevance of BRICS as a potential catalyst for transformative change (Fardoust, 2023). As the global balance of power shifts, BRICS can capitalize on emerging partnerships and fortify ties with other developing nations to amplify its collective voice (Chin, 2021).

2.10 THE CURRENT GDP OF THE BRICS

The GDP of the BRICS nations, including India, has now exceeded USD 60 trillion, as the world's GDP is estimated at USD 113 trillion in 2025, signaling a profound transformation in the global economic order. In 1992, the Group of Seven (G7) countries held a commanding 45.5% share of global GDP, while the BRICS nations accounted for a modest 16.7%. By 2023, however, BRICS had substantially expanded its economic footprint, capturing 37.4% of global GDP, whereas the G7's share had receded to 29.3%. The nine BRICS countries collectively encompass 28.3% of the world's landmass and represent 44.6% of its population. In nominal terms, their combined GDP reached USD 29.06 trillion in 2023, constituting 27.4% of global output, while the G7 economies accounted for USD 45.92 trillion, or 43%. When measured in terms of purchasing power parity (PPP), the BRICS achieved a GDP of USD 65.79 trillion, representing 35.43% of global GDP, in contrast to the G7's GDP in PPP terms, which stood at USD 55.02 trillion, or 29.63%.

According to the *IMF World Economic Outlook* (2025), emerging and developing economies collectively account for over 60% of global GDP measured at purchasing power parity (PPP), while advanced economies contribute about 39% (IMF, 2025). Within this context, the BRICS bloc (Brazil, Russia, India, China, and South Africa, with recent expansions to include several new members) has surpassed the G7 in terms of global output share at PPP since 2023. Estimates indicate that BRICS now accounts for roughly one-third of world GDP at PPP, compared to the G7's share of about 29–30% (Desjardins, 2023). Thus, while popular narratives sometimes describe BRICS as holding "about 50% of global GDP (PPP)," the more precise range is closer to one-third.

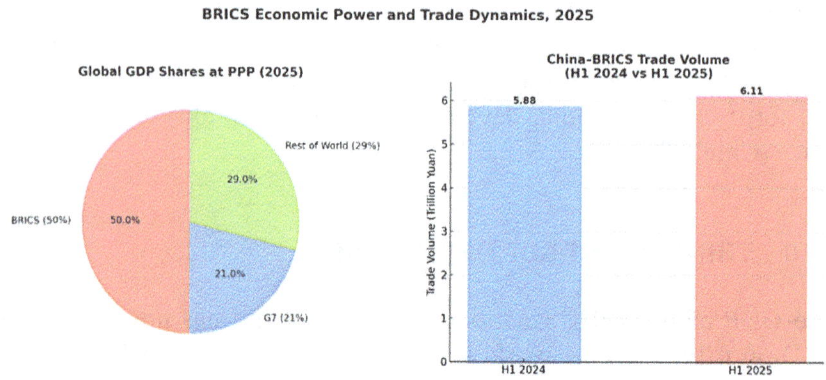

Left panel (pie chart): BRICS contributes 50% of world GDP (PPP), G7 holds 21%, and the rest of the world makes up 29%.

Right panel (bar chart): China's trade with BRICS increased from 5.88 trillion yuan in H1 2024 to 6.11 trillion yuan in H1 2025.

China's trade with BRICS members has grown significantly. In the first half of 2025, China's trade volume with BRICS partners reached 6.11 trillion yuan (≈ USD 855 billion) (Guru, 2025), representing a 3.9% year-on-year increase and accounting for over a quarter of China's total foreign trade (TASS, 2025). This trend highlights deepening South–South economic linkages and reflects Beijing's broader strategy to strengthen intra-BRICS supply chains and reduce dependence on Western markets.

The rising economic influence of BRICS is further underscored by its growing weight within the IMF, where the bloc's quota share surged from 8.4% in 2001 to 25.8% by 2022, while the G7's share contracted from 64.6 to 42.9%. The admission of new members has not only expanded the bloc's economic scale but also enhanced its strategic assets. With the inclusion of the UAE and Iran, BRICS' share of global oil production increased by 8.9%, from 18.62 million barrels per day to 26 million barrels. Despite these significant developments, the US dollar's dominance within the international financial system remains largely unchallenged, with 88% of global transactions conducted in dollars and the currency comprising 58% of global foreign exchange reserves. From 2000 to 2023, the BRICS+ group's share of global merchandise exports rose significantly, from 10.7 to 23.3%, representing an impressive gain of 12.6 percentage points.

In contrast, the G7's share declined sharply from 45.1 to 28.9%, while the rest of the world maintained a relatively stable position, with a modest increase from 44.2 to 47.9%. The G7, comprising advanced economies—the United States, Canada, France, Germany, Italy, Japan, and the United Kingdom—reflects the world's traditional economic powerhouses.

In 2023, the BRICS marshalled a combined populace of 3.2 billion individuals, constituting a commanding 41% slice of the global population. Beyond demographic magnitude, the expanse of BRICS territories collectively encompasses 26.7% of the Earth's land surface. This formidable coalition further underscores its influence through a combined GDP towering at US$35 trillion in the annals of 2023, a commanding share representing no less than 30% of the global economic output.

At the helm of this economic juggernaut, China commands preeminence with a towering GDP tally of US$19.3 trillion, trailed by India at US$3.7 trillion, Brazil at US$2.1 trillion, Russia at US$2 trillion, Saudi Arabia at US$1 trillion, and Argentina at US$0.6 trillion. Complementing this economic mosaic, the United Arab Emirates (UAE), South Africa, Egypt, Iran, and Ethiopia complete the roster, showcasing GDPs ranging from US$0.15 trillion to US$0.4 trillion. The expanded ambit of the BRICS alliance thus showcases a consolidated GDP tally of US$30.51 trillion, a formidable testament to its collective economic clout, projected to burgeon by 50% come 2030.

The individual member states of the BRICS consortium epitomize a diverse tapestry of resource endowments and economic capabilities. Brazil is rich in natural bounty; India boasts the second-largest reservoir of technically skilled manpower globally and commands one of the most expansive markets worldwide; Russia stands as a veritable repository, possessing a quarter share of the world's oil and gas reserves;. South Africa, abundant in natural riches, serves as a pivotal conduit to the African continent; and, China, renowned for its technological prowess, commands an imposing manufacturing base. China's economic ascent has been meteoric, evidenced by a steadfast GDP ascent from USD 6 trillion in 2010 to nearly USD 18 trillion in 2022.

Underscoring its commitment to global development and cooperation, China has initiated the establishment of the Global Development and South–South Cooperation Fund, with an earmarked funding corpus of $4 billion (sh14.9 trillion), alongside plans for the establishment of a dedicated special fund totaling $10 billion (sh37.3 trillion) to spearhead the implementation of the Global Development Initiative (GDI). Over 200 collaboration projects have been actualized, with cooperative frameworks expanding across domains such as poverty alleviation, educational enhancement, and healthcare provisioning across Asia, Africa, Pacific Island countries (PICs), and the Caribbean.

Furthermore, China has anchored its strategic focus on green development, novel industrialization paradigms, and digital economic proliferation, exemplified through its pioneering Partnership on New Industrial Revolution, aimed at catalyzing high-quality development trajectories. Moreover, China's proactive initiatives span a spectrum of domains, ranging from agricultural technology dissemination through the Food Production Enhancement Action to spearheading a Global Clean Energy Cooperation Partnership geared toward enhancing energy security. Notably, China's developmental largesse extends to Africa, underscored by its substantial assistance to the continent over the past decade (BRICS SUMMIT: China to launch special fund for GDI, 2023).

Amidst the economic landscape, Brazil, South Africa, and Russia witnessed a stagnation in growth trajectories, juxtaposed against India's commendable ascent from a GDP of $1.7 trillion to $3.1 trillion. Nonetheless, India's growth narrative was eclipsed by the meteoric rise witnessed in China's economic sphere. In a pivotal juncture in 2014, the BRICS nations collectively unveiled the NDB, endowed with an initial corpus of $50 billion (equivalent to approximately €46 billion) as a viable alternative to the established financial bastions of the World Bank and the IMF. Concurrently, they forged a robust liquidity mechanism christened the CRA, designed to furnish vital support to member states grappling with imminent payment exigencies (Prange, 2023).

The BRICS has instituted a formidable NDB, boasting a robust asset base amounting to US$100 billion. In a marked departure from convention, the consortium has recently embraced gold as a pivotal commodity within its foreign reserve currency framework, signaling a deliberate shift away from reliance on the US dollar. Beyond merely catering to the fiscal exigencies of the BRICS member nations, the NDB stands resolute in extending its financial mantle to encompass other developing and emerging economies. These nations, oftentimes grappling with the deleterious aftermath of the IMF's abbreviated liberalization programs, characterized by constricted public budgets and the privatization of state-owned enterprises, find solace in the NDB's resolute commitment to steering clear of such detrimental repercussions. Instead, the NDB avows a steadfast dedication to engendering positive economic outcomes through the implementation of enduring structural adjustment initiatives and judicious austerity measures. This institutional ethos of inclusivity is underscored by the NDB's welcoming stance toward new members, as evidenced by the 2021 inclusion of Egypt, the UAE, Uruguay, and Bangladesh into its esteemed ranks.

Moreover, a constellation of nations, including Saudi Arabia, the UAE, Egypt, Algeria, Argentina, Mexico, and Nigeria, have aligned themselves with the BRICS bank, further enhancing its global footprint and fostering a climate of collaborative economic stewardship. Against the backdrop of geopolitical flux, the diplomatic arena stands witness to the stark delineation between an Eastern-backed Russia and the USA-backed West. The conflagration in Ukraine and the protracted turmoil in Palestine serve as poignant fulcrums, accentuating the chasm that delineates these polarized geopolitical spheres (Prange, 2023).

At the forefront of this transformation are India and China, which ranked third and first, respectively, by PPP in 2023—positions both countries are projected to hold through 2030.

China's contribution to BRICS+ exports soared from 36.1% in 2000 to 62.5% in 2023, while India's share also increased considerably, reaching 7.9% in 2023.

The BRICS+ group has made remarkable advances in high-tech exports as well, with its share climbing from just 5% of the global market in 2000 to 32.8% in 2022. This growth reflects a strategic pivot toward technology-intensive sectors, solidifying BRICS+ nations as essential contributors to the global high-tech economy.

On the currency front, BRICS+ currencies are gaining traction worldwide. While the Chinese Yuan has remained relatively stable with slight appreciation, the Indian Rupee has depreciated, particularly since 2018. Concurrently, the US dollar's share as a global reserve currency has declined from 71.5% in 2000 to 58.2% in 2024, indicating a gradual shift toward a more diversified currency landscape.

Amid rising geopolitical tensions, coordinated policies among BRICS+ members could pose a challenge to the established dominance of the G7 and the US dollar, advancing a new multipolar economic framework. The BRICS+ group is actively developing a platform for international trade and investment transactions, which could serve as a cost-effective alternative to the SWIFT system. Furthermore, the group is progressing toward a trade and reserve currency backed by gold and other strategic commodities.

The widening economic gap between BRICS and the G7 appears to be a continuing trend, fueled by BRICS' concerted initiatives to accelerate socioeconomic development and promote sustainable growth. These efforts are poised to deliver tangible benefits to the quality of life and well-being of their citizens, positioning BRICS as a pivotal force in reshaping the future trajectory of the global economy (Prabhakar, 2014). Over the past few decades, BRICS has contributed to over 40% of global GDP growth, solidifying its role as a key driver of the world economy. For the current year, BRICS is projected to achieve an average economic growth rate of 4%, significantly outpacing the G7's 1.7% and the global average. Moreover, the bloc now accounts for approximately a quarter of global goods exports, with companies from these nations leading in critical sectors such as energy resources, metals, and food—markets that are vital for sustainable economic development.

2.11 FACTS, FINDINGS, AND RESULTS

Formation and Composition: Established in 2009 as an alliance of major emerging economies—Brazil, Russia, India, China, and South Africa—BRICS (initially BRIC) was founded to foster economic cooperation and address common challenges faced by developing nations. The bloc's composition reflects a strategic alignment of diverse economic and political interests, aimed at enhancing global influence.

Economic Significance: Together, the BRICS nations account for approximately 42% of the world's population and nearly 50% of global GDP, signifying their substantial economic weight. The bloc's economic significance is projected to grow, underscoring its increasing influence on the international stage and its role in shaping global economic dynamics.

Strategic Initiatives: The NDB, launched in 2014, serves as a pivotal financial institution committed to supporting infrastructure development and sustainable growth within member states and other emerging economies. The NDB provides a compelling alternative to traditional Western-dominated financial institutions, aiming to diversify funding sources for the Global South.

Geopolitical Context: BRICS operates within a complex geopolitical environment marked by intensifying tensions among member countries, particularly the enduring rivalry between China and India. These geopolitical dynamics pose significant challenges to the coalition's unity and its ability to act as a cohesive force in global governance.

Internal Divisions: The analysis reveals significant internal obstacles, including varying political systems, economic disparities, and conflicting national priorities. Such heterogeneity complicates consensus building and often impedes decisive action, reflecting the inherent diversity of interests within the alliance.

Geopolitical Tensions: Ongoing geopolitical frictions, especially the strained relations between China and India, continue to hinder BRICS's efforts to project a united stance on major international issues. This disunity undermines the bloc's effectiveness in championing a multipolar global order and dilutes its bargaining power.

Latent Potential: Despite the internal and external challenges, BRICS possesses considerable latent potential. Its vast demographic base, abundant economic resources, and firm commitment to sustainable development provide a solid foundation for the bloc to shape a reimagined global order, particularly by promoting South–South cooperation and alternative development models.

Emerging Opportunities: The research identifies strategic opportunities for BRICS to expand its influence through the potential inclusion of additional emerging economies and by strengthening ties with nonmember states. Such expansion could enhance the coalition's capacity to advocate for a more equitable and inclusive global governance framework.

Strategic Recommendations: The study highlights the need for BRICS to align its divergent interests and prioritize collective action to address contemporary international challenges. Achieving this alignment will require strategic foresight and cohesive policymaking to maximize the bloc's potential and fulfill its objectives effectively.

Implications for Global Governance: The findings emphasize BRICS's ability to shape global governance structures by advocating for reforms that mitigate the imbalances inherent in the current international system. The bloc's focus on representing the interests of the Global South can facilitate the emergence of a more balanced and inclusive world order, with a stronger voice for developing nations.

Increased Relevance: As the global geopolitical landscape evolves toward multipolarity, BRICS is increasingly recognized as a critical actor in international affairs. Its initiatives, particularly in sustainable development and infrastructure investment, bolster its legitimacy and position it as a viable alternative to established Western-led institutions.

Future Prospects: The results suggest that BRICS has the potential to become a transformative force in the global political and economic arena by effectively navigating both internal and external challenges. Strategic initiatives and a commitment to cohesive action will be essential for the bloc to realize its foundational vision of reconfiguring the global order in favor of a more multipolar and just system.

2.12 THE DEBATE ON THE BRICS: A NEW GLOBAL ORDER

The agenda for the 2024 BRICS Summit is centered on reinforcing multilateralism, expanding trade, and deepening cooperation across diverse domains such as technology, health, energy, and sustainable development among its member nations—Brazil, Russia, India, China, and South Africa. Collectively, the BRICS countries account for approximately 35% of the global economy in terms of PPP, with China alone contributing more than half of this economic strength. This year, BRICS is poised to challenge the preeminence of the US dollar by advocating for its reduced usage in international transactions, thereby mitigating the impact of US sanctions. The bloc functions as a forum for fostering economic and military alliances while exploring alternatives to dollar-centric global trade.

Collectively, BRICS members cover 30% of the world's landmass and represent 45% of the global population. As participants in the G20, their combined economic power is formidable, boasting a nominal GDP of $28 trillion—equivalent to 27% of the world's total—and a PPP GDP of $65 trillion, which accounts for one-third of the global figure. By the end of the decade, BRICS's share of global GDP is projected to rise to 37%, while the share held by the Group of Seven leading Western economies is anticipated to decline from 30% to approximately 28%. With over 30 nations, including NATO member Turkiye, expressing interest in joining, the summit is set to make pivotal decisions that could significantly reshape international relations. A key highlight will be the discussion of alternatives to the US dollar and the SWIFT payment system.

2.13 GLOBAL SOUTH/G77

Established in 1964 by 77 nations from the Global South, the G77 has expanded to encompass 134 member states, including China, collectively representing 80% of the global population. The G77 convened a landmark summit in Havana, Cuba, on September 15–16, 2023, attended by approximately 30 heads of state and government from Africa, Asia, and Latin America. The summit sought to articulate and advance shared economic interests, enhance collaborative negotiating strength, and champion multilateralism, cooperation, and equitable development. A central aim was to assert the right to development within an increasingly exclusive and inequitable international system, addressing the systemic obstacles faced by developing nations under the USA-led Western hegemonic order and advocating for the establishment of a new economic world order.

The Global South plays an increasingly pivotal role in the global economy, contributing over half of the world's GDP. Intra-trade among these nations surged to USD 6.1 trillion in 2022, up from USD 5.3 trillion in 2021, reflecting a robust 13% growth in trade value. Developing regions, encompassing Asia, Latin America, Africa, and Oceania, accounted for 42.08% of total global merchandise exports in 2018. Notably, intra-regional trade in Asia reached 32.78%, while Africa's intra-trade under the African Continental Free Trade Area (AfCFTA) constituted approximately 14% of total African trade—a stark contrast to Europe's 60% and North America's 40%.

Despite these strides, developing nations continue to trade predominantly with developed economies, amounting to USD 8.9 trillion annually, compared to USD 6.1 trillion in South–South trade. This disparity underscores the enduring dominance of North–North trade, valued at USD 9.5 trillion, highlighting the challenges developing nations face in achieving greater economic independence and integration within the Global South (South–South Trade Increases; UNCTAD, 2023).

TABLE 2.1 Intra-Trade and Rest of the World Trade of Global South Countries in 1995–2018, Percentage by Destination.

Countries	1995		2000		2005		2010		2015		2018	
	IG	W	IG	W	IG	W	IG	W	IG	W	IG	W
Africa	12.01	87.99	9.38	90.62	9.53	90.47	13.81	86.19	17.94	82.06	15.26	84.74
America	20.50	79.50	17.84	82.16	18.66	81.34	19.97	80.03	17.26	82.74	16.14	83.86
Asia	42.22	57.78	41.65	58.35	46.58	53.42	51.46	48.54	53.60	46.40	53.85	46.15
Oceania	0.35	99.65	2.41	97.59	3.99	96.01	2.90	97.10	2.81	97.19	2.62	97.38

Source: Authors' development based on UNCTAD (2019).

IG, intra-group; W, rest of the world.

South–South trade stands as the foremost contributor to global commerce in communication equipment, chemicals, electric and other machinery, and basic metals. Notably, South–South trade represents approximately 50% of the world's trade in communication equipment. Furthermore, a distinctive characteristic of South–South trade, particularly evident in exports, is the reliance on primary commodities, notably oil, gas, coal, and petroleum products. This reliance is particularly pronounced among developing nations in Latin America, Africa, and the Middle East. Primary products constitute approximately one-third of exports in both South–South and South–North trade (as illustrated in Table 2.1).

In terms of investment, the outflows of foreign direct investment (FDI) from the Global South have accounted for a third of global flows. Prevailing global sentiment suggests a shifting balance of power away from the West, which has held sway for the past three to four centuries, toward the East in the 21st century. The GDP ratio and trade performance of the South have tripled, accompanied by the acquisition of technological and financial capacities by select emerging nations such as China, Russia, India, Brazil, South Africa, Iran, North Korea, Cuba, Vietnam, and Venezuela. The South, in conjunction with Latin America, Africa, and Asia, has exceeded the corresponding benchmarks of Western Europe and the USA, poised to exert a transformative influence on the global economy in the 21st century (Prabhakar, 2020b).

Historically, the peoples of Asia, Africa, and Latin America have borne the brunt of Western imperialism. Regions densely populated, such as China, India, Indonesia, Pakistan, Iran, Afghanistan, Iraq, Yugoslavia, Syria, Libya, Palestine, and Yemen, alongside numerous African and Latin American nations, have endured devastation at the hands of Western colonial masters and imperialist forces spanning three to four centuries. Presently, emerging nations like China, India, South Africa, Brazil, Russia, Iran, Venezuela, Cuba, North Korea, and others harbor clear aspirations to challenge the prevailing iteration of the USA-led global order, aiming to supplant Western dominance in various spheres including currency, technology, trade, finance, and military with their envisioned "New World Order."

In the waning years of the 20th century, coinciding with the collapse of the Soviet Socialist Block, a new liberal international economic system, often dubbed the globalization project, was initiated. This paradigm shift was shaped by institutions such as the World Bank, the IMF, and the

TABLE 2.2 Intra-Trade and Extra-Trade of Global South Countries By-products in 1995–2018, Percentage by Destination.

Countries	1995		2000		2005		2010		2015		2018	
	IG	W	IG	W	IG	W	IG	W	IG	W	IG	W
Africa												
Food items	15.05	84.95	17.47	82.53	18.46	81.54	26.66	73.34	26.04	73.96	23.77	76.23
Ores and metals	5.02	94.98	7.90	92.10	8.13	91.87	6.55	93.45	6.26	93.74	11.97	88.03
Fuels	6.03	93.97	5.01	94.99	5.29	94.71	6.62	93.38	10.26	89.74	9.08	90.92
Manufactured goods	24.44	75.56	18.66	81.34	19.78	80.22	33.70	66.30	33.62	66.38	25.52	74.48
Chemical products	30.33	69.67	27.62	72.38	26.64	73.36	32.88	67.12	39.16	60.84	29.13	70.87
Machinery	28.87	71.13	20.13	79.87	16.83	83.17	36.81	63.19	29.35	70.65	19.96	80.04
Electronic goods	55.61	44.39	64.53	35.47	47.43	52.57	49.21	50.79	44.31	55.69	37.47	62.53
Iron and steel	20.59	79.41	12.37	87.63	15.98	84.02	23.29	76.71	28.49	71.51	28.28	71.72
Textile and clothing	9.54	90.46	7.09	92.91	7.13	92.87	11.88	88.12	15.20	84.80	12.53	87.47
Latin America												
Food items	17.56	82.44	18.51	81.49	14.43	85.57	16.80	83.20	15.12	84.88	14.21	85.79
Ores and metals	12.00	88.00	12.64	87.36	12.30	87.70	9.26	90.74	7.45	92.55	5.96	94.04
Fuels	26.56	73.44	28.28	71.72	21.66	78.34	19.46	80.54	24.80	75.20	24.32	75.68
Manufactured goods	22.50	77.50	15.49	84.51	20.79	79.21	26.88	73.12	19.63	80.37	17.80	82.20
Chemical products	48.44	51.56	49.32	50.68	47.35	52.65	50.08	49.92	49.09	50.91	44.59	55.41
Machinery	15.81	84.19	9.53	90.47	15.90	84.10	20.21	79.79	12.76	87.24	11.85	88.15
Electronic goods	9.57	90.43	6.16	93.84	10.93	89.07	10.27	89.73	7.30	92.70	6.16	93.84
Iron and steel	21.36	78.64	23.88	76.12	25.00	75.00	33.03	66.97	24.80	75.20	23.72	76.28
Textile and clothing	21.48	78.52	11.72	88.28	15.29	84.71	28.90	71.10	23.22	76.78	23.55	76.45

TABLE 2.2 *(Continued)*

Countries	1995		2000		2005		2010		2015		2018	
	IG	W	IG	W	IG	W	IG	W	IG	W	IG	W
Asia												
Food items	45.27	54.73	44.99	55.01	45.61	54.39	54.16	45.84	56.91	43.09	58.05	41.95
Ores and metals	61.64	38.36	62.35	37.65	70.08	29.92	70.03	29.97	67.90	32.10	66.83	33.17
Fuels	40.73	59.27	45.42	54.58	49.88	50.12	59.32	40.68	66.02	33.98	64.71	35.29
Manufactured goods	41.42	58.58	39.91	60.09	44.44	55.56	47.95	52.05	50.10	49.90	50.57	49.43
Chemical products	69.25	30.75	65.41	34.59	62.82	37.18	62.24	37.76	60.04	39.96	62.88	37.12
Machinery	40.88	59.12	41.56	58.44	47.10	52.90	51.16	48.84	54.93	45.07	55.47	44.53
Electronic goods	22.33	77.67	20.84	79.16	27.88	72.12	31.84	68.16	34.89	65.11	33.84	66.16
Iron and steel	64.97	35.03	58.42	41.58	64.09	35.91	62.14	37.86	59.05	40.95	59.16	40.84
Textile and clothing	39.29	60.71	34.31	65.69	30.79	69.21	30.29	69.71	33.68	66.32	32.39	67.61
Oceania												
Food items	0.22	99.78	4.34	95.66	9.42	90.58	6.18	93.82	5.03	94.97	6.08	93.92
Ores and metals	0.01	99.99	2.62	97.38	0.17	99.83	0.11	99.89	0.47	99.53	0.24	99.76
Fuels	0.39	99.61	0.91	99.09	4.46	95.54	5.05	94.95	2.65	97.35	2.28	97.72
Manufactured goods	1.21	98.79	2.58	97.42	3.99	96.01	6.34	93.66	7.49	92.51	5.79	94.21
Chemical products	3.09	96.91	7.62	92.38	22.87	77.13	15.93	84.07	7.95	92.05	8.12	91.88
Machinery	1.86	98.14	9.09	90.91	5.68	94.32	9.09	90.91	8.25	91.75	6.90	93.10
Electronic goods	0.85	99.15	1.78	98.22	4.88	95.12	26.44	73.56	17.79	82.21	9.97	90.03
Iron and steel	0.03	99.97	0.29	99.71	0.36	99.64	0.34	99.66	0.57	99.43	0.33	99.67
Textile and clothing	0.15	99.85	0.45	99.55	1.41	98.59	5.78	94.22	11.05	88.95	14.97	85.03

Source: Authors' development based on UNCTAD (2019).
IG, intra-group; W, rest of the world.

General Agreement on Tariffs and Trade (GATT) until its conversion into the WTO in 1995. These establishments have long been under the sway of the United States and Western Europe. However, the prevailing globalization, or global economic system/order, is undergoing a metamorphosis and realignment owing to the multilateralization of initiatives like the Chiang Mai Initiative, BRICS, and large-scale regional free trade negotiations such as the SCO-East Asian Cooperation (EAC), and the Regional Comprehensive Economic Partnership (RCEP).

The world now finds itself sharply divided into two blocs: the USA and European Union, along with 52 other nations, leading the First Block, while Russia and China, supported by 12 countries, lead the Second Block. A total of 127 countries have yet to align with either the USA-led first block or the Russia–China-led second block. Nineteen countries have expressed interest in joining BRICS, including Saudi Arabia and Iran. Thirteen countries have already applied for BRICS membership, with another six countries seeking to join the forum.

Ideologically and politically, the "neoliberalism" and "privatization" projects signify a resurgence of classical economist Adam Smith's doctrines, an ideology rebuffed by modern economists such as Keynes and Nobel Laureate Amartya Sen. Nonetheless, this classical ideology, once again championed by the conservative Thatcher and Reagan administrations in Great Britain and the United States during the 1980s, found practical implementation in South America before expanding to Canada, New Zealand, Australia, Japan, and South Korea. By the final decade of the 20th century, it had been globally embraced under the guise of the so-called "globalization project."

The neoliberal approach posits that the welfare state is generally undesirable, contending that it often exacerbates rather than resolves social problems. The overarching goal is the dismantling of state structures responsible for public service provision, to be supplanted by market-driven, private-sector activity. Proponents advocate for the market, with minimal or no regulation, as the optimal mechanism for delivering human services. This philosophy is predicated on the belief that such an approach maximizes efficiency, fosters competition, and enhances individual choice and accountability of services to their users. In this paradigm, the government's role is minimized, with policy directives leaning toward privatization, the "user pays" principle, private insurance mechanisms, voucher systems, and similar strategies (Ife, 2006).

The notion that a new construction necessitates positive destruction is deeply entrenched in history. Throughout the ages, the "World Order" has undergone transformative shifts catalyzed by conflict and war. Historically, the Western-dominated "Global Order" rested upon pillars of military supremacy, currency hegemony (exemplified by the dominance of the dollar), trade superiority in both capital goods and commodities, and extensive control over global oil reserves.

However, the landscape of the global order is experiencing profound upheaval in 2022. Since the late 20th century, following the collapse of the USSR-led socialist bloc and the discrediting of socialist ideologies in welfare states across the developing world, the USA emerged as a purported "unipolar superior power." Under the banner of so-called "globalization," the "Capitalistic Project" was swiftly inaugurated, championed by the largest Western Multinational Corporations (MNCs) who wield substantial influence in advancing capitalist agendas worldwide.

These MNCs and their transnational counterparts have come to dominate the global economy, reshaping the nature of international trade, FDI, and technology transfer. Leveraging instruments, such as the WTO, World Bank, and IMF, they have directly influenced the liberalization of economic policies, implementing structural adjustment programs across nations.

The proliferation of global supply chains and value chains orchestrated by these MNCs and TNCs, purportedly in the pursuit of global competitiveness and efficiency, has become ubiquitous. These corporations structure their global operations through outsourcing and offshoring, exploiting the natural resources, labor, and markets of developing countries in the former periphery and semi-periphery.

Remarkably, while representing a mere fraction of the total number of businesses, these Western corporate giants command a disproportionate share of global GDP, trade volumes, research and development activities, and employee compensation. For instance, a single MNC may accumulate more wealth than the combined GDP of 48 sub-Saharan African countries.

The influence of these MNCs extends far beyond the economic realm, permeating into foreign and economic policy domains such as taxation, trade regulations, foreign investment, immigration, and exchange rate determinations. In the USA, these corporations form the bedrock of the "military-industrial complex," exerting substantial sway over global conflicts and wars, contributing over a quarter of private sector GDP and employee compensation.

The preeminence of USA-based MNCs is reflected in their dominance of both exports and imports, shaping national and global economic trajectories. With a significant share of revenue generated from overseas operations, MNCs wield considerable influence, accounting for half of global exports, nearly a third of world GDP, and a substantial portion of global employment.

The dynamics of capital flows, particularly in the form of FDI by MNCs, have undergone notable shifts in recent years. Since the 1990s, there has been a discernible trend of capital flowing from the West to the East, notably toward Asia, with a particular emphasis on East and Southeast Asia, as indicated by IMF data. However, this trend witnessed a downturn starting in 2019, attributable to the disruptive impacts of the COVID-19 pandemic and escalating geopolitical tensions among global superpowers.

Nevertheless, it is noteworthy that despite the overall decline in capital flows from the West to the East, investments by China and China have remained resilient amid these challenges. Notably, Western MNCs have increasingly directed their FDI toward countries perceived as allies, constituting approximately 50% of total FDI inflows since 2008. Moreover, a significant portion, approximately 38%, of total FDI inflows have been directed toward geographically proximate countries.

Despite these trends, there has been a concerning decline in FDI in Africa, notwithstanding the region's acute need for development. This decline underscores the complex interplay of factors influencing capital allocation and investment decisions in the global landscape (Enoghase, 2023).

The prevailing global geopolitical and geo-economic landscape has once again delineated into two distinct blocs, each vying for supremacy and influence:

The Group of Seven (G7), comprised of the world's wealthiest industrialized nations, retains a commanding 44% share of global GDP despite constituting a mere 10% of the world's population. Its dominance is further reinforced through the USA-led North Atlantic Treaty Organization (NATO), an alliance encompassing 30 member states, predominantly European nations.

On the opposing front, the combined forces of China and Russia, bolstered by alliances with nations such as North Korea, Iran, and Venezuela, constitute a formidable bloc challenging the traditional hegemony of the West.

This epoch marks the culmination of an era dominated by Western imperialism and ushered in the dawn of a new paradigm, catalyzed by

Russia's decisive military intervention in Ukraine on February 24, 2022, aimed at demilitarization.

The ramifications of these seismic geopolitical shifts reverberate across various facets of global affairs, profoundly impacting international trade, food and energy security, investments, and technological collaboration. The escalation of tensions, epitomized by the China-USA trade war, the disruptive effects of the COVID-19 pandemic, the Russia-Ukraine conflict, and the imposition of economic sanctions by the West against nations like Iran, North Korea, Venezuela, Russia, and China, has prompted a realignment of major global powers and a transition from unipolarity to multipolarity in the global order.

These geopolitical and economic dynamics have disrupted the trajectory of globalization projects initiated in the late 20th century, leading to a resurgence of protectionism, right-wing corporate nationalism, and strains on the global economy. Nations across Asia, Africa, Europe, and the USA grapple with economic recessions, soaring inflation, disruptions in food and energy supplies, and unemployment woes.

The spectre of food insecurity looms large not only over countries like Sri Lanka and Pakistan, grappling with inflationary pressures, but also extends to regions spanning Africa, Europe, the Pacific Islands, and the Middle East. Addressing agricultural trade barriers and fostering regional economic blocs could ameliorate global food security challenges, ensuring equitable access to diverse and nutritious food, particularly in low-income African and Asian nations.

The current global food crisis is exacerbated by geopolitical conflicts, economic sanctions, and trade barriers imposed by dominant powers, underscoring the urgent need for initiatives aimed at de-dollarization, de-corporatization, and de-globalization. Such endeavors would prioritize food and energy security, as well as foster economic and financial stability on a regional scale.

The escalation of conflicts such as the China-USA trade war, the Russia-Ukraine military confrontation, and various other geopolitical flashpoints underscores the inherent contradictions within the existing global order. These tensions epitomize the clash between entrenched Western imperialist forces, spearheaded by the USA and its European allies, and emerging powers like China, Russia, India, Iran, Brazil, and South Africa. The emergence of this new global order, championed by China and Russia, reflects the growing discontent and divergence of interests between erstwhile colonial powers and rising nations.

The BRICS has spearheaded initiatives aimed at "de-dollarization," challenging the Western-dominated global order perpetuated by former colonial powers and supported by the Group of Seven (G7), the World Bank, and the IMF. Concurrently, efforts to assert control over crucial sea trade routes have been initiated as part of new geopolitical realignments. Central to these endeavors is the establishment of a productivity platform by the BRICS, focusing on fostering "decent work, dignity, and respect for all." This platform seeks to promote collaboration in employment creation and labor market governance among BRICS partners, emphasizing labor rights, universal access to social protection, skills development, and the promotion of sustainable enterprises to drive inclusive and sustainable economic growth.

The geopolitical landscape is further complicated by the emergence of three pivotal "Blue Battle Grounds" spanning the Indo-Pacific, Asia-Pacific, and Arctic regions. From the Baltic Sea and the Black Sea to the Arctic Sea, South China Sea, East China Sea, and the Arabian Sea, these strategic zones have become focal points of contention.

Amidst ongoing Eurasian and Middle Eastern conflicts, the Indo-Pacific region has emerged as a key arena where major powers vie for influence. Here, the combined forces of China, Russia, and North Korea present a formidable challenge to the longstanding military dominance of the USA. Since the latter half of the 19th century, the USA has wielded influence through military, financial, trade, technological, and currency supremacy. Its strategies encompass a range of tactics, including direct military intervention in developing and impoverished nations such as Yugoslavia, Iraq, Afghanistan, Libya, and Syria. Additionally, the USA has often fomented military conflicts between Asian and African nations, such as India–Pakistan and India–China disputes, as well as the North Korea–South Korea standoff. Moreover, the USA has been known to instigate civil wars within countries and supply arms and weaponry to various factions. As the world's largest arms supplier, the USA exported weapons totaling $150 billion to nations, like Ukraine, Poland, Germany, Japan, South Korea, Israel, and others in 2022.

2.14 THE ECONOMIC AND FINANCIAL SANCTIONS IMPOSED BY WESTERN IMPERIALISTS

The Group of Seven (G7), the European Union (EU), and the World Economic Forum (WEF) have enacted a series of economic, trade, and financial sanctions targeting several nations, including Russia, Iran, Syria, North Korea, Venezuela, and Myanmar. Notably, the G7 and EU have collectively frozen Russian assets totaling USD 630 billion, concurrently excluding Russian banks from the SWIFT system. In response, Russia has defiantly confronted the US-led NATO and Europe, showcasing its formidable military prowess while strategically navigating economic and financial repercussions. To mitigate the impact of sanctions, Russia has diversified its trade alliances, forging robust partnerships with BRICS nations, notably India and China, circumventing the use of the US dollar and Western-dominated SWIFT system for financial transactions.

In a strategic move, European countries have turned to India as a conduit, importing a substantial 42% of their oil and gas from Russia through this channel in 2022. Demonstrating a concerted effort to challenge Western hegemony, Russia and India have brokered agreements to conduct trade using the Ruble and Indian currencies for oil and gas exports from Russia, as well as for Indian commodities. Likewise, China and Russia have solidified their trade relations, opting to employ the Yuan and Rubal for bilateral transactions. Consequently, China and India emerge as the primary importers of Russian oil and gas, cementing their status as pivotal investors and trade partners for Russia.

These intricate triangular dynamics among Russia, China, and India, coupled with the collaborative endeavors of Latin American, African, and Asian nations, underscore the collective capability of these nations to usher in a new era of multipolarity across global economic, financial, technological, political, and military domains.

2.15 IRAN–CHINA–RUSSIA COOPERATION

Iran, renowned for its vast gas and oil reserves ranking second and fourth globally, respectively, has faced considerable constraints in freely accessing and distributing these resources due to stringent economic and financial sanctions imposed by the USA. Nevertheless, Iran maintains a production capacity of 0.6 million barrels of oil per day, with its oil exports predominantly directed to Malaysia (46%), China (28%), the UAE (10%), and Syria (9%), yielding a substantial revenue of $40 billion in 2022.

Since the era of Barack Obama's administration, Iran has weathered a barrage of economic, trade, financial, and technological sanctions. In response, Russia and China have solidified their ties with Iran across various sectors, spanning defence, mining, railways, automobiles, machinery, and industrial equipment. Noteworthy among these engagements are the recent signings of two memorandums of understanding (MOUs) between China and Iran, collectively valued at over $8.1 billion, signaling a deepening of bilateral cooperation, particularly in agriculture.

The first MOU, valued at $3.5 billion, centers on collaboration in the fishery sector and agricultural mechanization, alongside initiatives for greenhouse development, rainfed cultivation, and knowledge exchange. Meanwhile, the second MOU, amounting to approximately $4.6 billion, is earmarked for financing a substantial irrigation project in southwestern Iran. Additionally, agreements in transportation and industry, valued at $12 billion and $3.5 billion, respectively, have been inked, encompassing joint endeavors such as the establishment of a high-speed rail link connecting Tehran and Mashhad, as well as investments in the development of Imam Khomeini Airport City. Moreover, strategic discussions have outlined investments along Iran's south eastern Makran Coast and the acquisition of Iranian oil reserves.

Trade between Iran and China has surged, reaching a noteworthy $24 billion. Notably, during the period spanning from March 21, 2022, to January 20, 2023, China emerged as Iran's principal trading partner, with exchanges totaling 29.2 million tons of goods valued at $25.3 billion, underscoring the robustness of their economic collaboration.

2.16 CHINA-SAUDI ARABIA-IRAN COOPERATION

A pivotal partnership has emerged among China, Saudi Arabia, and Iran, marked by a series of MOUs totaling $30 billion. These MOUs span various domains, including physical infrastructure, educational advancement, and security, signifying a deepening of collaboration between the three nations. China has positioned itself as a prominent importer of petroleum oil from Saudi Arabia, with the kingdom accounting for 18% of China's total oil imports. In reciprocation, China exports goods valued at $30 billion to Saudi Arabia as of 2022. Conversely, Saudi Arabia's exports to China amount to a substantial $50 billion, constituting a quarter of its overall exports. Notably, China is actively advocating for Saudi Arabia to adopt the Yuan currency for oil transactions.

This trilateral alliance carries profound strategic implications for the geopolitical dynamics of the Middle East, promising to wield considerable influence over the region's balance of power. The accord between Saudi Arabia, Iran, and China holds the potential to usher in stability, prosperity, and enhanced security across the Arab world. China's status as the preeminent global consumer of oil and gas further underscores the significance of this partnership. Moreover, both Iran and Saudi Arabia stand to benefit from investment opportunities in China, with transactions increasingly being denominated in local currencies, thereby diminishing reliance on the US dollar.

The collapse of the Bretton Woods System marks a pivotal juncture in the trajectory of the global monetary landscape, emblematic of three distinct epochs delineating the evolution of international finance. The inaugural phase denoted as Bretton Woods-1, was inaugurated in 1944, where the anchorage of the US dollar to the gold standard became the cornerstone. Subsequently, Bretton Woods-2 unfolded in 1971 under the auspices of President Nixon's decision to extricate the dollar from its gold moorings, thereby inaugurating a partial linkage to oil. Presently, the ongoing transition to Bretton Woods-3 signifies a paradigmatic shift toward a recalibrated global economic order, poised to redefine the hegemonic sway historically wielded by the US dollar.

Emanating from Latin America's triptych of Argentina, Brazil, and Mexico, extending across the vast expanse of Africa and Asia, encompassing the likes of Russia, China, India, Saudi Arabia, and Iran, the impetus for this epochal transition finds its vanguard in China. Embodied in the digital Yuan, meticulously underpinned by the auspices of the Chinese Central Bank and a constellation of goods and commodities, China assumes a pioneering role in reshaping the contours of global finance.

As Yuefen astutely observed, the Bretton Woods Accord of 1944 bestowed upon the US dollar a preeminent status within the international fiscal architecture, thereby concretizing the preponderance of American global hegemony. Nevertheless, the intervening decades have borne witness to a burgeoning dissonance between the economic prowess of the United States and the hegemonic sway exercised by the dollar. The attendant pitfalls of an overarching reliance upon the dollar have been palpably discerned, particularly among the burgeoning economies of the Global South. Recent endeavors to wield the dollar and its accompanying payment clearance apparatus as instruments of geopolitical coercion have galvanized a sweeping reevaluation of the dollar's incumbent role, precipitating an unparalleled de-dollarization endeavor spanning the vast swathe of Southeast Asia, Latin America, and the Middle East.

While strides have been undertaken to mitigate reliance upon the dollar through the diversification of foreign exchange reserves and the adoption of alternative currencies for trade invoicing, formidable hurdles persist. Imperatives for reform within the international fiscal arena, notably encapsulated by the de-dollarization thrust, demand concerted leadership from multilateral entities such as the BRICS consortium (Li, 2023).

The geopolitical and geo-economic landscape has been dynamically evolving since the turn of the millennium, as evidenced by the inception of the Quadrilateral Security Dialogue (QUAD) in the early 2000s. This alliance, fashioned as a bulwark against China's ascension in the South China Sea, East China Sea, Indo-Pacific, and Asia Pacific regions, signifies a paradigmatic shift in global power dynamics. Spearheaded by the United States and Japan, and subsequently bolstered by the inclusion of Australia and India, this realignment has engendered a novel geopolitical milieu, characterized by the crystallization of power blocs pitting China against the United States, and Russia against the United States.

The world is currently transitioning from a unipolar to a multipolar structure, a process that is both gradual and fraught with challenges. This shift will inevitably entail significant adjustments and disruptions in international relations and the framework of international law, which is presently under considerable strain.

Prominent emerging powers—Russia, India, and China—have opted to pursue alternative pathways within the global financial and trading systems, exemplified by their involvement in BRICS. These nations have demonstrated the capacity to engage effectively both bilaterally and multilaterally. Russia, in particular, places substantial value on its relationships with both India and China, underscoring its commitment to the idea of a genuinely multipolar world. When Russia advocates for a multipolar global order, it does so with authenticity. It refrains from interfering in regional matters, a principle it expects other powers, notably the United States, to uphold as well.

India, historically entrenched in a robust alliance with Russia, now finds itself ensnared in the precarious interstices between these burgeoning superpowers. India-Russia trade is poised to exceed the $60 billion benchmark in 2024, reflecting the deepening economic alliance between the two nations. This remarkable surge in bilateral trade is fueled by India's substantial import of discounted Russian crude oil amidst global energy market fluctuations, alongside steadfast collaboration in key sectors such as defence, pharmaceuticals, fertilizers, and machinery.

This burgeoning partnership signifies a strategic pivot in India's economic policy, emphasizing diversification of energy and commodity supply chains while solidifying ties with a historically trusted ally. The notable growth in trade volume, despite the imposition of Western sanctions on Russia following the Ukraine crisis, underscores the resilience and adaptability of this relationship. In a further step to fortify economic cooperation, both countries are advancing efforts to establish trade mechanisms utilizing local currencies, thereby reducing dependency on dollar-denominated transactions. These initiatives aim to enhance trade efficiency and mitigate exposure to geopolitical and financial uncertainties. As India and Russia venture into emerging domains such as technology, infrastructure, and renewable energy, their economic synergy is expected to expand further, laying a robust foundation for sustained and mutually beneficial trade growth in the years to come. Meanwhile, China and Russia have solidified an accord for untrammelled collaboration, with Iran emerging as Russia's veritable "nuclear shield." The confluence of interests has birthed an alliance encompassing Iran, Russia, Pakistan, China, and North Korea, meticulously crafted as a counterweight to the burgeoning political, economic, and military entente between India, the United States, Japan, and Australia.

Iran, a potent economic juggernaut within the Middle Eastern milieu, poised to burgeon into an economic behemoth by 2025, stands as a stalwart ally of Russia, China, and North Korea. The strategic trilateral ententes forged among Russia, China, and Iran have radiated their influence to encompass other regional stalwarts such as Saudi Arabia, the UAE, Iraq, and Syria, heralding a seismic geopolitical shift and portending the emergence of formidable power blocs within the realms of energy, trade, and military hegemony. This epochal development portends a deepening of the strategic quagmire between the United States and the amalgamated might of China and Russia.

Iran's entrenchment within China's ambitious New Silk Road Project, underscored by initiatives aimed at modernizing their naval and aerial armaments, as well as the development of the Chabahar port, has elicited consternation from India and the United States. The strategic import of the Chabahar port and its ancillary railway conduits looms large, holding the potential to metamorphose into a pivotal nexus for global trade, facilitating maritime transit routes from the Middle East to Africa and Europe, and extending to Central Asian hinterlands via Afghanistan.

India, occupying the mantle of presidency within the SCO, finds itself at a crossroads, pondering the prospect of aligning with China's Silk Road Project. The envisioned linkage between Pakistan's Gwadar port and Iran's Chabahar port, stretching forth to encompass Afghanistan and Central Asia, presents a tantalizing opportunity for regional connectivity and economic integration. Simultaneously, multilateral entities such as BRICS, SCO, EAC, and RCEP stand poised to counteract the unilateralist predilections propagated by the USA-led Western world. Among these burgeoning alliances, the confluence of skilled labor pools, burgeoning populations, copious natural endowments, and expansive territorial sprawls offers fertile ground for the cultivation of regional and international trade, technological synergies, economic prosperity, and security integration. The BRICS consortium, inaugurated in 2009, collectively represents a staggering 42% of the world's populace, commandeers approximately 27% of global GDP, and orchestrates nearly 20% of international trade, thus underlining its pivotal role in shaping the contours of the contemporary geopolitical milieu.

As per the pronouncements of the IMF, the collective GDP of the BRICS nations—comprising Brazil, Russia, India, China, and South Africa—stood at a formidable $27.3 trillion in the annals of 2022. Delineating further, the discrete GDPs of Egypt, Iran, the UAE, Saudi Arabia, and Argentina for the same temporal epoch manifested as $3.2 trillion, $730 billion, $402 billion, $813 billion, and $456 billion, respectively.

Upon the proclamation of these quintet nations' accession to the BRICS consortium, the aggregated GDP of this formidable alliance is poised to surge to a staggering $38.1 trillion. This anticipated augmentation in economic clout would effectively anoint the BRICS as the paramount economic entity on the global stage, eclipsing the G7—a constellation of advanced economies—whose cumulative GDP rests at a slightly lesser $36.8 trillion.

Such a projected confluence of economic might, encapsulated within the envisaged $38.1 trillion GDP, portends a seismic augmentation in both purchasing prowess and trade leverage on the international arena. This ostensible paradigm shift underscores a tangible amplification in the economic sway wielded by the BRICS member states, thereby heralding a reconfiguration of the global economic order (Rantao, 2023). The BRICS, comprised of Brazil, Russia, India, China, and South Africa, have inaugurated the NDB, colloquially known as the BRICS bank, a multilateral financial institution fortified with a substantial capital endowment of US$50 billion (€45.6 billion). This corpus is earmarked for the financing of infrastructural projects and climate-centric initiatives within developing nations. Counting among its stakeholders not only BRICS member states but also Bangladesh, Egypt, and the UAE, the bank has already disbursed loans surpassing $30 billion since its establishment in 2015. By comparison, the World Bank extended commitments exceeding $100 billion in the calendar year of 2022 alone. Furthermore, the BRICS have introduced a $100 billion Contingency Reserve Arrangement, a mechanism facilitating foreign currency liquidity to member states during periods of global financial tumult.

In a strategic manoeuvre aimed at challenging the dollar's preeminence, the BRICS have initiated steps toward the development of a unified currency. Simultaneously, the SCO, instituted in the year 2001, commands a formidable demographic footprint, representing 42.49% of the global populace and laying claim to 24.2% of the world's GDP. Initially encompassing eight member states, namely China, India, Kazakhstan, Kyrgyzstan, Russia, Tajikistan, Pakistan, and Uzbekistan, the SCO is on the cusp of welcoming Iran into its fold. Concurrently, Afghanistan, Belarus, and Mongolia assume observer status, while Armenia, Azerbaijan, Cambodia, Nepal, Sri Lanka, and Turkiye partake as dialogue partners.

As underscored by Ojha, the United States' policy of containment vis-à-vis Iran, epitomized by stringent economic and trade sanctions, has obstructed India's endeavors to foster bilateral ties with Iran in the energy domain. Traditionally, the United States, as a preponderant global power, has espoused an adversarial stance toward Iran—a regional entity commonly categorized as a "middle power"—deeming it a menace to American-Israeli dominance within the West Asian purview. The burgeoning ascendancy of Iran in the Middle Eastern echelons portends a formidable challenge to the established hegemony perpetuated by the USA-led global order. Consequently, the United States has enforced an array of economic and financial strictures, including curbs on the Iranian petroleum trade. Before the imposition of US-led sanctions in January 2012, India stood as Iran's second-largest consumer of crude oil within the West Asian panorama, trailing only behind China in this regard.

In response to the evolving landscape precipitated by the withdrawal of American forces, China, Russia, Iran, Pakistan, and neighbouring regional entities have embarked upon a concerted endeavor to ally, aimed at redressing the multifaceted challenges that have arisen within the Afghan milieu (Ojha, 2022)."

2.17 FINANCIAL REQUIREMENTS FOR INFRASTRUCTURAL DEVELOPMENT IN DEVELOPING COUNTRIES

The imperatives surrounding infrastructural development in developing nations, encompassing regions such as Africa, dictate an annual financial requisition of no less than two trillion dollars. Yet, in the wake of the inception of seminal financial institutions like the IMF and the World Bank within the Bretton Woods framework at the denouement of World War II in 1945, the collective efforts of these international financial bastions have faltered in furnishing even a quarter of the requisite funding requisite for the comprehensive ambit of industrialization, educational enhancement, health infrastructure augmentation, transportation modernization, digital marketing infrastructure fortification, employment proliferation, and poverty alleviation initiatives within the domains of developing countries.

The burgeoning phenomenon of the "Global South" encapsulates the constellation of developing and underdeveloped nations primarily located in the Southern Hemisphere, with a predominant presence spanning the continents of Africa, Asia, and Latin America. Coined initially in 1969 by the discerning political activist Carl Oglesby, the term serves as a poignant commentary on the historical narrative of northern dominance over these regions, with Oglesby contending in the liberal Catholic magazine Commonweal that the Vietnam War epitomized the culmination of such hegemonic tendencies.

Central to the operational dynamics of the Global South is the Global System of Trade Preferences (GSTP), an institutional framework fostered among developing nations under the aegis of the G77 bloc. Designed to catalyze trade facilitation, financial cooperation, and technology transfer, the GSTP primarily operates through preferential tariff concessions. At present, its expansive membership, spanning 42 nations across the expanses of Africa, Asia, and Latin America, collectively represents a formidable market force commanding a staggering US$16 trillion in economic value. Notably, this conglomeration generates an estimated US$4.4 trillion in import demand for diverse goods, constituting nearly 20% of the global merchandise import landscape (The Global Trade Preferential System among the Global South, 2023).

Alfred Sauvy, a distinguished French demographer, economist, and historian, is acclaimed for his seminal contribution in introducing the conceptual lexicon of "First World," "Second World," and "Third World" in 1952. Within this paradigm, the "First World" denoted the vanguard of advanced capitalist industrial nations, while the "Second World" encompassed the socialist bloc, notably including Eastern European nations under the aegis of the Soviet Union. Conversely, the "Third World" epitomized the cohort of developing nations, delineating their socioeconomic milieu amidst the post-World War II epoch. The resonance and dissemination of the term "Third World" were further amplified by the eminent sociologist Peter Worsley through his seminal work "The Third World: A Vital New Force in International Affairs," published in 1964. Worsley's portrayal juxtaposed these nations against a backdrop of impoverishment, destitution, and political instability, often portrayed in Western media as enclaves governed by autocratic regimes. This conceptualization of the "Third World" found its antecedents in the Non-Aligned Movement, an ideological bulwark that emerged as a counterfoil to the bipolar alignments of the Cold War era.

Concomitantly, the "Third World" was characterized by a plethora of socioeconomic malaises, ranging from endemic poverty, malnutrition, and homelessness to acute land scarcity, pervasive income disparities, and entrenched unemployment. These nations often found themselves relegated to the peripheries and semiperipheries of the global economic order, serving as erstwhile colonies subjected to the hegemony of Core Colonial Masters, predominantly emanating from North America and Western Europe. Conversely, the "Global North" emerged as a conglomeration of affluent nations predominantly situated in North America and Europe, with peripheral extensions into Oceania and beyond.

The dissolution of the Soviet Union and the concomitant demise of the Second World precipitated a waning usage of the term "Third World" throughout the 1990s. The nations comprising the Global South had historically borne the brunt of imperialism and colonial subjugation, with African nations serving as poignant exemplars. This historical trajectory significantly informed their perspective on the dynamics delineating the interface between the Global North and the Global South, colloquially epitomized as "the West and the rest" or "the North and the South."

Against this backdrop of entrenched disparities and historical imbalances, it is discernible why many nations of the Global South may evince reluctance in aligning with emergent superpowers, whether it be the "China-Russia-led BRICS-SCO-EAC-RCEP" consortium or the "America-led NATO" alliance. Such inclinations reflect a steadfast pursuit of autonomy and sovereign agency in the domain of international relations.

With the advent of the 21st century, there has been an observable recalibration in global power dynamics, a phenomenon underscored by both the World Bank and the United Nations. This transformative paradigm shift, often characterized as a pivot from the North Atlantic toward the Asia-Pacific realm or from the West to the East, has garnered widespread acknowledgment within the echelons of international discourse. Prabhakar encapsulates this paradigm shift succinctly, affirming the prevailing consensus regarding the discernible transition of power dynamics away from the Western hegemony toward the burgeoning ascendancy of the East (Prabhakar, 2020c). It is prognosticated that by the year 2030, three of the globe's four preeminent economies will emanate from the Global South, constituting a notable shift in economic power dynamics. The anticipated hierarchy will be led by China, followed by India, the United States, and Indonesia. Furthermore, the metric of PPP underscores the ascendancy of the BRICS nations, predominantly hailing from the Global South, over the Group of Seven (G7)—a consortium of affluent nations predominantly representing the Global North. Notably, the collective sum of billionaires in China, India, and Russia eclipses the tally present solely within the confines of the United States.

Since the juncture of 2022, international scrutiny has discerned a palpable contestation between China, Russia, and the United States, along with the latter's 31 NATO member nations and an additional 50 allied entities. This contestation unfolds across multiple theatres of engagement, including the Black Sea, the East China Sea, the South China Sea, the Indo-Pacific region, and the Arabian Sea. This challenge manifests through a confluence of military encounters, the forging of regional economic and trade blocs, and concerted initiatives aimed at mitigating the predominance of the US dollar—commonly referred to as dedollarization—in global financial transactions (Heine, 2023).

2.18 GLOBAL GEOPOLITICAL GAMES

The United States and Russia find themselves enmeshed in a devastating proxy war that, in numerous respects, eclipses the tensions experienced during the Cold War. Simultaneously, relations between the United States and China are steeped in profound mutual distrust and uncertainty. In stark contrast, the dynamic between India and China remains notably tranquil, especially when juxtaposed against the recent upheavals and violent shifts in the international order. Paradoxically, even the unconventional nature of India-China relations has proven to be more peaceful, stable, and predictable than those among other major powers.

The United States has articulated its position unequivocally: it views India primarily as a strategic asset in a potential confrontation with China, rather than as a sovereign nation with legitimate geopolitical interests and aspirations. This patronizing attitude has unsettled many in India, who harbor doubts not only about America's ability to execute its stern rhetoric regarding China should a serious clash erupt in the Himalayas, but also about the risk of India being inadvertently drawn into a perilous US-China military conflict in the Western Pacific. Further complicating this scenario, the United States has lost its unchallenged military supremacy relative to China, rendering the enforcement of a security framework in Asia unattainable without Beijing's acquiescence. The occupant of the White House in the coming years will be unable to alter these fundamental realities. This encapsulates a hard security argument, whereby India's national interests necessitate adept management of its relationship with China in alignment with a rapidly evolving international landscape.

Since the 1950s, various geopolitical contexts have shaped the trajectory of the India-China rivalry. Throughout this period, phases of détente, modus vivendi, Cold War-like conditions, controlled competition, peaceful rivalry, and collaboration have emerged. While the underlying structural challenges in India-China relations have never entirely receded, both nations have consistently adapted to the ebb and flow of the global order. New Delhi and Beijing have pragmatically managed their ties, even during more tense and ideologically hostile phases than the current one, driven by a shared recognition of mutual self-interest. This historical tapestry of conflict, competition, and cooperation management offers contemporary policymakers a nuanced template for navigating the months and years ahead.

2.19 GEOPOLITICAL SIGNIFICANCE OF BRICS

Among BRICS members, India adopts a dual approach in its geopolitical strategy, balancing relationships with both China and Russia while simultaneously engaging with the US-led Western bloc. Through BRICS, India endeavors to uphold its strategic autonomy by fostering multilateralism and precluding any single nation from dominating the group's agenda. In contrast, China employs BRICS as a vehicle to establish a global order that reflects the burgeoning influence of emerging economies. While asserting its leadership within the bloc, China seeks to forge partnerships with developing nations, particularly in Africa and Latin America, as part of its broader objective to challenge US-led global structures. For Russia, BRICS serves as a critical platform for maintaining global relevance amid escalating tensions with the West. The bloc not only fortifies its strategic partnership with China but also acts as a counterweight to Western-dominated institutions such as NATO and the European Union.

2.20 GLOBAL GEOECONOMICS

The earlier phase of India-China relations was characterized by globalization defined by distinct dynamics, wherein the primary focus was not on the accumulation of national power. Instead, economic policies pursued growth without adequate consideration for qualitative aspects such as industrial advancement, technological progress, and job creation. During this period, the collective West reigned as the preeminent force in the global economy. However, over the past decade, this open yet unequal international economic order has yielded to a fragmented, competitive, and uncertain form of globalization. Faced with a global power transition, major powers have reverted to industrial strategies, trade wars, and economic sanctions—tools once considered relics of the "flat world" paradigm of the early 2000s.

Consequently, India cannot rely solely on a strategy centered around growth, modernization, and job creation in the hope that external economic conditions will become favorable. Rather, it must proactively script the next chapter of globalization, ensuring that the rules and norms reflect the interests of large developing economies. This is particularly pertinent in light of the unabashed misuse of global public goods by Western powers to serve narrow geopolitical ends. As the West retreats from its leadership role, India and China have emerged as stabilizers of the system. This presents a compelling rationale for India to rediscover shared interests and seek collaboration with China in clearly defined areas that may serve as future public goods underpinning economic interdependence in a multipolar world. Naturally, other partners are also engaged in steering globalization toward a more inclusive, non-Western direction, with BRICS standing as the most prominent multilateral cooperation format at present. However, new opportunities for collaboration may arise in the future.

The evolving global economic order is intricately linked to the realities of trade, technology, and investment flows. China's dominant position in global industry and commerce renders it an indispensable factor in the economic strategies of rising powers. Despite this, India has reaped little geopolitical or economic benefit from its dealings with China. Efforts to leverage economic veto power have failed to elicit concessions from Beijing, and over the past four years, economic ties have subtly expanded without a coherent blueprint for sector-specific or national-level engagement. As a result, existing trade imbalances and manufacturing asymmetries have largely persisted, if not worsened.

The time has come for a more sophisticated economic approach, one driven by well-structured plans to enhance India's domestic capabilities. Although this is an incremental process, without unequivocal clarity and decisive policy signals, economic stakeholders in both countries will remain hesitant to commit to a renewed framework for interdependence. It is evident that global manufacturing supply chains, particularly in industrial and consumer electronics, cannot function without China's involvement. Aspiring to localize a greater share of global production inevitably necessitates the inclusion of Chinese firms, components, and technologies in national capacity-building efforts.

A nuanced strategy may draw insights from the United States "small yard, high fence" approach to China, wherein restrictions target specific critical areas with known security implications while allowing a broader range of interdependence to evolve organically across various economies and regions. Ultimately, India's policy cannot be uniform; it must involve a diverse array of stakeholders capable of articulating the detailed aims and considerations pertinent to different sectors of the economy. As Modi and Xi engage in dialogue at the BRICS summit in Kazan, Russia, the India-China relationship stands at a pivotal juncture. The cross-talk of the past four years, marked by opposed views on détente, must give way to a dynamic approach that is realistic in its security objectives, ambitious in its vision for world order, and confident enough to prioritize the core national interests of both nations. Under the prevailing international conditions, the prospects for constructive and responsible competition between India and China are within reach, awaiting refinement through earnest bilateral negotiations.

2.21 TECHNOLOGICAL INNOVATION

India aims to leverage BRICS to enhance technological cooperation in digital infrastructure, healthcare, and space technology, aligning with its aspirations to emerge as a global leader in the digital economy. China's dominance in sectors such as 5G, artificial intelligence, and manufacturing positions it as an innovation leader within BRICS, where it seeks to establish technology collaborations, including the development of smart cities. Despite facing sanctions, Russia remains a significant player in cutting-edge fields such as nuclear energy, and BRICS presents opportunities to expand cooperation in these sectors. Prime Minister Narendra Modi's forthcoming visit to Russia, at President Vladimir Putin's invitation, will further solidify ties between the two nations.

2.22 ENERGY AND CLIMATE CHANGE

Energy security is central to India's BRICS agenda, with a pronounced emphasis on cooperation in clean and renewable energy. The bloc also provides a platform for discussing sustainable development initiatives aimed at addressing climate change. As the world's largest energy consumer and a leading producer of renewable energy, China regards BRICS as pivotal for advancing its clean energy goals and consolidating its leadership in climate diplomacy. Russia, as a significant energy exporter, views BRICS as a means to reinforce its role in global energy markets and explore new projects, particularly in oil and gas, despite Western sanctions.

2.23 SECURITY AND COUNTER-TERRORISM

For India, BRICS serves as a stage to advance its counter-terrorism agenda, particularly in addressing crossborder terrorism emanating from Pakistan. India emphasizes the necessity for enhanced coordination in combating terrorism financing, cyber threats, and transnational crime. China's focus on security within BRICS aligns with its Belt and Road Initiative, aiming to safeguard overseas investments. Meanwhile, Russia utilizes the bloc to deepen military and intelligence cooperation, seeking to counter Western military influence.

2.24 GLOBAL SOUTH: TOWARD DE-DOLLARIZATION AND MULTIPOLARITY

The Global South's quest for economic autonomy and political sovereignty finds a powerful ally in BRICS, as it champions the principles of multipolarity and de-dollarization. India leverages its leadership role within BRICS to deepen engagement with Africa and Latin America, presenting a development model anchored in mutual respect and noninterference. This diplomatic thrust not only bolsters India's economic footprint but also fortifies its campaign for a permanent seat on the United Nations Security Council.

China complements these efforts by using BRICS as a conduit for advancing its strategic interests across Africa, Latin America, and Asia. Its emphasis on robust bilateral and multilateral ties with developing nations strengthens its influence while promoting a multipolar global order. For Russia, BRICS represents a vital platform for asserting its position as a key player in the Global South, countering Western hegemony, and advocating for diversified global governance.

For India, China, and Russia, BRICS serves as an indispensable mechanism for advancing economic, geopolitical, and strategic objectives. While united by a shared vision of multipolarity and the reformation of global governance structures, each nation navigates the bloc with distinct priorities, reflecting their unique regional and international ambitions.

2.25 GLOBAL FINANCIAL INSTABILITY AND THE SHIFT TOWARD MULTIPOLARITY

The dominance of the US dollar in the global financial system has long been a cornerstone of international economic architecture, dating back to the 1974 Petro-dollar agreement between OPEC and the United States. This accord mandated the exclusive use of the dollar for oil transactions, cementing its role as the global reserve currency. Over decades, Saudi Arabia directed approximately 77% of its oil exports to burgeoning Asian economies, including China, India, Pakistan, and Japan, reinforcing the dollar's supremacy.

However, recent geopolitical and economic shifts signal a profound recalibration of global financial dynamics. Saudi Arabia, along with the UAE and Iran, has begun selling petroleum to China exclusively in Yuan, signaling a strategic pivot toward alternative currencies. Russia has further catalyzed this trend by mandating that its oil and gas exports be purchased in Rubles, with major importers such as India, China, and North Korea complying. In 2022 alone, Russian gas exports to Europe surged by 42%, with payments predominantly executed in Rubles, exemplifying the growing momentum toward de-dollarization.

This movement extends beyond hydrocarbons. Venezuela has adopted the "Petro" cryptocurrency for oil transactions, while historical precedents, such as Libya's use of gold under Gaddafi and Iraq's preference for the Euro under Saddam Hussein, illustrate the geopolitical volatility surrounding currency diversification. Both leaders' attempts to shift away from the dollar were met with aggressive interventions, underscoring the entrenched resistance to altering the status quo.

Today, the de-dollarization campaign is championed by a coalition of nations including Russia, China, Iran, Venezuela, North Korea, and India, reflecting a collective resolve to dismantle the dollar's hegemony. This coalition is joined by the Global South—spanning Asia, Africa, and Latin America—and even European actors like France, which are increasingly vocal in their opposition to dollar dominance.

The European Union has made significant strides toward financial autonomy through initiatives such as the Indigenous European Payment Initiative (EPI), aimed at reducing dependence on the dollar. Concurrently, Europe's heavy reliance on China for trade—estimated at 98%—has prompted a shift toward settling transactions in Yuan, further eroding the dollar's preeminence in international trade.

The transition from a dollar-centric system to a more diversified and multipolar financial architecture represents a seismic shift in global economic governance. As the Global South, in conjunction with emerging powers and European allies, coalesces around de-dollarization, the stage is set for a reimagined international monetary order that champions equity, resilience, and regional empowerment.

2.26 SHIFTING TIDES: THE RISE OF THE ASIAN MONETARY FUND IN CHALLENGING DOLLAR DOMINANCE

Since the watershed year of 1974, OPEC, led by pivotal oil supplier Saudi Arabia, inked a seminal agreement with the United States and christened the "Petro-dollar" accord. This pivotal pact mandates that any procurement of petroleum products or crude oil necessitates payment solely in USDs. Over the ensuing decades, Saudi Arabia has directed a significant 77% of its petroleum oil exports toward burgeoning Asian markets, encompassing economic powerhouses such as China, India, Pakistan, and Japan.

In a monumental paradigm shift that underscores the recalibration of global economic dynamics, recent developments have witnessed Saudi Arabia, the UAE, and Iran converging to vend their petroleum products exclusively in Yuan currency to China. Simultaneously, Russia has made resounding proclamations, decreeing that any nation can procure Russian oil and gas while effectuating payments solely in Ruble. Noteworthy importers of Russian hydrocarbons, namely India, China, and North Korea, have unequivocally acceded to this stipulation, thus facilitating payments exclusively in Ruble. A tangible manifestation of this transformative trend is the surge in Russian gas supplies to Europe, which burgeoned by a formidable 42% in 2022, with Europe reciprocating by remitting payments in Ruble.

Beyond the realm of hydrocarbon transactions, Venezuela has embraced the "Petro" currency for its petroleum oil dealings. Echoes of past geopolitical upheavals reverberate in Libya's erstwhile sale of petroleum products in "Gold" during Gaddafi's regime and Iraq's transactional preference for "Euro" under Saddam Hussein's rule, culminating in their lamentable demises at the hands of American interventionism.

Notwithstanding the entrenched dominance of the US dollar in global financial corridors, a groundswell of dissent has coalesced, spearheaded by a coalition comprising Russia, China, Iran, Venezuela, North Korea, and India. This formidable amalgamation vehemently advocates for the imperative of de-dollarization, underscoring a collective resolve to dismantle the prevailing hegemony.

Against this backdrop, the Global South, encompassing the expansive swathes of Asia, Africa, and Latin America, alongside European nations, have allied in the pursuit of the "de-dollarization" campaign. The European Union, including stalwart members such as France, has emerged as a vociferous protagonist in challenging the unassailable dominion of the US dollar within the international financial and monetary arena. Endeavors to establish an indigenous EPI underscore the concerted efforts to diminish the overarching supremacy of the dollar. Concurrently, European nations, ensconced in a staggering 98% dependency on China for trade, have arrived at a consensus to transact payments in Yuan, further underscoring the seismic shift away from dollar-centric trading paradigms.

The technological trade war between the USA and China inaugurated in 2017 during the tenure of President Donald Trump, has intensified, exemplified by the protracted battle between tech behemoths Huawei and Apple. The ensuing repercussions have seen the Chinese mobile brand Huawei facing bans not only in the USA but also in Canada, Japan, India, Australia, Britain, and many other nations, despite the veneer of "free competition, free market, free trade" espoused during the era of globalization.

The geopolitical arena now witnesses a confluence of strategic manoeuvrings by Russia, China, Iran, Turkiye, and India across key battle-grounds such as the Black Sea, the South China Sea, the Indian Ocean (Indo-Pacific), and the Asia-Pacific. These nations endeavor to fortify trade and military alliances with Russia, eschewing the Western systems and prevailing global order. This burgeoning constellation of trade blocs, spanning from the Middle East through Central Asia to Southeast Asia, and extending into Latin America, underscores the burgeoning imperative to bypass Western frameworks and strengthen ties with China, Russia, and India, leveraging their vast capabilities.

The Indo-Pacific region, which represents the second-largest market for both the USA and the European Union, has become a focal point of contention. A majority of European and American trade, approximately 75% of total trade, traverses the sea lanes of the South China Sea to reach top trading partners in the EU, such as Taiwan, the Philippines, Malaysia, South Korea, Japan, and other ASEAN countries. Characterized by a complex web of strategic fault lines and historic mistrust, the Indo-Pacific stands as the crucible of China's quest for preeminence as the dominant superpower. Spanning from the east coast of Africa to the west coast of the Americas, the Indo-Pacific epitomizes a geostrategic fulcrum and the epicenter of a burgeoning global power struggle, encircled by major population centers and hosting eight of the top 20 economies, thereby underscoring its immense geo-economic significance (Mukherji, 2022).

2.27 PACIFIC INTEGRATION: THE ROLE OF FIPIC AND CPIDF FOR SUSTAINABLE, INCLUSIVE, AND SELF-RELIANT DEVELOPMENT

The term "Pacific Ocean" finds its origin in the Latin phrase Mare Pacificum, denoting a "peaceful sea," attributed to the Portuguese explorer

Ferdinand Magellan. Geographically, this vast expanse is flanked by the Arctic to the north and the Antarctic to the south, bordered by Asia and Australia to the west, and the Americas to the east. The Pacific Ocean hosts 18 sovereign nations, including Australia, Fiji, Japan, Kiribati, Marshall Islands, Micronesia, Nauru, New Zealand, Palau, Solomon Islands, and Papua New Guinea (PNG).

Furthermore, 23 nations hold membership in the Indian Ocean Rim Association, encompassing Australia, Bangladesh, Comoros, France, India, Indonesia, Iran, Kenya, Madagascar, Malaysia, Maldives,

Mauritius, Mozambique, Oman, Seychelles, Singapore, Somalia, South Africa, Sri Lanka, Tanzania, Thailand, the UAE, and Yemen. The Indo-Pacific region spans the Pacific Rim, Southeast Asia, South Asia, West Asia, and Eastern and Southern Africa, hosting approximately 2.5 billion individuals, and constituting 64% of the global populace.

The Pacific and Indian Oceans harbor extensive natural resources, particularly oil and gas reserves. Additionally, they serve as primary conduits for 70–80% of global trade routes, facilitating seamless commerce flow between hemispheres. Nonetheless, their Blue Economy faces formidable challenges, notably climate change, widespread ocean pollution, unsustainable marine resource exploitation, and alarming biodiversity loss.

Historically, the South Pacific, with its cluster of island nations, has attracted global powers' attention due to its geopolitical significance and abundant natural resources. This expansive and diverse region, comprising numerous island nations and territories, relies predominantly on agriculture, tourism, and fisheries. However, it is increasingly becoming a focal point for geopolitical initiatives.

India and China have been intricately involved in economic integration endeavors within the Pacific region, albeit with nuanced disparities in their approaches and focal points. Both nations have sought to foster economic integration through mechanisms such as the Forum for India-Pacific Islands Cooperation (FIPIC) and the China-PICs Economic Development and Cooperation Forum (CPIDF), alongside engaging in bilateral trade and investment ventures.

India's approach is notably underscored by its emphasis on capacity building, sustainable development, and the cultivation of strategic partnerships. Through initiatives like FIPIC, India prioritizes empowering Pacific nations with the necessary skills and resources for long-term prosperity.

Moreover, India leverages bilateral trade agreements and investment engagements to foster mutually beneficial economic ties and regional stability.

Conversely, China's engagement strategy is marked by substantial infrastructure investments, economic aid, and expansive connectivity projects, prominently epitomized by the Belt and Road Initiatives (BRI). By spearheading large-scale infrastructural developments, China aims to bolster connectivity and economic growth across the Pacific region, thus exerting considerable influence on regional dynamics.

These differing approaches wield significant implications for the economic development, geopolitics, and broader regional landscape of the Pacific region. While India's focus on capacity building and sustainable development aligns with the Pacific nations' aspirations for self-reliance and inclusivity, China's infrastructure-centric approach has the potential to reshape regional dynamics and foster closer economic ties with Pacific nations. The interplay between these contrasting strategies underscores the evolving dynamics of economic integration and geopolitical competition within the Pacific region.

India and China have both markedly increased their engagement with the Pacific Islands in recent years, albeit with contrasting approaches and objectives.

2.28 INDIA'S ENDEAVORS IN THE PACIFIC ISLANDS

India spearheaded the FIPIC in 2014, establishing a platform for dialogue and collaboration with 14 Pacific Island nations. FIPIC is geared toward augmenting cooperation across diverse domains such as climate change mitigation, sustainable development, trade facilitation, investment promotion, and capacity enhancement. India has unveiled a myriad of initiatives under FIPIC, encompassing lines of credit for infrastructure development, scholarships for educational pursuits, and multifaceted capacity-building programs.

2.28.1 MARITIME COLLABORATION

India has been actively engaged in fostering maritime security cooperation with Pacific Island nations, endeavoring to safeguard vital sea routes, combat piracy, and ensure maritime safety. Initiatives such as coordinated patrols, maritime surveillance initiatives, and capacity-building endeavors in maritime domain awareness have been initiated to bolster maritime security in the region.

2.28.2 HUMANITARIAN ASSISTANCE AND DISASTER RELIEF (HADR)

India has extended HADR to PICs grappling with natural calamities, including cyclones and earthquakes. India's HADR endeavors encompass the provision of relief supplies, medical aid, and support for disaster response and recovery undertakings. India has consistently provided substantial humanitarian aid and disaster relief to PNG. Notably, India dispatched a consignment of 7.2 million doses of anti-retroviral drugs, valued at US$3 million, in addition to supplying computers and peripherals worth approximately US$760,000 under India's Regional Assistance to PICs. Moreover, financial assistance totaling US$1 million was extended to PNG for earthquake relief and restoration efforts following the Ulawun volcano eruption. Additionally, a donation of 132,000 doses of the Astra-Zeneca Vaccine, valued at USD 450,000, was facilitated by M/s. Mysore Paints and Varnish Ltd.

2.28.3 PATTERNS OF TRADE AND INVESTMENT

India has been actively involved in fostering trade and investment ties in the South Pacific region. As a member of the South Pacific Community (SPC), India benefits from access to the Pacific Agreement on Closer Economic Relations (PACER) Plus, which facilitates economic integration among PICs. India has been exploring avenues for trade and investment in PNG and other South Pacific nations, particularly focusing on sectors such as agriculture, mining, renewable energy, infrastructure development, healthcare, education, and information technology. Bilateral trade agreements and preferential trade arrangements have been deliberated to foster economic cooperation and integration between India and the Pacific Islands.

TABLE 2.3 Bilateral Trade Figures Between India & PNG for the Last Few Years Are as Follows.

Year	Export from India to PNG (USD Million)	Import into India from PNG (USD Million	Total Bilateral Trade in USD Million
2018–2019	14.72	88.97	138.69
2019–2020	56.02	55.70	111.72
2020–2021	56.17	125.85	82.02
2021–2022	69.95	357.58	427.53
2022–2023	85.84	643.36	729.20

Source: Department of Commerce, Government of India (2023).

India's Export Items to PNG:

Textiles

India boasts a significant export share in textiles, comprising garments, fabrics, and yarn to cater to PNG's textile requirements. Renowned for its quality and diverse offerings, the Indian textile industry stands as a preferred choice for PNG's apparel and textile demands.

Merchandise

Diverse consumer goods, including electronics, household essentials, and personal care products, constitute India's merchandise exports to PNG. Leveraging its robust manufacturing capabilities and competitive pricing, India emerges as an attractive sourcing destination for such commodities within the PNG market.

Machinery and Equipment

India's proficiency in manufacturing machinery and equipment spans across various sectors, encompassing agriculture, construction, and industrial machinery. These products find resonance in PNG's infrastructural and developmental endeavors, driving demand for India's machinery exports.

Food Items

Indian culinary delights, ranging from spices, tea, rice to processed foods, enjoy popularity in PNG, owing to their superior quality and distinct flavors. The Indian food industry's diversity caters to PNG's varied culinary preferences, further solidifying India's foothold in PNG's food imports.

Pharma and Surgical Items

India emerges as a leading exporter of pharmaceutical products and surgical instruments to PNG, propelled by its hallmark attributes of quality and affordability. India's pharmaceutical prowess positions it as a preferred source for healthcare products in PNG.

Rubber

India's exports encompass rubber and rubber-based products, including tires, hoses, and allied items, to meet PNG's demands. Renowned for its premium quality and competitive pricing, India's rubber industry serves as a key contributor to PNG's import portfolio.

India's Import Items from PNG:

Nickel

PNG, as a prominent nickel producer, supplies India with this valuable metal, essential for various industries such as electronics, aerospace, and automotive. India imports nickel from PNG to meet its industrial requisites.

Copper

India imports copper from PNG, recognizing its significance across diverse industries including construction, electronics, and telecommunications. Copper imports from PNG contribute significantly to India's industrial and infrastructural landscape.

Pearls

PNG's reputation for high-quality pearls resonates with Indian consumers, driving imports for jewelry and luxury items production. Indian markets value the superior quality and allure of PNG pearls, facilitating their importation.

Copper Ores

In addition to refined copper, India imports copper ores from PNG, critical for various industrial applications including electronics, construction, and manufacturing processes.

Wood and Its Articles

India sources wood and wood-based products, such as furniture and handicrafts, from PNG, capitalizing on the latter's rich timber resources. PNG's wood products, renowned for their quality and craftsmanship, find resonance in India's import market.

Cocoa

PNG's cocoa bean production serves as a vital source for India's cocoa-based products, particularly chocolate and confectionery items. India imports cocoa beans from PNG to meet domestic demand for cocoa-derived products.

India's Investment Cooperation in PNG

India's investment endeavors in PNG have reached a substantial scale, amounting to US$100 million, primarily directed toward infrastructural development projects. A noteworthy allocation of US$60 million has been earmarked for the Bayer-Madang Road project, with the remaining US$40 million dedicated to the Hoskins-Kimbe Road project.

During Prime Minister Narendra Modi's visit to PNG from May 21st to 23rd, 2023, in conjunction with the 3rd FIPIC, a comprehensive 12-step action plan was unveiled. This action plan underscores India's commitment to fortifying its partnership with PICs, encompassing initiatives spanning healthcare, renewable energy, information technology, and education.

FIPIC's focal domains, spanning trade, investment, climate change, and capacity building, underscore India's multifaceted support to Pacific Island nations. India's endeavors extend beyond financial assistance, encompassing grants, concessional credit, and technical expertise, epitomizing its commitment to fostering sustainable development and mutual prosperity in the region.

Despite commendable efforts, India's engagement with the South Pacific faces notable challenges, notably the lack of connectivity impeding trade and investment. Moreover, India contends with stiff competition from other global players, including China, the USA, Japan, the UK, Germany, and Australia, who demonstrate heightened activity across various sectors, amplifying the competitive landscape in the region.

2.28.4 CULTURAL COLLABORATION AND PEOPLE-TO-PEOPLE EXCHANGES

India has conscientiously nurtured cultural ties and facilitated people-to-people exchanges with South Pacific nations. Manifesting its steadfast commitment, India has extended scholarships to students from South Pacific countries, enabling them to pursue education in Indian academic institutions. Moreover, India has orchestrated a plethora of cultural events and exhibitions throughout the region, meticulously curated to showcase the diverse tapestry of Indian culture and heritage.

In addition to these cultural initiatives, India has intricately embedded itself in conservation efforts within the South Pacific. With a discerning eye toward preserving the region's abundant biodiversity and natural splendor, India has taken proactive measures to contribute to conservation initiatives. This unwavering involvement underscores India's dedication to safeguarding the environmental treasures of the South Pacific, ensuring their enduring existence for generations to come.

2.29 CHINA'S ENGAGEMENT IN THE PACIFIC ISLANDS

China's presence in the South Pacific, particularly in PNG, has been propelled significantly by its extensive economic endeavors, chiefly epitomized by the Belt and Road Initiative (BRI). The BRI serves as a conduit through which China aims to cultivate connectivity and enhance economic collaboration across diverse geographies, including the Pacific region.

Established in 2006, the China-Pacific Island CPIDF stands as a pivotal mechanism for fostering economic cooperation and developmental initiatives among Pacific Island nations. Central to CPIDF's mandate is the facilitation of infrastructure development, investment facilitation, trade enhancement, and capacity building across various sectors, encompassing agriculture, fisheries, tourism, and telecommunications.

The overarching goal of CPIDF is to cultivate a conducive environment for sustainable economic growth and mutual benefit among participating nations. Through targeted initiatives and collaborative efforts, CPIDF endeavors to bolster the socioeconomic fabric of PICs, including PNG, by addressing critical developmental needs and promoting inclusive prosperity.

Within the ambit of the Belt and Road Initiative (BRI), Chinese investment in PNG has materialized through multifarious channels, prominently embodied by the China-Pacific Island CPIDF. Established in 2006, CPIDF stands as a pivotal conduit for fostering trade and investment, infrastructure development, and cultural exchanges between China and Pacific Island nations, encompassing PNG.

Chinese investment in PNG under the auspices of the BRI has predominantly concentrated on infrastructure development. This entails the construction of vital transportation arteries such as roads, bridges, and ports, geared toward amplifying connectivity and expediting trade. Additionally, China's engagement has extended to the energy and telecommunications sectors, thus contributing to the overarching socioeconomic advancement of PNG.

Nevertheless, amid the infrastructural strides catalyzed by Chinese investment, challenges have arisen. Paramount among these challenges is the opacity enshrouding China's aid endeavors, giving rise to apprehensions regarding debt sustainability and environmental ramifications. The dearth of transparency has spurred scrutiny from various quarters, including international observers and select Pacific Island nations, prompting an interrogation of the enduring implications of Chinese investment in the region.

Furthermore, China's involvement in PNG has intermittently encountered censure, with allegations of leveraging aid as a tool for political influence. Such apprehensions underscore the intricate dynamics inherent in navigating the socio-political landscape of the region, emphasizing the imperative of fostering transparent and mutually beneficial partnerships in engendering sustainable development.

In essence, Chinese investment through the BRI in PNG presents a dichotomy of opportunities and challenges. While it possesses the potential to ignite economic growth and infrastructural development, the imperative of ensuring transparency, accountability, and mutual respect looms large in nurturing sustainable and inclusive development in the Pacific region (Liqiang, 2023).

2.29.1 CHINA'S CONTRIBUTION TO GLOBAL ENVIRONMENTAL INITIATIVES

The urgency of the climate crisis has underscored the need for a unified global effort to mitigate carbon emissions. Recognizing this imperative, China has embarked on a significant journey to promote green and low-carbon development across 43 developing nations directly engaged in the

Belt and Road Initiative (BRI). These efforts entail a multifaceted approach, encompassing environmental protection measures, legislative enactments, regulations, and standards, as well as comprehensive environmental policies and management protocols. Furthermore, China has actively fostered technical exchanges and industry collaborations, all aimed at forging a cleaner and aesthetically enriched global landscape.

China's steadfast commitment to environmental stewardship is evident in its remarkable economic expansion, which has consistently averaged a commendable 6% annually. Notably, this growth has been achieved while maintaining an average annual energy consumption growth rate of a mere 3%. Particularly impressive is China's substantial reduction of carbon dioxide emissions per unit of GDP by approximately 35%, resulting in a commendable reduction of approximately 3.7 billion metric tons of carbon dioxide emissions. This remarkable achievement is further underscored by China's leadership in renewable energy, with installed capacity surpassing 1.2 billion kilowatts in 2022, marking a significant milestone by surpassing that of coal-fired power for the first time.

Aligned with its resolute emphasis on green energy and finance, China is actively positioning itself to seamlessly integrate into the global green industry and value chains. This endeavor includes enhancing capacities in advancing green investment and financing mechanisms while sharing its paradigm on green development and innovative solutions for pollution mitigation and carbon dioxide emissions abatement.

Through the Belt and Road Initiative, China has facilitated an augmentation of people-to-people connectivity and heightened integration among more than 140 nations. With investments exceeding USD 200 billion, these efforts aim to foster the development and scalability of clean energy solutions and allocate resources toward carbon sequestration initiatives. This holistic and far-reaching approach to green cooperation not only benefits China but also makes a substantial contribution to global initiatives aimed at combating climate change and realizing sustainable development objectives.

2.30 CHINA-AFRICA ECONOMIC PARTNERSHIP: A MULTIFACETED ALLIANCE FOR MUTUAL PROSPERITY

The burgeoning economic and trade rapport between China and Africa continues to deepen, showcasing remarkable growth and resilience. In

2022 alone, China's trade volume with Africa surged by an impressive 42.8%, culminating in a substantial revenue of USD 55.6 billion. Rooted in principles of mutual benefit and cooperation, the symbiotic China-Africa partnership has yielded significant dividends, with the total revenue generated eclipsing the monumental sum of USD 2 trillion.

Recent endeavors have seen China and Africa solidify their collaboration through monumental contracts valued at a staggering USD 700 billion. These agreements encompass a diverse array of sectors, ranging from infrastructure development and technology transfer to industrial projects. Moreover, both parties have committed to bolstering capacity-building initiatives, epitomized by the implementation of over 1000 specialized training programs tailored specifically for African professionals. These comprehensive programs are meticulously designed to augment skills, knowledge, and expertise across various domains, thereby catalyzing Africa's long-term development trajectory and fostering self-sustainability.

Against the backdrop of the 60th anniversary of the Organization of African Unity (OAU), African leaders convened in Addis Ababa for the 36th Ordinary Session of the Assembly of the Heads of State on February 18 and 19, 2023. This landmark occasion underscored the unwavering commitment of both China and Africa toward fostering robust diplomatic ties and nurturing a collaborative ethos. China's steadfast commitment to multilateralism in Africa harks back to a rich historical legacy, underscored by the Afro-Asian solidarity of the 1950s–1960s, epitomized by seminal gatherings such as the Bandung Conference, wherein China played a pivotal role.

Moreover, China's multifaceted engagement with the African Union (AU) in its nascent years was galvanized by its unwavering support for liberation movements across the African continent. Notably, by 1972, China's military aid to the OAU accounted for a staggering 75% of total military assistance extended to the organization's African Liberation Committee. Beyond ideological motivations, China's foray into African affairs has been driven by strategic imperatives, including the safeguarding of the one China policy and the consolidation of diplomatic isolation against Taiwan, in tandem with Russia, aimed at countering Western imperialism.

As China continues to navigate its evolving role on the global stage, its burgeoning engagement with Africa underscores its burgeoning appetite for raw materials and its aspirations to emerge as a preeminent international player. In forging a robust alliance with Africa, China is poised to exert a transformative impact on the global economic landscape, fostering prosperity and development across the African continent while consolidating its own position as a pivotal global player.

At the 20th National Congress of the Communist Party of China (CPC) convened in October 2022, the Chinese trajectory toward modernization crystallized into five key tenets: the modernization of a populous nation, the pursuit of common prosperity, advancement in material and cultural-ethical spheres, the fostering of harmony between humanity and nature, and the promotion of peaceful development. Central to these aspirations is the overarching vision of national rejuvenation, epitomizing China's collective ambition.

Concurrently, the African Union (AU) has delineated seven core aspirations within its Agenda 2063 blueprint. These encompass the realization of a prosperous Africa, the integration of the continent, the promotion of democracy, good governance, and human rights, the attainment of peace, the cultivation of a robust cultural identity and shared heritage, the pursuit of people-driven development, and the emergence of a formidable Africa as an active and influential global participant. In this convergence of objectives, mutual interests between the two entities emerge palpably.

Firstly, both China and Africa converge on the pursuit of common prosperity through people-centric development paradigms. For Africa, this entails the attainment of a "second liberation" through robust economic development strategies mirroring China's emphasis on inclusive and sustainable growth trajectories. Furthermore, there exists a shared recognition of the pivotal role of culture in fostering development. African scholars have long posited culture as the linchpin of Africa's developmental trajectory, a sentiment echoed by China's acknowledgment of culture as a cornerstone of national rejuvenation.

Moreover, the overarching objective of rejuvenating the Chinese nation resonates with Africa's ambition to emerge as a significant global player. Amidst a burgeoning international consensus advocating for enhanced representation and influence for Africa within multilateral fora, China's support assumes paramount significance. This year's summit, themed "Year of AfCFTA: Acceleration of the African Continental Free Trade Area Implementation," underscores the pivotal role of trade dynamics in Africa's developmental narrative.

As African stakeholders deliberate on continental trade dynamics, cognizance of China's pivotal role in regional trade over the past two decades is imperative. China's substantial investments in critical infrastructure such as roads, ports, airports, railways, and communication networks have significantly bolstered connectivity within Africa, thereby facilitating continental and sub-regional trade integration. However, challenges persist, notably, the trade imbalance skewed in favor of China. Despite China's recent measures to redress this imbalance by opening its markets further to African goods, concerted efforts toward policy coordination between African regional and sub-regional entities and China are imperative to surmounting extant challenges and fostering mutually beneficial trade relations (Shangwe, 2023).

Some scholars posit that China's approach to Africa diverges from the traditional Western paradigm of development assistance. Whereas Western discourse prioritizes the promotion of human rights, the rule of law, and democratic governance, China's engagement places greater emphasis on fostering economic development and stability. This focus on infrastructure development and resource extraction resonates deeply with many financially strained African nations, who view it as a pragmatic means to advance their own development objectives.

The goods, services, and technologies imported from China to Africa are often deemed more suitable for the local context. Chinese products typically offer a more cost-effective solution, making them accessible to a broader segment of the African population. Construction techniques and methodologies employed by Chinese entities tend to be less reliant on advanced technology, rendering them comparatively simpler for African entities to adopt, manage, and sustain. This stands in contrast to the more intricate and capital intensive approaches employed by Western counterparts.

Moreover, Chinese enterprises generally exhibit a higher degree of coordination, often with government support, enabling them to offer competitive pricing strategies and effectively penetrate and capture market share. This coordinated approach enhances the efficiency and efficacy of Chinese businesses operating in Africa, facilitating their ability to navigate complex local dynamics and emerge as key players in various sectors (Burke, China V. EU: Power Dynamics And Competition In Africa, 2023).

The Russia-Africa Summit convened in St. Petersburg with the aim of fostering a "new level of mutually beneficial partnership." This gathering sought to advance comprehensive and equitable collaboration between Russia and African nations spanning politics, security, economics, science and technology, as well as cultural and humanitarian realms. Termed "Africa +1," this summit mirrors analogous gatherings such as the Forum on China-Africa Cooperation (FOCAC), Japan's TICAD, and the US-Africa Leaders' Summit. The inaugural Russia-Africa Summit, held on October 23–24, 2022, in Sochi, brought together 45 African heads of state, two vice presidents, 109 ministers, and leaders from the African Union (AU) Commission, the African Export-Import Bank, and various regional economic communities. This summit underscored the principles of the Africa-Russia strategic partnership, accentuating potential collaboration in agriculture, natural resource development, industry, trade, infrastructure, energy, military affairs, and political cooperation. A final declaration was adopted, outlining plans for subsequent summits every three years.

Simultaneously, the Russia-Africa Summit hosted a Russia-Africa Economic Forum, where 92 contracts and memoranda of understanding, valued at $12.5 billion, were signed. Facilitating 569 meetings, the forum drew over 6000 participants, including 1100 international business representatives, 1400 Russian business delegates, 1900 official foreign delegation members, and 300 Russian delegation members. The 2023 edition of the forum will incorporate a humanitarian dimension.

Meanwhile, numerous African nations have initiated ambitious natural gas projects to monetize resources, bolster energy security, and catalyze long-term socioeconomic progress. Notably, Mozambique is spearheading several large-scale LNG developments.

The European Union (EU) maintains significant economic and political interests in Africa, contributing 43% of global aid in 2021, amounting to €70.2 billion. Over 70% of this aid is directed to Africa through the EU's development cooperation budget, supporting sustainable development, poverty alleviation, good governance, peace, and stability. EU initiatives, including Economic Partnership Agreements (EPAs), foster trade and economic collaboration. Additionally, the EU aids African nations in attaining Sustainable Development Goals (SDGs), concentrating on poverty eradication, education, healthcare, gender parity, agriculture, infrastructure, and renewable energy.

The EU actively engages in conflict prevention, peacebuilding, and security cooperation, endorsing peacekeeping missions, mediation endeavors, and regional stability initiatives. It prioritizes good governance, human rights, and democracy, reinforcing institutions, combating corruption, upholding human rights, and advocating for free and fair elections. While European policies aim to bolster EU business interests, market access, and resource extraction from former colonies, they are articulated within the framework of human rights, the rule of law, and democratic principles, signifying a commitment to liberal values. Nevertheless, the EU's endeavors to sustain relevance in a shifting global landscape encounter challenges as production capacities migrate to Asia, accompanied by a surplus of financial resources (Burke, 2023).

2.31 CONCLUSION

BRICS has emerged as a formidable alternative to the Western imperialist-dominated global order, which has prevailed for centuries. In the 21st century, it represents the potential to usher in a New Global Order that favors the Global South—comprising developing nations in the East and South.

By fostering strategic collaboration among rising powers, including China, India, Russia, South Africa, Brazil, Iran, Saudi Arabia, Turkiye, North Korea, and Vietnam, BRICS underscores the transformative vision of a multipolar world.

The coalition of Brazil, Russia, India, China, and South Africa transcends a mere alignment of nations. It symbolizes a shared aspiration for a sustainable, inclusive, and equitable global framework that addresses the intricate economic, political, and environmental challenges of our times. Grounded in historical insights, nuanced analysis, and a forward-looking perspective, this discourse highlights BRICS' contributions, complexities, and goals in reshaping global governance, promoting sustainable development, and enhancing cooperation across diverse regions and cultures.

In an era of rapid transformations and pervasive uncertainty, BRICS' role as a catalyst for systemic reforms and as a voice for the Global South is increasingly vital. Its unwavering commitment to innovation, equity, and unity suggests that the construction of a new global paradigm is not merely a distant ideal but an evolving reality. For policymakers, academics, business leaders, and globally conscious citizens, *BRICS: A New Global Order in the 21st Century* provides essential insights into the forces driving changes in international relations, global economics, and sustainable development. It urges active engagement with these transformative processes shaping the modern world.

The foundation of the Global South's resurgence, led by the trilateral alliance of China, Russia, and India, aims to redefine the global economic framework. Over the 21st century, developing nations have demonstrated remarkable economic growth, nearing parity with the Group of Seven (G7) industrialized economies. China, poised to become the world's largest economy by 2024, has spearheaded transformative initiatives like the Belt and Road Initiative (BRI) and the Asian Infrastructure Investment Bank (AIIB). These projects challenge US economic dominance, reshaping regional and global economic geographies while adhering to existing international regulations and institutions.

The evolving global economic architecture reflects a collective demand for an inclusive growth model. Emerging powers advocate for tolerance and mutual respect in recognizing diverse developmental trajectories, rejecting the entrenched hegemony of a single power.

BRICS, comprising 14 emerging economies—including Iran, Venezuela, Saudi Arabia, and North Korea—has established strong ties across Africa, Latin America, and Asia. Initiatives like China's expansive BRI exemplify the southward and eastward shift in geopolitical influence. These collaborations aim to address critical challenges, including poverty, unemployment, inequality, and climate change.

Developing nations are increasingly prioritizing renewable energy, sustainable agriculture, and technological innovation to drive self-reliance and resilience. Efforts to ensure equitable development have become central, fostering inclusivity by empowering marginalized communities and expanding access to education, healthcare, and political participation.

Despite its progress, BRICS faces the challenge of navigating internal diversity and aligning member states' priorities. Balancing divergent interests while fostering unity will be crucial to strengthening its influence in international forums and addressing global challenges effectively.

Recent geopolitical tensions, including conflicts in Ukraine and the Middle East, underscore the shifting global order. BRICS must navigate these complexities to assert its role in advocating for equitable governance and promoting the interests of the Global South. The coalition's commitment to systemic reforms, sustainable multilateralism, and inclusive economic growth positions it as a central player in shaping the trajectory of a multipolar world.

The forthcoming 16th BRICS Summit in Kazan, Russia, with its theme *"Strengthening Multilateralism for Just Global Development and Security,"* offers a critical platform for advancing these goals. With growing interest from nations seeking affiliation with the bloc, BRICS is poised to further consolidate its position as a leading advocate for a fairer and more balanced global order.

As BRICS continues to rise in geopolitical significance, its vision of fostering equitable cooperation and sustainable development resonates strongly within the Global South. This transformative initiative holds the promise of a more inclusive and resilient world, underpinned by a commitment to shared prosperity and collective progress.

China stands poised to ascend as the world's largest economy by 2024. China's strategic initiatives, such as the AIIB and the Belt and Road Initiative, seek to challenge the prevailing dominance of the United States in the global economic order. These ambitious endeavors aim to redefine economic geography in the regions they impact and exert substantial influence on the global economic stage. China, while adhering to existing global regulations and institutions, also seeks to assume commensurate responsibilities commensurate with its international stature.

This paradigm shift is not solely attributable to the substantial gains emerging powers, including China, have realized from the postwar global economic order and a tranquil international milieu, but also reflects the growing advocacy within the international community for a novel growth approach and a competitive outlook that espouses tolerance for the development trajectories of other nations. This underscores the imperative for an end to absolute hegemony in the global economic architecture.

The coalition of 14 emerging economies, led by China, Russia, India, Brazil, and South Africa, alongside nations such as Iran, Venezuela, Saudi Arabia, and North Korea, is forging robust ties with countries across Africa, Latin America, and Asia. This gradual shift of the geopolitical center of gravity toward the south and east is exemplified by China's expansive "One Belt and One Road Project Initiative," spanning Asia, Africa, Europe, and Latin America.

Collaborative endeavors and partnerships can be expanded and deepened across diverse domains encompassing infrastructure investment, trade, sustainable agricultural development, defence, cybersecurity, technology, healthcare, education, climate change mitigation, and environmental conservation across Africa, Latin America, Asia, and the

Asia-Pacific regions. These concerted efforts are geared toward fostering self-reliance and addressing pressing challenges such as poverty, malnutrition, hunger-related diseases, illiteracy, homelessness, unemployment, inflation, and inequality. Particularly promising avenues for collaboration include green tech entrepreneurship and the development of green and clean energy solutions. Vast opportunities and potential abound for India, China, Russia, Brazil, South Africa, Iran, North Korea, Vietnam, Bangladesh, Pakistan, Venezuela, and other developing nations to synergize their efforts in tackling the multifaceted challenges confronting their societies.

The Global South is presently undergoing a profound realignment, spearheaded by emerging powers like Brazil, Russia, India, China, and South Africa (BRICS). At the 15th annual conference convened in Johannesburg (South Africa) from August 22 to 24, 2023, 45 nations from the Global South showcased their keen interest in affiliating with the BRICS Bloc. This strategic manoeuvre aims to overhaul the prevailing global order by nurturing sustainable multilateralism and fostering inclusive economic growth and development. The BRICS member states are resolutely committed to catalyzing trade and investment initiatives, poised to challenge the prevailing Western hegemony.

Since its inception, the BRICS nexus has been forecasted to encompass 40% of the global populace and is anticipated to account for 45% of the global GDP in terms of PPP by 2030. The Global South is progressively pivoting toward industrialization, self-sufficiency, sustainability, and inclusivity. This transformative trajectory is underpinned by the acknowledgment that conventional development paradigms, often reliant on external aid or resources, are inherently unsustainable in the long run. Instead, Global South nations are channelling their energies toward fortifying indigenous industrial bases, fostering technological innovation, and cultivating autonomous revenue streams.

A pivotal facet of this evolution is a steadfast emphasis on sustainability. Many Global South nations are embracing renewable energy reservoirs, such as solar and wind power, to diminish their reliance on fossil fuels. Concurrently, there is a concerted push toward investing in sustainable agricultural methodologies, encompassing organic farming and agroforestry, to engender environmentally sound and resilient food production systems.

Moreover, inclusivity has emerged as a cornerstone of the Global South's developmental ethos. This entails ensuring that the dividends of progress are equitably distributed across all strata of society, including historically marginalized cohorts such as women, ethnic minorities, and persons with disabilities. This endeavor encompasses facilitating universal access to education and healthcare, while concurrently fostering avenues for socioeconomic participation and political empowerment.

The Global South is embracing a novel developmental blueprint predicated on principles of self-reliance, sustainability, and inclusivity. This paradigm shift is undergirded by cognizance of the inadequacies inherent in traditional development frameworks, coupled with an aspiration to engender a more equitable and sustainable global landscape for posterity.

The Kazan Declaration, adopted at the 16th BRICS summit under Russia's leadership, voices significant concern over the "disruptive effect of unlawful unilateral coercive measures, including illegal sanctions" on the global economy, international trade, and SDGs. According to the declaration, such sanctions undermine the UN Charter and the multilateral trading system, while also stifling economic growth, energy security, healthcare, and food security worldwide.

Sources report that, as chair, Russia proposed establishing an economic "fencing" mechanism to shield BRICS members from the effects of unilateral Western sanctions. Allegedly, no member opposed the proposal, and Russia has offered to prepare a concept note for detailed review and potential adoption at the next BRICS summit in Brazil in 2025. This note, expected to circulate among BRICS members "within a month or two," aims to outline an economic defence system for the bloc, although it has yet to be included in the Kazan Declaration.

BRICS members have previously maintained economic ties with Russia despite US sanctions imposed following Russia's actions in Ukraine. India, for instance, continued purchasing Russian oil, while trade between China and Russia remained strong. However, Russia's exclusion from the SWIFT financial transaction system has severely disrupted its trade. To address this, BRICS members are currently developing a mechanism to ensure continuity in trade among member states amid external economic threats.

Finance ministers and central bank governors from BRICS nations have been tasked with facilitating payment settlements in local currencies and creating alternative payment platforms and instruments in anticipation of the 2025 summit.

IMF Managing Director Kristalina Georgieva has voiced concerns over the global economy's path toward stagnant growth and escalating debt, warning of potential public discontent and a decline in governments' fiscal capacities. Though she noted the possibility of a "soft landing," Georgieva remarked that persistent inflation and limited job opportunities contribute to public pessimism. The IMF projects a dip in global GDP growth to 3.1% by 2029, down from a pre-pandemic average of 3.8%. Additionally, global debt is expected to exceed $100 trillion this year, with a potential rise to 100% of global GDP by 2030. Such debt trajectories, she cautioned, could hamper long-term investments, especially in climate initiatives, while escalating geopolitical tensions—particularly concerning the Middle East and China—threaten global stability. Further, China's economic growth, forecasted by the IMF to fall below 5% by 2025 in the absence of structural reforms, poses additional challenges to global resilience.

Russian Foreign Minister Sergey Lavrov hinted in 2022 that "World War III" may already be underway, underscoring how NATO—a 31-member alliance rooted in imperialism and colonialism—has consistently opposed Russia with economic sanctions against countries such as Russia, Iran, North Korea, Venezuela, and Cuba. In response to these pressures, Russia initiated a "special military operation" in Ukraine to preserve its sovereignty.

The ongoing conflicts in Ukraine and the Middle East, combined with the strengthening ties between Russia, China, North Korea, and Iran, signal an extraordinary global risk. This potential World War III could inflict severe human suffering and profoundly impact the global economy.

Recent developments in the Middle East further exemplify these tensions, with the United States intervening directly in support of Israel, while Russia has aligned with Iran, Lebanon, and Palestine. This volatile landscape suggests that the Western-dominated world order established by the United States after World War II is shifting toward a more multipolar world. BRICS—comprising Brazil, Russia, India, China, and South Africa—now stands at a critical juncture, facing complex challenges and seizing substantial opportunities. As the global political dynamic increasingly tilts toward multipolarity, BRICS's role in advocating for the Global South and promoting equitable governance becomes even more crucial.

For BRICS, navigating internal diversity and aligning member priorities will be vital for shaping a more balanced and inclusive global order.

Prioritizing cooperation and strategic initiatives could enable BRICS to strengthen its influence in international forums and tackle pressing global issues effectively. The 16th BRICS Summit, scheduled for October 22–23, 2024, in Kazan, Russia, promises to be a key platform for discussions on critical international issues. The summit's theme, "Strengthening Multilateralism for Just Global Development and Security," reflects BRICS's commitment to collaborative efforts for a fairer, more secure world order.

The escalating conflict in Gaza is expected to be a central topic at the summit, with President Vladimir Putin extending an invitation to Palestinian President Mahmoud Abbas. As a platform dedicated to championing the interests of the Global South, BRICS continues to rise in geopolitical importance. Its growing influence reflects not only a reaction to global uncertainties but also an increasing demand for equitable forms of cooperation within an evolving multipolar world.

2.32 RECOMMENDATIONS

1. Enhancing Internal Cohesion: BRICS should prioritize initiatives aimed at reconciling internal divergences through the cultivation of dialogue among member states. Establishing mechanisms for conflict resolution and joint decision-making will facilitate a more unified approach to global challenges.
2. Expanding Membership: To amplify its influence, BRICS ought to consider broadening its membership to include additional emerging economies. Such enlargement could enhance the coalition's legitimacy and bolster its voice in advocating for reforms in global governance structures.
3. Strengthening South–South Cooperation: BRICS should actively promote and invest in South–South cooperation initiatives, with a focus on trade, technology transfer, and capacity building. By nurturing partnerships with other developing nations, BRICS can solidify its leadership role in championing the interests of the Global South.
4. Leveraging Strategic Partnerships: Building strategic alliances with nonmember countries, particularly those in regions of mutual interest, can significantly enhance BRICS's geopolitical influence. Collaborative projects that address shared challenges—such

as climate change and food security—will foster goodwill and strengthen the coalition's standing.

5. Advocating for Global Governance Reforms: BRICS must adopt a proactive stance in championing reforms in international governance structures to rectify systemic inequities. By promoting a multipolar world order that values diverse perspectives, BRICS can position itself as a catalyst for meaningful change in global governance.
6. Focusing on Sustainable Development: Emphasizing sustainable development as a core principle can augment BRICS's appeal and effectiveness. Initiatives prioritizing environmental sustainability, social equity, and economic growth will resonate with both member states and the broader international community.
7. Conducting Regular Assessments: Establishing a framework for the regular evaluation of BRICS's strategies, initiatives, and outcomes is essential for adapting to the evolving geopolitical landscape. Continuous assessment will empower the coalition to respond dynamically to emerging challenges and opportunities.

The successful navigation of the challenges confronting BRICS, coupled with strategic actions and a commitment to cohesive collaboration, has the potential to redefine its role in the global order. By embracing these recommendations, BRICS can enhance its effectiveness and contribute to a more equitable and inclusive international system, ultimately fulfilling its foundational objectives.

KEYWORDS

- **BRICS**
- **climate change**
- **economic power**
- **GDP**
- **Global South**
- **sustainability**

REFERENCES

Banga, R. (2020). BRICS and the global south: Opportunities and challenges. *International Journal of Emerging Markets*, *15*(1), 32–49.

BRICS Joint Publication. (2024). *BRICS in figures*. National Bureau of Statistics of China.

Cardoso, F. H. (1979). *Dependency and development in Latin America*. University of California Press.

Chaudhuri, S. (2021). The new development bank and its role in BRICS: Financing development in a changing world. *Asian Journal of Comparative Politics*, *7*(3), 250–267.

Chin, G. T. (2021). Emerging powers and global governance: BRICS as a catalyst for change. *Global Governance*, *27*(4), 475–492.

Desjardins, J. (2023, April 18). Visualizing the BRICS vs. G7 GDP (PPP). Visual Capitalist: https://www.visualcapitalist.com.

Fardoust, S. (2023). Navigating geopolitical shifts: BRICS and the future of global governance. *Review of International Political Economy*, *30*(2), 197–214.

Gonzalez, L. F. (2020). BRICS: An alliance in the making? Historical perspectives and future directions. *Third World Quarterly*, *41*(8), 1302–1321.

Guru, W. (2025). China settles $855 billion worth of deals with BRICS countries in 2025. https://watcher.guru/news/china-settles-855-billion-worth-of-deals-with-brics-countries-in-2025.

Hill, C. B. (2019). The BRICS phenomenon: A critical appraisal. *Journal of International Relations and Development*, *22*(3), 518–540.

Hopewell, K. (2015). Different paths to power: The rise of Brazil, India and China at the world trade organization. *Review of International Political Economy*, *22*(2), 311–338.

Ikenberry, G. J. (2003). *International relations theory and the Asia-Pacific*. Columbia University Press.

IMF. (2025). *World economic outlook database*. Washington, DC: IMF.

Kupchan, C. A. (2012). *No one's world: The west, the rising rest, and the coming global turn*. Oxford University Press.

Mishra, P. (2021). The geopolitical dynamics of BRICS: Challenges and prospects. *Asian Security*, *17*(1), 45–62.

Prabhakar, A. C. (2011). An overview of the new emerging balance of forces-'The BRICS, G 20 and G 7'response to the global financial crisis. *Dynamics of Public Administration*, *28*(1), 10–32. https://scholar.google.com/citations?view_op=view_citation&hl=en&user=eWMChdoAAAAJ&citation_for_view=eWMChdoAAAAJ:9yKSN-GCB0IC.

Prabhakar, A. C. (2015). Foreign direct investment, trade and economic growth: A new paradigm of the BRICS. *Modern Applied Science*, *9*(12), 32–42. https://scholar.google.com/citations?view_op=view_citation&hl=en&user=eWMChdoAAAAJ&citation_for_view=eWMChdoAAAAJ:YsMSGLbcyi4C.

Prabhakar, A. C. (2016a). BRICS: A new world economic order. In *The current global recession: A theoretical and empirical investigation into developed and BRICS economies*. UK: Emerald Publishing Group.

Prabhakar, A. C. (2016b). *The current global recession: A theoretical and empirical investigation into developed and BRICS economies*. UK: Emerald Publishing Group.

https://scholar.google.com/citations?view_op=view_citation&hl=en&user=eWMChdoAAAAJ&citation_for_view=eWMChdoAAAAJ:MXK_kJrjxJIC.

Prabhakar, A. C. (2020). Trade and economic integration in BRICS: Towards multi-polarity. In: *Foreign direct investments: Concepts, methodologies, tools, and applications*. USA: IGI Global.

Prabhakar, A. C. (2024). Colonial echoes: Unraveling economic legacies and geopolitical shifts in the south pacific islands. *African and Asian Studies*, *1*(aop), 1–29. https://scholar.google.com/citations?view_op=view_citation&hl=en&user=eWMChdoAAAAJ&cstart=20&pagesize=80&citation_for_view=eWMChdoAAAAJ:bEWYMUwI8FkC.

Stuenkel, O. (2015). *The BRICS and the future of global order*. Lexington Books.

Stuenkel, O. (2016). *The BRICS and the future of global order: In global governance and the emergence of BRICS*. Palgrave Macmillan.

TASS. (2025). China's trade with BRICS countries tops $855 bln in H1 2025. TASS Russian News Agency: https://tass.com/economy/1989115 (accessed July 11, 2025).

Waltz, K. N. (1979). *Theory of international politics*. McGraw-Hill.

Wilson, J. D. (2015). The Eurasian economic union and BRICS: Emerging partnerships in global economic governance? *International Politics*, *52*(3), 405–419.

Zhang, Y. (2022). China-India relations and the future of BRICS: Opportunities and challenges. *Pacific Review*, *35*(1), 73–89.

CHAPTER 3

Political and Diplomatic Strategies of BRICS

ABSTRACT

This chapter offers a critical exploration of the strategic paradigms and foreign policy trajectories pursued by the BRICS alliance—comprising Brazil, Russia, India, China, and South Africa—as it endeavors to recalibrate the architecture of global governance and assert a genuinely multipolar international order. This study interrogates the modalities through which BRICS operationalizes political dialogue, multilateral engagement, and institutional synchronization to contest the entrenched asymmetries of a Western-centric global system. By forging issue-based coalitions, championing the principles of state sovereignty and non-intervention, and advancing structural reforms in key international institutions, such as the United Nations and the International Monetary Fund, BRICS articulates a counter-hegemonic vision grounded in equity, mutual respect, and inclusivity. Through a meticulous analysis of summit communiqués, joint diplomatic initiatives, peacebuilding interventions, and regional alignments, this research underscores the bloc's emergence as a coherent yet pluralistic diplomatic entity—one that is actively reshaping the discursive and normative contours of international relations in the 21st century.

3.1 INTRODUCTION

The emergence of BRICS (Brazil, Russia, India, China, and South Africa) as a formidable global coalition has profoundly altered the political and

The BRICS Coalition and a New Global Order: Akhilesh Chandra Prabhakar (Authors)
2026 Apple Academic Press, Inc. Co-published with CRC Press (Taylor & Francis)

DOI: 10.1201/9781779642936-3

diplomatic landscape of the 21st century. Formed with the collective aim of challenging entrenched global power structures, BRICS embodies the concerted efforts of five of the world's largest emerging economies to assert their influence in shaping international affairs. The political and diplomatic strategies of BRICS are underpinned by a commitment to multilateralism, a drive to address pervasive global inequalities, and an aspiration to establish a more just and equitable global order. As a bloc, BRICS seeks to reform international institutions, such as the United Nations Security Council (UNSC) and the Bretton Woods institutions, which are widely perceived as outdated and disproportionately reflective of Western interests.

Central to BRICS' diplomatic strategy is its vision of a multipolar world, one in which global governance structures are more inclusive and better aligned with the aspirations of the Global South. Through its collective action, BRICS aims to counterbalance the unipolar dominance of the United States and Western powers, advocating for a redistribution of influence within established global institutions. This vision is grounded in a commitment to economic diplomacy, regional security cooperation, and a multilateral approach to international relations, all anchored in mutual respect for sovereignty and non-interference in the domestic affairs of states.

This chapter delves into the political and diplomatic strategies employed by BRICS as it navigates the multifaceted and often contentious terrain of global governance. By examining its engagement in multilateral forums, its advocacy for institutional reforms, and its efforts to redefine security paradigms, BRICS positions itself as a pivotal player in the ongoing reconfiguration of global power dynamics.

3.1.1 POLITICAL COOPERATION AMONG BRICS NATIONS

BRICS has distinguished itself as a singular platform where countries with disparate political systems and rich cultural diversity converge to address shared global imperatives. Anchored in the principles of national sovereignty, multipolarity, and regional stability, its political strategy enables it to adeptly navigate the complexities of contemporary international relations. This chapter scrutinizes the intricate dynamics of political relations among BRICS members, focusing on their collective endeavors to tackle pressing global issues, including security, climate change, and human rights.

3.1.2 A COMMITMENT TO SOVEREIGNTY AND MULTIPOLARITY

At the heart of BRICS' political synergy, lies an unwavering commitment to safeguarding national sovereignty and championing a multipolar global order. Each member state appreciates the criticality of maintaining autonomous policy-making insulated from external pressures, a principle that binds them despite ideological divergences. This shared conviction has empowered BRICS to challenge unilateralism and advocate for a balanced distribution of power in global governance.

The bloc has been a persistent proponent of reforming global institutions such as the United Nations to foster equitable representation and inclusivity for developing nations. By championing multipolarity, BRICS endeavors not only to decentralize global decision-making but also to foster a fairer and more participatory international framework.

3.1.3 COLLABORATIVE EFFORTS ON GLOBAL SECURITY

Security cooperation remains a foundational pillar of BRICS' political agenda. The bloc prioritizes addressing transnational threats, including terrorism, cybercrime, and organized crime. Through mechanisms such as the BRICS Counter-Terrorism Working Group, member states have fortified intelligence-sharing frameworks and coordinated strategies to combat security challenges effectively.

Furthermore, BRICS has played a pivotal role in promoting regional stability by utilizing diplomatic channels to mediate conflicts and foster peace in volatile regions like the Middle East, Africa, and Central Asia. The bloc's unified presence in international forums underscores its dedication to conflict resolution and the pursuit of global peace.

3.1.4 CLIMATE DIPLOMACY AND ENVIRONMENTAL GOVERNANCE

BRICS' political collaboration extends to the domain of environmental governance, where it addresses the dual challenges of climate change and sustainable development. As major contributors to global greenhouse gas emissions, member states have worked collaboratively to advance climate action, balancing developmental aspirations with environmental stewardship.

Their unified approach to climate negotiations emphasizes equity and the principle of common but differentiated responsibilities, advocating for fairer climate policies that account for the historical contributions of developed nations to environmental degradation. Platforms such as the BRICS Energy Research Cooperation Platform have been instrumental in promoting renewable energy adoption and sustainable practices, solidifying the bloc's role as a key player in global climate governance.

3.1.5 HUMAN RIGHTS AND SOCIAL JUSTICE

Despite their ideological differences, BRICS nations have converged on a common approach to human rights, prioritizing dialogue and cooperation. The bloc consistently opposes the politicization of human rights issues as instruments of external interference, advocating instead for a balanced framework that respects cultural diversity and national sovereignty.

This cooperative stance underscores the bloc's broader commitment to fostering global social justice, where rights and freedoms are contextualized within the socio-political realities of individual nations.

3.1.6 A DIPLOMATIC FORCE ON THE GLOBAL STAGE

Through coordinated political initiatives, BRICS has established itself as a formidable diplomatic force in international affairs. Acting collectively in global negotiations, the bloc amplifies the voices of the Global South, advancing policies that reflect the priorities and aspirations of developing nations.

Annual summits and engagements with multilateral organizations have strengthened BRICS' influence, enabling it to champion initiatives such as the reform of global financial institutions and equitable resource distribution. This cohesive diplomatic presence has fortified its role as an indispensable actor in shaping global political discourse.

3.1.7 CHALLENGES AND THE PATH FORWARD

Despite its achievements, BRICS faces challenges in harmonizing diverse national priorities and regional interests, which at times impede consensus-building. However, the bloc's demonstrated ability to bridge differences on critical issues highlights its resilience and steadfast commitment to cooperative progress.

As the contours of global politics continue to shift, BRICS' emphasis on sovereignty, inclusivity, and multipolarity positions it as a transformative force in international diplomacy. By deepening their political cooperation, BRICS nations stand poised to redefine the parameters of global governance and contribute to a more balanced and equitable world order.

3.2 BRICS AND THE REFORM OF GLOBAL GOVERNANCE

At the core of BRICS' diplomatic agenda lies an unwavering commitment to redefining global governance structures to better mirror the complexities of an increasingly multipolar world.

Central to this transformative vision is the coalition's sustained advocacy for the overhaul of key institutions such as the United Nations Security Council (UNSC) and the Bretton Woods system. These institutions, conceived in the post-World War II era, have often been criticized for their archaic frameworks and their tendency to disproportionately serve the strategic and economic interests of Western powers.

BRICS champions a paradigm shift toward a more inclusive and equitable global governance model, vehemently advocating for the incorporation of perspectives from the Global South regions—historically marginalized within international decision-making arenas. By emphasizing the redistribution of influence within these institutions, BRICS aspires to empower emerging economies, ensuring that global governance mechanisms are more attuned to the realities of the 21st century.

This reformist trajectory epitomizes BRICS' broader aspiration to forge a more just and balanced international order, one rooted in the principles of sovereignty, equity, and inclusivity, thereby reshaping the foundational dynamics of global interactions.

3.2.1 REGIONAL AND GLOBAL SECURITY DYNAMICS

BRICS has solidified its position as a pivotal actor in regional and global security affairs, engaging robustly with institutions such as the Shanghai Cooperation Organization (SCO) and asserting its voice in international security dialogues. This active participation reflects a unified commitment to addressing pressing security challenges, including conflict resolution, peacekeeping, and counterterrorism.

The Shanghai Cooperation Organisation (SCO) summit scheduled for August 31 to September 1, 2025, in Tianjin, China, stands as a significant multilateral event aimed at deepening cooperation among member states and expanding partnerships with countries across Central Asia, the West Asia, South Asia, and Southeast Asia. Established in 2001 by China, Russia, Kazakhstan, Kyrgyzstan, Tajikistan, and Uzbekistan, the SCO has evolved from a primarily security-focused alliance into a comprehensive regional organization promoting political, economic, cultural, and security collaboration (Elite Plus Magazine, 2025).

The 2025 Tianjin summit, the 25th Heads of State Council meeting, is anticipated to be the largest in the organization's history, convening leaders from over 20 nations alongside representatives from more than ten international organizations. This scale reflects the SCO's growing geopolitical importance as a strategic fulcrum for Eurasian cooperation and a pillar for Global South solidarity (Contributors, 2025). Tianjin's status as a major northern Chinese port city is emblematic, connecting key Belt and Road Initiative corridors, such as the New Eurasian Land Bridge, which underscores the summit's focus on enhancing regional connectivity and infrastructural integration (Qazinform, 2025).

A central agenda item pertains to strengthening the nexus between SCO and BRICS, facilitating synergies across political, economic, and security domains to bolster multipolar governance frameworks. The active engagement of Central Asian states, West Asian participants, and representatives from South and Southeast Asia exemplifies the summit's inclusive approach, positioning the SCO as a vehicle for augmenting South–South cooperation on a broader scale (Izvestia, 2025). This convergence aligns with the resolutions outlined during the July 2025 XVII BRICS summit convened in Brazil, which emphasized the imperative of fostering Global South cooperation to promote equitable and sustainable governance models (India, 2025).

Moreover, the summit reinforces strategic commitments to regional economic integration, evidenced by efforts to advance major projects, like the China–Pakistan Economic Corridor and initiatives promoting green, low-carbon development. The promotion of cross-border e-commerce, coordinated public health frameworks, cultural exchange programs, and joint scientific research projects further reflect the SCO's evolution into a multidimensional cooperative institution (Mepei.com, 2025).

The Tianjin Summit epitomizes the SCO's trajectory toward becoming a robust pillar of Eurasian regionalism and a significant constituent of the broader Global South geopolitical architecture. Its focus on inclusivity, pragmatic cooperation, and sustainable development positions it as a critical strategic forum capable of enhancing peace, stability, and prosperity across the participating regions in an increasingly multipolar world order (Elite Plus Magazine, 2025; Wikipedia, 2025).

The BRICS approach to regional security is firmly rooted in the principles of stability, proactive conflict prevention, and an uncompromising respect for national sovereignty. By prioritizing cooperative frameworks and advocating for non-interventionist strategies, the bloc has adeptly positioned itself as a stabilizing force, particularly in regions where traditional powers have often faltered in delivering effective or enduring solutions.

This nuanced diplomatic strategy not only amplifies BRICS' influence within global security governance but also aligns seamlessly with its overarching vision of fostering a multipolar world order. Through its concerted efforts, BRICS persistently advances a holistic and inclusive approach to security, ensuring that the imperatives of regional stability and global peace remain integral to its strategic objectives.

3.3 SURVEY OF LITERATURE

The political and diplomatic strategies of BRICS (Brazil, Russia, India, China, and South Africa) have garnered substantial scholarly attention, given the bloc's concerted efforts to challenge the longstanding dominance of Western powers in global governance. Scholars have examined various facets of BRICS' collective diplomacy, from its commitment to multilateralism to its aspiration for a multipolar world order.

3.3.1 MULTILATERALISM AND GLOBAL GOVERNANCE

BRICS' engagement with multilateralism has been a focal point of academic inquiry. Stephen (2014) argues that BRICS epitomizes South-South cooperation by promoting collaboration among emerging economies to counterbalance the dominance of the Global North in institutions like the United Nations and the Bretton Woods system (Stephen, 2014). Similarly, Hopewell highlights the bloc's adept use of multilateral forums to advocate for governance reforms, particularly within the International Monetary Fund (IMF) and the World Bank, emphasizing the imperative for greater representation of the Global South (Hopewell, 2015).

3.3.2 REGIONAL AND GLOBAL SECURITY

The role of BRICS in regional and global security dynamics has been extensively analyzed.

Kornegay and Bohler-Muller (2013) underscore BRICS' dedication to peace and security, demonstrated through initiatives in counterterrorism, conflict prevention, and cooperative security mechanisms (Kornegay, 2013). Cooley elaborated that BRICS' collaboration with entities such as the Shanghai Cooperation Organization (SCO) reflects its strategic engagement in enhancing regional stability (Cooley, 2012).

3.3.3 ECONOMIC DIPLOMACY

Economic diplomacy is a cornerstone of BRICS' political strategies. Stuenkel contends that the establishment of the New Development Bank (NDB) underscores BRICS' ambition to provide an alternative to Western-dominated financial institutions (Stuenkel, 2016). Through the promotion of infrastructure development and sustainable growth, the bloc seeks to redefine the financial architecture of the Global South, thereby fostering economic sovereignty among its members.

3.3.4 ADVOCACY FOR A MULTIPOLAR WORLD

The pursuit of a multipolar world is a recurring theme in BRICS-related literature. Vieira and Alden emphasize BRICS' efforts to create a more balanced global power structure, challenging the unipolar dominance of the post-Cold War United States (Vieira, 2011). Thakur further notes BRICS' collective advocacy for reforms in the United Nations Security Council (UNSC) as a reflection of this ambition, aiming to enhance the representativeness and equity of global decision-making processes (Thakur, 2014).

3.3.5 *CHALLENGES AND CRITIQUES*

Despite its transformative potential, BRICS faces significant obstacles in realizing its diplomatic objectives. Hurrell highlights the internal divergences among member states, particularly in their geopolitical priorities, which frequently undermine the bloc's cohesion (Hurrell, 2013). Abdenur and Folly critique the bloc's limited success in achieving substantive reforms in global governance, attributing this to disparities in its member's economic and political capacities, as well as resistance from entrenched global powers (Abdenur, 2015).

This chapter illustrates that BRICS, through its political and diplomatic strategies, represents a formidable effort by emerging economies to reshape the global governance landscape. While the bloc's emphasis on multilateralism, regional security, and economic diplomacy highlights its capacity to influence global affairs, its internal tensions and the inertia of existing power structures pose significant challenges. Future research should explore the evolving internal dynamics of BRICS and its potential to sustain its influence in a rapidly changing geopolitical environment.

3.4 CONCLUSION

The political and diplomatic strategies of BRICS manifest the bloc's unwavering resolve to redefine the architecture of global governance in a manner that more effectively reflects the interests of emerging economies and the Global South. Through its steadfast commitment to multilateralism, economic diplomacy, and regional security cooperation, BRICS has positioned itself as a formidable counterweight to the entrenched dominance of Western powers. The bloc's concerted efforts to challenge the prevailing global order, notably through advocating for institutional reforms within the United Nations and the Bretton Woods system, underscore its ambition to foster a more inclusive and multipolar world order.

However, despite these significant strides, BRICS faces considerable challenges in consolidating its influence. Internal divisions, arising from divergent geopolitical priorities and economic disparities among member states, present ongoing hurdles to its cohesion, and long-term viability. Additionally, the resistance of established global powers, coupled with the intricate complexities of international diplomacy, further complicate the realization of BRICS' bold objectives.

Ultimately, BRICS' political and diplomatic strategies represent a concerted endeavor to reshape global power structures, yet their success hinges on the bloc's capacity to effectively navigate internal discord and external opposition. As the geopolitical landscape continues to evolve, the future of BRICS will likely depend on its ability to adapt to shifting dynamics while steadfastly upholding its foundational principles of cooperation, sovereignty, and equitable representation in global affairs.

KEYWORDS

- **conflict prevention**
- **counterterrorism**
- **cybercrime**
- **climate change**
- **economic diplomacy**
- **multilateralism**
- **UNSC**

REFERENCES

Abdenur, A. E. (2015). The new development bank and the institutionalization of the BRICS. *Revista Brasileira de Política Internacional*, *58*(2), 66–92.

Contributors. (2025, April 17). 2025 Tianjin SCO summit. https://en.wikipedia.org/wiki/2025_Tianjin_SCO_summit.

Cooley, A. (2012). *Great games, local rules: The new great power contest in Central Asia.* Oxford University Press.

Elite Plus Magazine. (2025). SCO Tianjin summit 2025: Shaping the future of global governance. https://www.eliteplusmagazine.com/Article/1195/SCO_Tianjin_Summit_2025___Shaping_the_Future_of_Global_Governance.

Hopewell, K. (2015). Different paths to power: The rise of Brazil, India and China at the world trade organization. *Review of International Political Economy*, *22*(2), 311–338.

Hurrell, A. (2013). Narratives of emergence: Rising powers and the end of the third world? *Brazilian Journal of Political Economy*, *32*(2), 203–221.

India. (2025, July 6). BRICS Rio de Janeiro declaration. https://www.pib.gov.in/PressReleasePage.aspx?PRID=2142786.

Izvestia. (2025, August 25). SCO 2025 summit in Tianjin: Participants, goals and challenges. https://en.iz.ru/en/node/1943038.
Kornegay, F. A. M. (2013). *Laying the BRICS of a new global order: From Yekaterinburg 2009 to eThekwini 2013.* Africa Institute of South Africa.
Qazinform. (2025, August 25). SCO in action: What is known about the venue and agenda of the anniversary summit. https://qazinform.com/news/sco-in-action-what-is-known-about-the-venue-and-agenda-of-the-anniversary-summit-5cdd28.
Stephen, M. D. (2014). Rising powers, global capitalism and liberal global governance: A historical materialist account of the BRICs challenge. *European Journal of International Relations*, *20*(4), 912–938.
Stuenkel, O. (2016). *Post-western world: How emerging powers are remaking global order*. Polity Press.
Thakur, R. (2014). How representative are BRICS? *Third World Quarterly*, *35*(10), 1791–1808.
Vieira, M. A. (2011). India, Brazil and South Africa (IBSA): South-south cooperation and the paradox of regional leadership. *Global Governance*, *17*(4), 507–528.

CHAPTER 4

Comparative Analysis of Emerging Economics

ABSTRACT

This chapter presents a rigorous and multidimensional investigation into the structural underpinnings, developmental trajectories, and policy architectures that shape the evolving landscape of emerging markets. Centering on a heterogeneous array of economies—including, but not confined to, the BRICS, MINT (Mexico, Indonesia, Nigeria, and Turkey), and the Next Eleven—this study interrogates patterns of convergence and divergence in their socioeconomic evolution amid intensifying global economic turbulence, shifting trade regimes, and fluid geopolitical realignments. Adopting an integrative analytical framework that synthesizes macroeconomic indicators, institutional robustness, demographic dynamics, innovation potential, and integration into global value chains, the research elucidates the intricate interplay between internal governance paradigms and exogenous economic forces. Through the deployment of both quantitative metrics and qualitative assessments, the study critically evaluates the strategic policy decisions that have either bolstered or constrained sustainable development, systemic resilience, and international competitiveness. In doing so, it offers nuanced insights into the capacities and constraints of emerging economies as pivotal agents of global economic reconfiguration in the 21st century.

4.1 INTRODUCTION

The term "emerging economies" denotes nations currently undergoing rapid industrialization and experiencing substantial economic growth.

The BRICS Coalition and a New Global Order: Akhilesh Chandra Prabhakar (Author)
2026 Apple Academic Press, Inc. Co-published with CRC Press (Taylor & Francis)

DOI: 10.1201/9781779642936-4

These economies are delineated by their heightened levels of investment, the burgeoning ascent of a burgeoning middle class, and a pronounced emphasis on export-oriented industries. Emerging economies are frequently hailed as the linchpins of global growth, garnering mounting attention from both investors and policymakers due to their pivotal role in shaping the contours of the global economic landscape.

Emerging economies constitute a substantial segment of the global economic sphere, assuming ever-greater significance as formidable participants in the international market arena. Marked by rapid economic expansion, industrialization, and the burgeoning emergence of a middle class, these nations epitomize dynamism and potential. Among the illustrious ranks of emerging economies stand China, India, Russia, Brazil, and South Africa, each encapsulating its distinctive array of challenges and prospects, further accentuating their individuality within the broader context of global economic dynamics.

China, the world's second-largest economy, has undergone a technologically propelled surge in economic growth and development over recent decades. This trajectory has been propelled by a confluence of factors, including substantial levels of investment, the rapid expansion of a sizable and burgeoning middle class, and a robust emphasis on export-oriented industries. Facilitating this growth is China's favorable business milieu, characterized by low levels of corruption and a stable political framework. Integral to China's economic ascendancy is its strategic investment in infrastructure, epitomized by the expansive network of roads, railways, and ports, which serves to enhance trade facilitation and bolster overall economic expansion. Additionally, substantial investments in education and research and development (R&D) have catalyzed innovation, driving heightened productivity levels.

India, the world's third-largest economy, has similarly experienced rapid economic expansion in recent years. Analogous to China, India's growth narrative is underpinned by considerable investment levels and the burgeoning emergence of a middle class. However, India grapples with formidable challenges, including entrenched poverty and inequality, compounded by a less favorable business climate. A primary engine propelling India's economic growth lies in its robust services sector, encompassing IT, finance, and healthcare industries. Coupled with substantial investments in education, India boasts a well-educated workforce driving innovation and enhancing productivity.

Russia, the largest nation by land area, boasts a diverse economic landscape spanning extractive industries, manufacturing, and services. The country has witnessed periods of rapid economic expansion, particularly during the early 2000s, propelled by soaring oil prices and a favorable global economic climate. However, Russia contends with significant hurdles, including pervasive corruption, limited economic diversification, and geopolitical tensions with Western counterparts. Central to Russia's economic trajectory is its formidable oil and gas sector, leveraging vast reserves to drive exports. Furthermore, substantial investments in infrastructure, particularly in transportation and energy, have bolstered trade and stimulated economic growth.

Brazil, South America's largest economy, has charted a course of rapid economic growth akin to China and India, propelled by substantial investment and the burgeoning middle class. Nonetheless, Brazil grapples with challenges including rampant corruption and a less conducive business environment. A pivotal driver of Brazil's economic expansion lies in its focus on the agribusiness sector, boasting a robust presence in agriculture, food processing, and biofuels industries. Complemented by investments in infrastructure and a well-educated workforce, Brazil's trajectory underscores a commitment to innovation and productivity enhancement.

South Africa, the largest economy on the African continent, has witnessed notable economic growth in recent years. However, the nation confronts entrenched poverty and inequality, compounded by an inhospitable business environment. Key to South Africa's economic narrative is its focus on the mining sector, leveraging abundant mineral reserves including gold, platinum, and diamonds to drive exports. Strategic investments in infrastructure, particularly in transportation and energy, further amplify trade facilitation and stimulate economic expansion.

Emerging economies are fundamentally reshaping the global economic landscape, ushering in a transition from a unipolar to a multipolar world order. Under the dollarization regime, encompassing practices like "dollar for trade payments" and "Petro-dollar," spearheaded by the United States, the unipolar world order has served as the backdrop for three major financial crises: the 1971–1973 oil and financial crisis, the 1997 Asian financial crisis, and the 2008 global financial crisis. These crises, compounded by trade deficits and balance of payments issues, have notably reverberated across developing and the least developed countries.

However, spanning the past 25 years, a cohort of 14 emerging economies, inclusive of the BRICS (Brazil, Russia, India, China, and South Africa), alongside others such as Argentina, Mexico, Chile, Turkey, UAE, Saudi Arabia, Indonesia, Israel, and Iran, have significantly steered the trajectory toward a multipolar world. The economic prowess exhibited by these emerging economies is striking. Brazil's gross domestic product (GDP) soared to 2.5 trillion dollars in 2023, forecasted to burgeon to 12 trillion dollars by 2050. Russia's GDP, standing at 1.9 trillion dollars in 2023, is projected to surge to 40 trillion dollars by 2050. India's GDP ascended to 3.3 trillion dollars in 2023, with prognostications pointing to a towering 34 trillion dollars by 2050. China, boasting an impressive GDP of 19.9 trillion dollars in 2023, is slated to escalate to a staggering 58 trillion dollars by 2050.

Contemporary empirical evidence demonstrates that the combined economic output of the BRICS nations has achieved unprecedented significance in the global economic architecture. According to the International Monetary Fund's World Economic Outlook data analyzed by the BRICS Presidency, the expanded eleven-member BRICS bloc accounts for 40.2% of global GDP measured in purchasing power parity (PPP) in 2024, with projections indicating growth to 40.7% in 2025 (Brasil, 2025). This represents a substantial shift from historical economic distributions, as academic research by Sadovnichiy, Akaev, and Davydova (2024) confirms that the GDP share of the BRICS countries reached 31.5% of world GDP in 2023, while that of the G7 countries declined to 30.7%. Carnegie Endowment research further corroborates that the bloc generates more than 35% of global GDP (as measured in PPP) (Peace, 2025) and boasts approximately 45% of the world's population (Akaev, 2024).

In comparative terms, the BRICS collective substantially exceeds both the European Union and approaches parity with the United States in economic significance. The World Bank's economic data indicates that the European Union maintained a GDP of approximately $19.4 trillion in 2024, representing 18.29% of the global economy, while the United States sustained its position with a GDP of $29.2 trillion in 2024, accounting for 27.49% of global GDP. The International Monetary Fund's April 2025 World Economic Outlook projects that BRICS nations collectively achieved 4% GDP growth in 2024 compared to 3.3% worldwide growth, with projected 3.4% growth in 2025 versus 2.8% global average (International Monetary Fund, 2025).

4.1.1 CHINA'S ECONOMIC INDICATORS AND GLOBAL CONTRIBUTIONS

China's macroeconomic indicators reflect substantial evolution from previously cited figures. The World Bank's China Economic Update (June 2025) reports that China's GDP reached $18.8 trillion in 2024, with real GDP growth of 5%. However, growth projections indicate moderation to 4.5% in 2025 and 4% in 2026, attributed to global trade restrictions and domestic structural challenges, including slower productivity growth, high debt levels, and demographic transitions (World Bank, 2025).

Regarding foreign exchange reserves, China's position requires substantive revision from earlier data. According to Georgetown University's Americas Program analysis, China's foreign exchange reserves totaled $3.261 trillion as of October 2024, maintaining the world's largest reserves position for consecutive years (Stisman, 2024). The People's Bank of China reported that reserves increased to $3.32 trillion by June 2025, representing the highest level since December 2015. Academic research by The Economic Review emphasizes that China's foreign currency reserves are nearly three times larger than Japan's $1.26 trillion and significantly exceed Switzerland's $831 billion.

4.1.2 CHINA'S MULTILATERAL INSTITUTIONAL CONTRIBUTIONS

China's contributions to international organizations demonstrate exponential growth trajectories, though specific metrics require academic precision. Research by the Center for Global Development reveals that China more than quadrupled its discretionary contributions to multilateral institutions over the past decade, with total contributions to the UN development system growing from approximately $100 million in 2010 to $451 million in 2020 (Center for Global Development, 2021). China's assessed contributions to the UN regular budget increased from 1% in 2000 to 15% for the 2022–2024 period, establishing China as the second-largest contributor behind the United States at 22% (Gwin, 2021).

In peacekeeping operations, academic analysis confirms that China's contributions witnessed a 20-fold increase since 2000, evolving from fewer than 100 peacekeepers to becoming the 14th largest contributor to UN peacekeeping operations by 2008. The Stockholm International Peace Research Institute documents China's expanding role in multilateral institutions (Gill and Huang, 2009), noting significant increases in both financial contributions and institutional leadership positions (Patrick, 2025).

4.1.3 CHINA'S GLOBAL ECONOMIC GROWTH CONTRIBUTION

Economic analysis confirms China's substantial contribution to global economic expansion. The China Daily Hong Kong reports that China accounts for nearly 30% of global economic growth in 2024. This contribution reflects China's maintenance of its position as the world's largest manufacturing economy, contributing approximately 30% of global manufacturing added value and sustaining its manufacturing leadership for fifteen consecutive years. However, independent economic assessments, including analysis by the Rhodium Group, suggest potential discrepancies between official growth figures and actual economic performance, estimating China's 2024 growth at 2.8%, significantly below official claims.

4.1.4 METHODOLOGICAL CONSIDERATIONS AND FUTURE PROJECTIONS

Academic research by multiple institutions, including the International Journal of Creative Research Thoughts, projects continued BRICS economic expansion with forecasts indicating constant growth for all BRICS countries through 2028, with China and India maintaining their positions as the bloc's largest economies (Yan, 2025). World Economic Forum analysis confirms that BRICS countries are home to roughly 3.3 billion people—over 40% of the global population—with economies accounting for an estimated 37.3% of global GDP based on PPP.

The empirical evidence demonstrates that BRICS nations have achieved economic parity with G7 countries when measured in PPP, representing 40.2% versus 28.8% of global GDP in 2024. This transformation validates academic projections regarding the rise of emerging economies and represents a fundamental shift in global economic power distribution, with implications for international governance structures and multilateral institutional arrangements.

Nevertheless, this seismic shift in the global economic terrain toward a multipolar world is not devoid of challenges. The ascent of emerging economies precipitates geopolitical tensions, evidenced in the standoff between Russia and the West, alongside economic exigencies such as the imperative for heightened financial stability and economic reforms within emerging economies. Nonetheless, it concurrently ushers in prospects for augmented trade and investment, heightened economic collaboration, and the potential for a more inclusive paradigm of global economic growth.

China and India, two of the globe's most densely populated nations, have undergone rapid economic evolution in recent decades. Both have witnessed substantial advancements in various spheres including infrastructure, trade, technology, finance, and poverty alleviation. However, each nation has grappled with distinct challenges in areas such as healthcare, education, and income inequality. This essay endeavors to juxtapose the development trajectories of China and India across key domains in the year 2024.

4.2 INFRASTRUCTURE DEVELOPMENT

Significant investments in infrastructure have been a shared priority for both China and India in recent years. China's infrastructure is widely perceived as more advanced, boasting a comprehensive network of high-speed railways, modern airports, and cutting-edge ports. In contrast, India's infrastructure is generally regarded as less developed, characterized by deficiencies in roads, railways, and ports. Nevertheless, India has embarked on initiatives aimed at upgrading its transportation networks and initiating new infrastructure projects.

4.3 ECONOMIC TRENDS

China's economy has exhibited robust growth, with GDP expanding at an average rate of 6–7% annually. India's economic growth, while steady, has been more moderate, averaging around 4–5% per year. However, India is poised to outpace China in terms of growth rate in the near future, with some analysts projecting it to become the world's fastest-growing major economy by 2024.

4.4 TRADE PATTERNS

Both China and India hold significant positions in the global economy, with China serving as the largest exporter and India as the largest importer of goods. China maintains a considerable trade surplus, exporting more than it imports, whereas India grapples with a trade deficit, importing more than it exports. However, India's trade deficit has shown signs of narrowing in recent years owing to heightened exports and reduced imports.

4.5 TECHNOLOGY

China has emerged as a global leader in technology, emphasizing innovation and robust R&D efforts. Investments in emerging technologies such as artificial intelligence (AI), robotics, and biotechnology have been substantial. India, on the other hand, has witnessed notable advancements in the technology sector, with a burgeoning startup ecosystem and a focus on digitalization.

4.6 FINANCE

Both nations boast well-developed financial systems, characterized by a plethora of banks and financial institutions. China's financial landscape is more centralized and tightly regulated, with significant government intervention. India's financial system, while decentralized, offers greater autonomy to banks and financial entities.

4.7 POVERTY REDUCTION

Both China and India have made remarkable strides in alleviating poverty, with China witnessing a precipitous decline in its poverty rate from over 80% in the 1980s to less than 2% in 2024. India has also made substantial progress, with its poverty rate plummeting from over 40% to approximately 12% during the same period. However, both nations continue to contend with a considerable number of individuals living below the poverty line.

4.8 HEALTH AND EDUCATION

Investments in healthcare and education have been prioritized by both China and India. China boasts a well-established healthcare system with an emphasis on preventive care and public health initiatives. In comparison, India's healthcare system faces challenges including a dearth of medical personnel and facilities. In the realm of education, China exhibits a robust system with a high literacy rate and a focus on scientific and technological education. India's education system, while less developed, has witnessed efforts aimed at enhancing accessibility and quality.

4.9 MINIMIZATION OF INEQUALITY

Both China and India have witnessed a reduction in income inequality, with China's Gini coefficient decreasing from around 0.5 to 0.4 and India's from around 0.4 to 0.3 during the period under consideration. Despite this progress, income inequality remains a significant challenge for both nations.

China and India have made commendable strides across various facets including infrastructure, economic growth, trade, technology, finance, poverty alleviation, healthcare, education, and income equality in 2024. Nonetheless, persistent challenges persist, necessitating continued investments and concerted efforts to ensure sustainable and inclusive development.

China's economy, propelled by technological innovation, has witnessed a remarkable ascent, climbing from the 34th rank in 2012 to the 11th position in 2022. With the capacity to rival the United States as the second largest economy, China has set ambitious targets, achieving around 5% annual GDP growth and contributing a staggering 18% to global GDP in 2023. The cornerstone of China's industrial growth lies in its accelerating digital transformation, a process that has revolutionized production norms and ushered in a new era of efficiency and productivity.

The integration of digital technology into traditional industries has been pivotal, particularly in sectors such as automotive, electrical machinery, and chemicals, where it has fundamentally reshaped manufacturing paradigms. This digital metamorphosis is not confined to major conglomerates; it permeates through the entire industrial spectrum, enhancing the performance of state-led enterprises, cooperatives, and private entities alike.

China's proactive role in financing projects under the "One Belt One Road (OBOR)" initiative spanning 150 countries underscores its commitment to stabilizing global economic growth and fostering sustainable financial investment. Internationally, China emerges as the engine propelling the world's economy forward, demonstrating resilience and adaptability amidst evolving global dynamics.

In 2023, industrial enterprises above designated size witnessed a 4% year-on-year increase in value-added, indicating a steady resurgence in industrial production post the economic shocks induced by the COVID19 pandemic. Notably, investments in high-tech manufacturing surged by 11.3%, a testament to China's unwavering dedication to technological advancement and innovation.

The rapid growth witnessed in sectors such as new energy vehicles, photovoltaic products, and aerospace equipment not only underscores China's technological prowess but also signals a transformative shift toward sustainability and innovation. These burgeoning sectors are not merely expanding; they are redefining China's industrial landscape, steering it toward a more sustainable and innovative trajectory (Khatoon, 2023).

China has consistently addressed the needs of its vast population, exceeding 1.4 billion people, while simultaneously promoting inclusive development for all. By ensuring access to fundamental amenities such as education and healthcare, China has instilled confidence in global economic stability and predictability. The nation's economic growth has been nothing short of remarkable, boasting an average annual growth rate of 6.6% between 2013 and 2021, and initiating 2023 with a trade surplus of USD 25 billion.

China's prowess in international trade was evident in March 2023, with goods and services trade reaching approximately 3.94 trillion yuan or 570.5 billion US dollars, marking a 2% year-on-year increase. Notably, exports surged by 14.8% to $315.6 billion, rebounding from earlier declines, while imports saw a smaller contraction of 1.4% to $227.4 billion. Despite the economic challenges posed by COVID-19 and geopolitical tensions, China's politically significant trade surplus widened by 82% to $88.2 billion.

The United States and the European Union remain China's largest export markets, albeit with some decline due to monetary policy adjustments. However, this dip was counterbalanced by robust sales to Canada, Indonesia, Russia, and other markets. China's strategic partnership with Russia, in particular, has flourished, with bilateral trade reaching record highs, totaling US$190 billion in 2022 and surging by over 40% in the first quarter of 2023.

The Reserve Bank of India's (RBI) economic research department highlights India's aspirations for sustained growth, aiming for a real GDP compound annual growth rate (CAGR) of 7.6% over the next 25 years. Despite past achievements, India faces the challenge of transitioning into a high-income nation, requiring substantial investments and sectoral reforms across various domains, including education, healthcare, infrastructure, and technology.

While India pursues its growth trajectory, the Asia-Pacific region has emerged as a favored destination for Western investors, with countries like India, Australia, Japan, and South Korea capturing significant capital inflows. However, China has experienced a notable downturn in Western capital inflows, reaching a 10-year low of only US$500 million.

Europe's economic dependence on China is palpable, with Chinese exports to European countries surpassing Euro 472 billion in 2021, while European exports to China amounted to Euro 223 billion, resulting in a trade deficit of –248.9 billion euros for the EU. China remains committed to advancing its economic structures, prioritizing high-quality manufacturing, modern infrastructure, and industrial system construction to drive sustainable growth and prosperity.

TABLE 4.1 China: Global Manufacturing Factory of the World.

Sectoral-Wise Production and Supply		2022 (in %)
Electronics	Mobile	17
	Air conditioner	80
	Solar plates	72
Shoes		60
Cement		60
Sheep		65
Steel		7
Apple		50
Branded luxury items		70
GDP growth rate		49 times
GDP growth ratio		10
Pollution share		20

Source: Authors' development based.

The economic reforms undertaken in both India and China have wrought profound changes in the socioeconomic and cultural landscapes, affecting the lives of rural and urban populations alike. China, in particular, has emerged as a major beneficiary of globalization, securing the second-largest rank globally, trailing only behind the USA. Both nations, characterized by vast populations, have embraced openness to trade, investment, talent, and knowledge exchange, attracting major multinational corporations (MNCs) eager to tap into their burgeoning markets and consumer base. This influx of foreign investments has left an indelible mark on various industries, including information technology/business processing outsourcing (IT/BPO), finance, pharmaceuticals, petroleum, fast-moving consumer goods (FMCG), and manufacturing.

Over the past three decades of globalization, MNCs have concentrated their efforts on providing a plethora of products and services ranging from electronics and entertainment to finance and transportation, thereby driving urbanization while also benefiting rural populations. In densely populated countries like China, India, Indonesia, Bangladesh, and Pakistan, there is a growing emphasis on "people centered agriculturally based industrial development strategies," alongside the commercialization of agriculture and the expansion of agro-industries to propel economic advancement.

The deepening of financialization, privatization, corporatization, digitalization, liberalization, marketization, and globalization of economies has spurred labor migration from rural to urban areas, exacerbating income and wealth inequality both within and among nations, while also giving rise to unemployment and inflation. While countries like China and India have reaped the rewards of these trends, others, particularly in Africa, have found themselves marginalized in international trade and marketing, despite advancements in information and communication technology.

The metamorphosis of metropolitan-urban areas in China and India, fueled by communication and consumerism, has precipitated mass migrations from rural to urban locales in the pursuit of improved job prospects and lifestyles. However, the higher cost of living in urban centers has exacerbated disparities in income, wealth, and resource distribution. India's service sector, experiencing exponential growth in urban regions, has become a magnet for foreign direct investment (FDI) in startups and businesses, second only to China. Projections suggest that India will surpass China in this aspect by 2025. The Indian government's initiatives to establish special economic zones (SEZs) and small/medium industry corridors across the northern and western regions of the country underscore its ambition to become a manufacturing powerhouse for high-quality products. With a youthful population of 356 million individuals aged 10–24, India stands as the nation with the world's largest youth demographic, offering a wealth of labor and knowledge skills. However, the key challenge remains in providing quality education and skill development to equip the workforce for success in a fiercely competitive global economy.

TABLE 4.2 Size of GDP in 2023.

Country	GDP (US$ Trillion) in 2023	Expected to Grow (US$) in 2050
China	19.9	58
India	3.3	34
Russia	1.9	40
Brazil	2.5	12
USA	25.3	34
European Union	15.2	17

Source: World Bank Report (2023).

China has cemented its status as a global manufacturing juggernaut across diverse industries, notably high technology sectors. Its rapid economic growth, technological advancements, and strategic initiatives have propelled it to the forefront of the global manufacturing arena. This discourse delves into China's trajectory toward manufacturing preeminence, its prowess and hurdles in high-technology domains, and the ramifications of its global manufacturing supremacy.

4.10 THE ASCENDANCY OF CHINA AS A MANUFACTURING HUB

China's ascent as a manufacturing powerhouse can be attributed to several factors:

1. Economic Reforms: Pioneering economic reforms initiated in the late 1970s laid the groundwork for China's manufacturing surge. Emphasis was placed on opening up the economy, attracting foreign investment, and fostering industrialization.
2. Abundant Labor Force: China's expansive and cost-effective labor pool has been instrumental in driving its manufacturing prowess, particularly in labor-intensive sectors.

3. Infrastructure Advancements: China's substantial investments in infrastructure, spanning transportation, energy, and telecommunications have bolstered connectivity and facilitated the smooth flow of goods and services.
4. Foreign Direct Investment (FDI): The influx of substantial FDI, especially in manufacturing, underscores China's allure as a production hub. Foreign enterprises have established manufacturing facilities in China, leveraging its vast market, skilled workforce, and supportive governmental policies.
5. Integration into Global Supply Chains: China's integration into global supply chains has bolstered its manufacturing prowess, with the nation assuming a pivotal role in the production networks of MNCs, serving as a crucial manufacturing base for products destined for global markets.

4.11 CHINA'S ADVANTAGES IN HIGH-TECHNOLOGY SECTORS

In recent years, China has made remarkable strides in high-technology fields, including:

1. Innovation Drive: China has intensified efforts in R&D, yielding breakthroughs in areas such as AI, 5G technology, and renewable energy. The nation's emphasis on innovation has fueled its competitiveness in high-technology sectors.
2. Skilled Workforce: China boasts a burgeoning pool of skilled professionals in STEM disciplines (science, technology, engineering, and mathematics), nurtured by its esteemed universities and research institutions.
3. Government Backing: The Chinese government has thrown its weight behind high-technology industries, offering incentives such as tax breaks, R&D funding, and support for tech startups, fostering an environment conducive to innovation and entrepreneurship.
4. Manufacturing Proficiency: China's manufacturing capabilities have transcended conventional industries to encompass high-technology domains. Equipped with advanced manufacturing infrastructure and adeptness in production processes, China churns out top-notch, technologically advanced products.

4.12 CHALLENGES IN HIGH-TECHNOLOGY SECTORS

Despite its strides, China grapples with several challenges in high-technology domains, including:

1. Intellectual Property Protection: Criticisms abound regarding China's lax enforcement of intellectual property rights (IPR), prompting concerns among foreign entities. Efforts to fortify IPR protection are underway, but more stringent measures are imperative to instill confidence among international stakeholders.
2. Talent Retention: China's rapid economic expansion has precipitated a dearth of skilled professionals in high-technology sectors, necessitating a concerted focus on talent retention and attraction to sustain innovation-driven growth.
3. Global Competition: China contends with stiff competition from other nations, particularly in high-technology spheres. Continuous investment in R&D, fostering innovation, and enhancing the business climate are indispensable for maintaining competitiveness.

4.13 IMPLICATIONS OF CHINA'S GLOBAL MANUFACTURING DOMINANCE

China's ascendancy in global manufacturing carries multifaceted implications for the global economy:

1. Supply Chain Resilience: China's pivotal role in global manufacturing underscores the imperative of supply chain resilience. The COVID-19 pandemic laid bare vulnerabilities in global supply chains, prompting calls for diversification and reshoring of manufacturing activities.
2. Geopolitical Dynamics: China's manufacturing prowess has exacerbated geopolitical tensions, notably with the United States, sparking a trade war characterized by tariffs and technology restrictions.
3. Environmental Imperatives: China's manufacturing endeavors have exacted a significant environmental toll, manifesting in air and water pollution, deforestation, and greenhouse gas (GHG) emissions. Addressing these environmental challenges is paramount for achieving sustainable development.

China's journey to manufacturing preeminence, especially in high-technology sectors, epitomizes a confluence of economic reforms, infrastructure development, innovation, and governmental support. While China boasts formidable strengths in manufacturing and burgeoning capabilities in high-tech realms, it faces formidable challenges, including intellectual property protection, talent retention, and global competition. Effectively addressing these challenges will be pivotal for China to sustain its manufacturing dominance and propel innovation and growth in high-technology domains.

4.14 CHINA'S ECONOMIC MIRACLE

China's economic transformation continues to captivate the world, evolving from extreme poverty into the world's second-largest economy with a per capita income exceeding $12,500, classifying it among upper middle-income countries. As it progresses toward becoming a great modern socialist nation over the next 27 years, China is guided by the "Chinese path to modernization." This vision encompasses a vast population, common prosperity, material and cultural-ethical advancement, harmony between humanity and nature, and peaceful development.

Amid this historic journey, the global community often poses the question: What underpins China's economic miracle? The answer lies in its collective action, strategic planning, and unwavering commitment to progress, all driven by the resilience and determination of the Chinese people.

4.14.1 ROOTED IN ASPIRATIONS

Deng Xiaoping, the architect of China's reform and opening up, provided the theoretical framework that catalyzed this transformation. He emphasized making economic development the central task while adhering to the Four Cardinal Principles: maintaining the socialist path, upholding the people's democratic dictatorship, affirming the Communist Party's leadership, and adhering to Marxism-Leninism and Mao Zedong Thought. These principles, coupled with a relentless pursuit of reform, have guided 75 years of dedicated effort, proving that China's achievements are far from a sudden miracle.

4.14.2 EQUALITY AS A CORNERSTONE

Another cornerstone of China's success is its enduring commitment to equality. For over 2000 years, Chinese society has pondered the question: Are kings and nobles born to their status? This belief in meritocracy has culminated in an inclusive society where equality is not merely a principle but a lived reality.

China boasts world-class public education and healthcare systems, universal access to essential services, and the largest infrastructure network globally. Remote villages enjoy electricity, clean water, and internet connectivity. These foundational elements ensure that every citizen has equal access to opportunities and resources, turning a population of 1.4 billion into a development asset rather than a liability.

4.14.3 REFORM AND INNOVATION

Reform and innovation have been integral to China's evolution. The ethos of self-improvement, deeply rooted in its cultural heritage, drives continuous progress. A bronze bathtub from the Shang Dynasty bears the inscription: If you can improve yourself in a day, do so each day.

Since the Communist Party of China's (CPC) founding, reform has advanced through integrating Marxism with China's realities and cultural traditions. This has led to the creation of socialism with Chinese characteristics and a unique path to modernization. The CPC's practice of self-reform ensures accountability and adaptability, enabling it to address challenges and push forward societal progress.

4.14.4 UNITY IN ACTION

Unity, another critical factor, is both a principle and a practice in China. The Chinese ethos of "1 + 1>2" underpins a collective strength where democracy and discipline coexist. Historical examples, such as soldiers' rights to voice opinions in the Soldier Committee, highlight this participatory approach.

Major policies, such as the Resolution on Further Deepening Reform to Advance Chinese Modernization, undergo extensive public consultation before implementation. This collective involvement unites the populace, channeling the power of 1.4 billion individuals into transformative change.

4.14.5 GLOBAL ENGAGEMENT

China's openness to the world has also played a pivotal role in its development. From Zhang Qian's pioneering Silk Road expeditions 2100 years ago to Admiral Zheng He's maritime journeys six centuries ago, China has a long history of international engagement.

Today, initiatives like the Belt and Road Initiative (BRI) exemplify China's commitment to globalization and peaceful development. By fostering international trade and cooperation, the BRI not only benefits China but also contributes to global economic stability and prosperity, standing as a testament to China's enduring spirit of openness and collaboration.

In sum, China's economic miracle is a product of aspiration, equality, reform, unity, and global engagement—an enduring testament to the power of strategic vision and collective effort.

4.15 THE RUSSIAN ECONOMY

The Russian economy finds itself ensnared within a web of formidable challenges stemming from the relentless imposition of financial, trade, technological, and travel sanctions orchestrated by the United States-led Western coalition. Anchored by a military–industrial complex intricately interwoven with a petroleum-centric economic framework, Russia's fiscal landscape has encountered formidable headwinds. The ripple effects of Russia's engagement in hostilities with NATO not only reverberate within its own borders but also reverberate across the European and American economic spheres.

Since the advent of 2021, Russia's GDP has sustained a precipitous decline, estimated between 11 and 15%, with the overall economy retracting by 2.1% in 2022. Forecasts from the International Monetary Fund (IMF) paint a picture of cautious optimism, predicting a meager growth of 0.3% for Russia in the year 2023. The hemorrhaging of approximately half of Russia's oil and gas revenue, coupled with a staggering plunge in trade surplus from $257 billion to $80 billion, underscores the severity of the economic tumult. Moreover, oil tax revenue plummeted by a staggering 48% in 2022. Yet, amidst this tempest of tribulation, Russia's tenacity manifests through its attainment of record fossil fuel earnings, tallying an impressive US$325 billion in 2022.

In a bid to mitigate the punitive repercussions of sanctions, Russia has pivoted its commercial focus toward Africa, Latin America, and Asia, with particular emphasis on burgeoning markets such as China, India, South Africa, and Brazil. This strategic maneuver has enabled Russia to stave off cataclysmic scenarios of mass unemployment, currency devaluation, and financial sector upheavals. Despite the exodus of 191 foreign enterprises from Russian soil, 1169 companies persist in their operations, while 496 companies bide their time in anticipation of a more conducive business environment. Noteworthy among these transitions are the acquisitions of renowned foreign brands like McDonald's and Starbucks by local proprietors, resulting in negligible alterations to menus albeit with slightly inflated prices.

Evidencing astute financial stewardship, Russia has managed to sustain robust foreign currency reserves denominated in US dollars and Euros, thus fortifying the economy against the punitive strictures of Western sanctions. Furthermore, Russia has adeptly navigated its traditional trade partnerships across Asia, Latin America, and Africa, thus circumventing the specter of economic stagnation.

The discontinuation of online sales of Apple iPhones within Russia notwithstanding, the void is swiftly filled by domestic giant Wildberries, offering the iPhone 14 at commensurate prices to those prevalent in Europe. Concurrently, Chinese-manufactured smartphones alongside a plethora of other goods, including vehicles, inundate the Russian market. The symbiotic relationship between Russia and its trading partners, notably China and India, continues to burgeon, with bilateral trade experiencing exponential growth despite the draconian strictures imposed by the US and EU.

Notably, the nexus between Russia and India has transcended mere economic symbiosis, with both nations committing to an intensified collaboration across a diverse spectrum encompassing IT, Cyber Security, Defense, Pharmaceuticals, Health Service, Technological Sovereignty, Smart City initiatives, Transportation, Food, and Agriculture. Emblematic of this burgeoning partnership is India's ascendance as the second-largest importer of oil from Russia, with bilateral trade projected to escalate from US$31 billion in 2022 to an estimated US$50 billion in 2023.

In the intricate tapestry of Sino-Indian trade dynamics, a discernible pattern emerges, characterized by India's importation of capital goods and essential commodities from China. Conversely, India's exports to China predominantly comprise raw materials such as mineral ores and unprocessed cotton. This bilateral exchange paradigm evokes historical echoes of a bygone era, reminiscent of the classic dichotomy between developed nations specializing in sophisticated manufactures and underdeveloped nations serving as purveyors of primary products and conventional manufactures (Chandrasekhar, 2022a, b).

India's trade liaison with China embodies a multifaceted and ever-evolving narrative. Throughout the annals of time, India has been a recipient of a diverse array of Chinese imports spanning machinery, electronics, textiles, and chemical commodities. Notably, China stands tall as a preeminent wellspring of imports for India, constituting a substantial proportion of the nation's aggregate inbound trade.

Conversely, India has reciprocated this exchange by dispatching an eclectic mix of goods to Chinese shores, encompassing raw materials such as iron ore, cotton, and sundry agricultural products. Moreover, India has ventured into the exportation of manufactured goods, including pharmaceuticals, chemicals, and machinery. However, the quantum of India's exports to China remains comparatively diminutive vis-à-vis its voluminous imports from the East.

Central to the dynamics of India's commercial entanglement with China is the specter of a persistent trade deficit. India perennially finds itself in the throes of a trade imbalance with China, whereby the magnitude of imports dwarfs that of exports. This incongruity has emerged as a focal point of apprehension for Indian policymakers, precipitating a burgeoning disparity in the bilateral trade milieu.

In tandem with tangible goods, India's import portfolio extends to encompass the procurement of raw materials essential for pharmaceutical production from Chinese origins. China emerges as a pivotal purveyor of these crucial raw materials, facilitating the sustenance of India's pharmaceutical industry through the provision of active pharmaceutical ingredients (APIs) and assorted chemical intermediates. These foundational elements serve as the lifeblood of India's pharmaceutical landscape, fostering the synthesis of an extensive array of medicinal formulations, including generic pharmaceuticals.

Broadly construed, India's commercial rapport with China is underscored by a conspicuous trade deficit, accentuating the nation's proclivity toward importation from its Eastern counterpart. Nevertheless, China's pivotal role as a primary supplier of raw materials to India's pharmaceutical sector engenders a symbiotic relationship that bolsters the vitality of India's pharmaceutical domain.

However, supposing India were to eschew imports from China owing to heightened competition and the undercurrents of geopolitical and geoeconomic tension characterizing the two nations' relationship, the ramifications would reverberate across Indian domestic industries, most notably within the pharmaceutical realm. The profound reliance on China for the supply of raw materials would precipitate severe repercussions, jeopardizing the operational efficacy of India's pharmaceutical sector. Indeed, the trajectory of India's pharmaceutical importations from China has witnessed an exponential ascent since 2003, coinciding with an era of accelerated industrial expansion and overall economic ascension within India's purview.

This epoch of growth assumes particular significance as it marks a departure from India's erstwhile "Mahal Nobis-model" of import-substitution industrialization, which espoused the attainment of self-reliance through the apportionment of substantial investments toward the heavy industrial machine tools sector. However, the efficacy of this industrial strategy has been persistently beleaguered over the past six and a half decades, underscoring the imperative for India to recalibrate its approach toward achieving economic self-sufficiency (Chandrasekhar, 2022a, b).

India has ascended to the zenith of remittance recipients globally, boasting an unprecedented influx of foreign currency exceeding the $100 billion threshold for the inaugural time in 2022. This revelation stems from comprehensive analyses conducted by both the RBI and the World Bank's Migration and Development Brief of November 2022.

Notably resilient amidst the tempest of the pandemic, remittance inflows have exhibited commendable fortitude, experiencing a marginal contraction of a mere 3% from $76 billion in the prepandemic fiscal year 2019–2020 to $73 billion in 2020–2021. However, the subsequent fiscal year bore witness to a remarkable surge, catapulting remittance inflows to an impressive $80 billion mark in 2021–2022 (Chandrasekhar, 2023).

A consortium comprising 13 burgeoning economies, notably encompassing the BRICS nations (Brazil, Russia, India, China, and South Africa), alongside Argentina, Chile, Indonesia, Israel, Mexico, Saudi Arabia, Turkey, and the United Arab Emirates, of which 10 hold membership within the esteemed G20 cohort, has amassed considerable reservoirs of foreign exchange assets, judiciously ensconced within Sovereign

Wealth Funds. Their collective contributions to the coffers of multilateral financial bastions, exemplified by the New Development Bank (NDB), have undergone a notable metamorphosis, surging from a modest US$1 billion to a robust US$6 billion over the past decade. Should this trajectory persist unabated, the economic ascendancy of these emergent powers could conceivably yield funds within the NDB in the forthcoming quarter century that overshadow the cumulative holdings of both the World Bank and the IMF. Such an epochal development would herald a seismic recalibration within the global economic and developmental paradigms, heralding the dawn of a multipolar epoch. Moreover, these emerging juggernauts possess the potential to furnish indispensable assistance to low-income developing nations, particularly in the realm of infrastructural development.

Notwithstanding a litany of tribulations ranging from the protracted aftermath of the global economic recession since 2007 to the convulsions of trade and geopolitical discord between China and the USA, China and India, and Russia and the USA (NATO) since 2017, not to mention the unprecedented disruptions wrought by the COVID-19 pandemic and the harrowing specter of total warfare between Russia and the USA (NATO) since 2022, these nascent economies have demonstrated remarkable resilience, amassing formidable capabilities while exerting a palpable impact on the global GDP landscape. Indeed, a discernible testament to their ascendancy lies in the perceptible dwindling of the share of the global populace domiciled within low-income developing and impoverished nations, which has dwindled by a substantive 7% since 1990, contrasting sharply with the burgeoning prevalence of middle-income developing countries, whose demographic footprint has burgeoned from 30% in 1990 to a staggering 73% in the annus horribilis of 2020.

The imperative for developing nations across Africa and Asia looms large, necessitating a formidable infusion of capital, projected at a staggering US$2 trillion annually, directed toward the augmentation of physical infrastructure in pivotal sectors such as agriculture, manufacturing, and tertiary/service industries. This concerted investment endeavor must be underpinned by a resolute commitment to fostering more ecologically sustainable modalities of inclusive development.

The inexorable ascent of China and India toward the echelons of global superpower Dom is an incontrovertible reality, poised to exert profound influence across realms encompassing science, technology, trade, finance, and military prowess. Endowed with vast populations and bounteous natural endowments, both nations find themselves strategically positioned to chart the course of the global economy in the foreseeable future. Evidencing this ascendant trajectory, China commands a commanding presence within the upper echelons of the corporate stratosphere, boasting a formidable contingent of 129 enterprises among the esteemed ranks of the top 500 global companies, whereas India's representation stands at a comparatively modest seven entities. China has firmly entrenched itself as a preeminent locus of global manufacturing prowess.

In the annals of political history, India's emergence as a sovereign entity dates back to 1947, with China following suit in 1949. The Chinese Communist regime has not only made robust investments in domestic infrastructure, thereby furnishing a conducive environment for both Indigenous and foreign enterprises but has also directed significant resources toward the amelioration of public education and healthcare provisions. This concerted endeavor extends to the provision of pragmatic vocational training programs, aimed at nurturing and fortifying a vast reservoir of skilled human capital. A testament to China's global ambitions is exemplified by the expansive OBOR Corridor initiatives, spanning continents from Asia to Africa, Latin America, and the Pacific Islands, alongside extensive penetration into European territories.

China's prodigious provision of infrastructure financing to other nations engenders a symbiotic relationship wherein recipient countries not only service their debt obligations to China but also engage Chinese enterprises, thereby engendering employment opportunities for Chinese laborers. Beyond its stature as a preeminent economic and financial juggernaut, China has emerged as a crucible of technological innovation, progressively augmenting its capacity to challenge the prevailing hegemony of the Western-led Washington Consensus. Evidencing this transformative trajectory is the establishment of the NDB under the aegis of the BRICS consortium, which portends a seismic realignment of the global financial landscape. The convergence of interests between Western powers, spearheaded by the United States, and the burgeoning BRICS constellation, inclusive of China and India, within the G-20 framework, underscores the inexorable march toward a multilateral or multipolar financial and political order, wherein China is slated to assume a pivotal role of paramount significance.

TABLE 4.3 Comparative Data Analysis of China and India.

S.No.	Variables Indicator	China	India	Year
1.	Total population	1.41 (billion)	1.39 (billion)	2021
2.	Population growth	0.1 (%)	1.0 (%)	2021
3.	Life expectancy at birth	77 (years)	70 (years)	2020
4.	Human capital index (HCI) (Scale 0–1)	0.7	0.5	2020
5.	Net migration	−1,741,996	−2,663,434	2017
6.	Poverty head count ratio at $2.15 a day (2017 PPP) (% of population)	0.1	10.0	2019
7.	Global multidimensional poverty index		415 million	2021
8.	Gross domestic product (GDP in US$ trillion)	17.73	3.17	2021
9.	GDP per capita (current US$)	12,556.3	2277.4	2021
10.	GDP growth (annual %)	8.1	7.4	2021
		8.9	6.8	2022
		10.1	6.1	2023
11.	Inflation, consumer prices Index (annual %)	1.0	7.41	2021
			12.17	September 2022
12.	Unemployment, total (% of the total labor force) modeled ILO estimates	4.8	6.0	2021
13.	Personal remittances	0.1	3.1	2020
14.	Foreign direct investment (FDI net inflows in % of GDP)	1.7	2.4	2020
15.	Central government debt, (total in % of GDP)	–	46.5	2018
		–	51.4	2020
		–	58.8	March 2022
		–	84	By the end of 2022
16.	Black money in Swiss bank	–	400 lakh crore (INR)	1990–2021
17.	Forest area (% of land area)	23.3	24.3	2020
18.	CO_2 emission (metric tons per capita)	7.6	1.8	2019
19.	Access to electricity (% of population)	100	87	2022
20.	Electricity production from renewable sources, excluding hydroelectric (% of total)	4.9	5.4	2015
			Total 403.759 GW (39.2% from renewable sources)	2022
21.	Individuals using the Internet (% of the population)	70	43	2020
		ONE users billion	658 million users	2022
22.	People using safely managed sanitation services (% of population)	70	46	2020
23.	Literacy rate	98.84	79.1	2022

Sources: World Bank Group.

4.16 THE ECONOMIC TRAJECTORIES OF INDIA AND CHINA

As of 1990, the economic landscapes of India and China were strikingly comparable. However, fast forward to the year 2022, and the narrative has dramatically diverged, with the Chinese economy surging ahead by a staggering 5.46-fold in comparison to its Indian counterpart. Presently, India's GDP hovers around the US$3.1 trillion mark, while China's economic juggernaut commands an imposing US$19.7 trillion. Prognostications from the IMF paint a nuanced picture of India's economic trajectory, forecasting a contraction in GDP growth from 7.4% in 2021 to 6.8% in 2022, followed by a further decline to 6.1% in 2023. IMF Managing Director Kristalina Georgieva has proffered an optimistic outlook, envisaging India maintaining a robust growth rate of 6.8% for the fiscal year spanning March 2022–March 2023. For the subsequent fiscal year of 2023/2024 (April 2023–March 2024), the IMF anticipates a growth rate of 6.1%, albeit exhibiting a marginal deceleration vis-à-vis the global economic milieu, yet remaining comfortably above the global average. Consequently, India is poised to contribute approximately 15% to the global growth trajectory in the year 2023.

India has adeptly leveraged digitalization as a pivotal catalyst for navigating the exigencies of the pandemic while concurrently fostering an environment ripe with opportunities for economic expansion and job creation. Capital investment has surged exponentially for the third consecutive year, ascending by an impressive 33% to reach ₹10 lakh crores. This augmentation in capital expenditure, constituting 3.3% of the GDP, represents the most substantial leap in recent memory, following a preceding surge of over 37% between the fiscal years of 2020–2021 and 2021–2022. Moreover, India has pivoted toward a strategic focus on channeling investments into the burgeoning green economy, particularly renewables, with the overarching objective of effectuating a transition toward sustainable energy and perpetuating economic growth. The potential looms large for harnessing this fiscal prudence into a medium-term framework that furnishes a robust foundation for India's public finances. Noteworthy is the annual influx of 15 million individuals into the labor force, highlighting the imperative of fostering a conducive investment climate that catalyzes job creation—a domain where India has historically underutilized its female workforce.

India's economic standing, currently occupying the 5th position, trailing behind Germany as of March 2022, is poised for a transformative ascent. Projections suggest that by 2027, India will ascend to the 4th position, trailing closely behind Japan, and by 2029, it is anticipated to trail just behind China. Conversely, India's global rank in terms of the human freedom index paints a more nuanced picture, with its position situated at 119 out of 165 nations worldwide. This index, predicated upon parameters encompassing individual liberties, citizen rights, and adherence to a rule-based economic framework, underscores the multifaceted nature of India's socioeconomic tapestry.

4.17 CHINA'S DISTINCTIVE PARADIGM OF PEOPLE-CENTERED DEVELOPMENT

Since its inception in 1949, China has been steadfastly committed to a "people-centered development model," spearheading a transformative trajectory that has propelled Chinese society from the agrarian confines of yore toward a modern, scientifically driven ethos characterized by rural–urban industrialization—a hallmark of scientific socialism. This model, with its resounding global resonance, has undergone iterative refinements since 1978, cementing China's reputation as a beacon of progressive socioeconomic transformation.

A pivotal milestone in China's trajectory is the resounding triumph in its battle against extreme poverty—a feat of unparalleled magnitude in the annals of human history. China's unwavering commitment to this cause has yielded substantial dividends, exerting a tangible impact on the global landscape of poverty alleviation.

The world stands to glean invaluable insights from the Chinese experience, wherein the interplay of resolute political will and concerted people-centric action has facilitated the attainment of seminal objectives such as self-reliance, rapid socioeconomic and cultural advancement, sustainability, and inclusive development. Key to this paradigm is the provision of qualitative public education and healthcare services, underpinning a concerted drive toward achieving universal literacy, eradicating extreme poverty, ameliorating malnutrition and hunger, mitigating unemployment, and dismantling socioeconomic and gender-based disparities—a holistic endeavor aimed at fostering a healthier, more equitable world.

Over the past several decades, dating back to 1978, China has steadfastly accelerated the construction of a modern economic edifice, leveraging the twin engines of scientific and technological innovation. This concerted endeavor, coupled with a relentless pursuit of state governance reform, has engendered transformative outcomes, including the eradication of extreme poverty, while concurrently championing the cause of green development—an ethos that underscores China's unwavering commitment to sustainability and environmental stewardship.

4.17.1 THE TENACITY OF THE CHINESE ECONOMIC APPARATUS

Under the astute stewardship of the CPC, China has successfully achieved the First Centenary Goal within the second phase of its socialist construction, heralding the eradication of absolute poverty, a marked improvement in living standards, the attainment of universal literacy, and the provision of qualitative and innovative education and healthcare services to its populace—all emblematic hallmarks of the realization of a moderately prosperous society. With this milestone firmly entrenched, China now sets its sights on the pursuit of the "Second Centenary Goal," propelling the nation toward new frontiers of development and prosperity.

The robustness of the Chinese economy finds vivid expression in the steadfast stability of prices. In the backdrop of a global inflationary surge reaching its zenith in over four decades, China's consumer price index has registered a mere 2% uptick in 2022—a figure markedly subdued in comparison to its counterparts in the United States and major European economies. Over the preceding 5-year period, the value-added contributions of China's high-tech and equipment manufacturing sectors have exhibited a commendable growth trajectory, averaging annual rates of 10.6 and 7.9%, respectively, while the digital economy continues its unabated expansion.

China's paradigm of innovation-driven development has not only catalyzed the metamorphosis and upscaling of its domestic economic landscape but has also engendered a concomitant localization and upgradation of foreign enterprises operating within its precincts. Initially conceived as a global manufacturing hub, China has since evolved into a nucleus for R&D activities, prompting foreign enterprises to establish R&D centers and integrate more value chains within the Chinese market.

This second wave of localization is characterized by foreign entities introducing advanced or novel products tailored to the discerning needs of Chinese consumers, thereby fortifying their competitive standing within the Chinese marketplace.

Embracing a high-standard socialist market economy and advocating for high-caliber opening up, China has embarked on a multifaceted reform agenda aimed at deepening institutional reforms in pivotal sectors, bolstering the construction of a modern infrastructure network, and nurturing a high-standard market ecosystem. Concurrently, China remains steadfast in its commitment to promoting institutional opening up—an endeavor that holds profound allure for foreign enterprises deeply entrenched within the Chinese market milieu. Firmly anchored in its support for multilateralism and the tenets of economic globalization, China has proactively spearheaded initiatives such as the Regional Comprehensive Economic Partnership and high-quality Belt and Road cooperation, fostering an environment conducive to win–win cooperation and active participation in global governance mechanisms.

4.18 DIGITAL ECONOMY: TRANSFORMING MODERN SOCIETY

The digital economy denotes economic activities underpinned by digital technologies and platforms. It encapsulates the production, distribution, and consumption of goods and services enabled through the internet, advanced communication tools, and transformative technologies such as AI, blockchain, and cloud computing. As an essential driver of globalization and innovation, the digital economy profoundly reshapes the interactions among businesses, governments, and individuals in today's interconnected world.

4.18.1 KEY COMPONENTS OF THE DIGITAL ECONOMY

1. **Digital Infrastructure**:

   Comprising hardware, software, and telecommunications networks, digital infrastructure forms the backbone of the digital economy. Examples include high-speed internet, robust cloud platforms, and cutting-edge 5G networks.

2. **Digital Platforms**:

   Serving as intermediaries, digital platforms facilitate seamless connections between users and service providers. Prominent examples include e-commerce giants such as Amazon, ride-sharing services like Uber, and streaming platforms like Netflix.

3. **Data**:

   Frequently likened to the "new oil," data constitute an invaluable resource for decision-making, personalization, and innovation. Advanced technologies such as big data analytics and AI leverage vast data repositories to create substantial economic value.

4. **Digital Services**:

   These encompass services delivered via digital networks, ranging from online banking and e-learning to telemedicine, enhancing convenience and accessibility.

5. **Workforce and Skills**:

   The digital economy demands a workforce proficient in areas such as coding, digital marketing, and data analytics. Furthermore, the gig economy and remote work paradigms are redefining traditional employment landscapes.

4.18.2 BENEFITS OF THE DIGITAL ECONOMY

1. **Enhanced Efficiency**:

   Automation and digital tools optimize operations, reducing costs and expediting processes.

2. **Global Reach**:

   Businesses gain unprecedented access to international markets, transcending geographical limitations.

3. **Innovation**:

   The digital economy spurs the creation of novel products, services, and business models, exemplified by fintech innovations and sustainable technologies.

4. **Job Creation**:

   Although automation supplants certain roles, it simultaneously generates employment opportunities in fields such as software development, data analysis, and IT management.

5. **Improved Accessibility**:

   Digital platforms democratize access to critical services like education, healthcare, and financial inclusion, particularly in underserved areas.

4.18.3 CHALLENGES OF THE DIGITAL ECONOMY

1. **The Digital Divide**:

   Disparities in access to digital tools and connectivity exacerbate socioeconomic inequalities.

2. **Cybersecurity Vulnerabilities**:

   Reliance on digital systems increases exposure to cyber threats, necessitating robust security measures.

3. **Data Privacy Concerns**:

   The pervasive use of personal data poses ethical and regulatory dilemmas, particularly regarding surveillance and misuse.

4. **Job Displacement**:

   Automation and AI may render certain traditional roles obsolete, compelling significant investment in workforce reskilling initiatives.

5. **Regulatory Complexities**:

   Balancing the dynamism of innovation with fair regulatory frameworks addressing digital monopolies, tax obligations, and competitive fairness remains a formidable challenge.

4.18.4 THE FUTURE OF THE DIGITAL ECONOMY

The digital economy is poised for exponential evolution as technologies such as the internet of things (IoT), blockchain, and quantum computing mature. Emerging trends include:

1. The proliferation of the **metaverse** and virtual economies, redefining digital interactions.
2. Accelerated adoption of **sustainable technologies** to combat climate change.
3. Wider integration of **AI-driven decision-making** across industries, enhancing efficiency and innovation.
4. The rapid expansion of **decentralized finance (DeFi)** and cryptocurrency markets, disrupt traditional financial systems.

To capitalize on the opportunities of the digital economy while addressing its inherent challenges, governments, businesses, and individuals must adopt adaptive strategies, ensuring equitable, inclusive, and sustainable progress.

TABLE 4.4 Digital Economy (Microsoft, Amazon, Google, etc.).

Country	Digital Economy Covers in % to GDP in 2021
World	4.5
USA	6.5
China	7
India	6

Mobile industries share USD 4.5 trillion in global GDP

Source: Statista.com, World Bank report, and so forth.

4.19 THE ASCENDANCY OF INDIA'S DIGITAL DOMINANCE

At a macroscopic level, Indian consumers are increasingly embracing digital payment platforms, encompassing Phone Pay, Credit Cards, Debit Cards, and Paytm, among a myriad of others, to orchestrate their purchasing transactions, both in the virtual realm and brick-and-mortar establishments. This seismic shift has catapulted India into the echelons of a services superpower. In the realm of commerce, India's bilateral trade nexus with the United States alone has burgeoned to approximately USD 150 billion annually, with a substantial fraction of this commerce gravitating toward the digital economy, which has surpassed the staggering threshold of USD 100 billion per annum.

India has notched significant milestones in the establishment of global value and supply chains. The nation has earmarked considerable financial incentives to galvanize producers into manufacturing high-value electronic commodities, spanning the gamut from iPhones, semiconductors, computers, and printers, to electric vehicles, within its territorial confines. The efficacy of these endeavors is palpable in the burgeoning share of domestically assembled electronic and digital products, particularly mobile phones, permeating the domestic market. This share has burgeoned from 11% in 2019 to a commendable 15% in 2022, with prognostications auguring that it will eclipse the 20% threshold within the ensuing 2–3 years.

In the annus mirabilis of 2022, India's electronic exports surged meteorically by an impressive 45% to attain the lofty summit of USD 20.45 billion, mirroring a robust uptick in imports, which witnessed a notable escalation of 19%. Nonetheless, the nation grapples with a persistent monthly electronics trade deficit, hovering around the USD 4 billion mark on average. In stark contrast, China's export juggernaut in December 2022 alone, culminated in the dispatch of electronic commodities valued at approximately USD 30 billion, underscoring the formidable might of its manufacturing prowess.

Moreover, India's exports of electronic components witnessed a commendable uptick of 29% in 2022, soaring to the tune of USD 3.7 billion, while imports registered a comparable ascent of 26% to reach USD 2.7 billion, with the lion's share of these components sourced from China. Notably, Foxconn's foray into India's electronics sector represents a colossus of investment unparalleled in scale, portending the creation of an estimated 100,000 employment opportunities (Global Economic Data, Indicators, Charts & Forecasts | CEIC, 2023).

4.20 INDIA'S ASCENDANT STATUS IN VARIOUS ECONOMIC ARENAS

India, asserting its prowess on the global stage, stands tall as the third-largest producer of electricity worldwide, with a robust national electric grid boasting an impressive installed capacity of 403.759 GW as of June 30, 2022. Notably, renewable power plants, inclusive of large hydroelectric facilities, constitute a notable 39.2% of this formidable installed capacity. Concurrently, India's manufacturing, supply chain, and e-commerce sectors are undergoing a metamorphosis, bearing witness to remarkable growth trajectories, thereby positioning the nation as a formidable force in these spheres.

With its burgeoning potential, India is primed to emerge as a veritable hub for software investments, a development that promises to engender a plethora of high-quality employment opportunities and inject a substantial impetus into global economic dynamics. Furthermore, the country is poised to ascend to the echelons of an agricultural superpower, courtesy of initiatives aimed at fostering an enabling environment for producers and farmers, with ambitious targets set at reaching the USD 500 billion mark. Services, particularly in domains such as manufacturing, supply chain management, and e-commerce, are poised to play instrumental roles across sectors encompassing pharmaceuticals, life sciences, defense, and aerospace.

India's capacity to mitigate its imports from China by an estimated 40% in the foreseeable future, as analyzed by the industry body PHD Chamber of Commerce and Industry, underscores the nation's strategic imperatives. Dynamic governmental schemes such as the production-linked incentive (PLI) initiative and PM Gati Shakti have invigorated sentiments among Indian producers, empowering them to enhance competitiveness and challenge the hegemony of Chinese imports.

The PLI scheme, in particular, has emerged as a catalyst for augmented production across a diverse spectrum of sectors, encompassing chemicals, automotive components, bicycle parts, agro-based commodities, handicrafts, drug formulations, cosmetics, consumer electronics, and leather goods. This surge in production not only mitigates India's reliance on Chinese imports but also augments exports within these product categories.

Approximately 36 subsectors harbor the potential to substantially curtail India's dependency on Chinese imports, collectively accounting for approximately $35 billion in India's import basket. These sectors, endowed with existing production capacities, stand poised to progressively reduce their reliance on China, facilitated by phased initiatives without necessitating exorbitant additional investments. The inaugural phase will prioritize sectors encompassed by the PLI scheme.

Furthermore, APIs, constituting a pivotal component in drug development, exhibit promising growth prospects, with the API market valued at USD 300,722.26 billion in 2021 and poised to burgeon to USD 540,335.81 billion by 2029 at a noteworthy CAGR of 7.6% during the forecast period of 2022–2029. This growth trajectory is propelled by factors such as the burgeoning prevalence of chronic ailments and an ageing populace—a confluence of factors underpinning the robust trajectory of the API market.

4.21 INDIA'S PHARMACEUTICAL PREDICAMENT: A TALE OF TRIUMPHS AND TRIALS

India, proudly bearing the mantle of the third-largest pharmaceutical industry globally, finds itself ensnared in a delicate dance of reliance and resilience. Despite its lofty status, China holds sway over approximately 70% of India's pharmaceutical requisites, encompassing the crucial APIs indispensable for drug formulation. In a bid to chart a course of diversification and mitigate reliance on a singular pharmaceutical niche, IOL Chemicals and Pharmaceuticals Limited— renowned for its commanding one-third market share in the painkiller drug ibuprofen API—announced in August 2023 a strategic pivot toward diversifying into other specialty chemical products and recalibrating the balance of its portfolio away from ibuprofen-centric ventures.

Looming large as the foremost producer of Ibuprofen in India, commanding a staggering 30% global market share, IOL Chemicals and Pharmaceuticals underscores the pivotal importance of diversifying its API portfolio to sustain growth and ameliorate risks associated with over-reliance on a singular pharmaceutical vertical. Notably, the company's non-Ibuprofen business witnessed a meteoric surge of approximately 70% in the preceding fiscal year compared to its antecedent, underscoring the dividends reaped from strategic diversification efforts.

India's robust capacity in medications such as Metformin and Clopidogrel serves as a beacon of promise, prompting fervent endeavors to augment market presence in a diverse array of APIs. In this vein, India has embarked upon an ambitious capital expenditure program to the tune of Rs 11 billion over the ensuing 3–4 years, with the overarching objective of broadening its API and Specialty Chemicals portfolio to align with burgeoning market exigencies. Encouragingly, the company's proactive strides are underscored by a flurry of regulatory approvals, including new Drug Master Files (DMFs) filed with the USFDA and applications submitted to the European Directorate for the Quality of Medicines (EDQM) for Certificate of Suitability to the Monographs of the European Pharmacopoeia (CEP).

India's overreliance on foreign shores for APIs and intermediates, particularly China, remains a vexing conundrum, underscoring the imperative of bolstering domestic manufacturing capabilities to mitigate import dependence. The PLI Scheme in India's pharmaceutical domain has emerged as a cornerstone initiative aimed at fostering indigenous manufacturing and alleviating import reliance. Nevertheless, challenges loom large, with pharmaceutical enterprises grappling with the formidable task of reducing reliance on Chinese imports, compounded by the prohibitive cost differentials between domestic production and imports.

Amidst this milieu of challenges, the global Ibuprofen market, valued at USD 400 million in 2020, holds promise for Indian pharmaceutical stalwarts, with India poised as the second-largest supplier of Ibuprofen worldwide, boasting a prodigious production market share nearing 50%. Despite the adversities, Indian pharmaceutical and chemical enterprises find solace in burgeoning outsourcing opportunities, underpinned by the burgeoning China + 1 strategy, heralding a silver lining amidst a tempestuous horizon (Panda, 2022).

4.22 THE APPRECIATION OF THE CHINESE YUAN: A GLOBAL PHENOMENON

China has assumed a pivotal role in the global landscape by spearheading the internationalization of the yuan, a feat substantiated by its gradual unfolding of the bond market to foreign investors, as meticulously delineated in a recent scholarly paper. The authors of the said paper cogently argue that Chinese bonds are now accorded treatment akin to debt emanating from a developed economy, eclipsing the traditional perception of emerging market debt. This incremental liberalization of China's bond market stands as a cornerstone in propelling the yuan toward heightened global prominence.

Nevertheless, the yuan finds itself at a juncture of monumental trial. Over the course of the past two decades, China has systematically broadened the aperture for traders and central banks to partake in its yuan-denominated bond market. While the yuan is yet to traverse the extensive terrain necessary to rival the hegemony of the US dollar on the global stage, its burgeoning internationalization is unequivocally palpable.

The recent conflagration between Russia and Ukraine, compounded by ensuing Western sanctions, has engendered a surge in the utilization of the yuan. Notably, Russia has emerged as the third-largest market for yuan transactions beyond mainland China, a testament to its acceptance of yuan-based payments for energy exports—a stark departure from its traditional reliance on the dollar, which historically served as the primary currency for most commodity transactions.

Presently, the yuan stands as the fifth most utilized currency in international payments markets, as per SWIFT data. While the US dollar retains its apex position, followed closely by the euro, British pound, and Japanese yen, the ascent of the yuan heralds a paradigm shift in global currency dynamics, underscoring China's burgeoning influence on the global economic stage (Yuan Appreciated, 2023).

4.23 POVERTY ALLEVIATION TRIUMPHS IN CHINA: A MONUMENTAL ACHIEVEMENT

As attested by authoritative bodies such as the United Nations, World Bank, and IMF, a mere 1% of China's vast populace grapples with poverty, a remarkable statistic emblematic of the nation's transformative journey. By the culmination of 2020, China had achieved the extraordinary feat of uplifting all 98.99 million impoverished rural denizens, ushering them into a realm of newfound opportunity and prosperity. This historic milestone not only resonates profoundly within the annals of Chinese history but also reverberates as a beacon of hope for humanity, encapsulating an unparalleled triumph of human endeavor.

In stark contrast, India finds itself grappling with a disquieting surge in its impoverished populace. The Modi Government's recent disclosure of an additional 430 million individuals slipping beneath the poverty line paints a stark picture, catapulting the total count of impoverished souls in India to a staggering 800 million. This precipitous rise in destitution is primarily attributed to the deleterious repercussions of the COVID-19 pandemic, which precipitated the loss of a staggering 210 million livelihoods.

Embarking on an ambitious trajectory of reform, China has orchestrated a multifaceted array of over 2000 reform initiatives spanning diverse sectors. These endeavors, meticulously calibrated to enhance basic living standards, educational access, healthcare provisions, and eldercare amenities, have coalesced to forge resilient institutional frameworks. This holistic metamorphosis underscores the maturation of China's distinctive socialist model, infused with quintessential Chinese characteristics, alongside the modernization of the nation's governance architecture and capacities.

Furthermore, China's outreach efforts extend far beyond its borders, entailing robust engagements with congenial political entities and organizations on a global scale. Anchored in the principles of parity, mutual esteem, and nonintervention, these diplomatic overtures have fostered a tapestry of extensive interactions and collaborations between China and its international counterparts. Such concerted endeavors have not only galvanized China's socioeconomic trajectory but have also elevated its global stature, resonating as a testament to its indomitable spirit of progress and cooperation on the world stage (Jingxi, 2022).

China is unequivocally dedicated to the construction of a sophisticated socialist market economy system, a commitment underscored by its unwavering resolve to fortify and propel forward the public ownership system while simultaneously nurturing and supporting the growth of the private sector. Central to this endeavor is the adept utilization of market forces to facilitate the efficient allocation of resources, thereby unleashing the full spectrum of economic potential.

At the heart of this vision lies the amalgamation of market dynamics with socialist principles, a symbiotic fusion aimed at engendering high-quality economic growth. China's steadfast efforts entail not only harnessing the dynamism of the market but also enhancing the government's role to ensure the attainment of economic objectives aligned with the overarching goal of constructing a modern socialist society.

Through a judicious blend of state intervention and market-driven mechanisms, China endeavors to foster an environment conducive to innovation, entrepreneurship, and sustainable development. The nation's unwavering commitment to this trajectory reflects its steadfast determination to realize the vision of a prosperous and harmonious socialist nation, where the fruits of progress are shared equitably among its populace.

China places paramount importance on environmental conservation, recognizing it as a pivotal element in its trajectory toward modern socialist development. The nation is steadfast in its commitment to promoting eco-friendly consumption, production, and lifestyles, acknowledging the indispensable role of safeguarding nature in fostering sustainable progress. Strides have been made in addressing environmental challenges, with a concerted focus on eliminating severe air and water pollution, alongside vigilant efforts to manage soil contamination effectively. Embracing a vision of a "green energy revolution," China champions renewable energy initiatives such as the "Solar Plan" while concurrently advocating for the clean utilization of coal.

Conversely, India grapples with daunting environmental adversities, with a substantial segment of its populace subjected to pollution levels surpassing those associated with prevalent diseases like HIV/AIDS, tuberculosis, malaria, and diarrheal ailments combined. The toll of pollution-induced illnesses exacts a significant economic toll, costing India between 0.3 and 0.9% of its GDP annually. Metropolises like Delhi find themselves ensconced under a veil of thick smog, a recurring phenomenon particularly pronounced across the Indo-Gangetic plain. Groundwater overexploitation, exacerbated by agricultural practices and subsidized electricity, emerges as a pressing concern, with water transference from arid regions like Punjab to water-rich locales exacerbating the crisis.

Notably, China showcases superior water management practices, employing water-efficient irrigation techniques like drip or sprinkler systems, while India grapples with reliance on flood irrigation. Urban centers in India grapple with substantial water loss, with 40–50% of piped water going to waste, attributable in part to inadequate infrastructure and administrative oversights. Furthermore, urban land utilization in India poses formidable challenges, with haphazard construction practices perpetuating spatial inefficiencies that may endure for generations.

To bridge the developmental chasm vis-à-vis China, India must sustain a robust growth trajectory of at least 6% over a quarter century, underscored by judicious land and water resource management. Forecasts by the IMF portend China's ascendance to the zenith of the global economic hierarchy by 2027, potentially surpassing the US economy in GDP magnitude. By 2040, China's economic prowess could burgeon to a staggering $50–55 trillion, markedly eclipsing current projections for the Indian economy, which is poised to emerge as the world's third-largest economy between 2025 and 2030, with a GDP hovering around USD 5 trillion. The erstwhile chasm between China and the US is anticipated to narrow, with China trailing the US by a mere 20% from 2023 to 2030, eventually outstripping the US by a commensurate margin.

China has spearheaded a circular economy paradigm aimed at mitigating the plastic waste crisis by repurposing it into sustainable concrete for the construction sector. Initiatives like Eco Bricks exemplify this approach, wherein China ingeniously rechannels plastic waste from construction endeavors, diverting it away from landfills and oceans. This innovative strategy not only diminishes waste accumulation but also furnishes a sustainable avenue for the construction industry. The objective is to upcycle local plastic waste into high-quality concrete components for indigenous construction ventures, subsequently subjecting them to full recycling into fresh bricks upon reaching the culmination of their lifecycle. This cyclic process epitomizes a broader endeavor to imbue the construction sector with sustainability throughout its entire value chain.

It is imperative to recognize the symbiotic relationship between achieving zero carbon and zero waste, as they are intertwined environmental imperatives. Tackling one often necessitates addressing the other. The built environment, encompassing buildings and infrastructure, stands as a significant wellspring of waste generation and GHG emissions. Carbon emissions ensue not merely during the construction phase but also across a structure's lifespan and operational tenure, along with the disposal of construction materials.

Furthermore, the construction industry's reliance on natural resources, notably sand for concrete production, poses a significant concern. Urbanization and construction activities fuel the demand for sand, precipitating environmental degradation and resource depletion. Projections indicate a substantial surge in new building stock between 2016 and 2060, exacerbating the conundrum of material consumption and waste generation.

Mitigating these challenges necessitates the pursuit of sustainable solutions for the built environment to actualize zero waste and zero carbon emission objectives. Sustainable materials like recycled plastic concrete hold immense promise in tackling these predicaments while catering to the escalating construction requisites in the forthcoming decades. It represents a mutually beneficial resolution that not only curtails waste accumulation but also fosters a trajectory toward a more sustainable future.

4.24 CLOSING THE LOOP: TRANSFORMING UNRECYCLED WASTE INTO SUSTAINABLE SOLUTIONS WITH ECOBRICKS

EcoBricks, an innovative initiative hailing from Hong Kong, China, has introduced a revolutionary concrete solution that harnesses local waste materials to supplant traditional virgin materials in construction endeavors.

This pioneering approach endeavors to either meet or exceed the performance benchmarks set by conventional concrete while substantially mitigating environmental repercussions. Crucially, the recycling process for plastic waste remains entirely cold and clean, eschewing the utilization of heat, melting, or chemical treatment. This results in diminished energy consumption and eradicates effluent pollution or chemical byproducts, rendering the manufacturing process both energy-efficient and environmentally benign.

A pivotal facet of EcoBricks lies in its harmonization with existing recycling endeavors, rather than instigating competition. By concentrating on plastic waste that currently eludes recycling and frequently finds its way into landfills (comprising 89% of collected plastic waste), EcoBricks collaborates with major waste management entities and recyclers to repurpose waste they are unable to process or recycle. The proportion of recycled plastic waste to unrecycled waste remains consistent worldwide, rendering this solution adaptable to diverse nations.

The plastic waste integrated into EcoBricks encompasses materials like PVC, which typically lack viable recycling avenues, alongside concrete and glass waste. Furthermore, the initiative is exploring locally sourced substitutes for cement, such as pulverized fly ash from coal power plants or granulated blast slag from steel mills, which could be employed in regions where these materials are abundant. By substituting raw materials with locally sourced waste materials, EcoBricks curbs the ecological ramifications of extensive mining, extraction, and transportation of hefty materials across extensive distances.

EcoBricks find application in local construction projects, serving as a testament to the imperative of recycling within local communities. Furthermore, any waste generated, inclusive of the bricks themselves, can be recycled back into bricks, fostering a zero-waste ethos from inception to fruition. To underscore the impact of plastic waste recycling, a solitary football pitch adorned with EcoBricks paving equates to upcycling 14.3 million plastic bottles.

EcoBricks embarked on its inaugural major endeavor at the Gold Coast Piazza development of the Sino Group in Tuen Mun, where they supplied over 15,000 bricks, derived from 5.4 tonnes of plastic waste sourced from 560 obsolete washing machines. This endeavor serves as a testament to the potential of EcoBricks to substantially curtail plastic waste while championing sustainable construction methodologies.

4.25 ADVANCING SUSTAINABILITY: CHINA'S CIRCULAR ECONOMY MODEL AND ECOBRICKS' CONTRIBUTION TO THE BUILDING SECTOR

In the pursuit of sustainability, China has emerged as a global leader in fostering a circular economy model, aimed at minimizing waste, reducing resource consumption, and maximizing material reuse and recycling. This strategic approach not only addresses environmental challenges spurred by rapid industrialization and urbanization but also enhances economic efficiency and competitiveness.

Since the issuance of the "Circular Economy Development Strategy and Action Plan" by China's State Council in 2002, the government has implemented a comprehensive framework to promote circularity. Through policies, tax incentives, subsidies, and regulations, China has encouraged the recycling and reuse of resources, laying the foundation for sustainable development.

A pivotal component of China's circular economy strategy is the establishment of eco-industrial parks. These parks function as closed-loop systems, where waste from one industry serves as a resource for another, fostering resource efficiency, pollution reduction, and economic opportunities.

Moreover, China has prioritized R&D in innovative technologies to support circularity. For instance, the country leads in the advancement of waste-to-energy technologies like anaerobic digestion and pyrolysis, which convert organic waste into energy or valuable products.

In tandem with these initiatives, China has undertaken extensive efforts to raise awareness among businesses and consumers about the importance of a circular economy. Through public education campaigns and technical assistance to businesses, the government aims to facilitate the adoption of sustainable practices across sectors.

In this landscape of advancing sustainability, EcoBricks has emerged as a pioneering solution, particularly within the building sector. By collaborating with partners to collect waste from existing buildings and repurpose it into concrete products for new construction, EcoBricks epitomizes circularity in action. This model not only reduces waste but also offers competitive pricing, thereby promoting circularity in a sector entrenched within one of the world's costliest real estate markets.

A life cycle assessment conducted by EcoBricks demonstrated the significant environmental benefits of using local waste materials over virgin materials in concrete production. By reducing the carbon footprint of concrete products by up to 41%, EcoBricks contributes to the industry's sustainability goals and aligns with global initiatives like the Paris Agreement.

In light of increasing investor activism and demands for enhanced sustainability credentials, EcoBricks' circularity proposition stands as a beacon of progress. By promoting transparency and accountability throughout the supply chain, EcoBricks fosters trust within local communities and promotes a circular economy ethos.

In essence, the partnership between China's circular economy model and EcoBricks' innovative contributions to the building sector exemplifies a harmonious synergy aimed at advancing sustainability and creating a more resilient future for generations to come.

4.26 A CIRCULAR ECONOMIC MODEL

China's concerted efforts in advancing toward a circular economy epitomize its commitment to sustainable development, aiming to mitigate waste, curtail resource consumption, and optimize material reuse and recycling. This strategic direction not only tackles the environmental challenges intertwined with swift industrialization and urban expansion but also bolsters economic efficiency and competitiveness.

The seminal "Circular Economy Development Strategy and Action Plan" issued by China's State Council in 2002 delineated a comprehensive blueprint for fostering circularity. Since its inception, the Chinese government has instituted an array of policies, ranging from tax incentives to subsidies and regulations, to bolster the circular economy. These measures are meticulously crafted to incentivize the recycling and repurposing of resources.

Central to China's circular economy strategy is the propagation of eco-industrial parks, engineered to establish closed-loop systems where industrial waste serves as a valuable resource for other sectors. These parks are ingeniously designed to optimize resource utilization, diminish pollution, and usher in novel economic prospects.

Moreover, China has earmarked substantial investments in R&D to spearhead innovative technologies that underpin a circular economy. For instance, the nation has emerged as a frontrunner in pioneering advanced waste-to-energy technologies like anaerobic digestion and pyrolysis, which transmute organic waste into energy or valuable commodities.

In tandem with these endeavors, China is actively engaged in elevating awareness about the significance of circular economy principles among businesses and consumers. Through multifaceted public education campaigns and tailored training initiatives, the government seeks to facilitate the adoption of sustainable practices across various sectors.

Overall, China's steadfast endeavors to cultivate a circular economy are pivotal components of its overarching strategy to champion sustainable development and mitigate environmental challenges. By championing resource efficiency and waste reduction, China aspires to foster a more sustainable and resilient economy capable of sustained growth and prosperity in the long haul.

In parallel, EcoBricks has embarked on a pioneering journey to develop solutions that not only embrace circularity but also cater to the exigencies of the building sector. Collaborating synergistically with partners, EcoBricks endeavors to harness waste from existing buildings and repurpose it into concrete products for new constructions, all while offering competitive pricing. This innovative model not only fosters circularity but also mitigates the burden of landfill levies in a sector entrenched in one of the world's most expensive real estate markets.

Conducting a rigorous life cycle assessment based on the ISO 14040 framework, EcoBricks has quantified the environmental advantages of utilizing local waste materials vis-à-vis virgin materials in conventional concrete production. The findings underscore a remarkable reduction in the carbon footprint of concrete products by up to 41%, thereby positioning concrete, the most widely utilized man-made material, on a more sustainable trajectory. This paradigm shift is imperative for the building sector, especially in light of the irreversible macroeconomic dynamics it confronts.

Furthermore, the burgeoning role of investor activism, coupled with mounting pressure from asset managers and stakeholders, underscores the industry's transition toward sustainability. The property development sector, grappling with its primary ESG reporting challenge—tracing the origins of building materials—faces an arduous task due to the fragmented and opaque nature of the supply chain.

Amidst these challenges, the circularity proposition shines as a beacon of hope. Proximity between raw material supply and end-product manufacture fosters transparency, easing the acquisition of verifiable and auditable data throughout the lifecycle—from inception to disposal. Driven by a blend of incentives and penalties, the industry is embracing transformational change, particularly in locales like Hong Kong, and China, where the private sector steers construction activities.

High rankings in sustainability assessments like LEED and BEAM Plus offer tangible and intangible benefits to companies, permitting them to expand operations while curbing their carbon footprint. Moreover, such initiatives play a pivotal role in mitigating plastic waste pollution, preserving the delicate balance of ecosystems and safeguarding human health. By fostering tangible products that seamlessly integrate into local infrastructure, the circular economy ethos not only engenders trust within communities but also galvanizes broader adoption of recycling practices, heralding a more sustainable future.

4.27 CHINA'S ONE BELT ONE ROAD INITIATIVE

China's historical narrative has been indelibly shaped by the notion of the Silk Road, an ancient trade network that originated approximately two millennia ago during the illustrious Han Dynasty. This intricate web of commerce interlinked China with the Mediterranean via Eurasia, serving as a pivotal conduit of trade and cultural exchange for countless centuries. The genesis of the original Silk Road can be traced back to the westward expansion of the Han Dynasty (206 BCE–220 CE), which engendered the development of robust sea and land trade routes traversing the vast expanse of the western terrain.

This maritime Silk Road, a manifestation of China's expansionist endeavors, intricately intertwined with the northern routes traversed by luminaries like Ibn Battuta and the southern maritime expedition routes pioneered by Ming dynasty admiral Zheng He. By circumventing the Malacca Strait, China charted a novel course, encompassing fueling stations, bustling ports, sturdy bridges, burgeoning industries, and expansive infrastructure spanning the South China Sea to Southeast Asia, and onward across the vast expanse of the Indian Ocean to the Asia Pacific region.

Moreover, contemporary China is forging new trade arteries, such as those extending from Gilgit-Baltistan—a region nestled within the disputed Kashmir territory—to Gwadar, an eminent port city nestled along the Arabian Sea, serving as a gateway to Europe. Additionally, burgeoning routes stemming from Baluchistan, traversing through Afghanistan and extending to Central Asian nations including Uzbekistan, Tajikistan, Kazakhstan, Kyrgyzstan, and Turkmenistan, extend over a prodigious span of 4000 miles, culminating in the European continent.

Central Asia, aptly dubbed the epicenter of one of the earliest waves of globalization, played a pivotal role in bridging the chasm between Eastern and Western markets, fostering unprecedented prosperity and facilitating the vibrant exchange of cultural and religious tenets. Coveted Chinese commodities, ranging from luxurious silk to exotic spices, coveted jade, and a myriad of other goods, embarked on a transcontinental odyssey toward the West, while China, in turn, welcomed a cornucopia of riches including gold, precious metals, ivory, and exquisite glassware.

The zenith of the Silk Road's prominence reached its apex during the first millennium, particularly flourishing under the aegis of eminent empires such as the Roman and Byzantine Empires, alongside the illustrious Tang Dynasty (618–907 CE) in China. This epoch marked an era of unparalleled cross-cultural pollination and economic dynamism, cementing the Silk Road's enduring legacy as an emblem of global connectivity and cultural diffusion.

4.28 MODERN ROUTES OF SILK ROAD ECONOMIC BELT INITIATIVE

The historical "BRI" inaugurated by China has been denoted as "OBOR" since its inception in 2013. The BRI encompasses two principal components: the Silk Road Economic Belt—a sprawling transcontinental corridor that interconnects China with Southeast Asia, South Asia, Central Asia, Russia, and Europe via land—and the 21st-century Maritime Silk Road—a maritime pathway that links China's coastal regions with Southeast Asia, the South Pacific, the Middle East, and Eastern Africa, culminating in Europe.

The maritime Silk Road, through which over half of the world's trade containers traverse to their ultimate destinations, mandates the expansion of deep-water ports, the establishment of logistical centers, and the development of new transport corridors in the hinterlands. This maritime expanse begins from the Chinese coastline, extending southward to encompass key waypoints such as Hanoi, Kuala Lumpur, Singapore, and Jakarta, before veering westward to encompass the Sri Lankan capital of Colombo and the Maldivian capital of Male. From there, it proceeds onward to East Africa, embracing the port city of Mombasa in Kenya. Subsequently, this connectivity extends northward to Djibouti, navigating through the Red Sea and the Suez Canal to reach the Mediterranean basin. This linkage incorporates pivotal ports such as Haifa, Istanbul, and Athens, eventually converging upon the Upper Adriatic region and the bustling northern Italian nexus of Trieste, renowned for its international free port and its extensive rail network connecting to Central Europe and the North Sea (Wilt, 2019).

Poland, the Baltic States, Northern Europe, and Central Europe have also become intricately interwoven into the maritime Silk Road, forging logistical linkages with East Africa, India, and China via the Adriatic ports and Piraeus. The ongoing restructuring of container transportation between Asia and Europe is poised to bring about substantial changes in maritime routes. In contrast to the conventional East Asian trade route traversing through northwest Europe, the southern sea passage via the Suez Canal and onward to the Trieste juncture is anticipated to markedly curtail the duration of goods transportation by a minimum of 4 days (Triest, 2018).

China's historical infrastructural endeavors, epitomized by the "Economic Corridor," "Silk Road Economic Belt," and "21st Century Maritime Silk Road," specifically delineate the Indo-Pacific Sea routes threading through Southeast Asia, South Asia, the Middle East, and Africa. Integral to the BRI, China's investments in infrastructure are multifaceted, encompassing ports, skyscrapers, railroads, roads, bridges, airports, dams, coal-fired power stations, and railway tunnels (Kuo and Kommenda, 2018).

Widely recognized as the "OBOR Initiative," this undertaking stands as one of the most ambitious infrastructural development ventures in contemporary history. China initially introduced the "One Road One Belt Initiative (OBOR)" in 2013, constituting one of three physical infrastructural development projects, notably dubbed the "Silk Road Economic Belt Project." Officially assimilated into China's national economic development strategy, this initiative spans approximately 8000 km, encompassing nearly 155 countries via land and sea routes. As of August 2023, the BRI is operational in 150 countries, collectively accommodating two-thirds of the world's population and contributing to 40% of global GDP. China's investment in the BRI has surged to USD 8 trillion. China's "Global Belt and Road Initiative," widely lauded as a visionary pursuit, intricately intertwines with a comprehensive infrastructure development program. This multifaceted initiative entails the construction of seaports, highways, railways, bridges, and airports, alongside energy pipelines, hydroelectric plants, solar farms, cyberinfrastructure, and telecommunications networks.

The objectives of the BRI encompass establishing the most extensive global market access by harnessing both international and domestic resources and integrating them through an innovative pattern of capital inflows, talent pools, and technology databases. The BRI is primarily focused on addressing the infrastructure gap across the Asia-Pacific, Africa, and Central and Eastern Europe. It is estimated that Asia, excluding China, requires up to US$900 billion in infrastructure investments annually over the next decade, a figure predominantly in the form of debt instruments, and represents a 50% increase over current infrastructure spending rates. The BRI aims to achieve its objectives through targeted investments in infrastructure, education, construction materials, railways, highways, automobiles, real estate, power grids, and iron and steel. These investments are channeled toward the following key areas:

1. Infrastructure connectivity: This initiative seeks to foster regional economic-trade-financial integration by enhancing infrastructure connectivity, thereby facilitating smoother movement of goods, services, and capital across borders.
2. Formation of geo-political, geo-economic, and geo-strategic alliances: The BRI endeavors to establish sustainable and inclusive multilateralism toward multipolarity by forging strategic alliances at both geopolitical and geoeconomic levels, aiming to promote mutual cooperation and prosperity.
3. People-to-people connectivity: The BRI aims to promote global people-to-people connectivity, fostering cultural exchange, educational collaboration, and interpersonal relationships across nations, thereby strengthening bonds and promoting mutual understanding and cooperation on a global scale.

4.29 CHINA'S DUAL CIRCULATION ECONOMY THROUGH THE BRI

Before 1978, China's global GDP share stood at a mere 2%, with around 90% of its populace living below the poverty line. However, with the adoption of a new economic reform policy in 1978, China's global GDP share surged to 18%, and the poverty ratio significantly plummeted to a mere 1% as of 2023. Today, China stands as a paramount manufacturing hub globally, boasting a GDP of $19 trillion, trailing only the United States.

China has meticulously developed state-of-the-art domestic infrastructures across all sectors, including modern highways, railways, and intelligent industrial cities. Moreover, since 2013, China has embarked on a global initiative known as the "BRI," spanning continents from Asia and Africa to Latin America, Europe, and Oceania. Under the BRI, participating nations have the opportunity to transact using the Chinese currency.

The Asian Development Bank has projected an annual infrastructure financing shortfall exceeding $900 billion across the Asian continent. In response, China has generously funded numerous SEZs and industrial areas to stimulate employment opportunities. Additionally, China has encouraged other nations to adopt its technological advancements, such as the 5G network pioneered by telecommunications giant Huawei.

Infrastructure corridors spanning 60 countries, primarily across Asia and Europe but also extending to Oceania and East Africa, are estimated to require investments ranging between US$4 and US$8 trillion. Management of these projects falls under the jurisdiction of the Silk Road Fund and the Asian Infrastructure Investment Bank (AIIB), with technical coordination provided by the B&R Summit Forum.

Land corridors include: The New Eurasian Land Bridge, traversing from Western China to Western Russia through Kazakhstan, features the Silk Road Railway through China's Xinjiang Autonomous Region, Kazakhstan, Russia, Belarus, Poland, and Germany.

Another corridor extending from Northern China through Mongolia to the Russian Far East, with the Russian government-established Russian Direct Investment Fund and China's China Investment Corporation partnering to create the Russia–China Investment Fund in 2012, focusing on bilateral integration opportunities.

1. The China-Central Asia-West Asia Corridor stretches from Western China to Turkey.

2. The China-Indochina Peninsula Economic Corridor links Southern China to Singapore.
3. The Trans-Himalayan Multi-Dimensional Connectivity Network aims to transition Nepal from a landlocked to a land-linked country.
4. The China-Pakistan Economic Corridor (CPEC), involves a US$62 billion array of infrastructure projects throughout Pakistan aimed at modernizing transportation networks, energy infrastructure, and the economy.

Initially, China's primary objective was to connect East Asia and Europe through comprehensive development and investment packages via physical infrastructure. However, the scope of the project has since expanded to encompass Africa, Oceania, Latin America, and Europe through land and maritime networks, aiming to enhance regional integration, bolster trade, and foster economic growth.

China has also outlined plans for the 21st Century Maritime Silk Road to accommodate burgeoning maritime trade traffic. Investments in port development along the Indian Ocean, spanning from Southeast Asia to East Africa and Western Europe, have been made to facilitate these routes, commonly referred to as the Silk Road Economic Belt. Furthermore, China's secondary objective is to establish a 21st Century Maritime Silk Road by linking the Southeast Asian region to China's southern provinces through ports and railways (Cai, 2017).

China's OBOR initiative, coupled with its technologically driven economy, reinforces stability within the domestic economy while simultaneously serving China's geo-economic, geo-political, and geo-strategic interests through regional economic integration. This initiative has led to the strengthening of ties with 150 countries across Asia, Africa, Latin America, and Europe.

OBOR is propelled by broad geostrategic aims, with a prime example being the China–Pakistan Economic Corridor, initially announced with a budget of US$46 billion, which was later expanded to US$62 billion in 2020. This corridor is expected to connect Kashgar in Xinjiang, China's far west, with the Port of Gwadar in the province of Baluchistan, providing a direct link to the Persian Gulf. This corridor could potentially serve as a transhipment point for China's energy supplies, bypassing the need to traverse the Strait of Malacca in Southeast Asia.

Justin Yifu Lin (2015) argues that China launched the OBOR initiative as a means to counterbalance US policies such as the pivot and the trans-Pacific partnership (TPP). China utilizes its economic resources, including its substantial foreign reserves and experience in infrastructure development, to enhance its position in the region. China's preferential policies, large-scale fiscal injections, state-directed investments, and technologically driven OBOR aim to create a regional production chain, with China positioned as a center of advanced manufacturing and innovation, focusing on quality improvements.

This initiative supports regional development in China by fostering better integration with neighboring economies, upgrading Chinese industry while exporting Chinese standards, and addressing the issue of Chinese excess capacity (Cai, 2017).

The construction of infrastructure, including roads, railways, airports, seaports, dams, and hydro-electricity projects, as part of the CPEC, is currently underway under the auspices of the BRI. This initiative, valued at USD 62 billion, aims to create a 4000–5000-km-long network covering an area of 2221 acres. It will connect China's coastal ports to Gilgit (Baltistan) in Pakistan-occupied Kashmir and further to the Gwadar port on the Arabian Sea, eventually reaching Europe. Additionally, the corridor will extend from Gilgit (Baltistan) via Afghanistan to Central Asia.

Another aspect of the OBOR initiative involves connecting and integrating the Chinese economy with the global economy by establishing global trade and supply-chain routes. This initiative aims to transform Asia from a backwards to a modern economy, thereby challenging the Western economic, trade, technology, currency, and military dominations that have maintained Western imperialist hegemony since the 18th century. The World Bank estimates that the BRI has the potential to increase trade flows in 155 participating countries by 4.1%, reduce the cost of global trade by 1.1–2.2%, and boost the GDP of developing countries in East Asia and the Pacific by an average of 2.6–3.9% (Belt and Road Initiative, 2022). The BRI, as forecasted by the London-based consultants Centre for Economics and Business Research, holds the potential to augment the global GDP by $7.1 trillion annually by the year 2040. This projection underscores the extensive advantages anticipated from the initiative, as enhanced infrastructure is poised to mitigate the "frictions that hold back world trade (Belt and Road Initiative to boost world GDP by over $7 trillion per annum by 2040, 2019)."

The emerging BRICS countries, collectively representing approximately 42% of the world's population, 30% of its territory, 27% of global GDP, and 20% of international trade, alongside about 6% of total intra-trade among the five members of BRICS, are assuming an increasingly pivotal role in the global economy. The NDB of the BRICS extends loans to its member countries for infrastructural development, with South Africa securing US$5.4 billion for five projects. BRICS affords its members greater flexibility in development financing, fosters collaboration on issues such as health, and facilitates a gradual departure from the dominance of the dollar.

The significance of BRICS is exemplified by the annual BRICS summit, slated to convene in Johannesburg, South Africa, from August 22 to 24, 2023. Sixty-seven representatives are anticipated to participate in this momentous event from the global south. Forty-five nations from the Global South have confirmed their attendance and expressed interest in joining the BRICS Bloc. Twenty-three of these countries formally submitted membership applications in May 2023 to partake in the 15th Annual Conference from August 22 to 24, 2023. These nations comprise Algeria, Argentina, Bangladesh, Bahrain, Belarus, Bolivia, Cuba, Egypt, Ethiopia, Honduras, Indonesia, Iran, Kazakhstan, Kuwait, Morocco, Nigeria, State of Palestine, Saudi Arabia, Senegal, Thailand, United Arab Emirates, Venezuela, and Vietnam.

BRICS is committed to galvanizing the Global South through initiatives like "South-South economic, trade, technology, and investment, including financial cooperation projects," aimed at diminishing global reliance on the US dollar-centric international financial and payment system. Additionally, it advocates for reforms of international financial institutions to afford developing countries greater voice and representation while endeavoring to foster sustainable and inclusive economic growth and development by promoting trade and investment.

China, in conjunction with the BRICS bloc, not only endeavors to achieve and manage global governance but also strives to provide the fundamental financial and technological requisites of BRICS nations and other developing countries for infrastructural and sustainable developmental projects. This entails the rollout of a US$32 billion package for green energy, urban mobility, and digital infrastructures, alongside the "OBOR" initiative, encompassing the construction of highway, railway, and seaport networks supported by the NDB initiative. The NDB serves as an alternative financial institution to the Western-dominated World Bank and IMF.

The Beijing Consensus, a term delineating China's novel approach characterized by a technologically and financially driven economy, infrastructural-centered development model, and export-oriented good governance, has drawn both acclaim and critique. This distinctive Chinese model, typified by a robust central government, embodies a form of "state-led market socialism." The communist regime in China vigorously safeguards "people's participation in economic activities," particularly through rural industrialization and urbanization, while prioritizing the augmentation of domestic demand and supply. It espouses an "export-oriented growth model" facilitated by economic and business alliances rooted in mutual interests and cooperation, notably exemplified by infrastructural development initiatives like the BRI across "BRICS-SCO-EAC-RCEP regions," alongside other economic and business partners in Asia, Africa, and Latin America, aimed at bolstering economic, financial, trade, and technological multipolarity and sustainability.

This collaborative Chinese approach stands in stark contrast to the "Washington Consensus," which aligns with the policies advocated by the IMF and the World Bank. The Washington Consensus emphasizes principles of free markets, privatization, liberalization of trade and financial sectors, and the dominance of big tech and MNCs in the economy.

"China's Massive BRI" published by the Council on Foreign Relations on February 2, 2023, present a critical perspective on the BRI (McBride, 2023). They characterize the BRI as an expansive China-led infrastructure project intended to span the globe. However, they express apprehension regarding the BRI's implications, viewing it as a mechanism for the extension of Chinese influence. Additionally, they highlight challenges faced by the US in articulating a competing vision. The BRI has encountered opposition in certain Belt and Road countries grappling with debt crises, further complicating the initiative's trajectory and impact.

4.30 CHINA–AFRICA INVESTMENT COOPERATION

The Chinese development model has garnered substantial global attention and serves as a focal point for emulation across the international community. China's Ministry of Commerce reports that the nation stands as the fourth-largest investor in Africa. As of 2022, Chinese investment in Africa has skyrocketed to an impressive $3.4 billion, showcasing its burgeoning economic influence on the continent. This substantial investment is buoyed by the active involvement of over 3000 Chinese enterprises, which are involved in a diverse array of business ventures and projects throughout Africa (Reporter, 2023).

In the initial quartile of this year, China's direct investment in Africa surged to $1.38 billion, reflecting a substantial year-on-year escalation of 24%. This surge serves as a testament to the robustness of economic and trade collaboration between China and Africa, reaffirming the steadfast confidence of Chinese enterprises in the African market. The third China-Africa Economic and Trade Expo, held from June 29 to July 2 in Changsha, the capital of Hunan province, provided further evidence of this trend. With the participation of 50 African nations and eight international organizations, the event underscored the burgeoning economic interdependence between China and Africa.

Over the past decade, total bilateral trade between China and Africa has exceeded $2 trillion, marking a significant milestone in their economic partnership. China's import and export volume with Africa reached 822.32 billion yuan (113.5 billion US dollars) in the first 5 months of 2023, reflecting a robust year-on-year increase of 16.4%. This upward trajectory in trade volumes has been consistent, with trade between China and Africa growing from under 100 billion yuan in 2000 to 1.88 trillion yuan in 2022, as official data indicate. This represents a cumulative surge of over 20 times, with an average annual growth rate of 17.7%. In 2022 alone, bilateral trade between China and Africa reached an impressive 282 billion US dollars.

Furthermore, the initial months of this year witnessed a substantial upsurge in China's new direct investment in Africa, amounting to $1.38 billion, marking a 24% increase year-on-year. Looking ahead, China Africa trade is poised to sustain its upward trajectory, with projections indicating a surge to USD 300 billion by 2025. This forecast underscores the enduring nature of the partnership between China and Africa, which is expected to further fortify and flourish in the years to come (Xinhua, 2023).

The impact of BRI projects across all 55 African nations is profound, characterized by the development of critical infrastructures such as bridges, dams, ports, railways, roads, airports, and seaports. These endeavors have

TABLE 4.5 Chinese Investment in Top 20 Destinations and Sectoral-Wise Number of Projects (1998–2012).

Country	Number of Projects	Sectoral-Wise	Number of Projects
Nigeria	404	Business service	1053
South Africa	280	Wholesale & retail	693
Zambia	273	Import and export	539
Ethiopia	255	Construction, transportation, storage, postal services	392
Egypt	197	Mineral products	319
Congo	193	Base metals and articles of base metals	148
Ghana	192	Articles of stone, plaster, cement	96
Angola	189	Machinery and electronics	76
Zimbabwe	167	Textiles and articles	75
Tanzania	149	Vegetable products	72
Sudan	148		
Kenya	137		
Algeria	123		
Mozambique	94		
Uganda	89		
Gabon	71		
Mali	68		
Namibia	66		
Mauritius	65		
Cameroon	60		

Source: http://brook.gs/1KWTFcX.

not only enhanced transportation networks and connectivity but have also engendered the creation of myriad job opportunities throughout the continent. For instance, the Entebbe Expressway in Uganda stands as a testament to this transformation, facilitating swift and streamlined travel between the capital city of Kampala and Entebbe National Airport, thereby alleviating traffic congestion in the urban center. Moreover, Uganda's Karuma and Isimba hydropower plants stand as beacons of progress, electrifying the lives of millions.

In Nigeria, the Lagos-Kano railway system has significantly augmented transportation efficiency, while Mozambique's Maputo-Katembe Bridge, Africa's largest suspension bridge spanning 3041 m, has notably enhanced intracountry connectivity. Similarly, Kenya's Mombasa-Nairobi Standard Gauge Railway (SGR), spearheaded by Chinese firms Road and Bridge Corporation (CRBC) and China's Communications Construction Company (CCCC), has not only linked the bustling Indian Ocean port city of Mombasa with the capital Nairobi but also bolsters the East African Rail Master Plan, aimed at establishing robust rail corridors connecting maritime hubs along the Indian Ocean with the region's hinterlands.

The port of Doraleh in Djibouti, a collaborative effort between China and the Djiboutian government, stands as a pivotal gateway equipped with terminals for handling containers, heavy cargo, and oil, seamlessly integrating with other critical infrastructures in neighboring Ethiopia, thereby granting the rapidly burgeoning nation access to maritime trade routes. Furthermore, the Addis Ababa-Djibouti railway also realized through Chinese investment has catalyzed enhanced connectivity between Ethiopia and Djibouti, facilitating over 90% of Ethiopia's trade through the strategic port of Djibouti. This railway system forms a cornerstone of Ethiopia's burgeoning National Railway Network. Additionally, China's partial financing of the Cherchell Ring Expressway and Port in Algeria, bridging the Mediterranean with Africa's heartland, underscores the pivotal role of China's BRI in fostering the development and interconnectivity of African nations.

China's BRI has extended its reach into the Asia Pacific region, which encompasses the vast expanse of the Pacific Ocean. The term "Pacific Ocean" traces its origins to the Latin phrase "Mare Pacificum," signifying a "peaceful sea," attributed to the Portuguese explorer Ferdinand Magellan. As the largest ocean on the planet, the Pacific Ocean delineates various geographic regions.

Positioned in the northern part lies the Arctic, while the southern segment hosts the Antarctic, flanked by Asia and Australia to the west, and the Americas to the east. Within this expansive realm reside eighteen sovereign nations, including Australia, Fiji, Japan, Kiribati, the Marshall Islands, Micronesia, Nauru, New Zealand, Palau, the Solomon Islands, and Papua New Guinea (PNG).

Additionally, the Indo-Pacific region encompasses twenty-three member states of the Indian Ocean Rim Association, spanning from the Pacific Rim to Southeast Asia, South Asia, West Asia, and the Eastern and Southern regions of Africa. This sprawling region is home to approximately 2.5 billion individuals, representing 64% of the global population.

Occupying approximately one-third of the Earth's surface, the Pacific Ocean boasts a staggering area of 179.7 million square kilometers (69.4 million square miles or 161 million cubic miles), surpassing the cumulative landmass of the planet.

Extending approximately 15,500 km (9600 mi) from the frigid waters of the Bering Sea in the Arctic to the icy boundaries of Antarctica's Ross Sea in the south, the Pacific Ocean's vast expanse transcends geographical boundaries. At its broadest point, situated around 5°N latitude, the Pacific Ocean spans approximately 19,800 km (12,300 mi), stretching from Indonesia to the shores of Colombia and Peru, traversing halfway across the globe and exceeding the diameter of the Moon fivefold.

The western demarcation of the Pacific Ocean is commonly acknowledged as the Strait of Malacca. Within its depths lies the Mariana Trench, the deepest abyss on Earth, plunging to unfathomable depths of 10,911 m (35,797 ft) below sea level. As China's BRI continues to unfold, its strategic expansion into the Asia Pacific region underscores the region's pivotal role in global trade, connectivity, and geopolitical dynamics (https://new.wikipedia.org/wiki, 2006).

The Pacific Ocean boasts a staggering array of approximately 25,000 islands, eclipsing the combined count of islands found in all other oceans worldwide. Predominantly positioned south of the equator, these islands punctuate the vast expanse of the Pacific, contributing to its unique geographical makeup. Among the notable seas nestled within its embrace are the Celebes Sea, Coral Sea, East China Sea, Philippine Sea, Sea of Japan, South China Sea, Sulu Sea, Tasman Sea, and Yellow Sea, each playing a pivotal role in the ocean's ecosystem and maritime dynamics.

On the western frontier, the Strait of Malacca emerges as a vital maritime corridor, seamlessly bridging the Pacific with the Indian Ocean, and facilitating trade and navigation between the two vast bodies of water. Conversely, on the opposite end, the eastern realm is delineated by the Strait of Magellan, serving as a pivotal conduit between the Pacific and the Atlantic Ocean, traversed by seafarers seeking passage between the two expansive oceans.

Heading northward, the Bering Strait emerges as a strategic gateway linking the Pacific with the Arctic Ocean, embodying a crucial juncture of maritime connectivity and ecological interaction. As these passages delineate the Pacific's periphery, they underscore its interconnectedness with neighboring oceans, facilitating global maritime trade, ecological exchange, and geopolitical dynamics (https://new.wikipedia.org/wiki, 2006).

The epoch of Western imperialist-dominated globalization is presently approaching its denouement. Commencing in the 1990s, the globalization of capital mobility, catalyzed predominantly by Big Tech conglomerates and financial behemoths, has engendered a notable surge in the propensity of developing economies to embrace FDI from MNCs. These corporate entities, driven by multifarious objectives, endeavor to exploit natural resources, capitalize on cost-effective labor pools, or circumvent import impediments, thereby leveraging their global reach for strategic economic gains (Imbun, 2006). The ocean has emerged as a contentious arena, wherein major global superpowers such as the USA, the UK, France, Germany, Japan, and Australia vigilantly oversee the Pacific's abundant reservoirs of oil, gas, gold, copper, silver, and other valuable minerals and resources with eagle-eyed scrutiny. Concurrently, emerging influential economic and military forces, notably China, Russia, India, and more recently, Iran, actively oppose and counteract the military hegemony of the USA and its strategic allies. These conflicting dynamics have precipitated a tumultuous landscape of geopolitical maneuvering, characterized by fierce strategic competition aimed at asserting dominance over oceanic routes, facilitating international trade and commerce, accessing rich natural reserves, including oil and gas deposits and fisheries, and ensuring overarching security objectives.

4.31 CHINA'S BRI INITIATIVE IN PACIFIC ISLANDS

China stands as one of the globe's paramount investors and primary contributors of foreign aid to the South Pacific Island nations. Over the span of 2008–2020, China injected a substantial sum totalling approximately US$3.148 billion into the Pacific region, with a vast majority, US$3.145 billion, being directed bilaterally and a nominal US$2.7 million earmarked for regional endeavors. The bilateral assistance and developmental financing from China to Pacific states saw a notable escalation from US$204 million in 2008 to US$334 million in 2016; however, due to the ramifications of the COVID-19 pandemic, this figure witnessed a decline to US$188 million by 2020. Moreover, China has allocated considerable funding, amounting to US$53 million, toward national sports stadiums, including a noteworthy US$21.4 million investment in the National University and a substantial US$66 million commitment to comprehensive medical infrastructure at the National Referral Hospital, alongside the establishment of 161 mobile phone towers. Presently, China is actively supporting more than 100 ongoing initiatives throughout the Pacific region.

In response to China's burgeoning influence, other significant players such as the United States, Australia, New Zealand, and the United Kingdom are augmenting their engagement in the Pacific domain. Nonetheless, China is further solidifying its ties with the Pacific Islands through the involvement of state-owned enterprises and corporations specializing in infrastructure, channeling efforts into six distinct focal points: agriculture, climate mitigation, poverty alleviation, disaster resilience, emergency assistance, and junco technology—a technique centered on cultivating mushroom grass. This multifaceted strategy, coupled with infrastructure financing, enables China to administer aid projects at reduced costs while integrating technical expertise and knowledge transfer, potentially bolstering involvement within local communities and refining its standing as a benefactor catering to both elite and grassroots sectors in the Pacific.

Chinese provinces and municipalities are also actively pursuing enhanced bilateral relations with Pacific Island counterparts. For instance, Shandong and Fujian provinces established sister-province relations with the Western Province and Isabel Province in the Solomon Islands in July 2021 and April 2022, respectively. Similarly, Liaocheng and Qingdao, situated in Shandong, inked agreements with Vava'u in Tonga and Tainainano in Kiribati to foster sister-city affiliations. Notably, in March 2022, Guizhou Province dispatched China's inaugural medical team to the Solomon Islands, while concurrently facilitating vocational and technical training in China for 80 students from the Islands under an educational scholarship program facilitated by the Tianjin Municipality. These Chinese regional administrations have also extended aid, encompassing machinery and COVID-related medical provisions, to their Pacific counterparts, emblematic of their burgeoning role in China's diplomatic endeavors.

In January 2022, the China International Development Cooperation Agency (CIDCA) conducted virtual training sessions tailored for Chinese enterprises and social entities concerning the utilization of an aid-reporting platform. China has pledged to provide 2500 government-sponsored scholarships and 3000 short-term professional training opportunities to candidates hailing from Pacific nations between 2020 and 2025 (Zhang, 2022a, b).

Between 2006 and 2017, China allocated approximately USD 1.5 billion in foreign aid to the Pacific Islands. Collaboratively, China and several South Pacific Island countries, including the Solomon Islands, Fiji, Kiribati, Samoa, Tonga, Vanuatu, PNG, and Timor-Leste, have devised a marine spatial plan to nurture the blue economy. Furthermore, China has escalated its investment endeavors through BRI initiatives, fostering the construction of diverse infrastructural projects encompassing roads, airports, seaports, bridges, dams, hydropower electric plants, solar plants, satellites, and cyber parks. Notably, Samoa, Kiribati, and Niue are among the South Pacific nations that have inked agreements with China, propelling cooperation toward shared developmental objectives.

China's initiatives extend beyond mere infrastructure development. The establishment of Confucius Institutes across the South Pacific Islands serves as a testament to China's commitment, providing invaluable resources such as Chinese-language consultants, teachers, and volunteers. The Confucius Institute at the National University of Samoa alone has trained over 1000 Samoans. Additionally, a comprehensive 5-year action plan has been outlined, featuring the appointment of a Chinese special envoy to the region, the establishment of laboratories, and the provision of numerous training opportunities for law enforcement personnel and high-level forums.

A prevailing sentiment pervades the South Pacific Islands, recognizing China as a steadfast partner to the Pacific community and a foremost investor in physical infrastructure development. Noteworthy scholars, including Chang (2017) and Denghua Zhang, contend that China's engagement in the region embodies the principles of the Beijing Consensus, epitomizing the importance of infrastructure investment and state-led development. They argue that China's presence has catalyzed economic growth, facilitated poverty reduction, and engendered political stability.

In stark contrast, the dominance of the United States and its strategic allies, including Australia, Japan, and England, has been characterized by the establishment of American military bases, the exploitation of natural resources, and the proliferation of American MNCs. This hegemonic influence extends beyond the Pacific region, encompassing Asia as a whole, perpetuating the promotion of liberal and capitalist ideologies from the Asia-Pacific to the Indo-Pacific (Prabhakar, 2020a, b).

4.32 THE BEIJING CONSENSUS: A BLUEPRINT FOR DEVELOPMENT IN THE PACIFIC ISLANDS

China's presence in the South Pacific, particularly in PNG, has been markedly propelled by extensive economic endeavors, notably exemplified through the BRI. Serving as a conduit for connectivity and economic collaboration across diverse geographies, the BRI epitomizes China's vision for the Pacific region.

At the core of China's engagement lies the China-Pacific Island Countries Economic Development and Cooperation Forum (CPIDF), established in 2006. This forum serves as a crucial mechanism for fostering economic cooperation and developmental initiatives among Pacific Island nations. Embracing infrastructure development, investment facilitation, trade enhancement, and capacity building across sectors like agriculture, fisheries, tourism, and telecommunications, CPIDF endeavors to cultivate a conducive environment for sustainable economic growth and mutual benefit.

Within the BRI framework, Chinese investment in PNG has primarily focused on infrastructure development. This encompasses the construction of vital transportation arteries such as roads, bridges, and ports, aimed at amplifying connectivity and expediting trade. Moreover, China's involvement extends to the energy and telecommunications sectors, contributing to the overarching socioeconomic advancement of PNG.

However, amidst infrastructural strides catalyzed by Chinese investment, challenges have emerged. Foremost among these challenges is the opacity surrounding China's aid endeavors, raising concerns regarding debt sustainability and environmental repercussions. The lack of transparency has prompted scrutiny from international observers and Pacific Island nations, necessitating a thorough examination of the enduring implications of Chinese investment.

Additionally, China's involvement in PNG has faced occasional criticism, with accusations of leveraging aid for political influence. Such apprehensions underscore the complexities inherent in navigating the sociopolitical landscape of the region, highlighting the importance of fostering transparent and mutually beneficial partnerships to foster sustainable development.

In essence, Chinese investment through the BRI in PNG presents a duality of opportunities and challenges. While it holds the potential to ignite economic growth and infrastructural development, ensuring transparency, accountability, and mutual respect is paramount in nurturing sustainable and inclusive development in the Pacific region.

4.33 CHINA'S TRADE WITH PAPUA NEW GUINEA (2018–2023)

The trade relationship between China and PNG has exhibited steady growth from 2018 to 2023, with the total trade volume between the two countries increasing significantly. In 2018, trade volume stood at approximately US$2.2 billion, with China emerging as PNG's largest trading partner. By 2023, this volume had surged to over US$3 billion, indicating robust growth in bilateral trade.

Trade composition has been diverse, with both nations exporting a range of goods and services to each other. PNG has served as a major exporter of natural resources to China, particularly minerals such as gold, copper, and nickel. In return, PNG has imported various Chinese goods, including machinery, electronics, textiles, and consumer products.

Furthermore, China has emerged as a significant investor in PNG, particularly in infrastructure and energy sectors. Chinese companies have played pivotal roles in constructing roads, bridges, ports, airports, hydroelectric power plants, and other energy projects in PNG. Notably, the Ramu Nickel project, one of the world's largest nickel and cobalt mining projects, stands as a testament to Chinese investment's impact on PNG's economy.

PNG possesses vast untapped potential in sectors like agriculture, tourism, and fisheries, which could further pique Chinese investors' interest. As such, continued collaboration between China and PNG holds promise for mutual economic growth and development.

4.34 CHINA'S ROLE IN GLOBAL GREEN PROJECTS

The escalating urgency of the climate crisis has underscored the imperative for concerted global efforts to mitigate carbon emissions. Recognizing this urgency, China has embarked on a significant endeavor to promote green and low-carbon development across 43 developing nations directly engaged in the BRI.

This multifaceted approach encompasses environmental protection measures, legislation, regulations, and standards, alongside comprehensive environmental policies and management protocols. Moreover, China has actively fostered technical exchanges and industry collaborations, all aimed at forging a cleaner and aesthetically enriched global landscape.

China's unwavering commitment to environmental stewardship is evidenced by its remarkable economic expansion, achieved while maintaining a commendably low annual energy consumption growth rate. Notably, China has substantially reduced carbon dioxide emissions per unit of GDP, precipitating a notable reduction in total emissions. Additionally, China's ascendancy in renewable energy further underscores its commitment to green development.

Aligned with its emphasis on green energy and finance, China is positioning itself to integrate seamlessly into the global green industry and value chains. This involves bolstering capacities in green investment and financing mechanisms, alongside sharing innovative solutions for pollution mitigation and carbon dioxide emissions abatement.

Through the BRI, China has facilitated heightened integration and cooperation among more than 140 nations, with investments exceeding USD 200 billion. These endeavors focus on advancing clean energy solutions and allocating resources toward carbon sequestration initiatives, thereby contributing substantively to global efforts to combat climate change and achieve sustainable development objectives.

4.35 WASHINGTON CONSENSUS

John Williamson elucidates how the "Washington Consensus" solidified its priorities under the auspices of the IMF and the World Bank, implementing a comprehensive set of 10 policy prescriptions on a global scale throughout the 1980s and 1990s. These tenets, constituting the core principles of the "Washington Consensus," encompassed fiscal discipline, the reallocation of public expenditures away from subsidies toward pivotal export-oriented programs aimed at fostering pro-growth GDP, tax restructuring, labor legislation reform aimed at broadening the tax base and adopting moderate marginal tax rates, interest rate liberalization, competitive exchange rates, trade liberalization, the opening up to inward FDI, state or public enterprise privatization, deregulation, property rights protection, as well as privatization initiatives concerning educational and healthcare systems, with a focus on infrastructural investment. The prescribed reforms imposed upon developing nations were firmly grounded in the liberal economic paradigm of the Western world, with the overarching objective of perpetuating economic dependencies on Western economies to facilitate their political, social, military, and cultural influence.

Eminent economist and former World Bank President Joseph Stiglitz contends that the Washington Consensus fell short in acknowledging the distinctive circumstances of developing nations and the transformative role of technology in shaping markets. Stiglitz posits that the market alone cannot adequately steer the economy in a desirable direction, as advocated by the Washington Consensus (Stiglitz, 2007).

4.36 INDIA'S ROLE IN THE PACIFIC REGION

India's relationship with China is characterized by a delicate interplay of cooperation and competition. Historically, the Indian bourgeoisie has navigated a nuanced path, oscillating between conflict and collaboration with both Western imperialist powers and Communist China. Following the dissolution of the Soviet Union, India pivoted toward strengthening its ties with the United States and the European Union, fostering bilateral trade and economic agreements. Simultaneously, India's rapport with China has deepened, marked by a blend of cooperation and rivalry.

India has historically assumed leadership in the nonaligned movement (NAM), advocating for self-reliance through state-owned joint ventures and MNCs, thereby advancing the agenda of industrialization.

In 2009, postindependence India forged a strategic partnership with Australia, solidifying their ties through a Civil Nuclear Cooperation Agreement inked in September 2014. By 2020, this relationship had evolved from a strategic partnership to a comprehensive strategic partnership (CSP). The India-Australia Economic Cooperation and Trade Agreement (IndAUS ECTA) entered into force on December 29, 2022. India stands as Australia's 9th largest trading partner, with bilateral trade in goods and services amounting to US$ 27.5 billion in 2021, comprising exports valued at US$ 10.5 billion and imports worth US$ 17 billion. India's merchandise exports to Australia surged by 135% between 2019 and 2021, with refined petroleum, medicaments, pearls and gems, jewellery, and textiles among the primary exports.

Key imports from Australia encompass coal, confidential trade items, copper ores and concentrates, natural gas, nonferrous waste and scrap, and education-related services. Defence collaboration between India and Australia encompasses research, development, industry engagement, and regular maritime exercises. India is a member of the Quadrilateral Security Dialogue (QUAD), comprising Australia, Japan, and the United States, aimed at countering potential military threats and trade influences posed by China in the East China Sea, South China Sea, Indo-Pacific, and Asia Pacific regions. The navies of these four QUAD members participated in Phase I of Exercise Malabar 2021 from August 26 to 29, 2021 off Guam, followed by Phase II in the Bay of Bengal from October 12 to 15, 2021.

A Maritime Partnership Exercise, featuring Royal Australian Navy (RAN) ships HMAS Adelaide and HMAS Anzac, alongside Indian Navy Ships Jalashwa and Kavaratti, along with their embarked helicopters, was conducted in the Bay of Bengal from November 02 to 03, 2022 as part of Australia's Indo-Pacific Endeavour 2022. Furthermore, the India-Australia Joint Military Exercise AUSTRAHIND 2022 took place in Rajasthan from November 28 to December 11, 2022, involving the Indian Army and the Australian Army, marking the inaugural exercise in the AUSTRA HIND series with participation from all arms and services contingents from both armies (India-Australia Bilateral Relations, 2023). Australia and India have reached an agreement to collaborate on endeavors aimed at mitigating the cost associated with ultra-low-cost solar and clean hydrogen technologies, as announced during the Official Visit to Australia by the Prime Minister of India in 2023 (Official Visit to Australia by the Prime Minister of India, 2023).

4.37 A CRITICAL NEW REALISTIC APPROACH TO ANALYZING THE GEOPOLITICAL SITUATION

The Indo-Pacific and Asia-Pacific regions, including the South Pacific Ocean, are endowed with rich natural resources, prominently including oil and gas reserves. These regions serve as vital international trade conduits, facilitating commerce from west to east and north to south. However, the Blue Economy of the Pacific and the Indian Ocean Rim face a myriad of challenges, ranging from climate change and ocean pollution to the overexploitation of marine resources and loss of biodiversity.

The Indo-Pacific and Asia-Pacific regions have emerged as focal points for geo-political and geo-economic endeavors. The Western-imperialist-led globalization project, which gained momentum in the late 20th century, is approaching its culmination, and a new world order is materializing following the Russia-NATO War of 2022 in Ukraine. Geo-political tensions manifest in various manifestations across the Black Sea, East and South China Sea, Indo-Pacific and Asia-Pacific Oceans, and the Arabian Sea. Nuclear tests and military maneuvers are concentrated in the Antarctic and Arctic regions, which have become arenas for conflict between Russia and America since 2022.

Encompassing an expanse of 169.2 million square kilometers, this largest division of the World Ocean comprises approximately 46% of the Earth's water surface and about 32% of its total surface area, surpassing the collective land area of the Earth (https://new.wikipedia.org/wiki, 2006).

The equator delineates two distinct realms: the North Pacific Ocean and the South Pacific Ocean. However, since the commencement of the "Russia-NATO War" in 2022 and the onset of "China-USA trade and military conflicts" in 2017, the geographic expanse spanning from the Baltic Sea to the Antarctic Sea, encapsulating the Black Sea, East China Sea, South China Sea, Asia-Pacific/Indo-Pacific regions, and the Arabian Sea, has experienced heightened volatility. Within these Pacific domains, geopolitical and geoeconomic tensions have surged, pitting the predominant superpower, the United States, against the amalgamated forces of China and Russia.

Since the 18th century, Western colonial powers have exerted dominion over the natural resources of the Pacific territories, leveraging labor and markets to fuel the expansion of their burgeoning industrial sectors through various projects spearheaded by MNCs. These initiatives have profoundly influenced the political and economic dynamics between European nations and the South Pacific Island nations, all with the objective of advancing their respective economic, political, cultural, and social agendas. Even subsequent to attaining sovereignty as independent nations, the dominant colonial powers persisted in wielding their traditional economic hegemony over the South Pacific Island nations, primarily through the instrumentalities of Big Tech and prominent multinational financial corporations (MNCs).

The vestiges of colonialism endure in the South Pacific nations, manifesting in the structures of production systems, the monopolization of natural resources and markets, and the perpetuation of inequitable and unjust trade practices. Historically, both preindependence and postindependence South Pacific nations have fallen prey to the exploitation of Western colonial masters, including the United States, the United Kingdom, Germany, and France, alongside their strategic allies such as Australia, New Zealand, and Japan. These entities have engaged in diverse economic and commercial ventures in the South Pacific region, steadfast in their pursuit of exploiting local resources to further their own economic interests.

TABLE 4.6 Foreign MNCs.

OK Tedi (Copper and Gold)	Western Province
Porgera (Gold and Silver)	Enga Province
Lihir (Gold and Silver)	New Ireland Province
Ramu (Nickel and Copper)	Madang Province
Hidden Valley (Gold and Silver)	Morobe Province
Tolukuma (Gold)	Central Province
Simberi (Gold)	New Ireland
Sinivit (Gold)	East New Britain Province

Source: Interview based.

TABLE 4.7 Sector-Wise Employment in 2018.

Variables	Construction	Transport andStorage	Administration and Support Services	Manufacturing Industry
No. of business	35	30	29	70
Total employment (in thousands/000)	10,000	7000	6000	23,000
Total full-time employment (in %)	69.2	89.3	92.0	85.2
Total casual / part-time	19.7	5.5	6.3	10.4
Total expatriate (in %)	11.1	5.2	1.7	4.3
Growth rate (2017–2018) in %	+3.4	+5.7	+19.2	−3.5

Source: National Business Statistical Office, Papua New Guinea.

As per the findings delineated by the National Business Statistical Office of PNG, the realm of international merchandise trade (IMT) has been notably characterized by a surplus in trade balances spanning the years 2015 through 2020. Commencing with the advent of the liquefied natural gas (LNG) project in mid-2014, PNG's export sector has demonstrated formidable resilience, while import figures have maintained a semblance of constancy, save for a marginal downturn in 2018 attributed to diminished exports of gold and crude oil.

Illustratively, PNG's exports witnessed a notable ascent from K25.4 billion in 2015 to K35.1 billion in 2020, thereby registering a robust 38.1% escalation. Conversely, import figures climbed from K14.2 billion in 2015 to K16.1 billion in 2020, reflecting a 13.7% uptick. Consequently, the trade balance surged by 68.7% from K11.3 billion in 2015 to K9.0 billion in 2020. However, exports experienced a marginal downturn from K35.3 billion in 2019 to K35.1 billion in 2020. Similarly, imports also witnessed a slight contraction from K16.8 billion in 2019 to K16.1 billion in 2020, notwithstanding the protocol lockdowns enforced amidst the COVID-19 pandemic. In percentage terms, exports experienced a nominal decrease of 0.4% in 2020, while imports saw a decline of 4.1%, ultimately resulting in a 3.0% augmentation in the trade balance for the year 2020.

Foreign MNCs engaged in mining operations, encompassing gold, silver, copper, and oil and gas, contribute to the national GDP of PNG to the extent of 25%, while also contributing 8% of the total revenue in taxes to the government. Furthermore, PNG exports primary commodities such as crude oil, fruits, vegetables, milk, and cocoa to Australia, with Australia reciprocating by exporting finished goods derived from the same commodities back to PNG. For instance, mineral products derived from bituminous minerals were imported for Kina 2.8 billion, LNG for Kina 12.9 billion in 2020, base metals and related articles in the form of aluminum casks, drums, cans, boxes, and similar receptacles were imported for Kina 1.4 billion, and machinery, mechanical, and electrical appliances were imported for Kina 4.1 billion in the same year.

4.38 INDIA-RUSSIA BILATERAL COOPERATION

In 2024, India and Russia significantly advanced their bilateral cooperation across trade, technology, energy, and finance, maintaining robust engagement despite prevailing global geopolitical challenges.

4.38.1 TRADE

Bilateral trade surged to an impressive $65.6 billion in FY2024, propelled by India's procurement of discounted Russian oil. Both nations have set an ambitious target of $100 billion by 2030. Strategies to diversify their trade portfolio encompass bolstering Indian exports in agriculture, pharmaceuticals, and technology. Moreover, streamlined customs procedures and ongoing discussions on a Free Trade Agreement (FTA) with the Eurasian Economic Union (EAEU) are expected to further enhance economic ties.

4.38.2 TECHNOLOGY

Technological collaboration has intensified, focusing on sectors such as digital infrastructure, space research, and defence technology. Both countries have committed to fostering high-tech partnerships in AI, cyber security, and advanced manufacturing. Plans are underway to develop industrial clusters and expand educational and research exchange programs, ensuring sustained innovation and progress.

4.38.3 ENERGY

Energy remains a linchpin of India–Russia relations. Their collaboration spans nuclear power, petrochemicals, and oil refining, epitomized by projects like the Kudankulam Nuclear Power Plant. Furthermore, renewable energy and low-carbon initiatives are gaining prominence, underpinned by agreements that align with global energy transition goals and climate change mitigation efforts.

4.38.4 FINANCE

Efforts to de-dollarize trade have gained momentum, with increasing reliance on local currency transactions, a move that mitigates the impact of Western sanctions on Russia and enhances trade flexibility for India. Additionally, frameworks promoting bilateral investments incentivize market entry for businesses from both nations, fostering deeper economic integration.

This multifaceted collaboration reflects a strategic partnership aimed at balancing geopolitical complexities while pursuing shared economic and developmental aspirations, reinforcing the enduring significance of India–Russia relations.

4.39 INDIA-SOUTH AFRICA BILATERAL COOPERATION

In 2024, India and South Africa elevated their collaboration across trade, technology, and finance, reflecting a deep-seated commitment to strengthening bilateral relations amidst shifting global economic and geopolitical landscapes.

4.39.1 TRADE

The trade dynamic between India and South Africa has flourished, driven by a well-balanced exchange of raw materials and manufactured products. Marking 30 years of diplomatic relations, the nations established the Indo-South African Chamber of Commerce, a pivotal platform designed to enhance economic ties, foster business collaborations, and champion youth and women's empowerment. This initiative seeks to streamline trade mechanisms, expand market access, and prioritize areas such as technology transfer and infrastructure development, fostering a more integrated and efficient trading ecosystem.

4.39.2 TECHNOLOGY

Technology cooperation stands as a cornerstone of this bilateral relationship, with a focus on digital innovation, telecommunications, and defence. India's "Make in India" program synergizes with South Africa's strategic investments in high-tech industries, paving the way for joint ventures that promise to revolutionize industrial and digital landscapes. These partnerships aim to develop cutting-edge ecosystems that leverage both nations' technological prowess.

4.39.3 FINANCE

The financial dimension of this partnership has been invigorated by significant investment flows. Notable contributions include South African entities like NASPA's $8 billion investment in Indian infrastructure and technology and Sanlam's active engagement in finance and insurance. Simultaneously, Indian firms are strategically entering South Africa's renewable energy and industrial markets. A progressive shift toward trade in local currencies further underscores their shared intent to enhance financial autonomy and adaptability, bolstering economic resilience.

These initiatives epitomize a dynamic and multidimensional partnership, leveraging the strengths of both nations in resource management, technological advancement, and financial strategy. They underscore a shared aspiration for sustainable development and mutually beneficial growth, laying the groundwork for a robust and enduring bilateral alliance.

4.40 INDIA–BRAZIL BILATERAL COOPERATION

In 2024, India and Brazil significantly enhanced their multifaceted cooperation across trade, technology, energy, and finance, underscoring a deepening relationship within bilateral and multilateral frameworks, including BRICS and the International Solar Alliance (ISA). This partnership reflects their shared commitment to addressing global challenges through mutual collaboration and innovation.

4.40.1 TRADE

Bilateral trade between India and Brazil demonstrated steady growth, reaching $15.2 billion in 2023, underpinned by a balanced exchange of agricultural products, industrial goods, and energy resources. Brazil's membership in MERCOSUR, coupled with India's Preferential Trade Agreement with the bloc, has facilitated increased trade flows. Mechanisms such as the India–Brazil Business Leaders Forum and the Trade Monitoring Mechanism have further catalyzed dialogue, focusing on resolving trade barriers and exploring untapped opportunities for expansion.

4.40.2 TECHNOLOGY

India and Brazil have strengthened technological cooperation across various domains, notably in space exploration and digital innovation. The 2004 agreement on space technology has been instrumental in fostering joint satellite launches and data-sharing initiatives. Both nations continue to explore synergies in emerging areas, including cybersecurity and digital infrastructure. Furthermore, traditional Indian practices like Ayurveda and Yoga are being integrated into Brazilian health policies, reflecting a broader cultural and scientific exchange.

4.40.3 ENERGY

Energy collaboration has emerged as a cornerstone of the India–Brazil partnership, particularly in biofuels, renewable energy, and clean technologies. Joint efforts to promote sustainable aviation fuel (SAF) production and ethanol blending highlight the strategic alignment of their agricultural capabilities with energy security goals. Indian firms have made significant investments in Brazil's oil and gas sector, solidifying Brazil's position as a vital partner in India's energy transition. The partnership is also aligned with global decarbonization efforts and the pursuit of sustainable energy solutions.

4.40.4 FINANCE

Financial ties have been bolstered through targeted investments in key sectors such as automobiles, IT, and renewable energy. Indian enterprises are leveraging Brazil's market for strategic joint ventures, while Brazilian businesses are exploring lucrative opportunities in India's expanding economy. Additionally, initiatives to streamline trade financing and promote local currency transactions are enhancing the financial flexibility of bilateral engagements.

This growing partnership exemplifies a robust and evolving alliance that leverages the strengths of both nations to address shared challenges. It underscores their collective aspiration for sustainable development, technological advancement, and economic resilience, positioning the India–Brazil relationship as a cornerstone of South–South cooperation in an increasingly interconnected global landscape.

4.41 CHINA-RUSSIA BILATERAL COOPERATION

In 2024, Russia and China significantly deepened their cooperation across trade, energy, finance, and technology, further cementing their strategic partnership and a shared vision for global economic influence.

4.41.1 TRADE

Bilateral trade between Russia and China surged to an estimated $220 billion in 2023, reflecting the growing interdependence of their economies. The increase was largely driven by China's higher demand for Russian energy, including oil and natural gas, as well as agricultural products. Concurrently, Russia continues to source Chinese industrial goods, technology, and electronics, helping diversify its supply chains. Both nations have worked to remove trade barriers and enhance logistical connections, aiming to expand trade in sectors such as machinery, electronics, and high-value agricultural commodities.

4.41.2 ENERGY

Energy cooperation remains a fundamental aspect of the Russia–China relationship. Russia is a major energy supplier to China, particularly through the Power of Siberia pipeline, which facilitates the delivery of natural gas. In 2024, the two countries signed new agreements focused on expanding renewable energy initiatives and nuclear power projects. The ongoing collaboration in these areas supports their long-term energy security and sustainability goals. The 6th China Russia Energy Business Forum, held in 2024, reinforced their commitment to accelerating green energy and ensuring mutual energy security.

4.41.3 FINANCE

Financial cooperation between Russia and China has grown significantly, with both countries moving toward settling trade in local currencies to reduce reliance on the US dollar. This shift is bolstered by the 10th Russia–China Financial Dialogue, which has fostered deeper integration in multilateral financial platforms, such as the NDB and the AIIB. By promoting green finance and infrastructure investments, both nations are fortifying their economic resilience and facilitating macroeconomic policy coordination in the face of global uncertainties.

4.41.4 TECHNOLOGY

Technological collaboration between Russia and China in 2024 has expanded across critical sectors, including advanced manufacturing, AI, and green technologies. Both countries are combining their respective strengths in digital infrastructure, energy-efficient systems, and defence technologies. Joint R&D initiatives in space exploration further demonstrate the strategic depth of their technological partnership, with significant investments in cutting-edge innovation.

The growing Russia–China alliance in 2024 highlights their shared commitment to addressing global challenges through economic, technological, and environmental cooperation. Their bilateral and multilateral engagements are crucial in mitigating global fragmentation while driving sustainable development and technological progress.

4.42 INDIA–CHINA BILATERAL COOPERATION

In 2024, India and China, despite enduring geopolitical complexities, continued to demonstrate resilient collaboration in trade, technology, energy, and finance, underscoring their prominence as leading global economies.

4.42.1 TECHNOLOGY

Technological collaboration between India and China advanced in 2024, particularly in digital innovation, green technologies, and emerging fields like AI and quantum computing. Through multilateral platforms such as BRICS, the two nations engaged in joint research initiatives addressing global challenges. The private sector has further augmented this cooperation, particularly in telecommunications and electronics manufacturing, strengthening technological ecosystems across both countries.

4.42.2 ENERGY

Energy cooperation remained a cornerstone of bilateral ties. China has been a prominent investor in India's renewable energy projects, especially solar and wind energy infrastructure. Conversely, India has shown growing interest in leveraging China's expertise in advanced energy storage solutions, aligning with its goals for a robust clean energy transition. These collaborations underscore a shared commitment to global decarbonization efforts.

4.42.3 FINANCE

India and China diversified their financial engagements in 2024, emphasizing mechanisms for trade settlement in local currencies, particularly through frameworks developed within BRICS. This move aims to mitigate dependence on the US dollar and fortify economic resilience. Furthermore, cross-border investments between financial institutions have targeted key sectors like infrastructure and green finance, fostering deeper economic integration.

While geopolitical tensions pose challenges, the evolving partnership between India and China reflects a pragmatic approach to mutual economic interests. By leveraging their combined strengths in innovation, trade, and sustainable development, both nations are laying the groundwork for a balanced and forward-looking bilateral framework.

4.42.4 TRADE

India–China trade remained robust, with the total trade volume exceeding $138 billion in 2023. China retained its position as India's largest trading partner, with imports predominantly comprising electronics, machinery, and industrial components. In return, India exported pharmaceuticals, raw materials, and agricultural products to China. Efforts to address trade imbalances have gained momentum, with both nations exploring enhanced access for Indian goods in Chinese markets and fostering bilateral trade through streamlined mechanisms.

The product utilized in the furniture industry was priced 49% lower than its domestic market value, prompting India to impose an antidumping duty of $614 (₹51,750) per tonne on its imports in October 2024. During the same month, India levied antidumping duties on five additional Chinese goods, including glass mirrors and cellophane film, with the tariffs set to remain in effect for 5 years. Additionally, a duty of $389 (₹32,790) per tonne was imposed on sulfur black imports, widely used in dyeing textiles, paper, and leather. Thermoplastic polyurethane, essential for applications in automotive, medical, and electronic industries, also faced antidumping duties ranging from $0.93 (₹78) per kg to $1.58 (₹133) per kg.

Since 2019, India has implemented stringent restrictions on Chinese investments and banned numerous mobile applications. However, these measures have not curtailed China's ability to penetrate the Indian market. In the first half of FY25 (April–September 2024), Chinese imports to India surged by 11.5%, rising from $50.5 billion (₹4.26 lakh crores) to $56.3 billion (₹4.74 lakh crores), while India's exports to China declined by 9.2%, falling from $7.6 billion (₹64,068 crores) to $6.9 billion (₹58,160 crores). This disparity further expanded India's trade deficit with China, which grew by 15%, from $42.9 billion (₹3.61 lakh crores) in H1 FY24 to $49.4 billion (₹4.16 lakh crores).

A major factor driving the increase in Chinese imports—and, in some cases, the dumping of goods—is the surging demand within the Indian industry, spurred by robust economic growth. In certain sectors, Indian manufacturers struggle to meet the required supply within a reasonable timeframe. Key imports from China include telecom equipment, electronics, and machinery, which collectively account for approximately 50% of the total imports in these categories. For instance, although India is a net exporter of mobile phones, it relies heavily on China for parts and components. The Indian government's PLI scheme, now extended to these parts and components, aims to bolster domestic manufacturing in the next 3–5 years, thereby reducing dependency on Chinese imports.

Similarly, while India aspires to become the pharmaceutical capital of the world, it remains heavily reliant on China for APIs, the raw materials essential for medicine production.

China, facing domestic economic challenges, has developed overcapacity in several industries. Sluggish domestic growth has compelled it to increase exports to sustain its economy. In the third quarter of China's fiscal year (July–September 2024), its economy grew at 4.6%—the slowest rate since early 2023 and below its 5% target. Stagnation in its real estate and infrastructure sectors has exacerbated overcapacity issues in allied industries such as steel, aluminum, ferroalloys, and other raw material sectors critical to construction.

China is strategically advancing its labor-intensive sectors by producing high-value goods at highly competitive prices, notably in the automotive industry. By capitalizing on its extensive labor resources and state-of-the-art production capabilities, China has solidified its position as a dominant global player in these industries. The seamless blend of superior quality and cost effectiveness has propelled the demand for Chinese products in international markets, with India being a prominent example.

This strategy not only bolsters China's export-driven economic framework but also escalates competition across global and regional markets. The surge of affordable, technologically sophisticated Chinese products is redefining consumer preferences and market dynamics, compelling domestic manufacturers to innovate and adapt to maintain their competitiveness. In the Indian automotive sector, this shift is particularly pronounced, as Chinese offerings continue to gain favor for their combination of cost-efficiency and perceived value.

TABLE 4.8 India's Trade with China (in US$ Billion).

Financial Year	Total Trade	Import From China (in %)	Export to China (in %)	Trade Deficit (in %)
FY2020	81.9	65.2	16.6	48.6
FY 2021	86.4	65.2	21.2	44
FY 2022	115.8	94.6	21.3	73.3
FY 2023	113.8	98.5	15.3	83.2
FY 2024	118.4	101.7	16.7	85

Source: Ministry of Commerce and Industry, Government of India.

TABLE 4.9 India's Import from China (April–August 2024).

Products	US$ Million	In %
Computer hardware, peripherals	3953	49
Telecom instruments	3618	47
Industrial machinery for dairy	3124	43
Bulk drugs, drug intermediaries	1,436	74
Accumulators and batteries	974	65
AC, refrigeration machinery	861	46
Consumer electronics	835	40
Iron and steel	831	41
Cranes, lifts and winches	780	65
Manmade yarn, fabrics	663	60
Plastic sheets, films	649	51
Glass and glassware	538	61
Other construction machinery	464	45

Source: Ministry of Commerce and Industry, Government of India.

4.43 INDIA'S CAPITALIST REVOLUTION: AN UNFINISHED TASK

India's quest for economic transformation through capitalism is an evolving narrative, marked by significant milestones yet tempered by enduring obstacles. Since the liberalization of its economy in 1991, the nation has adopted market-driven reforms designed to catalyze growth, reduce poverty, and integrate into the global economy. Despite this progress, the realization of a true capitalist revolution—encompassing widespread prosperity, a vibrant private sector, and equitable development—remains an incomplete endeavor.

4.43.1 ACHIEVEMENTS OF INDIA'S CAPITALIST REVOLUTION

1. Unprecedented Economic Growth: India has emerged as one of the fastest-growing major economies, with its GDP multiplying exponentially since liberalization. This economic surge has fueled urbanization, industrial expansion, and the burgeoning of a dynamic middle class.
2. Deeper Global Integration: Through its active participation in global trade and investment, India has become a prominent hub for IT services, pharmaceuticals, and manufacturing. The influx of substantial FDI underscores its rising global significance.
3. Thriving Entrepreneurial Ecosystem: A robust startup culture has taken root, buoyed by initiatives such as Startup India and Make in India, which have nurtured innovation, job creation, and global competitiveness.
4. Significant Poverty Reduction: Market-oriented policies have lifted millions out of poverty, though challenges of inequality persist.

4.43.2 CHALLENGES HINDERING THE COMPLETION OF THE REVOLUTION

1. Structural Inefficiencies: Bureaucratic hurdles, underdeveloped infrastructure, and an inconsistent regulatory environment impede the seamless functioning of markets and dissuade private sector participation.

2. Persisting Inequality: Economic growth has not been uniformly inclusive, with pronounced disparities in wealth and access to opportunities between rural and urban areas and across socioeconomic groups.
3. Labor Market Rigidity: Outdated labor laws and inadequate skill development initiatives stymie formal sector job creation, leaving a substantial portion of the workforce in vulnerable informal employment.
4. Limited Financial Inclusion: Despite strides in financial accessibility, a significant segment of the population remains outside formal banking and credit systems, constraining grassroots entrepreneurship.
5. Policy and Reform Challenges: Political and administrative inefficiencies often delay or dilute critical economic reforms, thereby impeding the pace of transformation.

4.43.3 THE ROAD AHEAD

1. Strengthening Infrastructure: Strategic investments in transportation, energy, and digital infrastructure are imperative for unlocking the full potential of the private sector and enhancing productivity.
2. Promoting Inclusive Growth: Policies must prioritize equitable access to quality education, healthcare, and financial services to bridge the rural–urban divide and mitigate income inequality.
3. Modernizing Labor Laws: A more flexible and inclusive labor market is essential to facilitate formal job creation, improve working conditions, and enhance workforce mobility.
4. Enhancing Governance and Transparency: Streamlined regulations, greater transparency, and accountability are critical for fostering investor confidence and ensuring market efficiency.
5. Nurturing Innovation and Entrepreneurship: Expanded support for R&D, coupled with robust incentives for entrepreneurship, will sustain India's competitive edge and drive long-term economic growth.

4.43.4 HISTORICAL BARRIERS TO THE CAPITALIST INDUSTRIAL REVOLUTION

India's capitalist revolution has unlocked extraordinary potential, positioning the nation as an emerging global economic powerhouse. However, this transformative journey remains incomplete, necessitating visionary leadership, sustained reforms, and a commitment to inclusive development. By addressing structural inefficiencies, promoting equity, and nurturing innovation, India can fully realize its capitalist aspirations. The completion of this revolution will not only redefine the nation's economic trajectory but also establish India as a model for dynamic and sustainable development in the 21st century.

India's capitalist industrial revolution necessitates the dismantling of feudal structures, much like Western Europe's experience during the 18th-century Industrial Revolution. However, in India's unique context, the trajectory of "building capitalism" rests on a foundation marked by historically contradictory "feudal-capitalist" structures—a complex framework led by the Indian industrial and financial bourgeoisie, aligned with international capitalist interests since independence (Prabhakar, 2024b). This coalition faces numerous obstacles: despite technological advancements and investments driven by debt-financed capital, robust economic growth and substantial job creation remain elusive. The resulting shortfall has left widespread unemployment and underemployment, with an alarming 83.6% of educated and skilled youth unable to fully utilize their potential within the workforce (Prabhakar, 2024a). This entrenched disparity poses an escalating threat to social stability as hunger and poverty continue to rise, with the UNCTAD report (October 17, 2024) estimating 104 million individuals in India living in poverty.

Stagnant wages, record-high inflation, and widening income and wealth gaps amplify the concentration of economic power within a narrow echelon of established corporate entities. India faces a severe wealth imbalance, with the top 1% controlling 49% of national resources, while the top 10% collectively command 58% of the country's wealth and income. Exacerbating these vulnerabilities is India's reliance on energy imports—meeting nearly 80% of its petroleum needs from abroad—making the nation acutely sensitive to global price fluctuations and geopolitical tensions. Additionally, India's public debt, now surpassing 80% of GDP, intensifies fiscal strains, constricting funds essential for infrastructure and social programs.

Another formidable challenge lies in India's limited integration into global supply chains, driven by an underdeveloped manufacturing and technology infrastructure. In pivotal sectors like AI, biotechnology, and semiconductor production, India has lagged in adopting advanced technologies and establishing a robust manufacturing base. This lag has entrenched dependency on foreign partnerships for technical expertise, investment, and critical resources, underscoring the urgent need for technological and industrial self-sufficiency.

Nonetheless, India's industrial transformation landscape holds considerable promise. Strategic alliances with global powers such as the United States, Europe, and Japan afford India access to advanced technologies and significant capital investments, both vital for accelerating modernization efforts. Additionally, India's leadership within the Global South strengthens its diplomatic leverage, enabling advantageous trade and investment agreements with emerging economies and resource-rich nations.

India's young workforce represents a unique demographic asset—a vast labor pool that, with adequate training and empowerment, could drive India's industrial and technological advancements. Moreover, the country's expanding consumer market provides a fertile landscape for growth in electronics, pharmaceuticals, green energy, and digital services. Investments in these sectors have the potential to generate domestic employment, enhance productivity, and diminish import dependency.

Navigating these complexities offers India a unique opportunity to reshape its economic trajectory through sustainable, inclusive, and self-reliant growth. This study explores how India can harness these opportunities to address its industrialization challenges, paving the way for the nation to solidify its role as a global economic leader and foster a more equitable and resilient economy.

4.44 REVIEW OF LITERATURE

India's industrial transformation has been the subject of considerable scholarly interest, particularly as it relates to job-oriented growth, economic self-reliance, and the implications of global geopolitical pressures. This literature review synthesizes key studies that examine the multifaceted challenges and opportunities within India's industrial growth narrative.

Scholars have extensively documented India's economic growth trajectory, highlighting the importance of job creation within its industrialization model. Mehrotra (2019) argues that while India has experienced substantial GDP growth, employment generation has not kept pace, creating a significant employment gap, particularly for skilled and semi-skilled youth. The study emphasizes that India's economic policies have largely favored capital-intensive sectors, limiting opportunities for labor-intensive industries that could offer widespread employment (Mehrotra, 2019). In their analysis of the "jobless growth" phenomenon, Papola and Sahu underline that India must reorient its policies to promote industries capable of absorbing its large workforce (Papola, 2012). Similarly, Hasan (2019) emphasizes that a sustainable industrial transformation requires India to focus on skill development and sectoral diversification to create a robust job-oriented growth model.

India's reliance on energy imports has been highlighted as a critical vulnerability in numerous studies. Krishnan notes that India's dependence on petroleum imports, which comprise nearly 80% of its energy requirements, exposes it to fluctuations in global energy prices, as well as shifts in international diplomatic relations (Krishnan, 2022). This reliance not only impacts domestic industry but also limits India's economic resilience in the face of geopolitical shocks (Krishnan, 2022). Additional research by Chaudhary points out that India's energy dependency constrains its ability to pursue a self-sustaining industrial base, as high import costs and supply chain uncertainties hinder the development of its manufacturing sector (Chaudhary, 2023). This literature underscores the need for investment in renewable energy infrastructure to reduce dependency and support sustainable growth.

India's limited integration into global supply chains is another significant barrier to industrial transformation (Balakrishnan, 2021). In their study, they argue that India's manufacturing sector suffers from a lack of advanced technological infrastructure, making it difficult to compete globally in high-tech sectors such as electronics, biotechnology, and semiconductor manufacturing. Kumar suggests that India's reliance on foreign expertise for advanced manufacturing and technology has impeded its ability to develop Indigenous capabilities (Kumar, 2020). These studies collectively point to the necessity for India to invest in high-tech innovation and foster partnerships to build a resilient domestic manufacturing ecosystem.

India's evolving geopolitical stance, characterized by its alliances with the United States, Europe, and Japan, plays a crucial role in its industrial ambitions (Prabhakar, 2024d). According to Chatterjee and Singh (2023), India's strategic alignment with these global powers provides access to advanced technology and capital, which are essential for driving industrial growth (Chatterjee, 2023). Their research highlights India's nuanced approach to foreign relations, whereby it balances its partnerships with Western countries while maintaining robust ties with Russia and other Global South allies. Similarly, Gupta argues that India's positioning within the Global South enhances its negotiating power, allowing it to secure favorable trade and investment agreements with emerging economies (Gupta, 2021). This geopolitical leverage is seen as a critical component of India's industrial strategy, as it enables India to diversify its resources and reduce its reliance on any single geopolitical bloc.

The widening income and wealth disparities in India, exacerbated by the growing influence of corporate entities, have also been the focus of several studies. Desai (2023) contends that wealth concentration among a few corporate conglomerates undermines equitable growth, as economic gains are disproportionately captured by a limited number of private actors. This phenomenon, often termed "crony capitalism," has created barriers to entry for small and medium enterprises, thereby restricting broader participation in India's industrial sector (Desai, 2023). According to Sharma (2024), government policies favoring privatization and deregulation in key sectors have contributed to this economic polarization, leading to social and political tensions. The literature suggests that addressing this inequality requires targeted policies to curb corporate dominance and promote inclusivity within India's industrial model.

Several researchers highlight the need for India to prioritize inclusive and sustainable growth within its industrialization efforts (Prabhakar, 2024c). In their analysis of India's demographic dividend, Joshi and Rao emphasize the importance of workforce development, arguing that India's young labor force is a powerful asset that, if properly harnessed, could drive economic growth for decades (Joshi, 2021). Their study advocates for large-scale investment in vocational training and education as a means of building a skilled workforce capable of supporting industrial transformation. Additionally, Mishra suggests that investment in green energy and digital infrastructure could position India as a leader in sustainable industrialization, creating jobs while reducing environmental impact (Mishra,

2022). These perspectives collectively underscore the importance of an inclusive growth model that balances economic, social, and environmental priorities.

4.45 INDUSTRIAL REVOLUTION: A COMPARATIVE STUDY OF INDIA AND CHINA

China, the world's second-largest economy, has made an estimated investment of USD 6 trillion in Africa, all while maintaining foreign currency reserves of approximately USD 5 trillion. In contrast, India aspires to achieve a USD 5 trillion economy by 2030, though this path to economic expansion is fraught with challenges. The deepening agrarian crisis, rising unemployment and inflation—reaching levels last seen 45 years ago—and a public debt surpassing USD 2.5 trillion underscore the complexity of India's situation. Although manufacturing growth saw a slight uptick to 6.8% in the last quarter from 6.7% in the April-to-June period, sustaining a consistent 7% growth trajectory remains elusive, mirroring a pattern of jobless growth.

The manufacturing sector, particularly within MSMEs (micro, small, and medium enterprises), faces significant challenges with minimal prospects for substantial job creation. Since adopting a neoliberal economic model in 1991, India has sought to attract FDI and incurred substantial loans from the World Bank and IMF, totalling approximately USD 2.5 trillion—nearly 80% of India's GDP. The implementation of the Goods and Services Tax (GST) has further pressured the average citizen while primarily benefiting a few influential corporations.

The government's economic strategy has increasingly leaned toward corporate-led growth, with key public assets—railways, roadways, defence, financial institutions, education, and healthcare— being gradually privatized, signaling a decisive shift toward a corporate-centric economy.

India, long recognized for its strong services sector, is now ambitiously positioning itself as a global manufacturing leader. However, aspirations to achieve global superpower status will remain constrained without energy self-sufficiency and advancements in financial and technological infrastructure. Launched in 2014, the "Make in India" initiative set the groundwork for a shift toward manufacturing by promoting domestic production and foreign investment. Supporting this, Production Linked

Incentive (PLI) schemes have attracted considerable global investment in critical industries such as electronics, pharmaceuticals, and automobiles. The COVID-19 pandemic revealed the risks of over-reliance on China, encouraging companies to diversify their supply chains. With competitive labor costs, expanding infrastructure, and a vast domestic market, India is emerging as an attractive alternative for global manufacturers. The country's adoption of Industry 4.0, integrating automation, AI, and the IoT, has fostered new efficiencies, while initiatives like Digital India are enhancing productivity and global competitiveness.

India's manufacturing resurgence offers vast economic potential, particularly as MNCs seek alternatives to China. However, formidable obstacles persist, including inadequate industrial infrastructure, logistical inefficiencies, and an outdated SME sector. Regulatory complexities, protracted land acquisition processes, and skill mismatches in advanced manufacturing roles further compound these challenges. While India boasts a large labor force, the need for enhanced vocational training in advanced manufacturing fields is pressing.

To support sustainable industrial growth, India must prioritize workforce skill development and infrastructure enhancement. Corporations could establish Centers of Excellence to cultivate a pipeline of talent adept in digital transformation, fostering a more innovative and competitive workforce. Coastal industrial clusters, offering accessible land, housing, and facilities for workers, could significantly bolster productivity. Implementing a plug-and-play model within these clusters would provide SMEs with ready-to-use infrastructure, promoting cohesive industrial ecosystems around larger operations.

Government policies should also focus on rationalizing tariffs to prevent the unintended export of taxes and duties. Lowering customs tariffs on essential commodities like aluminum, steel, and copper could elevate the global competitiveness of Indian industries, reinforcing domestic manufacturing and economic resilience.

India's manufacturing resurgence represents a promising avenue for economic growth. Through targeted government initiatives, workforce investment, and the resolution of infrastructure and regulatory challenges, India has the potential to assert itself as a key player in global supply chains. Embracing advanced technologies and establishing industrial clusters will be essential for enhancing productivity and competitiveness. By coordinating efforts among the government, industry leaders, and educational institutions, India can surmount current obstacles to creating a sustainable manufacturing ecosystem, positioning the nation as a global manufacturing hub, and driving innovation and prosperity.

In an era where both India and China are keen to avoid direct geopolitical confrontation, their roles within BRICS and the Shanghai Cooperation Organization (SCO) take on heightened significance. These economic blocs, recently expanded to include new members, are evolving as platforms for Global South collaboration, despite member nations' varying relationships with Western powers. Although BRICS discussions continue to explore reducing reliance on the US dollar, major shifts in the global financial system are unlikely in the short term, as the dollar's dominance in global trade has remained largely unchallenged since the 1990s.

In the geopolitical arena, the world may be experiencing what some perceive as a third world war. Russian Foreign Minister Sergey Lavrov suggested this in 2022, hinting that the ongoing conflicts may constitute a global struggle. NATO, a 31-member alliance historically rooted in imperialism and colonialism, has imposed sustained economic and financial sanctions on nations such as Russia, Iran, North Korea, Venezuela, and Cuba for decades. In response, Russia's "special military operation" in Ukraine was framed as a move to demilitarize Ukraine and protect its sovereignty.

The escalating conflicts in Ukraine and the Middle East, alongside closer cooperation among Russia, China, North Korea, and Iran, pose unprecedented risks. With the third world war looming, the global landscape appears increasingly precarious, potentially ushering in widespread human suffering and significant economic consequences. Recent events in the Middle East highlight the fragility of this landscape, with the US directly supporting Israel while Russia backs Iran, Lebanon, and Palestine. The US-dominated global order established post-World War II is gradually shifting, with power increasingly gravitating toward the East.

4.45.1 CASE STUDY OF TEXTILE INDUSTRIES

Each year, the fashion and textile industries inject billions of dollars into the global economy; however, they simultaneously inflict considerable harm on the environment. Approximately 20% of water pollution and 10% of GHG emissions can be attributed to textile production. Projections indicate that by 2030, GHG emissions from the fashion sector will escalate by over 50%. Notably, India stands as the world's largest textile and apparel manufacturer, with this sector contributing 2.3% to the nation's GDP. The industry aspires to achieve $250 billion in textile production and $100 billion in exports by 2030. Conversely, the textile sector generates an alarming 7793 kilotonnes of waste, of which 3944 kilotonnes is classified as postconsumer textile waste. Alarmingly, nearly 34% (1347 kilotonnes) of this postconsumer waste finds its way into landfills, where it may take over 200 years to decompose.

As climate change emerges as a pressing global crisis, an increasing number of consumers are demanding that apparel manufacturers prioritize sustainable production processes. According to the India Sustainability Report 2023, 45% of respondents expressed a desire for recyclable fashion, 49% aimed to adopt sustainable practices, and 22% preferred upcycled garments. In response, major brands are beginning to recognize the importance of sustainability, with over 40 leading companies in India committing to the Science-Based Targets Initiative (SBTi) framework to actively reduce GHG emissions. Similarly, prominent global brands are establishing ambitious GHG emission reduction targets while seeking sustainable suppliers. To promote sustainability effectively, textile firms must concentrate on mitigating Scope 1, Scope 2, and Scope 3 emissions. Scope 1 pertains to direct emissions from owned or controlled sources, which can be diminished through the adoption of renewable energy and energy-efficient processes. Scope 2 involves indirect emissions resulting from purchased electricity, which can be addressed through a transition to green energy. Scope 3 encompasses all other indirect emissions within the value chain, necessitating a comprehensive approach that incorporates sustainable farming practices, ecofriendly transportation, and responsible retail operations.

As Indian textiles transition toward sustainable practices, several universal sustainability standards have emerged as guiding frameworks. Among these is the Global Organic Textile Standard (GOTS), which provides a robust quality assurance system through the inspection and certification of the entire textile supply chain. The Better Cotton Initiative further promotes responsible cotton cultivation and consumption. On a national level, the Ministry of Textiles has established a task force to implement industry-specific interventions. For example, the Textile Export Promotion Council endorses sustainable practices through initiatives such as the Kasturi Cotton Bharat program, which emphasizes quality and responsible governance within India's textile sector. In light of the escalating climate threat, reducing emissions, implementing energy-efficient processes, and pursuing net-zero emission targets is imperative for fulfilling India's global climate commitments, including those stipulated in the Paris Agreement for 2050.

4.46 ECONOMIC DEVELOPMENT WITH SUSTAINABILITY: CHALLENGES AND OPPORTUNITIES

However, the United Nations Sustainable Development Goals (UN SDGs) present both challenges and opportunities in adopting these strategies. Notably, approximately 70% of countries in Asia are classified as developing or least developed, rendering it difficult for them to allocate resources for costly climate change mitigation and adaptation measures. Nations such as India, Bangladesh, Cambodia, Vietnam, and Myanmar will struggle to implement capital-intensive strategies to enhance the environmental sustainability of their textile industries, which significantly contribute to emissions and ecological degradation. While about 59% of India's textile waste is recycled annually, the remaining 41% either ends up in landfills or is disposed of improperly. Effective waste management remains a formidable challenge, particularly due to the absence of programs aimed at managing postconsumer waste. The most significant barrier to promoting recycling lies in the intricate task of sorting and segregating reclaimed textiles, especially since blended garments often comprise multiple diverse fibers, along with contaminants from dyes and colors. The rise of fast fashion has led cotton mills to blend polyester and viscose with cotton, preserving economic viability while meeting the demand for inexpensive garments; unfortunately, this practice contributes to an increase in discarded garments filling landfills.

Another challenge arises in bridging the skills gap related to sustainability within the textile industry. Despite producing 25% of the world's cotton, India faces intrinsic hurdles in providing a skilled workforce for jobs in the environmentally friendly ecosystem. This challenge is compounded by the necessity for sustainability to be managed across the entire sourcing, procurement, manufacturing, distribution, and sales ecosystem. Given the existence of both organized and unorganized players in the garment sector, addressing this skills gap proves to be a complex endeavor.

As global environmental awareness gains traction, both manufacturers and consumers are gradually transitioning from fast fashion to slow fashion, which emphasizes the principles of use, reuse, and recycling inherent in the circular economy. In this context, the circular economy's closed-loop system operates by designing, manufacturing, utilizing, and managing garments to ensure they circulate within consumer communities as long as possible. Promoting maximum apparel usage minimizes environmental impact while facilitating low waste generation and optimizing the utilization of energy, water, and other resources throughout the product lifecycle.

Moreover, textile manufacturers are adopting a variety of sustainability initiatives, including energy-efficient manufacturing processes, water conservation and management strategies, wastewater treatment and zero-liquid discharge practices, and the development of a collaborative and transparent supply chain network that guarantees sustainability throughout the entire production chain, from raw material sourcing to end products.

Nevertheless, opportunities for sustainability come with challenges, as eco-friendly garments and raw materials are often more expensive. To mitigate high costs, companies must explore cost-effective decarbonization alternatives while enhancing energy efficiency, optimizing supply chains, and refining production processes.

In support of sustainable fashion, the central government has launched initiatives such as the Handloom and Handicrafts Development Programme and the Sustainable Resolution (SU.RE) scheme. Additionally, the Saathi program, facilitated by the Ministry of Textiles, aims to foster sustainable textile production in collaboration with private entities. Furthermore, the Centre must establish clear sustainability standards and implement conducive policies that incentivize sustainable processes and products.

The establishment of a sustainable textile industry requires a holistic approach that integrates innovation with a pragmatic outlook to minimize resource wastage through a circular economy model. Embracing a closed-loop system will benefit consumers and communities alike. Ultimately, a pragmatic framework can ensure that the Indian textile industry adopts sustainable practices without compromising its global competitive edge.

4.46.1 KEY FINDINGS OF THE STUDY

The Indian economy currently grapples with significant challenges, as stagnant wages, high inflation, rising unemployment, and widening inequality threaten its long-term growth trajectory. According to the 2022–2023 Annual Survey of Industries (ASI), purchasing power has diminished considerably over the past decade. Structural issues—particularly wage stagnation, inflation, and a widening wealth gap—pose severe barriers to inclusive economic progress.

1. Consolidation of Wealth and Market Power: Over the last decade, five dominant conglomerates, including the Adani Group, have expanded across 40 sectors, forming quasi-monopolies in industries such as cement, chemicals, and construction. The average consumer today spends ₹100, of which ₹36 flows to these industrial titans, double the amount from 2015. This rising share of profits has strained household budgets, exacerbating economic inequality across the nation.
2. K-Shaped Economic Recovery Post-COVID-19: India's recovery from the pandemic has been marked by stark inequalities. Rural areas and low-income households have struggled, with key indicators—like rural two-wheeler sales—remaining below 2018 levels. Wealth disparity in India, now greater under Narendra Modi's "Billionaire Raj" than during the peak of British rule, underscores the economic imbalance. While luxury consumption rises, mass-market consumption lags, highlighting unequal growth.

Demographic Advantage: India's workforce is one of its strongest assets, with around 65% of the population under the age of 35. This young workforce presents significant growth potential if effectively harnessed through skill development and job creation initiatives.

1. Economic Indicators: As of 2024, India's GDP growth rate is projected at 6.5%. However, job creation has not kept pace, leaving unemployment around 8.1% and substantial underemployment, particularly among educated youth, impacting workforce productivity.
2. Income Inequality and Social Instability: Wealth disparity has reached critical levels, with the top 10% of the population owning over 77% of the nation's wealth. This widening gulf between the rich and the poor threatens social cohesion and economic stability.
3. Energy Dependency: India imports nearly 80% of its energy needs, rendering it vulnerable to global price fluctuations and geopolitical

tensions. This dependency is compounded by a public debt level exceeding 80% of GDP, further straining fiscal resources and limiting investments in infrastructure and social services.

4. Technological Lag: India lags approximately 50 years behind countries like the USA and China in key technological domains, such as AI, biotechnology, and semiconductor production. This lag impairs the nation's industrial competitiveness and capacity for high-value exports.
5. Geopolitical Positioning and Strategic Alliances: India has developed robust partnerships with the United States, Europe, and Japan, positioning itself as a leader in the Global South.

Nevertheless, India's intricate relationships with China and Russia require cautious diplomatic navigation to balance economic aspirations and strategic interests.

1. Sectoral Opportunities: Emerging fields such as green energy, digital services, and pharmaceuticals offer vast potential for job creation and economic growth. With targeted investments, India could capitalize on its consumer base and labor force to position itself as a global manufacturing hub.
2. Challenges in Employment Generation: Despite strong GDP growth, unemployment and underemployment remain persistent, particularly among educated youth. This mismatch between economic expansion and job creation highlights the need for targeted employment strategies.

Policy Innovation Imperative: Industrial policies must prioritize job-oriented growth to mitigate income inequality. Fostering an environment supportive of startups and SMEs is critical for ensuring equitable growth.

1. Resource Utilization and Energy Independence: India must reduce its energy reliance through renewable energy investments and alternative resources like hydrogen. This shift would enhance energy security and support sustainable industrialization.
2. Technological Advancement Needs: Accelerating technological adoption and infrastructure development in high-impact sectors is essential. Collaborations with advanced economies could facilitate technology transfer and boost industrial competitiveness.

3. Role of the Private Sector: India's corporate-driven growth model, dominated by a few conglomerates, risks entrenching economic inequalities. A more inclusive growth model, involving cooperatives and small businesses, is vital for sustainable development.

4.47 BROADER SOCIOECONOMIC CHALLENGES

1. Incomplete Industrial and Agricultural Transformation: Despite 76 years of independence, India's agricultural transformation and industrial revolution remain incomplete. As highlighted in the October 17, 2024 UNCTAD report, around 104 million people in India live in poverty, and 83.6% of educated youth remain unemployed. Consumer prices, especially for food, have surged by over 56% in the past year alone. Growing income disparities and high public debt are stifling development efforts, while the influence of crony capitalism further undermines equitable progress.
2. Technological Dependency and Potential: Advances in AI, robotics, and machine learning have demonstrated the potential to enhance productivity, efficiency, and workforce capabilities across sectors, as seen during the COVID-19 pandemic. However, without substantial domestic development in these fields, India risks being left behind in the global technology race.
3. Energy Dependence and Strategic Vulnerabilities: Energy remains essential for industrialization, but India's reliance on imported oil and gas—mainly from the Gulf, Middle East, and countries like Russia and Venezuela—creates strategic vulnerabilities. A robust energy strategy focused on renewable resources is crucial for reducing this dependency.
4. Financial Sector's Role: Access to finance is critical for driving production, trade, and infrastructure development. Biotech, AR/VR, and sensory technology advancements are reshaping healthcare, manufacturing, and other sectors. However, India's heavy reliance on foreign investments and technology in finance hinders its ability to independently drive sectoral innovation.

4.48 INDIA'S GLOBAL GEOPOLITICAL POSITION

India occupies a uniquely influential geopolitical position, adeptly balancing strong alliances with the United States, Europe, and Japan while emerging as a natural leader of the Global South. This duality has been particularly evident during India's G20 presidency, where it adeptly bridged varied interests and perspectives, fostering dialogue and cooperation across the international community.

Prime Minister Narendra Modi recently held a pivotal bilateral meeting with Chinese President Xi Jinping during the BRICS Summit, building on the historic border disengagement agreement between India and China. This engagement represents a critical step toward stabilizing relations between two of the world's largest economies and key trade partners.

Despite Western sanctions, India has strategically expanded its oil imports from Russia, navigating this arrangement without substantial international backlash. This contrasts sharply with China, which, while maintaining strong ties with Moscow, faces more frequent scrutiny. Additionally, India has successfully balanced its relationships with both Israel and Iran, even amid escalating tensions in the Middle East, underscoring India's sophisticated diplomatic agility in managing complex regional and global dynamics.

4.49 CONCLUSION

A comparative analysis of emerging economies, particularly focusing on populous nations such as China and India since the 1950s, reveals a captivating tapestry of socioeconomic progress shaped by divergent policy trajectories, institutional frameworks, and sociocultural dynamics.

Since the mid-20th century, both nations embarked on ambitious nation-building efforts to liberate their vast populations from poverty and underdevelopment. However, their paths diverged profoundly, reflecting their unique historical contexts, ideological underpinnings, and strategic policy choices.

In China, the Communist Party's rise to power in 1949 marked the advent of radical socioeconomic transformation under Mao Zedong's leadership. Through centrally planned economic policies, exemplified by the Great Leap Forward and the Cultural Revolution, China sought rapid industrialization and collectivization. Despite resulting in widespread social upheaval and economic stagnation, the late 1970s witnessed a paradigm shift under Deng Xiaoping's reforms. The adoption of market-oriented policies, encapsulated in the framework of "socialism with Chinese characteristics," initiated an era of economic liberalization, foreign investment, and export-driven growth. This transformation propelled China to global prominence, fostering rapid industrialization, urbanization, and poverty reduction.

India's trajectory, in contrast, was shaped by its democratic ethos, secularism, and commitment to a mixed economy model. Under Jawaharlal Nehru's leadership, India prioritized state-led industrialization and development through 5-Year Plans, focusing on public sector investments in industries such as steel, heavy machinery, and infrastructure. While these initiatives laid the groundwork for advancements in education, healthcare, and institutional democracy, they were often hindered by bureaucratic inefficiencies and regulatory hurdles. The liberalization reforms of the 1990s, spearheaded by Prime Minister Narasimha Rao and Finance Minister Manmohan Singh, marked a turning point, unleashing India's private sector potential and fostering integration with the global economy.

In terms of socioeconomic outcomes, China has achieved remarkable progress in poverty alleviation, infrastructure development, and human capital enhancement. Massive investments in education and healthcare, coupled with the rapid expansion of manufacturing industries, lifted hundreds of millions out of poverty and positioned China as a global economic leader. However, this progress has been accompanied by challenges such as environmental degradation, income inequality, and social disparities.

India, on the other hand, has made significant strides in education, healthcare, and social equity. Affirmative action programs, alongside the expansion of democratic institutions, have improved representation and inclusion for marginalized communities. Additionally, India's cultural diversity, entrepreneurial vigor, and burgeoning knowledge economy have established its prominence in industries like IT, pharmaceuticals, and renewable energy. Yet, persistent issues such as poverty, malnutrition, and regional disparities continue to demand sustained attention.

Since the 1990s, China's economic model has been characterized by rapid urbanization and industrialization, leveraging its abundant labor force and strategic infrastructure investments. Membership in the World Trade Organization (WTO) in 2001 further accelerated this trajectory, boosting foreign investment and technology transfer. Conversely, India's economic transformation during the same period, though slower, has been defined by its emphasis on sectors like IT and pharmaceuticals, supported by a burgeoning middle class and youthful population.

China's centralized approach to development has enabled swift execution of large-scale projects, but it also raises concerns about sustainability, social inequality, and human rights. In contrast, India's decentralized governance and democratic framework foster resilience and adaptability, albeit with slower decision-making and implementation.

China's BRI, an ambitious framework of global connectivity projects, underscores its pursuit of economic and geopolitical influence. Spanning 150 countries and involving investments across Africa, Asia, and Latin America, the BRI aims to bolster trade, infrastructure, and energy security while redefining global trade dynamics. Concurrently, China is transitioning toward advanced industries such as new energy vehicles, high-tech manufacturing, and the digital economy, solidifying its status as a global economic powerhouse.

India's developmental strategy focuses on leveraging its demographic dividend and fostering innovation. Its resilience, democratic values, and emphasis on inclusive growth, despite challenges, continue to position it as a key player in the global economy.

Ultimately, the comparative analysis of China and India underscores the complexity of socioeconomic development in emerging economies. While both nations have achieved remarkable progress, their distinct approaches highlight the importance of context-specific strategies in navigating the challenges of the 21st century. As they move forward, addressing socioeconomic disparities, harnessing innovation, and fostering sustainability will be crucial for achieving inclusive and equitable development (Caridi, 2023).

The South Pacific region faces an urgent imperative to prioritize the consolidation of economic and trade partnerships with the Global South, particularly through frameworks such as BRICS, the SCO, and ASEAN+5 (RCEP). Central to this strategy is the cultivation of robust ties with China and India, designed to attract substantial investments and advanced technologies for infrastructural development and industrialization. Key focus areas include Green Hydrogen, Renewable Solar Energy, infrastructure, science and technology, agriculture, and the promotion of small- and medium-sized enterprises (SMEs). Establishing a multisectoral production network is crucial for fostering sustained economic growth and regional resilience. Additionally, the development of the blue economy must adhere to principles of sustainability and inclusivity, ensuring long-term prosperity for the region.

India stands at a transformative juncture in its pursuit of industrial modernization, simultaneously grappling with significant challenges and leveraging unprecedented opportunities. The nation's demographic dividend, strategic geopolitical positioning, and potential in emerging sectors create a unique environment conducive to job-oriented growth. However, unless critical issues—such as unemployment, energy dependency, and technological stagnation—are addressed, India's aspirations to ascend to global economic leadership may remain unrealized.

China, as the world's second-largest economy, has strategically positioned itself as a global economic powerhouse, evidenced by approximately $6 trillion in investments across Africa and foreign currency reserves nearing $5 trillion. In contrast, India, while aspiring to achieve a $5 trillion economy by 2030, continues to confront structural vulnerabilities that complicate its path to industrial transformation.

India's industrial revolution unfolds against the backdrop of dynamic global and regional challenges. Advances in technology, particularly in AI, robotics, and machine learning, are reshaping productivity and enhancing workforce competitiveness. The transformative potential of these technologies was underscored during the COVID-19 pandemic, when robots were deployed in hospitals, hotels, and high-risk environments. Yet, realizing this potential requires India to secure critical resources in finance, technology, and energy, which are indispensable for sustained industrial growth.

Energy dependency remains one of India's most pressing vulnerabilities. Nearly 80% of the country's petroleum, oil, and gas is imported, primarily from the Gulf region, the Middle East, Russia, and Nigeria. This reliance exposes India to global energy market volatility. Concurrently, financial resources are essential not only for industrial growth but also for building the foundational infrastructure that underpins economic expansion. Although India has invested in sectors such as biotechnology, augmented reality (AR), and virtual reality (VR), a cohesive strategy integrating these technologies with job creation is essential for sustainable development.

To emerge as a superpower economy, India must achieve self-reliance in energy, financial independence, and technological innovation. Presently, the country remains heavily dependent on external sources for these critical inputs. India's reliance on international financial institutions, with loans from the World Bank and the IMF totalling approximately $2.5 trillion, alongside its significant dependency on oil and gas imports and foreign technology, underscores the challenges it faces in its journey toward self-sufficiency. Consequently, projections of India attaining superpower status by 2025 appear overly optimistic.

Nevertheless, India's geopolitical positioning significantly bolsters its industrial ambitions. Strategically aligned with key global powers such as the United States, Europe, and Japan, India has also solidified its role as a leader of the Global South, an achievement accentuated during its G20 presidency. Its nuanced diplomacy has enabled it to maintain balanced relationships with diverse stakeholders, including China. The recent bilateral engagement between Prime Minister Narendra Modi and Chinese President Xi Jinping at the BRICS Summit, following a landmark border disengagement agreement, signals a stabilization of relations with China, India's largest trade partner—a development of mutual importance.

India's adept diplomatic strategies are exemplified by its ability to navigate complex international dynamics. For instance, India has significantly increased oil imports from Russia amidst Western sanctions, managing to avoid substantial geopolitical fallout. Similarly, it has maintained balanced ties with both Israel and Iran, even amidst heightened tensions in the Middle East, showcasing its capacity for strategic agility.

To realize its industrial and economic aspirations, India must channel greater investments into education, healthcare, and renewable energy while prioritizing biotechnology, advanced technologies, and sustainable energy solutions. Key sectors such as banking, IT, infrastructure, energy, and consumer goods must receive enhanced focus, while ensuring that welfare-oriented areas like healthcare, education, and food security remain publicly accessible.

India's ambitious industrial and geopolitical strategies reflect its growing influence on the global stage and underscore its potential to spearhead an industrial revolution that promotes domestic prosperity while solidifying its leadership role within the Global South.

4.50 STRATEGIC RECOMMENDATIONS

1. Resource Allocation for Industrial Advancement: To realize its industrial ambitions, India must secure robust resources across finance, technology, and energy. Collaborating with oil

and gas-rich nations—such as Russia, Iran, Iraq, Saudi Arabia, Venezuela, Nigeria, and PNG—alongside forging partnerships with technological leaders like the US, China, and Germany will be crucial for sustained industrial growth.

2. Investment in Key Sectors: India should prioritize five essential areas—banking, IT, energy and utilities, consumer goods production, and infrastructure. While banking and technology have demonstrated high profitability globally, vital sectors like food, water, healthcare, and education should prioritize public welfare and resist commercialization.
3. Public Sector Leadership in Welfare Services: Public sectors must assume leadership roles in welfare-oriented services, while India's IT sector should diversify its service offerings to emulate global technology giants like Amazon, Nvidia, and Apple.
4. Advanced Sector Development and Skill Enhancement: Investing in scientific education, healthcare, and advanced technology sectors—such as AI, biotech, green energy, and hydrogen—will be instrumental in achieving India's economic self-sufficiency goals. Allocating a significant portion of the national budget to these areas is essential for sustaining industrialization.
5. Strategic Utilization of the Demographic Dividend: India's youthful population can serve as a transformative force if skill development and job creation are prioritized. Establishing Centers of Excellence and incentivizing vocational training can cultivate a workforce adept in advanced manufacturing, AI, and biotechnology.
6. India's industrial journey necessitates a balanced approach—one that aligns economic growth with social equity, technological advancement, and energy independence. Through coordinated efforts among government, industry, and academia, India can overcome existing barriers and realize its potential as a leading global economy.
7. Enhance Skill Development Programs: Invest in comprehensive skill development initiatives that align with industry requirements, particularly in emerging sectors such as AI, renewable energy, and biotechnology.

8. Promote Inclusive Growth: Implement policies that foster inclusive economic growth by supporting SMEs and cooperatives. This strategy will diversify the economy and broaden the base for job creation.
9. Strengthen Energy Security: Develop and invest in renewable energy sources and alternative technologies. Policies aimed at increasing energy efficiency and reducing dependence on fossil fuel imports will bolster national security.
10. Foster Technological Innovation: Create an ecosystem conducive to R&D in critical technology sectors. This should include facilitating partnerships between academic institutions and industry leaders to spur innovation.
11. Diversify Geopolitical Engagement: Continue to enhance diplomatic relations with a diverse range of global partners, ensuring that India maintains a balanced approach to its geopolitical relationships, particularly with major powers such as the USA, China, and Russia.
12. Implement Comprehensive Economic Policies: Formulate economic policies that address the underlying structural issues affecting industrial growth, encompassing regulatory reform, taxation policies, and infrastructure investment. By undertaking these strategic actions, India can adeptly navigate its industrial transformation, fostering a job-oriented growth model that is resilient, inclusive, and attuned to the demands of a rapidly evolving global landscape.

KEYWORDS

- **consumer market**
- **economic growth**
- **endeavors**
- **geopolitical tensions**
- **investment**
- **workforce**

REFERENCES

Akaev, A. A. (2024). Modeling and forecasting the evolutionary economic development of the BRICS and G7 countries in the first half of the twenty-first century. *Journal of Globalization Studies*, *15*(2), 7–33.

Brasil, B. (2025, May 1). BRICS GDP outperforms global average, accounts for 40% of world economy. https://brics.br/en/news/brics-gdp-outperforms-global-average-accounts-for-40-of-world-economy.

Center for Global Development. (2021). *Mapping China's rise in the multilateral system.* CGD Policy Analysis.

Gill, B., & Huang, C. H. (2009). *China's expanding peacekeeping role: Its significance and the policy*. Stockholm International Peace Research Institute.

Gwin, C. (2021). *Report reveals new data on China's growing power, influence at 76 global institutions*. Center for Global Development Research Brief.

International Monetary Fund. (2025). *World economic outlook: A critical juncture amid policy uncertainties*. IMF Publications.

McBride, J. M. (2023, February 2). *China's massive BRI. Council on foreign relations.* https://www.cfr.org/backgrounder/chinas-massive-bri.

Patrick, S. A. (2025). *BRICS expansion and the future of world order: Perspectives from member states, partners, and aspirants*. Carnegie Endowment for International Peace.

Peace, C. E. (2025). *BRICS expansion and the future of world order: Perspectives from member states, partners, and aspirants*. Carnegie Endowment Research Report.

Stisman, P. (2024). *China's rising international reserves signal economic strength.* Georgetown University Americas Program.

World Bank. (2025). *China economic update: Unlocking consumption.* World Bank Publications.

Yan, E. (2025, March 6). How China maintains the world's largest foreign exchange reserve. *The Economics Review*, *15*(2), 23–41.

CHAPTER 5

Automation and Digitalization: A Premature Deindustrialization in Developing Economies

ABSTRACT

This chapter critically interrogates the profound and disruptive ramifications of rapid technological advancement on the industrialization trajectories of the Global South. As automation and digital technologies progressively displace labor-intensive manufacturing, numerous developing economies confront the paradox of deindustrialization in the absence of having undergone full-scale industrialization—a condition conceptualized as "premature deindustrialization." This study explores the diffusion of capital-intensive innovations, the restructuring of global value chains, and the concomitant decline in manufacturing employment, all of which subvert conventional models of structural transformation and economic ascent. Drawing on comparative cross-national data, sector-specific analyses, and illustrative case studies, the research elucidates how automation not only constrains employment creation and deepens income inequality but also intensifies economic dualism within low- and middle-income countries. In response, the study examines a spectrum of policy interventions aimed at aligning technological adoption with inclusive growth—emphasizing strategic investments in human capital, digital infrastructure, and adaptive industrial policy frameworks. Ultimately, the analysis underscores the imperative to reconceptualize development strategies in a digital age where technological disruption increasingly delineates the boundaries of economic possibility and social equity.

The BRICS Coalition and a New Global Order: Akhilesh Chandra Prabhakar (Author)
2026 Apple Academic Press, Inc. Co-published with CRC Press (Taylor & Francis)

DOI: 10.1201/9781779642936-5

5.1 INTRODUCTION

Automation and digitalization are catalyzing transformative shifts in industries worldwide, propelled by unprecedented advancements in artificial intelligence (AI), robotics, and data analytics. While these innovations hold immense promise for accelerating economic growth and enhancing productivity, they simultaneously present formidable challenges for developing economies. Chief among these concerns is the risk of premature deindustrialization—a phenomenon where industrial activity wanes before economies achieve a stable and sustained trajectory of economic development.

5.1.1 THE PROMISE OF AUTOMATION AND DIGITALIZATION

Automation and digitalization herald a new era of industrial efficiency, characterized by heightened productivity, significant cost reductions, and expanded integration into global value chains. For industries, the adoption of automated systems diminishes reliance on manual labor, optimizes operational workflows, and enhances competitiveness on a global scale. From a consumer perspective, digital platforms significantly improve accessibility to goods and services.

In advanced economies, these benefits seamlessly complement established industrial and service sectors, yielding a net positive impact on economic growth and employment. However, the dynamics in developing economies present a more complex narrative.

5.1.2 THE RISKS OF PREMATURE DEINDUSTRIALIZATION

In developing economies, the precipitous transition to automation and digitalization threatens to upend conventional pathways to industrialization. Historically, manufacturing has served as the bedrock of economic development, offering employment opportunities, facilitating infrastructure development, and fostering innovation (Herrendorf, 2014). However, the premature integration of advanced technologies into industrial sectors presents distinct risks:

1. **Job Displacement**: Automation inherently reduces the demand for low-skilled labor, a critical pillar in the manufacturing sectors of developing economies. As machines supersede humans in

performing repetitive tasks, widespread unemployment ensues, leaving many workers grappling with the need for upskilling—a prospect that may remain inaccessible for large segments of the population.

2. **Stunted Industrial Growth**: The advantages traditionally afforded by low labor costs are eroded in an increasingly automated landscape, impeding the establishment of robust manufacturing sectors. This disruption challenges the conventional progression from agrarian to industrial and ultimately service-based economies, hindering developmental trajectories.

3. **The Digital Divide**: Many developing nations contend with significant disparities in digital infrastructure and technological proficiency. Inadequate investments in these domains exacerbate existing inequalities, relegating these economies further to the margins of global technological advancements.

4. **Technological Dependence**: The reliance on automation and digitalization technologies developed predominantly in industrialized nations fosters dependency. This dependency constrains domestic innovation, limiting the ability of developing economies to tailor solutions to their unique developmental contexts.

5.1.3 POLICY RESPONSES TO MITIGATE RISKS

Effectively navigating the dichotomy of opportunity and risk posed by automation and digitalization necessitates a nuanced policy approach:

1. **Invest in Education and Workforce Upskilling**: Comprehensive reforms in education systems are imperative, prioritizing digital literacy, vocational training, and lifelong learning to equip the workforce with skills aligned with future industrial demands.

2. **Adopt Incremental Automation**: A phased approach to automation allows for a balance between technological integration and employment generation. Small and medium enterprises (SMEs) can be encouraged to adopt digital tools in a manner that complements, rather than replaces, human labor.

3. **Promote Digital Inclusivity**: Expanding access to digital infrastructure and ensuring equitable participation in the digital economy are vital. Public–private collaborations can play a pivotal role in bridging the digital divide.
4. **Foster Indigenous Innovation**: Policies that incentivize research and development (R&D), establish innovation hubs, and promote knowledge sharing can build the capacity for localized technological adaptation and innovation.
5. **Regional and Sectoral Prioritization**: Developing economies should identify and invest in sectors where they hold comparative advantages, fostering regional collaborations to strengthen industrial resilience and competitiveness.

While the transformative potential of automation and digitalization is indisputable, their integration into developing economies necessitates a careful balancing act to forestall premature deindustrialization. Inclusive policy frameworks, substantial investment in human capital, and a robust commitment to fostering local innovation are essential to ensure that these technologies serve as enablers of sustainable and equitable development. The ultimate objective must transcend mere technological adoption; it should focus on leveraging these advancements to foster long-term resilience and shared prosperity.

5.2 CONCEPT OF DEINDUSTRIALIZATION

Deindustrialization constitutes a multifaceted and intricate process emblematic of the evolving landscape of economic development (Rodrik, 2016). It encompasses the gradual decline of the manufacturing sector within an economy relative to its overall economic output. This phenomenon is intricately linked with the transition of an economy away from traditional industrial pursuits toward a heightened emphasis on service-oriented and information-based activities.

While deindustrialization is often perceived through a lens of negativity, it is imperative to recognize its dual nature, replete with both positive and negative implications. On one hand, it signals a progression toward a more service-oriented and technologically advanced economy, indicative of economic growth and innovation. Conversely, it entails the displacement of traditional manufacturing jobs, potentially leading to social and economic upheaval within affected communities.

Nevertheless, amidst these complexities, deindustrialization emerges as an inevitable byproduct of economic evolution and technological progress. As nations traverse the path of development, it is foreseeable that deindustrialization will remain a pivotal force in reshaping the fabric of their economies. Thus, while it may evoke apprehension and concern, deindustrialization fundamentally embodies the essence of economic metamorphosis, propelling societies toward new horizons of prosperity and innovation.

The genesis of the concept of deindustrialization lies deeply entrenched within the realms of economic development and the epochal transition from agrarian to industrialized societies. At the nascent stages of economic advancement, nations invariably undergo a phase of rapid industrialization, wherein agriculture relinquishes its primacy to manufacturing as the principal catalyst of economic progress. This pivotal transition is often paralleled by the phenomenon of urbanization, as rural denizens gravitate toward urban centers in the pursuit of gainful employment within burgeoning factories and industrial complexes.

Nonetheless, as countries ascend to a certain echelon of economic maturation, the manufacturing sector undergoes a perceptible diminution in its significance vis-à-vis other economic domains. This trajectory is propelled by a constellation of factors, encompassing technological advancements engendering heightened productivity, shifts in consumer predilections, and the inexorable march of market globalization. Consequently, manufacturing evolves into a realm characterized by diminished labor intensity and augmented capital investment, precipitating a concomitant decline in employment opportunities within the sector.

Deindustrialization reverberates with a plethora of economic and social ramifications. On one hand, it can engender heightened productivity and elevated living standards, as laborers achieve greater output with diminished exertion. Conversely, it can precipitate job displacement and economic upheaval, compelling workers in waning sectors to seek alternative livelihoods within the broader economic landscape. This transition poses a formidable challenge, especially for individuals entrenched in industries heavily reliant on low-skilled labor, who may confront hurdles in acquiring the requisite skills and education requisite for transitioning into higher paying occupations. As the global tapestry becomes increasingly interwoven, the reverberations of technological advancements resonate with amplified resonance within developing nations. While technological innovation holds the potential to catalyze economic expansion and societal advancement, it concurrently presents formidable hurdles for countries yet to traverse the full spectrum of industrialization. At the global echelon, contentious discourse ensues, characterized by fervent debate surrounding the ramifications of "hi-tech," digitalization, corporatization, and financialization on developing economies. Particularly poignant is the ongoing dialogue surrounding premature deindustrialization, punctuated by its complex interplay with the evolving fabric of global economic dynamics.

The intricate nexus of hi-tech, digitalization, corporatization, and financialization stands as a linchpin in shaping the contemporary global economic landscape. Hi-tech epitomizes the integration of advanced technology across diverse sectors such as manufacturing, information technology, and telecommunications, heralding a paradigm shift in operational methodologies. Concurrently, digitalization emerges as the transformative process of transmuting analog data into digital formats, fostering unparalleled efficiency and adaptability in information governance.

Corporatization embodies the metamorphosis of public sector entities into corporate entities, orchestrated with the overarching objective of enhancing operational efficiency and bolstering profitability. Meanwhile, financialization delineates the ascendancy of financial markets and institutions, exerting an increasingly dominant influence on the economic milieu, often eclipsing traditional manufacturing and production sectors.

In recent years, a palpable trend of premature deindustrialization has taken root across numerous developing nations, wherein conventional manufacturing bastions yield ground to burgeoning hi-tech industries and service sectors. This seismic shift is propelled by an amalgam of catalysts, encompassing technological breakthroughs, evolving consumer predilections, and the pervasive forces of globalization. While hi-tech industries and services herald novel avenues for economic advancement, they concurrently pose formidable challenges for developing economies yet to traverse the full spectrum of industrialization.

This research undertakes an expedition into the profound impact of hi-tech, digitalization, corporatization, and financialization on developing countries, with a particular emphasis on the nuanced intricacies underlying the phenomenon of premature deindustrialization. Through a comprehensive exploration of these interconnected dynamics, it endeavors to unravel the intricate tapestry of challenges and opportunities confronting developing economies in an era characterized by rapid technological innovation and economic transformation.

Amidst the epoch of hi-tech, digitalization, corporatization, and financialization, developing nations grapple with a formidable challenge: the imperative to adapt to the tumultuous currents of a swiftly metamorphosing global economy. Traditional manufacturing bastions, erstwhile linchpins of many developing economies, find themselves eclipsed by the ascendant prominence of hi-tech industries and services. This paradigmatic shift precipitates a concomitant decline in the demand for low-skilled labor, juxtaposed against a surge in the requisition for highly skilled personnel. The resultant dissonance leaves many developing nations teetering on the precipice of economic recalibration, struggling to synchronize their labor force with the exigencies of an evolving economic order.

Central to the waning prominence of traditional manufacturing sectors within developing countries is the proliferation of automation and robotics within manufacturing processes. While these technological innovations herald heightened levels of productivity and operational efficiency, they simultaneously orchestrate a diminution in the requisition for low-skilled labor. This conundrum resonates with particular acuity within developing nations, where a substantial proportion of the workforce is ensconced in low skilled manufacturing vocations. Consequently, many developing countries grapple with soaring rates of unemployment and underemployment, notably among the burgeoning cohort of the youth populace.

In essence, the confluence of hi-tech advancements and economic restructuring engenders a crucible of challenges for developing nations, necessitating a nuanced approach toward labor market adaptation and economic diversification. The imperative lies in fostering an ecosystem conducive to nurturing a skilled workforce adept at navigating the exigencies of an increasingly technologically driven global economy. Only through strategic foresight and concerted efforts can developing countries hope to surmount the formidable hurdles posed by the relentless march of economic evolution.

Another salient factor precipitating the erosion of traditional manufacturing sectors in developing nations is the burgeoning significance accorded to services within the global economic milieu. Services, spanning a gamut from finance and information technology to telecommunications, burgeon in prominence within the global economic landscape, eclipsing erstwhile manufacturing strongholds. Developing nations find themselves ensnared in the throes of a relentless struggle to vie for competitive standing vis-à-vis their developed counterparts in these burgeoning service domains. The resultant confluence catalyzes a palpable migration away from conventional manufacturing bastions within many developing economies, spurred by a zealous quest to diversify economic portfolios and assert relevance within the echelons of the burgeoning global services market.

The phenomenon of premature deindustrialization unfolding within developing nations is undeniably propelled by a multiplicity of factors, among which lies the inexorable sway of shifting consumer preferences. As disposable incomes burgeon across developing landscapes, consumers exhibit a discernible proclivity toward the procurement of higher-quality goods and services, frequently sourced from developed economies. This escalating penchant for superior quality precipitates a perceptible decline in the requisition for low-quality commodities and services originating from developing nations, thereby amplifying the downward trajectory of traditional manufacturing sectors.

Moreover, the pervasive tendrils of globalization exert an indelible imprint upon the contours of premature deindustrialization. The advent of globalization ushers forth a milieu characterized by heightened competition within the global economic arena, wherein developing nations grapple with the arduous task of contending against their developed counterparts within traditional manufacturing spheres (Prabhakar, 2015b). This intensified competition catalyzes a palpable erosion in the demand for low-quality commodities and services emanating from developing economies, thereby perpetuating the downward spiral encroaching upon traditional manufacturing bastions.

In the contemporary landscape of the 21st-century global economy, the symbiotic interplay of hi-tech, digitalization, corporatization, and financialization emerges as a defining nexus. These intertwined concepts, while heralding novel avenues for economic expansion, concurrently pose formidable challenges for developing nations yet to traverse the full spectrum of industrialization. The spectre of premature deindustrialization looms large over these economies, propelled by a multifaceted array of catalysts including technological strides, shifts in consumer predilections, globalization imperatives, and the pervasive advent of automation and robotics (Prabhakar, 2015a).

As a consequence, a plethora of developing countries find themselves ensnared in a protracted struggle to acclimate to the exigencies of the burgeoning global economic order. The repercussions reverberate with particular acuity, manifesting in soaring rates of unemployment and underemployment, notably pronounced among the burgeoning cohort of the young populace. In essence, the confluence of these interconnected dynamics engenders a crucible of challenges for developing nations, mandating a paradigm shift in economic strategies and labor market paradigms. Only through astute foresight and concerted efforts can these economies endeavor to navigate the tumultuous currents of the emergent global economic paradigm, ensuring sustainable growth and equitable prosperity for generations to come.

The principal driver behind deindustrialization stems from the accelerated growth of productivity within the manufacturing sector relative to services. Contrary to popular belief, North–South trade has played a peripheral role in the overarching narrative of deindustrialization.

The narrative of the Industrial Revolution, in conjunction with the Agricultural Revolution, remains incomplete within the annals of developing nations, save for the notable exception of China. To supplant antiquated industrial frameworks and advance toward the attainment of Sustainable Development Goals, the imperative lies in erecting a novel industrial infrastructure imbued with sustainability principles, underscored by the harnessing of green (renewable) energy sources. Crucially, this entails the establishment of electric/battery charging stations, particularly tailored for transportation and telecommunications systems, alongside investments in water and sanitation, food and agriculture, biodiversity, health, and educational infrastructures.

Developing and least-developed countries find themselves ensnared within a labyrinth of investment challenges, precipitated by a dearth of domestic financial capital and technological resources. Compounded by the reverberations of successive global economic and financial shocks and crises, as well as the repercussions of military and geopolitical conflicts between major global superpowers such as the combined forces of Russia and China vis-à-vis America-NATO allies since 2022, the revitalization of investment endeavors has been stifled. This confluence of disruptions has imperiled the transition toward low-carbon energy systems, resilient health infrastructure, and bolstered supply chain resilience while impeding the growth of productive capacities.

Consequently, these developing and least-developed nations find themselves confronted with a dire dearth of investment, estimated to surpass an annual deficit of USD 4 trillion, as delineated by UNCTAD's World Investment Report 2023. Urgent remedial action is imperative to surmount these obstacles, heralding a renaissance of investment initiatives to steer these nations toward a trajectory of sustainable growth and equitable prosperity.

The imperative for transformative action looms ever more pressing, lest we find ourselves subject to the inexorable dictates of technological imposition. Forecasts suggest that AI and Robotics could potentially displace up to 800 million jobs by the year 2030. Yet, a staggering number of developing nations remain ill-prepared to safeguard their traditional socioeconomic and cultural frameworks, let alone adapt to the advent of these disruptive technologies.

Since their inception, many developing countries have charted a distinct trajectory characterized by socialist developmental paradigms, wherein the state assumed a pivotal role in orchestrating target-based planning and time-bound policies aimed at fostering industrialization. This approach hinged upon the establishment of state-run public enterprises as the bedrock of the national economy, alongside concerted efforts to bolster agricultural production to attain self-sufficiency objectives. Concurrently, public welfare initiatives were launched, encompassing poverty alleviation programs, employment generation schemes, and the provision of essential services such as food security through public distribution systems, housing initiatives for the marginalized, and improved healthcare and education services.

However, the denouement of the 20th century witnessed a seismic upheaval with the collapse of the Soviet Socialist Bloc, heralding a tectonic shift in the global geopolitical landscape in favor of free-market capitalism. This epochal transition precipitated an era characterized by the ascendancy of liberalization, privatization, corporatization, financialization, digitalization, and globalization initiatives—emblematic of a resurgence of classical economic precepts espoused by Adam Smith. Propagated by erstwhile Western colonial powers and propagated through various media, educational, and research channels, these initiatives purported to unlock new vistas of prosperity and opportunity, fostering global economic integration under the auspices of institutions like the World Bank, International Monetary Fund, and World Trade Organization.

However, the reality belies the lofty promises of this global project. The sweeping tide of globalization, privatization, liberalization, and digitalization has engendered a chasmic schism between a privileged cadre of the affluent and skilled, and the disenfranchised masses. Across nations and economic systems, integration into these processes has engendered the meteoric rise of a new echelon of military and financial elites, even as the vast majority grapple with persistent hardship. Public debt burgeons, inflation surges, and unemployment burgeons amplify socioeconomic disparities and sap domestic demand in key sectors. The consequence is an exacerbation of economic malaise, characterized by declining wages and widespread suffering. Across the past quarter century, the proportion of employment allocated to manufacturing within the world's most advanced economies has undergone a precipitous decline, a phenomenon widely recognized as "deindustrialization."

This trend manifests prominently within the United States and Europe, yet its reverberations have also been discerned in nations such as Japan, India, Pakistan, Bangladesh, Sri Lanka, Nepal, Southeast Asia, and East Asia (Rowthorn, 1997). Rowthorn further posited that deindustrialization has engendered significant consternation within the affected economies, catalyzing a spirited discourse concerning its underlying causes and anticipated ramifications. Many perceive deindustrialization through a lens of trepidation, attributing it to the exacerbation of income inequality in the United States and the exacerbation of unemployment rates in Europe. Some proponents argue that deindustrialization is a byproduct of market globalization, propelled by the rapid proliferation of North–South trade—the burgeoning exchange between advanced economies and the developing world. These critics assert that the rapid ascension of labor intensive manufacturing industries in the developing sphere precipitates job displacement within advanced economies.

Within the 23 most advanced economies, the prevalence of manufacturing employment has dwindled from approximately 28% of the workforce in 1970 to a meagre 18% by 1994. Deindustrialization has unfolded disparately across various economies, commencing at differing junctures and advancing at divergent paces. Its inception was earliest in the United States, where the proportion of manufacturing employment plummeted from its zenith of 28% in 1965 to a mere 16% by 1994. In stark contrast, Japan's trajectory commenced later and transpired with less dramatic fervor, with manufacturing employment cresting at 27% of total employment in 1973 (8 years subsequent to the U.S. zenith) before receding to approximately 23% by 1994. Across the 15 nations constituting the European Union, the proportion of manufacturing employment remained relatively robust, exceeding 30% in 1970, only to precipitously decline to a mere 20% by 1994.

Conversely, the ascendancy of services as a proportion of employment has been a consistent trend across advanced economies, with all witnessing a surge in service employment since 1960. The United States has been at the vanguard of this paradigm shift, with service employment accounting for approximately 56% of the workforce in 1960 and surging to around 73% by 1994—the highest among advanced economies. This augmentation in service employment has been concomitant with a commensurate decline in manufacturing employment across all advanced economies (Rowthorn, 1997).

The ascendant proportion of employment within the manufacturing sector during the industrialization phase of development serves as a poignant marker of the transition of labor from agrarian pursuits to industrial endeavors. Two pivotal factors underpin this pivotal realignment of employment dynamics. First, on the demand side, Engel's law assumes prominence, stipulating that as individuals' incomes escalate, the proportion of their income allocated toward sustenance diminishes relative to other expenditures. In practical terms, this translates to a shift in spending patterns as economies progress industrially, with a reduced portion of income earmarked for sustenance and a commensurate augmentation directed toward manufactured goods and services.

Concurrently, on the supply side, the rapid strides in agricultural productivity emerge as a pivotal catalyst, facilitated by technological innovations that amplify food production while diminishing the requisite labor inputs. This surge in agricultural efficiency precipitates a concomitant decline in employment within the agricultural sector. The confluence of these demands- and supply-side dynamics precipitates a profound reorientation of labor, catalyzing a palpable migration from agricultural pursuits to manufacturing roles.

Indeed, the aggregate proportion of employment within the agricultural sector across advanced economies witnessed a precipitous decline, dwindling from approximately 20% in the early 1960s to a mere 11% by the early 1970s. Given the pronounced contraction already witnessed within the agricultural domain, any further expansion in the share of employment allocated to services will invariably come at the expense of manufacturing employment, echoing the earlier transition from agriculture to manufacturing.

The persistent trajectory of deindustrialization bears profound ramifications for the long-term growth trajectory of advanced economies. It is widely recognized that as a greater proportion of the workforce transitions into the service sector, the trajectory of productivity growth within services assumes paramount significance in shaping the trajectory of overall living standards.

Certain industries inherently lend themselves more readily to technological advancement, characterized by high rates of productivity growth stemming from their potential for standardization. In contrast, other sectors exhibit a lesser propensity for technological progress. Manufacturing, by its intrinsic nature, embodies a propensity toward technological advancement, evincing a systematic inclination toward discovering means to augment production efficiency, thereby achieving more with fewer workers. However, not all service industries conform to a uniform pace of technological progress. Indeed, certain service sector domains—such as telecommunications—exhibit attributes akin to manufacturing, manifesting a predisposition toward technological advancement. Conversely, personal services, exemplified by certain forms of medical care, defy easy standardization and remain impervious to the mass production techniques inherent in manufacturing. Consequently, these service sectors are poised to experience slower rates of productivity growth.

The long-term trajectory of average growth is predicated upon the pace of growth exhibited by the sector with the slowest progression. This principle, encapsulated within the theory of asymptotic stagnancy, finds illustration within the realm of the computer industry. For instance, if hardware production experiences technological advancement while software production remains stagnant, the overall productivity growth within the computer industry will inevitably plateau. This phenomenon arises due to the burgeoning ratio of software to hardware producers, resulting in hardware production exerting a diminishing influence on overall productivity growth within the industry.

Expanding this analogy to encompass the broader economy yields intriguing insights. In a scenario where manufacturing exhibits technologically progressiveness while services, as a whole, lag behind in technological advancement, the economy-wide growth trajectory, in the long run, will increasingly hinge upon productivity growth within services. This portends a departure from conventional wisdom, whereby the productivity growth in manufacturing wields diminished influence in ameliorating living standards within advanced economies. Thus, as deindustrialization continues unabated, the overarching trajectory of productivity growth will progressively pivot toward being contingent upon advancements in service sector productivity (Rowthorn, 1997).

As developed nations burgeoned in prosperity, they underwent a profound process of "structural transformation." This metamorphosis entailed a transition from agrarian-based economies to manufacturing centric ones, culminating in the ascendancy of service-based economies. Analogously, densely populated developing nations, often in nascent stages of industrialization, exhibit a similar trajectory. Manufacturing industries, renowned for their labor-intensive nature, serve as prolific providers of employment opportunities. The absence of a robust manufacturing sector can engender efficiency ramifications, constraining growth potentials by forgoing participation in the "manufacturing bandwagon." Manufacturing industries are renowned for their propensity for productivity augmentation, a feat often more readily attainable than in agriculture or services. This stems from the manufacturing sector's inherent predisposition toward assimilating foreign technology and fostering the creation of high-productivity job roles.

Rodrik posits that industrialization has served as a linchpin in fostering labor movements within agriculturally dominated, impoverished nations—erstwhile constituents of the periphery or semi-periphery. These labor movements have played a pivotal role in agitating for expanded voting rights and the establishment of welfare states. Literature within the realm of political economy proffers that negotiations between societal elites and organized labor constituencies constitute a fulcrum in the evolution of democratic institutions. Consequently, premature deindustrialization may undermine the potency of organized labor within contemporary low-income countries, potentially steering political development toward less propitious trajectories, antithetical to the ideals of liberal democracy (Lippolis, 2017).

Despite the sweeping tide of "digitalization-financialization-liberalization-privatization-corporatizationmarketization and globalization" permeating the global economic landscape, it becomes evident that nations do not uniformly traverse the same trajectory of economic development nor do they progress through identical stages of structural transformation from agrarian-based economies to manufacturing-centric ones. A poignant illustration lies in the disparate trajectories witnessed between China and India. In 1990, their GDPs stood on comparable footing; however, over three decades, China emerged with a substantially augmented share of employment within the manufacturing sector, whereas India pivoted toward a more pronounced presence in the service sector. Notably, China's GDP surged to USD 19 trillion, dwarfing India's GDP of around INR 3 trillion.

Akin to this dichotomy is the case of South Africa, which in 2007 boasted a GDP per capita akin to Italy's in 1960. Despite this semblance of economic development, South Africa exhibited a disproportionately larger share of employment within the service sector.

Many emerging, transitional, and economically challenged developing nations, spanning from India and Indonesia to various Asian countries, Eastern Europe, and Africa, grapple with a phenomenon termed "premature deindustrialization." This phenomenon signifies an accelerated transition into the services sector relative to the evolutionary trajectory experienced by early-industrialized nations at comparable stages of economic development.

Indeed, the prevalence of "premature deindustrialization" does not permeate all corners of the globe uniformly. However, the overarching cross-country pattern is emblematic of the burgeoning concentration of global manufacturing activities in nations such as China. Nevertheless, the incontrovertible truth remains that industry has wielded a more pronounced impact on the growth trajectories of today's affluent nations than on their economically disadvantaged counterparts.

Consider Africa, replete with vast reserves of critical minerals encompassing aluminum, cobalt, manganese, graphite, copper, nickel, lithium, and iron. These invaluable resources underpin the production of high-tech and environmentally sustainable products such as smartphones, solar panels, and electric vehicles. Consequently, developing nations across Africa, Asia, Latin America, and the South Pacific Islands are impelled to recalibrate their industrial policies, prioritizing Indigenous sourcing initiatives and directing concerted efforts toward the spheres of science and technology, human capital development, infrastructure augmentation, and capacity-building endeavors (UNCTAD's Economic Development in Africa Report 2023, 2023).

The pursuit of job-oriented industrialization, concomitant with technological advancement, poses a formidable challenge in the quest for sustainable and inclusive economic growth, progress, and development. Dani Rodrik contends that premature deindustrialization can be ascribed primarily to two pivotal factors: technological progress and international trade dynamics. In recent decades, technological strides have precipitated a diminution in the competitive edge of low-income nations characterized by a paucity of skilled labor. Historically, many nations penetrated the manufacturing realm by commencing with rudimentary, labor-intensive endeavors, subsequently ascending the industrial echelons. Nonetheless, this erstwhile viable strategy has encountered impediments in contemporary times owing to heightened skill requisites within the industrial milieu. The erstwhile facile transition from agricultural to industrial pursuits, sans substantial investments in supplementary training, has become increasingly untenable.

Globalization has accentuated these challenges, further complicating the plight of low-income nations endeavoring to ingress into a fiercely competitive global manufacturing arena. Rodrik asserts, "It is now well documented that manufacturing has become increasingly skill-intensive in recent decades. Along with globalization, this has made it very difficult for newcomers to break into world markets for manufacturing in a big way and replicate the experience of Asia's manufacturing superstars. Except for a handful of exporters, developing economies have been experiencing premature deindustrialization. It seems as if the escalator has been taken away from the lagging countries." It is plausible that these constraints will persist as binding shackles for the foreseeable future: unless there is a drastic expansion in skills acquisition and training initiatives, the advent of automation and further technological advancements will render it increasingly arduous for today's impoverished nations to traverse the trajectory charted by early industrialized counterparts.

5.3 GLOBAL FOREIGN DIRECT INVESTMENT FLOWS

In the realm of foreign direct investment (FDI), the year 2023 witnessed a modest uptick of 3% compared to its antecedent, reaching an estimated US$1.37 trillion on a global scale. However, this panorama was not uniformly mirrored across all regions; rather, FDI inflows to developing nations encountered a discernible downturn, experiencing a 9% contraction to the tune of US$841 billion. This downturn was notably pronounced in Asia, witnessing a 12% decrease, and in Africa, where it dwindled by 1%. The rationale behind this decline was attributed to economic uncertainty and escalated interest rates. Conversely, FDI in Latin America and the Caribbean remained steadfast, with Central America even counteracting the prevailing downward trajectory.

One sector that underwent a conspicuous downturn was renewable energy, with novel international project finance deals dwindling by 17% in terms of frequency and 10% in value. This decline mirrored the broader downturn in project finance. However, it is imperative to underscore that these figures are estimations and subject to revision as additional data become available.

FDI assumes a pivotal role in the global economic landscape by facilitating the fluidity of capital across borders, thereby buttressing economic growth and development endeavors. It heralds the infusion of novel technology, expertise, and managerial methodologies, while concurrently engendering employment opportunities and galvanizing domestic industries. Nevertheless, the ebb in FDI to developing nations in 2023 begets apprehensions regarding its potential ramifications on their economic advancement and their capacity to attain sustainable growth.

Multiple factors could have contributed to the contraction in FDI flows to developing nations. Economic instability, precipitated by factors such as the lingering COVID-19 pandemic, geopolitical tensions, and trade frictions, may have dissuaded investors from committing to long-term ventures. Additionally, escalated interest rates in certain jurisdictions may have rendered it less enticing for investors to procure funds for investment endeavors.

The downturn in renewable energy project finance deals is also disquieting, indicative of a deceleration in the transition toward a more sustainable and eco-friendly energy paradigm. This could bear implications for endeavors to combat climate change and realize the objectives delineated within the Paris Agreement.

It is incumbent upon policymakers in developing nations to undertake measures aimed at enticing and retaining FDI, given its pivotal role in propelling economic expansion and development. This may entail instituting policies to enhance the business milieu, encompassing measures to curtail bureaucratic hurdles and streamline regulatory frameworks.

Furthermore, investment in infrastructure and education is imperative to nurture a skilled workforce and enhance productivity levels.

While the contraction in FDI flows to developing nations in 2023 is disconcerting, it is imperative to contextualize FDI as merely one facet within the broader economic vista. Policymakers ought to pivot toward fostering an environment conducive to investment and fostering sustainable economic growth and development endeavors (Global Investment Trends Monitor [Foreign Direct Investment in 2023 was weak, with lower flows to developing countries], 2024).

5.4 CONCLUSION

Japan, the USA, and China stand as stalwarts with formidable industrial bases, harnessing highly sophisticated, advanced-level Hi-Tech capabilities. Particularly noteworthy is China's expansive industrial infrastructure, not confined solely to urban landscapes but extending its reach into vast rural terrains, boasting an approximate tally of 58 million SMEs in collaboration with global MNCs. Presently, China's conventional industrial frameworks are swiftly metamorphosing into digital realms. The infusion of digital technology into traditional industries heralds a revolutionary shift in production paradigms, ushering in a new era of efficiency and productivity. This digital revolution casts its profound impact, notably within sectors such as the automotive, electrical machinery, and chemical industries, where digital technologies are redefining manufacturing standards.

This transformative wave is not exclusive to major industries or corporations; rather, it permeates across the entire industrial spectrum. The data flux facilitated by digital technology accentuates productivity, efficiency, and overall performance across state-led public enterprises, cooperatives, communities, and private firms. UNCTAD, relying on the UNCTAD-WTO common dataset on international trade in services, discerned a 3% uptick in worldwide exports of digitally deliverable services in 2022, reaching a formidable USD 3.94 trillion. This denotes a moderation compared to the 16% surge witnessed in 2021 amidst the COVID-19 pandemic. However, the majority of developing nations grapple with inadequate digital infrastructures and financial resources to harness the potential of digitally delivered trade. These nations predominantly adhere to agricultural economies, encompassing emerging nations such as India, South Africa, Russia, Brazil, and Indonesia.

India and Indonesia, with their dense populace, witness a substantial proportion engaged directly or indirectly in rural agricultural economies. The prevalent trends of atomization, digitalization, financialization, corporatization, marketization, privatization, and urbanization within burgeoning economies foster an inevitable "rural–urban migration" surge. Rural agrarian laborers, en masse, migrate alongside their families to urban domains in quest of livelihood opportunities. Traditional unskilled labor faces jeopardy, encountering challenges in securing employment due to automation and the digital paradigm shift. Conventional industries confront closure or stiff competition in both rural and urban precincts, ensnared by the monopolistic clutches of big corporate entities and MNCs dictating natural resource control, production, supply chains, and market dynamics.

Enterprises in the micro, small, and medium-sized categories, historically responsible for generating 70–80% of job opportunities, grapple with the dominance exerted by big corporate entities and MNCs not only in production but also in supply chain management and product distribution through the establishment of malls and superstores across urban landscapes. Consequently, the advent of Hi-Tech, automation (embracing AI), robotics, machine learning, digitalization, and other advanced technological modalities by big corporate entities/MNCs accentuates the phenomenon of deindustrialization. This, in turn, exacerbates unemployment and inflation within developing countries, reflective of an incipient industrial base or the unfulfilled vestiges of the initial industrialization thrust within densely populated, agrarian-dominated, economically disadvantaged, and underdeveloped nations, where poverty remains endemic.

KEYWORDS

- **automation**
- **deindustrialization**
- **digitalization**
- **economies**
- **manufacturing**
- **unemployment**

REFERENCES

Herrendorf, B. R. (2014). Growth and structural transformation. In P. Aghion & S. N. Durlauf (Eds.), *Handbook of economic growth* (Vol. 2). Elsevier.

Lippolis, E. O. O. (2017, October 30). Are emerging economies deindustrializing too quickly? https://ourworldindata.org/growth-and-structural-transformation-are-emerging-economiesindustrializing-too-quickly.

Prabhakar, A. C. (2015a). Evaluation of technology, trade, and inclusive development: Chinese experiences. *Investment Management and Financial Innovations, 12*(3), 180–186.

Prabhakar, A. C. (2015b). A critical appraisal of comparative advantage theory under free market crony capitalism. *Investment Management and Financial Innovations, 12*(3), 93–95.

Rowthorn, R. (1997). *Deindustrialization: Causes and implications: IMF's research department* (IMF Working Paper 97/42). International Monetary Fund.

CHAPTER 6

Self-Reliance and Industrialization Goals: An Unfinished Task

ABSTRACT

This chapter offers a critical interrogation of the enduring impediments and unrealized ambitions surrounding the pursuit of self-reliance and industrialization in developing economies. Notwithstanding decades of targeted policy interventions, strategic planning, and international cooperation, numerous countries across Asia, Africa, and Latin America remain mired in structural dependencies, constrained technological capacities, and underdeveloped industrial infrastructures. The analysis traces the post-independence industrial trajectories of these nations, elucidating the intricate interplay between global economic asymmetries, internal policy deficits, and institutional vulnerabilities. It further scrutinizes the extent to which neoliberal globalization, trade liberalization, and the burden of external debt have curtailed prospects for autonomous industrial development. Through the lens of comparative case studies, this chapter accentuates the imperative for revitalized, state-driven industrial policies, robust investment in indigenous innovation, strengthened regional integration, and a reoriented development paradigm grounded in inclusivity, sustainability, and contextual relevance. The study ultimately posits that the quest for genuine self-reliance remains an unresolved and multifaceted challenge—yet one that is essential for fostering equitable growth and securing long-term economic sovereignty in the Global South.

The BRICS Coalition and a New Global Order: Akhilesh Chandra Prabhakar (Author)
2026 Apple Academic Press, Inc. Co-published with CRC Press (Taylor & Francis)

DOI: 10.1201/9781779642936-6

6.1 INTRODUCTION

The concept of self-reliance and industrialization has long stood as a central pillar for developing nations endeavoring to attain economic sovereignty and minimize dependence on external aid and resources. Rooted in the philosophy of "people-centered development," this paradigm underscores the empowerment of local communities and individuals to steer their own developmental trajectories. While notable advancements have been achieved across various sectors, the quest for genuine self-reliance and comprehensive industrialization remains an elusive goal for many nations.

These twin objectives—self-reliance and industrialization—represent the aspiration for economic autonomy, technological sophistication, and the establishment of resilient industrial systems capable of fostering innovation, productivity, and sustainable growth. For emerging economies, they are not merely aspirations but imperatives to escape the cyclical traps of dependency and marginalization in a competitive global landscape.

Yet, despite decades of progress, the path toward fulfilling these ambitions is fraught with persistent challenges. Inadequate infrastructure, dependence on imported technologies, underfunded research and development, and entrenched global economic dependencies continue to stifle progress. Moreover, the rapid currents of globalization, technological upheavals, and shifting geopolitical realities compound these obstacles, further complicating the realization of these goals.

In this context, the pursuit of self-reliance transcends economic necessity to become a strategic imperative, central to safeguarding national interests in an increasingly interconnected yet volatile global economy. This essay seeks to unravel the intricate nexus between self-reliance and industrialization, delving into historical milestones, enduring challenges, and the adaptive strategies that can propel nations toward completing this unfinished mission.

6.1.1 UNDERSTANDING SELF-RELIANCE AND INDUSTRIALIZATION

Self-reliance denotes a nation's capability to meet its own needs and demands without excessive reliance on external support or assistance. In contrast, industrialization refers to the systematic development of manufacturing and industrial sectors, enhancing production capacity and fostering economic growth. Together, these twin goals embody a transformative vision of economic and societal advancement, particularly for developing nations aspiring to reduce dependency and achieve sustainable progress.

Rooted in the philosophy of "people-centered development," self-reliance emphasizes the role of local communities and individuals as active agents in shaping their developmental trajectories. This approach empowers societies to make decisions that directly impact their lives while strengthening their economic foundations. In tandem, industrialization drives the structural transformation of economies, shifting them from agrarian reliance to diversified industrial and technological frameworks. These concepts are not merely complementary but foundational to achieving resilience and long-term prosperity.

6.1.2 THE CONCEPT OF SELF-RELIANCE

Self-reliance transcends the notion of economic independence; it embodies a nation's ability to harness its resources, foster local innovation, and minimize dependence on external aid. This multifaceted ideal is realized through strategies such as:

1. **Strengthening Domestic Production**: Prioritizing the production of essential goods domestically, particularly in critical sectors such as agriculture, manufacturing, and energy.
2. **Reducing Import Dependency**: Developing local alternatives to imported commodities, thereby conserving foreign exchange reserves and invigorating domestic industries.
3. **Promoting Innovation and Indigenous Technology**: Investing in research and development to craft homegrown solutions tailored to specific local challenges.
4. **Empowering Human Capital**: Prioritizing education, skill development, and community participation to cultivate a capable and innovative workforce.

Self-reliance, however, does not advocate for isolationism. Instead, it seeks a balanced engagement with globalization, enabling nations to participate in international trade while retaining the capacity to sustain themselves in vital areas.

6.2 THE ROLE OF INDUSTRIALIZATION

Industrialization serves as the driving force behind economic modernization and diversification. By transitioning economies from traditional agricultural systems to robust manufacturing and industrial bases, it unlocks a host of transformative benefits:

1. **Economic Diversification**: Reducing excessive reliance on singular economic sectors, such as agriculture or resource extraction, and spreading risk across a broader spectrum of industries.
2. **Technological Advancement**: Facilitating the adoption of modern technologies that enhance productivity, competitiveness, and innovation.
3. **Employment Generation**: Creating vast employment opportunities, particularly in urban areas, while fostering skill acquisition and workforce development.
4. **Infrastructure Development**: Catalyzing improvements in transportation, energy, and communication systems, which further enable economic activities and industrial growth.

6.3 THE INTERDEPENDENCE OF SELF-RELIANCE AND INDUSTRIALIZATION

Self-reliance and industrialization are intrinsically intertwined, each reinforcing the other. A self-reliant nation necessitates a robust industrial base to manufacture essential goods, stimulate innovation, and reduce external dependencies. Conversely, industrialization thrives on the foundations of self-reliance, which mobilizes local resources, skilled labor, and institutional support. Together, they create a self-sustaining cycle of economic stability and growth, equipping nations to withstand external shocks while competing equitably in the global arena.

6.3.1 CHALLENGES TO ACHIEVING SELF-RELIANCE AND INDUSTRIALIZATION

Despite their significance, achieving self-reliance and industrialization presents formidable challenges:

1. **Resource Constraints**: Many developing nations face limited access to capital, raw materials, and skilled labor.
2. **Technological Dependence**: Over-reliance on foreign technologies stymies the development of indigenous innovation.
3. **Global Economic Pressures**: Trade imbalances and entrenched dependencies within global supply chains hinder local development.
4. **Policy and Governance Inefficiencies**: Poor planning, corruption, and bureaucratic hurdles exacerbate developmental delays.

6.4 THE WAY FORWARD

To overcome these obstacles and realize the dual goals of self-reliance and industrialization, nations must adopt integrated and forward-looking strategies:

1. **Investing in Education and Skills**: Building a workforce equipped to meet the demands of modern industries and technologies.
2. **Encouraging Public–Private Partnerships**: Leveraging resources and expertise from both sectors to accelerate industrial growth.
3. **Promoting Indigenous Research and Innovation**: Cultivating a culture of scientific and technological creativity to develop locally tailored solutions.
4. **Fostering Inclusive Development**: Actively involving local communities in the development process to ensure equitable benefits.

Understanding the intricate relationship between self-reliance and industrialization is vital for nations aiming to assert autonomy, uplift living standards, and secure sustainable progress. By addressing persistent challenges and embracing opportunities, these goals hold the potential to transform economies and empower societies in transformative and enduring ways.

6.5 CHALLENGES TO SELF-RELIANCE AND INDUSTRIALIZATION

Despite the significant progress made by many developing countries in recent decades, several challenges persist in achieving self-reliance and industrialization. These challenges include:

1. Economic Dependency: Many developing countries remain heavily reliant on external aid and resources, which can hinder their ability to achieve self-reliance. This dependency can be exacerbated by factors such as debt, trade imbalances, and unequal access to global markets.
2. Lack of Infrastructure: Inadequate infrastructure, including transportation, energy, and communication networks, can limit a country's ability to industrialize and achieve self-reliance. This lack of infrastructure can also hinder the development of rural areas and limit access to basic services such as healthcare and education.
3. Limited Access to Technology: Access to technology is essential for industrialization and economic growth. However, many developing countries lack the necessary infrastructure and resources to adopt and implement new technologies, which can hinder their ability to achieve self-reliance.
4. Political Instability: Political instability and conflict can disrupt development efforts and hinder a country's ability to achieve self-reliance and industrialization. These challenges can be exacerbated by factors such as corruption, weak governance, and lack of political will.
5. Environmental Degradation: Environmental degradation, including deforestation, soil erosion, and water pollution, can undermine efforts to achieve self-reliance and industrialization. These challenges can be exacerbated by factors such as climate change, unsustainable resource use, and lack of environmental regulation.

6.6 REVIEW OF LITERATURE

The pursuit of self-reliance and sustainable industrialization has been extensively explored in academic literature, focusing on the strategic pathways, inherent challenges, and emerging opportunities in the realization of these objectives. This review synthesizes seminal studies that address the interconnections between self-reliance, industrialization, and their alignment with the broader principles of sustainable development.

Conceptual Foundations of Self-Reliance in Industrialization: The concept of self-reliance in industrial development gained prominence in the mid-20th century as newly independent nations sought to break free from colonial dependencies and promote autonomous economic growth. Amin contends that self-reliance is not confined to resource independence; rather, it entails the nurturing of internal capacities in innovation, technology, and governance, enabling nations to design unique development trajectories (Amin, 1990). Sen argues that self-reliance plays a pivotal role in enhancing human capabilities, which, in turn, serve as the bedrock for equitable and sustainable industrial growth (Sen, 1999). Thus, self-reliance is portrayed as a comprehensive framework that extends beyond mere economic independence to encompass broader socio-political dimensions of development.

Sustainable Industrialization—A Synergistic Framework: Sustainable industrialization is conceptualized as the integration of economic, social, and environmental objectives, emphasizing inclusive growth while safeguarding ecological integrity. The United Nations Industrial Development Organization defines sustainable industrialization as the adoption of technologies and practices that minimize environmental impact while enhancing economic resilience (UNIDO, 2018). Sachs underscores the importance of harmonizing industrial policies with the Sustainable Development Goals (SDGs), particularly Goal 9, which advocates for the promotion of inclusive and sustainable industrialization, innovation, and infrastructure (Sachs, 2015). Sustainable industrialization, thus, is not merely an economic imperative but a multidimensional approach that integrates innovation and environmental stewardship.

Self-Reliance through Technology and Innovation: Technological self-reliance is a critical pillar in achieving industrial autonomy and sustainability. Dunning (2000) posits that the development of Indigenous technologies not only reduces reliance on external systems but also fosters adaptability to local contexts, ensuring the sustainability of industrial endeavors. Yao and Zhou reinforce this argument by highlighting China's efforts in cultivating technological self-reliance, which has enabled the nation to strike a balance between rapid economic growth and the imperative of environmental sustainability (Yao, 2020). Technology, therefore, becomes both a tool for self-reliance and a means to achieve industrial sustainability in the global context.

Challenges in Aligning Self-Reliance and Sustainability: The journey toward self-reliant and sustainable industrialization is fraught with numerous challenges, including limited resources, technological gaps, and institutional constraints. Evans identifies that the lack of access to advanced technologies often compels developing nations to adopt practices that, while conducive to short-term industrial growth, may prove environmentally detrimental in the long run (Evans, 2014). Similarly, Dasgupta and Ghosh argue that the path to sustainability in self-reliance demands robust policy frameworks capable of integrating environmental safeguards into industrial strategies (Dasgupta, 2019). The challenge, therefore, lies in reconciling industrial growth with environmental sustainability while ensuring that the benefits of industrialization are broadly distributed.

Policy Interventions and Global Cooperation: Scholarly literature emphasizes the critical role of effective policy frameworks and international cooperation in facilitating self-reliant, sustainable industrialization. Rodrik advocates for adaptive industrial policies that prioritize the development of local capabilities while concurrently drawing from global best practices (Rodrik, 2018). The role of global partnerships, such as those promoted by the Paris Agreement and the SDGs, is deemed essential for providing both technical and financial support to nations pursuing sustainable self-reliance (Meadows et al., 2018) . Thus, global cooperation serves as a complement to national efforts, facilitating the exchange of knowledge and resources vital for sustainable industrialization.

Case Studies: India and China: India and China present contrasting yet instructive case studies in the pursuit of self-reliance and sustainable industrialization. India's strategy emphasizes democratic governance and gradual economic reforms, but its reliance on imported energy and technology remains a significant impediment to full industrial autonomy (Chaturvedi, 2020). On the other hand, China's state-led model has been characterized by rapid industrialization and substantial investments in renewable energy, although concerns persist regarding the social inclusivity of its growth model and the environmental implications of its industrial policies (Liu, 2019). These cases illustrate the diverse pathways nations can adopt in balancing industrial growth, technological self-reliance, and environmental sustainability.

The literature unequivocally highlights that the attainment of self-reliance in industrialization with sustainability is a complex and multi-faceted challenge, demanding a nuanced balance between economic growth, environmental preservation, and social equity. The path forward necessitates the fostering of technological innovation, the strengthening of institutional frameworks, and the promotion of international cooperation. By aligning self-reliance goals with sustainable development objectives, nations can pave the way for resilient and equitable industrial futures.

6.7 STRATEGIES FOR ACHIEVING SELF-RELIANCE AND INDUSTRIALIZATION

To address the challenges of self-reliance and industrialization, developing countries can adopt several strategies:

1. Promoting Local Entrepreneurship: Encouraging local entrepreneurship can help create jobs, increase incomes, and reduce poverty. Governments can support local entrepreneurs by providing access to credit, training, and technical assistance.
2. Investing in Infrastructure: Improving infrastructure, including transportation, energy, and communication networks, can facilitate industrialization and economic growth. Governments can invest in infrastructure projects that benefit local communities and promote sustainable development.
3. Enhancing Access to Technology: Improving access to technology can help developing countries adopt and implement new technologies that support industrialization and economic growth. Governments can support technology transfer and provide incentives for technology adoption.
4. Strengthening Governance: Strengthening governance and promoting transparency and accountability can help address political instability and conflict. Governments can promote good governance practices, such as transparency, accountability, and the rule of law.
5. Promoting Sustainable Development: Promoting sustainable development can help address environmental degradation and support self-reliance and industrialization. Governments can adopt policies that promote sustainable resource use, protect natural ecosystems, and mitigate climate change.

Achieving self-reliance and industrialization is an unfinished task for many developing countries. Despite significant progress in various sectors, several challenges persist, including economic dependency, lack of infrastructure, limited access to technology, political instability, and environmental degradation. To address these challenges, developing countries can adopt several strategies, including promoting local entrepreneurship, investing in infrastructure, enhancing access to technology, strengthening governance, and promoting sustainable development. By implementing these strategies, developing countries can achieve true self-reliance and industrialization and improve the well-being of their populations.

The pursuit of self-reliance in developing countries is a multifaceted endeavor that encompasses a range of economic, social, and developmental aspects. At its core, self-reliance refers to a nation's ability to meet its own needs without excessive reliance on external aid or resources. Achieving self-reliance is widely considered a crucial step toward sustainable development, as it empowers countries to control their destinies, reduce vulnerability, and build resilience.

Here are some key aspects and benefits associated with the pursuit of self-reliance in developing countries:

1. Economic Independence: Developing countries strive to diversify their economies, reducing dependence on a few key sectors. A diversified economy is more resilient to external shocks.

2. Financial Sustainability: A focus on self-reliance involves managing and reducing external debt, ensuring that a country's financial obligations are sustainable.

3. Innovation and Technology Transfer: Self-reliant nations invest in research and development to foster innovation and technological advancements, reducing reliance on foreign technologies.

4. Human Capital Development: Developing a skilled and educated workforce is crucial for self-reliance. It enables nations to meet their labor needs domestically and reduces dependence on foreign expertise.

5. Infrastructure Development: Investing in robust infrastructure is essential for self-reliance. Adequate infrastructure supports economic activities and reduces dependence on external sources for essential services.

6. Agricultural Self-Sufficiency: Achieving self-sufficiency in food production is a common goal. This involves promoting sustainable agriculture practices, improving productivity, and reducing reliance on food imports.
7. Healthcare and Social Services: Building strong healthcare systems ensures that countries can address health challenges internally, reducing the need for extensive external assistance during crises.
8. Environmental Sustainability: Self-reliance involves sustainable management of natural resources, ensuring that a country can meet its needs without depleting essential resources.
9. Political and Governance Stability: Developing strong institutions and governance structures is vital for self-reliance. Stable political environments foster economic growth and development.
10. Trade and Economic Partnerships: While pursuing self-reliance, countries also engage in mutually beneficial economic partnerships. This involves fair trade agreements and collaborations that enhance economic growth.
11. Resilience to External Shocks: Self-reliant nations are better prepared to handle economic downturns, natural disasters, or global crises without suffering severe consequences.
12. Cultural Preservation: As countries develop, they often seek to preserve and promote their cultural heritage, ensuring that economic progress does not come at the expense of cultural diversity.
13. Challenges and Considerations: Achieving self-reliance is a complex and long-term process that requires careful planning and execution. It may involve overcoming historical legacies, systemic challenges, and global economic inequalities. Balancing self-reliance with international collaboration is essential for addressing global challenges that require collective efforts.

The industrialization process remains an unfinished task in developing countries, despite abundant natural resources, technological advancement, and wealth creation (except in emerging countries like China). The majority of Asian, African, and Latin American countries have not completed even the first phase of industrialization, making self-reliance goals far from reach. Africa is particularly marginalized in this regard. Among the eighteen independent nations located in the Pacific Ocean, including Australia, Fiji, Japan, Kiribati, Marshall Islands, Micronesia, Nauru, New Zealand, Palau, Solomon Island, and Papua New Guinea, along with twenty-three (23) member countries of the Indian Ocean Rim Association, including Australia, Bangladesh, Comoros, France, India, Indonesia, Iran, Kenya, Madagascar, Malaysia, Maldives, Mauritius, Mozambique, Oman, Seychelles, Singapore, Somalia, South Africa, Sri Lanka, Tanzania, Thailand, United Arab Emirates (UAE), and Yemen (excluding Japan, Singapore, and Australia), have not achieved industrialization.

The Indo-Pacific region, which spans the Pacific Rim, Southeast Asia, South Asia, West Asia, and Eastern and Southern Africa, covering about 2.5 billion (64%) of the global population in its member states, faces challenges such as unemployment, inflation, economic deficiencies, heavy debt burdens, poverty, malnutrition, and heavy dependence on Western countries for foreign direct investment (FDI), foreign aid, technology, and foreign currency like the dollar to correct their imbalances of payments and trade. This indicates that since gaining political independence, developing countries' economic and trade linkages have continued with their former colonial masters' countries, which are referred to as "colonial legacies." Without breaking down or delinking from these existing colonial practices, achieving the goals of self-reliance in developing countries is almost impossible. This is evident in the patterns of unequal relationships between Core Nations and Periphery and Semi-Periphery Nations.

6.8 CONTRADICTORY ARGUMENTS SURROUNDING POPULATION AND INDUSTRIALIZATION

There is a common argument that a vast population poses a burden and creates barriers to industrial development. However, this is not entirely true. For instance, China, a country with a vast population, has efficiently mobilized and utilized its workforce, leading to significant industrial development over the past few decades. This has also resulted in poverty reduction and the resolution of issues related to backwardness and unemployment. According to a report released by the United Nations on

November 15, 2022, the global population has reached 8 billion, and it is projected that India will surpass China in population size by 2023. The UN report suggests that the global population could grow to around 8.5 billion by 2030, 9.7 billion by 2050, and it could peak at around 10.4 billion between 2080 and 2100. More than half of this projected population growth will be concentrated in eight countries: India, Pakistan, the Philippines, Ethiopia, Congo, Egypt, Nigeria, and Tanzania. Sub-Saharan African (SSA) countries are expected to be the center of population growth by 2050.

Liu Zhenmin, the UN Under-Secretary-General for Economic and Social Affairs, argues that rapid population growth poses a barrier to achieving the industrialization process and ultimately achieving self-reliance. He emphasizes that achieving the SDGs, such as eradicating poverty, combating hunger and malnutrition, and improving health and education systems, are major challenges in developing and poor countries. The COVID-19 pandemic has also had a significant impact on global life expectancy, child mortality rates, and the sustainability of social security and pension systems.

The era of Western imperialist-dominated globalization is coming to an end. Since the 1990s, globalization, led by Big Tech and Big Financial Houses, has made developing economies more open to FDI from multinational companies seeking to extract natural resources, access cheap labor, or circumvent import barriers. However, it is important to note that this form of globalization has often been exploitative and has not necessarily led to sustainable development in developing countries (Imbun, 2006).

The ocean has been a contentious zone, with major superpowers such as the USA, the UK, France, Germany, Japan, and Australia closely monitoring the Pacific's richly endowed basin, which includes oil, gas, gold, copper, silver, and other natural minerals and mining resources. Emerging influential economic and military players like China, Russia, India, and now Iran are also resisting and countering the USA and its strategic allies' military influences. These conflicting forces have created a volatile nature of "geopolitical" strategic games aimed at controlling ocean routes for international trade and business, as well as securing abundant natural resources such as oil and gas reserves, fisheries, and for security purposes.

Periphery and semi-periphery developing countries, including South Pacific nations like Papua New Guinea, primarily supply raw materials to core nations like the USA, European countries, Australia, England, and

Japan. These core nations then manufacture these raw materials into final products and export them, along with capital goods, to the periphery and semi-periphery nations. This inter-relationship is referred to as "unequal patterns of trade." Thousands of Western multinational corporations (MNCs) and their branches (outsourcing companies) operate in East Asia, Southeast Asia, West Asia, South Asia, and Africa. For example, more than fifty thousand MNCs are operating in India, where they control natural resources, exploit cheap labor, and dominate the markets. Consequently, local domestic industries, particularly small- and medium-sized enterprises (SMEs and MSMEs), struggle to compete with these large MNCs due to a lack of financial capital, hybrid technology, and marketing networks. SMEs face challenges such as access to markets, training, financial resources, capacity building, excessive bureaucracy, high taxes, and complex legal frameworks, all of which hinder their efficient operation and limit their growth potential.

In the present day, China is actively countering Western influences worldwide, including in Africa, Latin America, Asia, and the South Pacific region. For instance, the Solomon Islands serve as a prime example, where China has not only established a military base but also invested significantly in infrastructural development projects such as roads, bridges, airports, and seaports. The geopolitical strategic partnerships in the South Pacific region must be analyzed from the perspective of the South Pacific Islands, examining what can be referred to as the "Washington Consensus" versus the "Beijing Consensus."

The views of the people of the South Pacific Islands are varied and complex. One narrative argues that China's engagement with the South Pacific region is positive, serving as a means to counter the influence of the Western former colonial powers and supporting the historical independence movements of the people against Western colonialism/imperialism. Another narrative suggests that China's involvement in the region, as per the "Beijing Consensus," is motivated solely by its narrow economic interests and could potentially lead to the reversal of democratic and human rights gains in the region.

The first narrative asserts that China provides unconditional developmental financial aid, concessional loans/debt to the region, and technology transfers on a complementary basis, with a commitment to neutrality in the domestic affairs of the South Pacific Island countries. However, the historical colonial legacies persist since independence, continuously interlinked with the economic sectors, including international trade. This Western influence is still present due to the "dual characters" of the ruling class, comprising the domestic comprador bourgeoisie and their petty traders bourgeoisie. Additionally, postcolonial Australian military presence and a colonial mindset, exemplified by donor dependency or economic, financial, and technological dependencies on others, have influenced the local people's values and norms, impacting their life approaches.

Africa possesses 60% of the world's unexploited arable land and abundant mineral resources, offering vast potential for green growth. These resources must be utilized for sustainable and inclusive development, with an emphasis on increasing green finance or green investments. The large areas of virgin land can be used to build low-carbon infrastructure without incurring large-scale expenditure.

According to the World Bank's 2023 report, economic growth in SSA slowed to 3.6% in 2022 from 4.1% in 2021, with further projections indicating a slowdown to 3.1% in 2023. In Western and Central Africa, GDP growth is estimated to decline to 3.4% in 2023 from 3.7% in 2022, while in Eastern and Southern Africa, it is expected to decline to 3.0% in 2023 from 3.5% in 2022. Growth across SSA continues to be sluggish, influenced by global economic uncertainty, underperforming large economies, high inflation, and a significant deceleration of investment growth.

The world has experienced significant economic and trade shocks, including disruptions in global supply chains (particularly in food and energy supplies) due to the COVID-19 pandemic and subsequent lockdowns, the war between Russia and NATO in Ukraine and Palestine, a global economic recession, and climate change. For instance, the World Bank has estimated that global economic growth will average 2.9%, with Europe at 1.1%, Asia at 4.3% (with China and India as major contributors), and Africa's economic growth declining from 4.1% in 2021 to 3.8% in 2022 to 3.1% in 2023, before climbing to 4.1% in 2024. Countries such as China, India, Russia, Iran, and Saudi Arabia possess the capacity to support other countries in Asia, Latin America, and Africa through technology transfer and financial investment funding to enhance capacity-building in physical and digital infrastructures for green growth, including abundant renewable energy sources, fostering a mutually beneficial relationship.

Economic players and policymakers should focus on boosting domestic resource mobilization, restraining inflation, reducing debt distress, and increasing domestic demand and supply to stabilize macroeconomic stability. Rapid global decarbonization presents significant economic opportunities for the South Pacific Indo-Pacific regions, Africa, Asia, and Latin America. The increased demand for metals and minerals for low-carbon technologies like batteries, coupled with appropriate policies, could boost fiscal revenues, create job opportunities through regional value chains, and accelerate economic transformation. Maximizing government revenues from natural resources would offer a dual benefit by increasing fiscal space and removing implicit production subsidies (Enoghase, 2023).

6.9 SOCIAL ENTREPRENEURSHIP DEVELOPMENT TO ACHIEVE "SELF-RELIANCE" GOAL

Social entrepreneurship is an emerging field that combines business principles with social goals. It involves the use of innovative business models to address social and environmental challenges, with the aim of creating positive social change and achieving SDGs. Social entrepreneurs leverage market-based approaches to create solutions to social problems, often focusing on marginalized communities or underserved markets.

The concept of social entrepreneurship is rooted in the idea that businesses can be a force for good, and that social and environmental issues can be addressed through market-driven solutions. Social entrepreneurs seek to create sustainable business models that generate both financial and social values, often using their profits to reinvest in their social mission.

6.10 THE PRINCIPLES OF SOCIAL ENTREPRENEURSHIP

1. Social Impact: Social entrepreneurs prioritize social impact over profit, seeking to create positive change in society. They measure their success not only in terms of financial returns but also in terms of the impact they have on the lives of the people they serve.
2. Innovation: Social entrepreneurs are often innovators, developing new approaches to solving social problems. They may use technology, business models, or other tools to create scalable and sustainable solutions.

3. Collaboration: Social entrepreneurship often involves collaboration with other organizations, including government agencies, nonprofits, and businesses. Social entrepreneurs recognize that complex social problems require collective action, and they work to build partnerships and networks to achieve their goals.
4. Sustainability: Social entrepreneurs aim to create sustainable solutions to social problems, both in terms of environmental sustainability and financial sustainability. They seek to create businesses that can generate revenue and support their social mission in the long term.
5. Empowerment: Social entrepreneurs empower individuals and communities to take control of their own destinies. They seek to build the capacity of people to solve their own problems, rather than providing handouts or temporary solutions.

Overall, social entrepreneurship is a dynamic and evolving field that seeks to harness the power of business to create positive social change. It is driven by a commitment to social impact, innovation, collaboration, sustainability, and empowerment.

Self-reliance is a critical goal for developing countries, as it enables them to meet their economic, social, and developmental needs without excessive dependence on external aid, resources, or support. Achieving self-reliance is often seen as a crucial step toward sustainable development, as it empowers nations to control their destinies, reduce vulnerability, and build resilience. However, achieving self-reliance is a complex and multifaceted process that requires careful planning and execution. In this essay, we will explore the role of social entrepreneurship in driving self-reliance in developing countries.

6.11 SOCIAL ENTREPRENEURSHIP AND SELF-RELIANCE

Social entrepreneurship refers to the use of innovative business models to address social and environmental challenges. Social entrepreneurs leverage market-based approaches to create sustainable solutions to social problems, often focusing on marginalized communities or underserved markets. Social entrepreneurship has gained prominence in recent years as a powerful tool for driving positive social change and achieving SDGs.

Social entrepreneurship has the potential to play a significant role in driving self-reliance in developing countries. By empowering local communities to address their own social and economic challenges, social entrepreneurs can help reduce dependence on external aid and support. Social enterprises can also generate income and create jobs, contributing to economic growth and self-sufficiency.

In short, social entrepreneurship has the potential to play a significant role in driving self-reliance in developing countries. By empowering local communities to address their own social and economic challenges, social entrepreneurs can help reduce dependence on external aid and support. Social enterprises can also generate income and create jobs, contributing to economic growth and self-sufficiency. However, achieving self-reliance is a complex and multifaceted process that requires careful planning and execution. Social entrepreneurship is just one piece of the puzzle, and a holistic approach is needed to achieve SDGs.

Sustainability fundamentally hinges on a people-centered development model, epitomized by the networking of big-medium-small medium-sized villages (NBMS). Rural areas ought to be galvanized by the establishment of "production units" and the formation of production–distribution–consumption networks from the grassroots to the top (e.g., local to regional to global) levels. This model should be grounded in "people's science and techniques," facilitated by area-based organizations of the existing occupational rural populace, functioning as "community-based" production units.

It is feasible to create a viable, district-wide large-scale production system network for the rural poor based on local resources, capabilities, and markets through suitable organizational and S&T initiatives. This can be achieved if the rural poor are mobilized to strengthen their interconnections and advance the local economy by encouraging local value addition through the integration of primary and secondary production and the technological modernization of existing occupations. It is imperative to eschew mutual competition among small producers and to prioritize superior access to resources, markets, and technology transfer to organize landless laborers, artisans, and impoverished peasants for area-based multisectoral large-scale production systems.

Under competitive circumstances, self-employed small producers not only need to unite for resource access but also have to evolve into a multisectoral collective of producers, cooperating in production. Given that economies of scale are indispensable to surmount adverse competition, the rural poor must be consciously networked and technologically advanced in a mutually complementary manner. They need to pool their resources and capabilities to elevate the scale and scope of their collective production organization.

This augmentation in scale and scope can alone enable the participating members to diminish the barriers impeding them in the creation and adoption of more sophisticated and improved technologies that can render their production more competitive than before in local markets. The local economy operates as a taluka-wide, multisectoral network.

In the local economy, the range of occupations engaging the rural poor is extensive and diverse. It encompasses agricultural labor, small/marginal cultivators, hides and skins occupations spanning flaying, cloth weaving, dyeing, and printing; fiber collection/extraction, basket, and mat weaving; animal husbandry, poultry, fishing, etc., and allied secondary processing like food processing; carpentry, and other engineering artisans, or handicraft occupations. The networks of group enterprises comprising rural poor can be constructed around the principle of worker cooperatives, that is, worker ownership, collective appropriation of surplus, and full participation in decision-making.

6.12 CASE STUDY: GRAMEEN BANK

One of the most well-known examples of social entrepreneurship is the Grameen Bank, founded by Nobel laureate Muhammad Yunus in Bangladesh. The Grameen Bank pioneered the concept of microfinance, providing small loans to poor individuals and entrepreneurs who lack access to traditional banking services. By empowering individuals to start their own businesses and generate income, the Grameen Bank has helped lift millions of people out of poverty and achieve self-reliance.

The Grameen Bank's model has been replicated in many other countries, demonstrating the potential of social entrepreneurship to drive positive social change and economic development. By providing access to financial services and business support, social enterprises like the Grameen Bank can help individuals and communities build their own pathways to self-reliance.

6.13 SUMMING UP

It is true that the global consensus on the importance of self-reliance and industrialization for the advancement of developing and least-developed countries is still relevant today. Despite significant progress in various areas, many developing countries continue to face challenges in achieving true self-reliance and industrialization. These challenges include economic dependency, lack of infrastructure, limited access to technology, political instability, and environmental degradation.

It is important to note that the concept of self-reliance and industrialization has evolved over time. Initially, the emphasis was on achieving economic independence and reducing reliance on external aid and resources. However, as the understanding of development has evolved, there has been a greater focus on people's centered development, which emphasizes the importance of empowering local communities and individuals to drive their own development processes.

The global consensus on the importance of self-reliance and industrialization is reflected in various international agreements and initiatives. For example, the United Nations SDGs include targets related to economic growth, industrialization, and innovation. Similarly, the African Union's Agenda 2063 aims to achieve economic transformation and industrialization in Africa.

Despite the global consensus on the importance of self-reliance and industrialization, there is still much work to be done. Many developing countries continue to face significant challenges in achieving these goals, and there is a need for continued international cooperation and support to address these challenges. Additionally, it is important to recognize that self-reliance and industrialization are not ends in themselves but are means to achieve broader development goals, including poverty reduction, environmental sustainability, and social inclusion.

Developing countries can achieve the goal of self-reliance through inclusive and sustainable economic development. To achieve this, they must focus on building their internal resilience capacity, promoting wealth generation with job creation, and maintaining their biodiversity and ecosystems. They can reduce dependency on imported goods and services by expanding marine biotechnology, aquaculture, and renewable energy, while also focusing on sustainable business models that can create significant economic opportunities and millions of jobs.

However, achieving these goals requires significant investment in green finance and technology. Countries like India and China have the capacity to contribute to this effort by investing in infrastructure and transferring technology to other developing regions, including Africa, Asia, and the Pacific Islands. This investment and technology transfer can help these regions achieve self-reliance and meet the SDGs while also promoting sustainability and environmental preservation.

KEYWORDS

- **developing countries**
- **global consensus**
- **green growth**
- **industrialization**
- **self-reliance**
- **social entrepreneurship**

REFERENCES

Amin, S. (1990). *Delinking: Towards a polycentric world.* Zed Books.

Chaturvedi, S. A. (2020). Sustainable industrialization and energy systems transformation in India. *Energy Policy, 147*(111849).

Dasgupta, S. A. (2019). Environmental policy integration and sustainable development: An assessment of India's industrial sector. *Journal of Environmental Management, 243*, 81-89.

Evans, P. (2014). *Embedded autonomy: States and industrial transformation.* Princeton University Press.

Liu, W. W. (2019). Industrial policy, environmental sustainability and socioeconomic outcomes: Evidence from China. *Ecological Economics, 165*(106418).

Meadows, D., Randers, J., & Meadows, D. (2018). *The limits to growth: The 30-year update*. Chelsea Green Publishing.

Organization. (2018). *Sustainable Industrialization with appropriate technological adoptation.* UNIDO.

Rodrik, D. (2018). Premature deindustrialization. *Journal of Economic Growth, 21*(1), 1-33.

Sachs, J. D. (2015). *The age of sustainable development.* Columbia University Press.

Sen, A. (1999). *Development as freedom*. Oxford University Press.

UNIDO. (2018). Industrial development report 2018: Demand for manufacturing. United Nations. https://www.unido.org/resources-publications-flagship-publications-industrial-development-report/idr2018.

Yao, Y. A. (2020). Technological self-reliance and environmental sustainability: The dual challenge in China's industrial sectors. *Technological Forecasting and Social Change*, *158*(120142).

CHAPTER 7

BRICS: Emerging as an Alternative Global Financial System in the 21st Century

ABSTRACT

This chapter undertakes a critical examination of BRICS as an emergent counterweight to the Western-centric global financial architecture of the 21st century. In response to deepening discontent with the structural inequities embedded in the Bretton Woods institutions, the BRICS coalition—comprising Brazil, Russia, India, China, and South Africa—has articulated a cohesive agenda aimed at redefining the parameters of global economic governance. Through strategic undertakings, such as the New Development Bank (NDB), the Contingent Reserve Arrangement (CRA), and concerted moves toward the de-dollarization of trade, BRICS aspires to undermine the entrenched dominance of the U.S. dollar and ameliorate the systemic vulnerabilities disproportionately affecting developing economies. This study rigorously interrogates the structural dynamics, geopolitical motivations, and institutional mechanisms underpinning the bloc's financial initiatives, while critically engaging with the internal asymmetries and divergent national interests that challenge its coherence. Employing an interdisciplinary analytical framework, this chapter contends that although BRICS has yet to fully materialize a comprehensive alternative financial order, its evolving institutional architecture signifies a meaningful, albeit gradual, and contested departure from unipolar financial hegemony. Ultimately, the BRICS financial agenda reflects an incipient paradigmatic shift toward enhanced strategic autonomy,

The BRICS Coalition and a New Global Order: Akhilesh Chandra Prabhakar (Author)
2026 Apple Academic Press, Inc. Co-published with CRC Press (Taylor & Francis)

DOI: 10.1201/9781779642936-7

systemic resilience, and deepened South–South financial cooperation in the evolving global economic landscape.

7.1 INTRODUCTION

The 21st century has witnessed a profound reconfiguration of the global economic architecture, steadily eroding the longstanding dominance of Western-led financial institutions. The 2025 BRICS Summit, convened in Rio de Janeiro, Brazil, marked a critical inflection point in the ongoing geopolitical and economic realignment at the global level. The summit convened the five founding members—Brazil, Russia, India, China, and South Africa—alongside 21 new members, collectively representing over 40% of global GDP and more than 55% of the world's population (Ravi, 2025). This expansion underscores the bloc's intensifying capacity to challenge the entrenched hegemony of Western powers, notably the G7 countries, whose combined GDP contribution now constitutes less than 29% of the global total. BRICS, consequently, emerges as a formidable multipolar alternative, advocating a reconfiguration of global governance based on South–South cooperation and equitable representation (D'Auria, 2025).

One of the most salient manifestations of this transformation is the exponential growth in intra-BRICS trade, which has recently surpassed the $1 trillion threshold, signaling a strategic decoupling from the legacy of Western-dominated trade regimes. This shift reflects a deliberate reorientation toward enhancing economic interdependence among emerging economies, reinforcing a South–South paradigm of collaboration. As of June 2025, global trade volumes reached an unprecedented $33 trillion, with approximately 46% of cross-border transactions bypassing reliance on the U.S. dollar, thereby evidencing a move toward de-dollarization (Stimson Center, 2025).

The summit further evidenced an intensification of strategic alliances, accelerated intra-bloc commercial exchanges, and deepened financial integration. Institutional mechanisms, such as the New Development Bank (NDB) exemplify BRICS's evolution from a loose grouping to a cohesive institutional actor with substantive operational capacity. Established to promote infrastructure development and foster financial resilience, the NDB has cumulatively approved loans exceeding $40 billion since inception. In tandem, BRICS members have initiated concrete frameworks facilitating trade settlements in local currencies, a strategic effort aimed at mitigating dependence on the U.S. dollar-dominated financial architecture (Press India, 2025).

The 2025 Rio de Janeiro BRICS Summit illuminated the bloc's strategic vision of a multipolar world order predicated on inclusive, equitable, and sustainable development. Through a combination of expanded membership, economic integration, and financial institution-building, BRICS continues to recalibrate the architecture of global finance and diplomacy, positioning itself as a central agent in shaping the trajectory of international relations in the 21st century.

Founded in 2006 to promote cooperation among emerging economies and amplify their collective voice, BRICS has transitioned from a loosely connected grouping to a dynamic platform poised to reshape the global financial landscape. The establishment of key mechanisms such as the New Development Bank (NDB) in 2015 and the Contingent Reserve Arrangement (CRA) reflects the bloc's commitment to creating alternatives to Western-dominated institutions like the International Monetary Fund (IMF) and the World Bank. These initiatives address critical developmental gaps by fostering financial inclusivity, mitigating liquidity risks, and challenging the conditionalities often imposed by traditional lenders.

Amid escalating geopolitical tensions and economic fragmentation, BRICS has further solidified its role as a champion of multipolarity and economic sovereignty. The bloc's push for South–South cooperation, financial integration, and infrastructure development is not merely a response to entrenched financial hierarchies but a forward-looking strategy to establish a more resilient global economic order. Notably, BRICS nations have intensified efforts to reduce dependency on the U.S. dollar in international trade by promoting local currency transactions. This move underscores their aspiration for greater financial autonomy while offering a replicable model for other emerging economies.

BRICS' vision transcends its member states, resonating deeply with developing countries that seek to challenge traditional dependencies and reimagine the global financial system. The coalition's focus on sustainable growth, fairness, and shared prosperity positions it as a blueprint for redefining international finance in the 21st century. As BRICS continues to expand its influence, its initiatives signify not only a recalibration of economic power but also a commitment to fostering a global financial order that is inclusive, balanced, and attuned to the aspirations of the Global South.

This vision, rooted in principles of equity and partnership, signals a paradigmatic shift in global economic governance, laying the groundwork for a multipolar financial system better equipped to address the diverse challenges of the modern world. Through its strategic initiatives and advocacy for systemic reform, BRICS is carving out a critical role in shaping the contours of the 21st century global economic landscape.

7.2 SURVEY OF LITERATURE

The BRICS coalition—composed of Brazil, Russia, India, China, and South Africa—has gained significant scholarly attention for its emergence as an alternative to the established global financial system, largely represented by the IMF and the World Bank. These institutions, while foundational to post-World War II global financial governance, have faced criticism for policies that many argue serve Western interests, often at odds with the developmental priorities of emerging economies (Armijo, 2014). In response, BRICS has pursued a distinctive vision of an inclusive, equity-driven financial framework that advocates for regional autonomy and reimagines the international economic order.

Central to BRICS' strategy is the NDB, inaugurated in 2015. Scholars argue that the NDB is emblematic of BRICS' intent to challenge the Western-dominated financial system by offering development funding without the stringent conditionality typically imposed by institutions like the IMF and World Bank (Huang, 2018). This alternative model is particularly geared toward infrastructure development and sustainable growth, presenting an innovative and responsive financing mechanism that empowers BRICS members and allies. The NDB as a symbol of the shifting paradigms in global development financing, with BRICS actively striving to build a more balanced and equitable financial order (Griffith-Jones, 2016).

In addition to the NDB, the CRA provides a currency reserve pool among BRICS nations, designed to enhance financial stability and resilience during times of economic turbulence. Helleiner (2022) argues that the CRA reflects BRICS' commitment to a cooperative safety net that minimizes reliance on the IMF, fostering a new model of financial solidarity and resilience. Through the CRA, BRICS members can provide each other with emergency liquidity, which reduces exposure to the risks and political conditions associated with traditional IMF-led assistance programs.

BRICS has also promoted initiatives to diversify the global currency system, with a specific focus on decreasing dependency on the U.S. dollar. By facilitating intra-BRICS trade in local currencies, the coalition seeks to limit its vulnerability to dollar fluctuations and expand its financial sovereignty (Otero-Iglesias, 2019). Farooqui contends that this currency diversification effort is pivotal to BRICS' mission of advancing a multipolar financial landscape (Farooqui, 2021). This approach not only strengthens internal economic resilience but also serves as a model for other emerging markets seeking to reduce their dollar reliance and pursue greater monetary independence.

Moreover, BRICS' alternative financial model has implications that extend beyond its own members. The NDB's inclusion of non-BRICS countries as potential members illustrates its broad vision for a cooperative global financial framework, one that fosters development without the economic and political strings attached to Western-led institutions. Stuenkel interprets this inclusion as BRICS' commitment to supporting emerging economies globally, encouraging a more equitable financial system that fosters stability and growth through partnership rather than conditional aid (Stuenkel, 2020).

The literature reflects that BRICS, through the NDB, CRA, and currency diversification efforts, has strategically positioned itself as an alternative to the established financial order. This coalition not only empowers emerging economies with enhanced financial autonomy but also presents a challenge to the status quo by advocating for an inclusive, multipolar financial system. As BRICS continues to evolve and expand its influence, its alternative financial architecture may increasingly shape the future of international finance, advancing a model rooted in mutual benefit, inclusivity, and shared development.

7.3 DE-DOLLARIZATION INITIATIVES AND TRADING CAMPAIGNS BY BRICS: A STRATEGIC SHIFT IN THE GLOBAL FINANCIAL LANDSCAPE

In the evolving global financial order, BRICS nations—Brazil, Russia, India, China, and South Africa—have emerged as formidable proponents of economic sovereignty through their concerted efforts to de-dollarize. These initiatives, aimed at reducing reliance on the U.S. dollar for trade and financial transactions, reflect the bloc's strategic vision to mitigate systemic vulnerabilities, such as exchange rate volatility, sanctions-related risks, and dependencies on Western-led financial institutions. These efforts form a pivotal component of BRICS' broader ambition to establish a multipolar, equitable, and resilient financial system.

7.3.1 MOTIVATIONS FOR DE-DOLLARIZATION

The dominance of the U.S. dollar as the global reserve and trade currency has imposed systemic risks on emerging economies:

1. Sanction Vulnerabilities: The imposition of economic sanctions, particularly on Russia, has illuminated the geopolitical risks associated with dollar-centric trade mechanisms.
2. Exchange Rate Volatility: The dollar's fluctuations disrupt trade balances, fiscal stability, and growth trajectories in economies dependent on it for international transactions.
3. Policy Asymmetry: The U.S. Federal Reserve's monetary policies disproportionately affect global markets, often disadvantaging emerging economies.

Recognizing these challenges, BRICS nations have embarked on a series of initiatives to secure greater financial sovereignty and reduce exposure to the structural vulnerabilities inherent in a dollar-dominated system.

7.4 KEY DE-DOLLARIZATION INITIATIVES

1. Local Currency Trade Mechanisms: BRICS countries have increasingly utilized local currencies for bilateral and multilateral trade. Notable agreements between China and Russia, India and Russia, and other intra-BRICS arrangements underscore the viability of bypassing the dollar in critical economic transactions. This strategy reduces costs associated with currency conversions and minimizes exposure to dollar-induced economic shocks.
2. Alternative Payment Systems: CIPS (China's Cross-Border Interbank Payment System): Designed as an alternative to SWIFT,

CIPS facilitates transactions in the Chinese yuan and is steadily gaining global acceptance.

3. BRICS Payment Network: Proposed as a unified platform for cross-border transactions among member states, this initiative seeks to enhance financial autonomy by reducing dependence on Western-controlled payment systems.
4. Development of a BRICS Currency: The creation of a unified BRICS currency represents a long-term strategic objective aimed at challenging the dollar's dominance. By providing a common medium for trade and financial transactions, such a currency could bolster intra-BRICS trade, enhance financial integration, and mitigate exchange rate risks.
5. Expansion of the NDB: The NDB has increasingly extended loans in local currencies, significantly reducing reliance on dollar-denominated debt. This approach aligns with BRICS' commitment to promoting sustainable economic growth while circumventing the conditionalities often associated with Western-lending institutions.

7.5 CAMPAIGNS FOR TRADE INTEGRATION

1. Strengthening Intra-BRICS Trade: Efforts to enhance trade within the bloc focus on key sectors such as energy, infrastructure, and technology. Agreements to settle trade in local currencies have fostered greater economic interdependence and resilience within BRICS.
2. Expanding Partnerships with the Global South: BRICS has proactively engaged emerging economies and regional blocs across Africa, Latin America, and Southeast Asia. These partnerships extend the reach of de-dollarization efforts, fostering a coalition of nations advocating for financial systems that better serve their developmental needs.
3. Energy and Commodity Settlements: Yuan-Denominated Oil Trade: China's use of the yuan in energy transactions, particularly with Russia and the Middle East, underscores its role in diversifying financial flows.

4. Gold-Backed Trade Settlements: Russia has championed gold-backed transactions as a secure alternative to dollar-denominated trade.

7.6 CHALLENGES AND OPPORTUNITIES

BRICS' de-dollarization initiatives have gained traction, but they face significant hurdles:

1. Logistical Complexities: Transitioning from entrenched dollar-centric systems to alternative frameworks necessitates substantial infrastructural and regulatory reforms.
2. Geopolitical Resistance: Western powers, especially the United States, may view these initiatives as a direct threat to their economic dominance and respond with countermeasures.
3. Economic Divergences: Disparities in economic structures, monetary policies, and financial systems among BRICS nations complicate the implementation of unified strategies.

Nevertheless, the bloc's efforts to foster a multipolar financial order signify a transformative moment in global economics. By championing South–South cooperation, advancing financial integration, and promoting innovative trade mechanisms, BRICS is laying the groundwork for a resilient and equitable financial architecture.

7.7 CONCLUSION

BRICS' de-dollarization strategy embodies the aspirations of emerging economies to assert greater sovereignty and influence in shaping the future of international finance. By challenging entrenched financial hierarchies, fostering alternatives to the dollar, and enhancing financial integration, BRICS is not merely reshaping its own economic landscape but also offering a compelling vision for a more balanced and inclusive global financial order.

Through its efforts, BRICS continues to position itself as a pivotal force in redefining the 21st century global financial architecture, paving the way for a system that better reflects the economic realities and aspirations of the Global South.

KEYWORDS

- **commodity**
- **dollarization**
- **economy**
- **equity**
- **financial**
- **trade**
- **vision**
- **vulnerability**

REFERENCES

Armijo, L. E. (2014). The BRICS countries as analytical category: Mirage or insight? *Review of International Political Economy*, *21*(4), 969–1000.

D'Auria, M. (2025, July 6). The 17th BRICS summit: Strengthening global south cooperation for more inclusive and sustainable governance. https://brics.br/en/news/brics-summit-signs-historic-commitment-in-rio-for-more-inclusive.

Farooqui, S. (2021). Currency diversification and BRICS: Towards multipolar financial architecture. *Journal of Global Finance*, *12*(2), 45–61.

Griffith-Jones, S. A. (2016). The new development bank. *Global Policy*, *7*(2), 283–291.

Huang, Y. (2018). The rise of the "BRICS Development Bank" and Africa's new resource curse. *Global Policy*, *9*(4), 501–510.

Otero-Iglesias, M. (2019). BRICS and the politics of multipolarity: Currency diversification and financial sovereignty. *International Affairs*, *95*(3), 641–659.

Press India. (2025, July 6). *BRICS Rio de Janeiro declaration.* https://www.pib.gov.in/PressReleasePage.aspx?PRID=2142786.

Ravi, V. (2025, July 10). BRICS summit 2025: Highlights and strategic priorities. https://vajiramandravi.com/upsc-exam/brics-summit-2025/.

Stimson Center. (2025, August 3). 2025 BRICS summit: Takeaways and projections. https://www.stimson.org/2025/2025-brics-summit-takeaways-and-projections/.

Stuenkel, O. (2020). *Post-western world: How emerging powers are remaking global order*. Polity Press.

CHAPTER 8

Investments and Trade Patterns Among BRICS, Shanghai Cooperation Organization (SCO), and the Global South

ABSTRACT

This chapter critically investigates the shifting contours of investment and trade dynamics among BRICS, the Shanghai Cooperation Organisation (SCO), and the wider Global South, emphasizing their increasing interdependence and the strategic recalibration of economic relations within an evolving post-unipolar world order. Against the backdrop of intensifying geopolitical flux and growing disenchantment with Western-centric trade architectures, these emerging alliances have progressively foregrounded intra-bloc economic engagement, South–South cooperation, and the pursuit of alternative development pathways. The analysis engages with the underlying structural trajectories, sectoral alignments, and policy instruments that shape investment flows and trade interlinkages, while also scrutinizing the asymmetries, governance constraints, and institutional inertia that impede deeper economic convergence. Drawing upon empirical datasets and cross-regional case comparisons, this chapter highlights the catalytic role of regional mechanisms—such as the BRICS New Development Bank, SCO economic platforms, and a proliferating network of bilateral trade accords—in fostering macroeconomic resilience, expanding market access, and subverting entrenched hierarchies in the global trade regime. It contends that, notwithstanding persistent challenges, the converging geoeconomic strategies of these blocs embody a

The BRICS Coalition and a New Global Order: Akhilesh Chandra Prabhakar (Author)
2026 Apple Academic Press, Inc. Co-published with CRC Press (Taylor & Francis)

DOI: 10.1201/9781779642936-8

nascent paradigm rooted in multipolarity, reciprocity, and a more just and balanced global distribution of economic influence.

8.1 INTRODUCTION

Amid the shifting contours of the global economy, the investment and trade patterns among regional alliances and developing economies have assumed unprecedented significance. The BRICS nations (Brazil, Russia, India, China, and South Africa), the Shanghai Cooperation Organization (SCO), and the extensive network of the Global South collectively constitute a powerful coalition of economic and geopolitical influence. These entities, representing a substantial share of the world's population, abundant natural resources, and vast market potential, are instrumental in shaping global economic dynamics. Despite their diversity in composition and objectives, they converge on a shared ambition: to catalyze economic growth, enhance regional cooperation, and restructure the global trade architecture to better align with their collective aspirations.

Trade and investment dynamics among the BRICS, Shanghai Cooperation Organisation (SCO), and the wider Global South alliance have exhibited robust growth and multifaceted evolution through July 2025, reflecting deepening economic synergies and strategic cooperation aimed at redefining global economic governance.

In 2025, the BRICS+ coalition, now incorporating a broader array of members beyond the original five, commands a significant share of global economic output, population, and trade flows. Efforts to consolidate intra-BRICS trade have yielded substantial dividends, with intra-bloc commercial exchanges exceeding $600 billion. This expansion is supported by initiatives aimed at tariff reduction, harmonization of trade protocols, and the promotion of regional and inter-regional value chains, intended to mitigate overdependence on Western supply routes and foster resilient South–South trade ecosystems (EY, 2025). The New Development Bank (NDB), a pivotal institution within BRICS, continues to amplify financial cooperation by financing infrastructure projects and promoting lending in local currencies, thereby enhancing financial autonomy and reducing exposure to volatile global capital markets (Brasil, 2025).

The SCO complementarily underpins regional economic integration, particularly among Eurasian member states. Bilateral trade between China and SCO countries surged to $247.7 billion in the first half of 2025, with

Chinese investments surpassing $40 billion in key sectors, such as energy, mining, infrastructure, digital technologies, and green development (BRICS Today, 2025a). The SCO framework facilitates collaboration in emergent high-tech domains, including 5G, smart cities, and industrial modernization, which are transforming regional economies and enhancing integration into global value chains (Mepei.com, 2025). These efforts dovetail with broader Global South aspirations encompassing large swathes of Asia, Africa, and Latin America, amplifying demands for equitable international economic reforms and sustainable development.

UNCTAD's recent analyses reveal that foreign direct investment (FDI) inflows within the BRICS have experienced volatility, with a notable decline in cross-border M&A sales post-pandemic; however, significant transactions in vital sectors, such as technology, natural resources, and manufacturing underscore ongoing structural economic transformation (UNCTAD, 2023). The BRICS Economic Partnership Strategy 2025 emphasizes trade facilitation, investment promotion, digital technologies, and sustainable infrastructure as the pillars for future growth, envisaging a multipolar world economy enhanced through cooperative frameworks that align with the United Nations Sustainable Development Goals (BRICS Today, 2025b).

Collectively, trade and investment trends among BRICS, SCO, and the Global South manifest a concerted shift toward economic self-reliance, diversified financial architecture, and collaborative governance. These developments encapsulate a striving for inclusive globalization, where emerging economies exert greater agency in shaping international trade, investment, and development paradigms.

Over the past six decades, the G77 and China have played a pivotal role in advancing the global agenda for sustainable development and bolstering the United Nations' capacity to address critical international challenges. Acting as a crucial platform for representing the interests of the Global South, this coalition has steadily grown in influence. As of 2024, developing countries account for 86.4% of the global population and 58% of the world's GDP, underscoring the increasing economic and social clout of the Global South. This ascent, fueled by South–South cooperation, marks a significant shift in the global balance of power.

Trade and investment activities within and among these blocs transcend mere transactions; they reflect strategic initiatives aimed at addressing historical inequities in global commerce, reducing dependency on traditional economic hegemons, and fostering inclusive development. Initiatives like China's Belt and Road Initiative (BRI), frameworks for South–South cooperation, and the establishment of alternative financial institutions such as the new development bank (NDB) exemplify a deliberate shift toward a multipolar economic order. These efforts highlight a concerted push to redefine the rules of global engagement, amplifying the voices and influence of emerging economies in international governance.

The intricate interplay of investments and trade among BRICS, SCO, and the Global South, analyzing their synergies, challenges, and far-reaching implications for the global economic order. By exploring these dynamics, we gain a nuanced understanding of how these alliances are recalibrating the economic trajectory of their regions and the broader world.

8.2 HISTORICAL CONTEXT AND THE ESTABLISHMENT OF THE G77

The G77 was founded in 1964 during the first United Nations Conference on Trade and Development (UNCTAD), at a time when many nations in the Global South were emerging from colonial rule. These newly independent states faced systemic marginalization in the global economic order, which was dominated by the Global North. Policies rooted in the post-World War II institutional framework, led by the United States and Europe, perpetuated economic imbalances, with commodity dependence and unfavorable terms of trade undermining the South's development. The exploitation of natural resources and inequitable trade practices left many developing nations economically vulnerable and politically marginalized.

The G77 was thus established to unify the voices of developing nations, enabling them to collectively address these systemic inequities. The group aimed to reimagine international trade and economic policies to support the South's development aspirations, challenging their relegation to peripheral roles in global governance.

8.3 CHALLENGES AND SETBACKS IN SOUTH–SOUTH COOPERATION

The collapse of the Soviet Union and the socialist bloc in the late 20th century marked a significant setback for South–South cooperation. This period saw the rise of globalization, characterized by privatization, liberalization, and imperialist economic agendas driven by the U.S. and Europe. The absence of a counterbalancing force allowed Western-led economic structures to dominate, limiting the South's capacity to advance its collective goals.

The Bretton Woods Institutions (the World Bank and the International Monetary Fund (IMF)) became emblematic of this imbalance, with decision-making processes that excluded or marginalized developing countries. Structural reforms and policy prescriptions imposed by these institutions further constrained the policy autonomy of the Global South, exacerbating inequalities and triggering financial and developmental crises.

8.4 THE ROLE OF THE G77, CHINA, AND THE GLOBAL SOUTH IN REVITALIZING COOPERATION

Despite these challenges, the G77, supported by China, has persisted in its efforts to champion the interests of the Global South. Over the decades, it has worked to build a multipolar world order that emphasizes self-reliance, economic sovereignty, and sustainable development. Notable achievements include the formation of institutions and alliances such as the non-aligned movement (NAM), the organization of the petroleum exporting countries (OPEC), and advocacy for a new international economic order (NIEO) during the 1970s.

China has played a pivotal role in reinvigorating South–South cooperation, supporting initiatives to achieve economic independence and political sovereignty for the Global South. The BRICS, SCO, and platforms like RCEP have further bolstered collective efforts to address economic imbalances and amplify the voices of developing countries on the global stage.

8.5 SUSTAINABLE DEVELOPMENT AND CONTEMPORARY CHALLENGES

The Global South has been instrumental in integrating environmental concerns into the sustainable development narrative. Milestones such as the 1972 Stockholm Conference on the Human Environment and the 1992 Rio

Earth Summit highlighted the importance of balancing economic growth with environmental preservation. The G77 and China have continued to advocate for this balance, addressing urgent issues such as poverty reduction, hunger eradication, and equitable climate action.

However, the contemporary global order remains fraught with challenges. The COVID-19 pandemic, geopolitical tensions, and economic fragmentation have exacerbated vulnerabilities in the Global South. Trade and financial inequalities persist, with developed nations maintaining dominance over the multilateral financial architecture. Yet, there are signs of optimism, as developing nations grow increasingly assertive in demanding greater representation and equity in global governance.

8.6 THE PATH FORWARD: A UNIFIED GLOBAL SOUTH AGENDA

For the Global South to navigate these challenges effectively, deepening cooperation through trade, investment, technology transfer, and knowledge sharing is crucial. Platforms such as BRICS, SCO, and RCEP must take the lead in advancing inclusive and equitable global governance. The focus should remain on promoting sustainable development goals, addressing climate change, and reforming international financial systems to prioritize the needs of developing countries.

The G77 and China, as champions of the Global South, have a critical role in steering the multilateral agenda toward inclusivity and fairness. By fostering solidarity and self-reliance, they can ensure that the aspirations of developing countries are no longer sidelined but are central to the global discourse on sustainable development. The ultimate goal is to create a world order that is equitable, multipolar, and leaves no one behind (Li, 2023).

In the 21st century, the global economic landscape has undergone a transformative shift, characterized by heightened investments and trade collaborations among developing nations. Alliances such as BRICS (Brazil, Russia, India, China, and South Africa), the SCO, and the Global South—a term encompassing developing countries across Asia, Africa, and Latin America—are emerging as pivotal players in addressing the gaps left by traditional global institutions like the World Bank, the IMF, and the World Trade Organization (WTO). The SCO, established in 2001, evolved from the Shanghai Five mechanism, which was founded in 1996. The

Shanghai Five—comprising China, Kazakhstan, Kyrgyzstan, Russia, and Tajikistan— was initially created to enhance border security and promote demilitarization in the aftermath of the Soviet Union's collapse. The addition of Uzbekistan in 2001 transformed this group into the SCO, which has since become the world's largest regional organization, encompassing some of the globe's most populous and influential nations. The current roster of full member states includes:

1. China (founding member, 1996)
2. India (joined in 2017)
3. Kazakhstan (founding member, 1996)
4. Kyrgyzstan (founding member, 1996)
5. Pakistan (joined in 2017)
6. Russia (founding member, 1996)
7. Tajikistan (founding member, 1996)
8. Uzbekistan (joined in 2001)
9. Iran (admitted as a full member in 2023)
10. Belarus (admitted as a full member in 2024)

The SCO spans an impressive 24% of the world's land area and is home to 42% of the global population. As of 2024, it accounts for 23% of global nominal GDP and 36% of GDP based on purchasing power parity (PPP).

In recent years, economic integration among SCO members has experienced significant growth. Between 2019 and 2023, mutual trade within the bloc expanded 1.5 times, increasing from $336 billion to $490 billion. Key trading partners include China, which accounts for 64.6% of mutual trade, and Russia, contributing 26.2%. Kazakhstan, with a 3.3% share, also plays an increasingly important role in the region's trade dynamics.

The SCO's growing economic influence, combined with its commitment to multilateral cooperation, highlights its pivotal role in shaping the contemporary geopolitical and economic order. The SCO plays a pivotal role in fostering foreign trade and economic activity, with a core mandate to enhance economic cooperation and mutual trade interests. Its efforts are directed toward elevating the prosperity, living standards, and overall well-being of over four billion people. The SCO prioritizes sustainable economic development through expanded trade volumes, a diversified trade structure, the establishment of resilient supply chains, and collective endeavors to fortify an open, equitable, inclusive, and transparent multilateral trade system rooted in the norms and principles of the WTO.

Recognizing the transformative potential of digital technologies, the SCO underscores their decisive role in driving sustainable economic growth and advancing innovation within the region. It advocates for leveraging digital transformation, including the development of digital public infrastructure, to enhance financial inclusion and accessibility. These initiatives exemplify the SCO's commitment to integrating technological advancements into its economic framework to ensure robust and inclusive development across member states.

This evolving economic partnership reflects a shared ambition among these regions: to build robust physical infrastructure, advance industrialization, and establish more balanced and diversified trade networks. Such efforts aim to reduce dependency on Western economies while enhancing resilience against global economic uncertainties. These initiatives not only signify a reorientation of economic priorities but also underscore a collective commitment to shaping a more equitable and multipolar global economic order.

8.7 THE ROLE OF BRICS

The BRICS nations, as emerging global economic powers, have played a pivotal role in driving investments within and beyond their respective regions. By the mid-21st century, BRICS could be some 50% bigger than their advanced counterparts. Currently, BRICS contributes to more than 50% of the world's economic growth. The BRICS's NDB and the Contingent Reserve Arrangement initiatives make an effort to fulfill the financial requirements of developing countries. The NDB provided US$2.5 billion loans to member countries till 2019. Intra-trade stood at about US$500 billion in 2020 (Prabhakar, 2020a, 2020b, 2020c, and 2020d).

China and India, in particular, have emerged as significant sources of Foreign Direct Investment (FDI) across the Global South, investing heavily in infrastructure, manufacturing, and technology. China's BRI exemplifies this trend, linking Asia, Africa, and parts of Europe through infrastructure development, with extensive investments in transportation, energy, and digital infrastructure that connect regions across the Global South and the SCO. Russia has also expanded its investments across Central Asia, the Middle East, and Africa, largely in energy, defense, and resource extraction, contributing to a multipolar investment landscape that reduces reliance on Western capital flows.

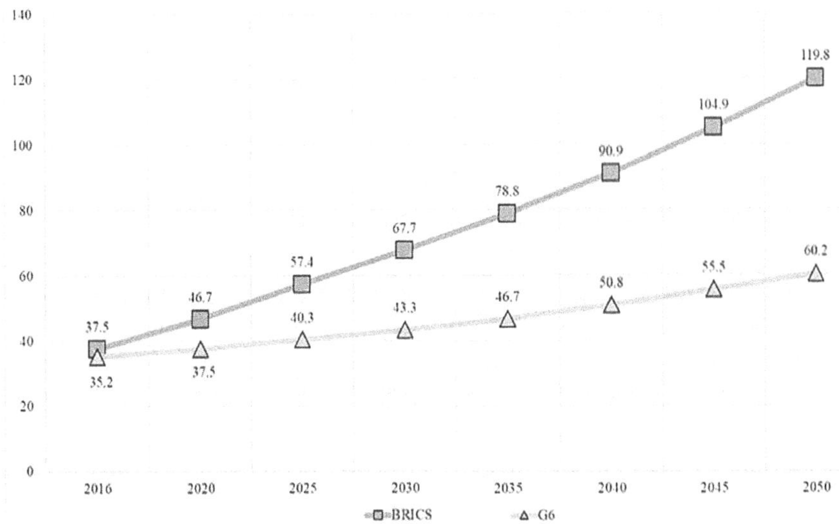

FIGURE 8.1 Projected GDPs in PPP of BRICS and G6 economies by 2050, $ trillion.
Source: Authors' development based on PricewaterhouseCoopers (2017).

The establishment of the NDB by BRICS has further bolstered investment flows, offering a financing mechanism for sustainable development projects without the conditionalities of traditional lenders like the IMF or the World Bank. Through the NDB, BRICS members and allied nations receive financing for infrastructure and development projects that align with local priorities and are less susceptible to foreign political influence, fostering a collaborative investment environment among BRICS, SCO, and the Global South.

8.8 TRADE PATTERNS

Trade among BRICS, SCO members, and the Global South is characterized by an increasing focus on regional trade agreements and bilateral trade settlements, often bypassing the US dollar in favor of local currencies. This shift is strategic, aimed at insulating these economies from the volatility of the dollar exchange rate and promoting financial sovereignty. Trade between China and India and other BRICS–SCO–Global South countries often includes critical sectors such as electronics, manufactured goods, raw materials, and agricultural products. South–South trade is rapidly expanding, with BRICS and SCO members collectively representing over 40% of the world's population and increasingly influential consumer bases.

In recent years, intra-regional trade has grown within the SCO, which includes China, Russia, and Central Asian nations such as Kazakhstan, Uzbekistan, and Tajikistan, alongside observer nations like Iran and affiliate members such as India and Pakistan. The SCO's initiatives to strengthen economic cooperation focus on sectors including energy, mining, agriculture, and industrial production. For example, Russia and China maintain a robust energy trade, with Russia supplying oil and natural gas to meet China's energy needs, while China provides manufactured goods and technology in return. Similarly, India has expanded its energy and mineral imports from Central Asia, supporting mutual economic interests across SCO member nations.

Approximately 90% of the economic and trade dependence of European nations rests upon China's expansive market. Despite initiating a "trade war" with China, the United States has exhibited a discernible loss of composure when confronting the vast potential of China's domestic consumer base. Indian industrialists and capital holders have similarly begun to acknowledge the critical significance of access to this market. The pervasive recessionary pressures engulfing the United States and European economies have imposed formidable challenges on Indian exporters attempting to penetrate these traditional markets. Compounding these difficulties are the exorbitant costs associated with maritime and logistical transportation to these regions. Furthermore, the imposition of tariffs under the present Trump administration has exacerbated anxieties within Indian capitalist circles (India Today, 2025).

In this context, Indian capitalists have wielded considerable influence over their political ally, Prime Minister Narendra Modi, pressing for intensified engagement with China to secure unfettered access to its burgeoning market. However, dissenting voices, exemplified by self-styled "capitalist intellectuals," such as Brahma Chellaney and others associated with American lobby interests in India, persist in expending considerable intellectual effort opposing China's ascendancy. This divergence raises a critical question regarding the political and intellectual viability of such perspectives amid the accelerating reconfiguration of the global economic order (New Indian Express, 2025).

The fiscal realities underpinning these developments are stark. India's trade deficit with China widened to a record $99.2 billion in the fiscal year 2024–2025, driven by surging imports primarily in electronics, electric batteries, and solar panels, while Indian exports to China contracted by approximately 14.5% to $14.3 billion (Reuters, 2025). This persistent trade imbalance engenders significant structural dependencies and supply chain vulnerabilities, reflecting a nuanced confluence of economic opportunity and geopolitical complexity (India Foundation, 2025).

8.9 SYNERGIES WITH THE GLOBAL SOUTH

The BRICS–SCO–Global South alliance creates a strategic platform for mutual growth through trade in commodities, technology exchange, and infrastructure development, offering a counterbalance to Western economic hegemony. With a shared interest in climate resilience and sustainable growth, BRICS and SCO nations have facilitated the transfer of green technology to Global South countries, fostering partnerships in solar, wind, and renewable energy that advance climate goals. Further, these alliances support developing economies through technology transfer, education, and capacity-building initiatives that prioritize local development agendas over imposed models.

8.9.1 CHALLENGES AND OPPORTUNITIES

While the alignment among BRICS, SCO, and the Global South has created significant economic opportunities, challenges remain. Regulatory disparities, political conflicts, and varying levels of economic development can complicate the coordination of trade policies and investment standards across diverse economies. Moreover, some Global South nations, while eager to embrace these new partnerships, may still contend with infrastructure limitations and political instability that hinder smooth economic integration.

Nonetheless, the growing economic interdependence and cooperative framework among BRICS, SCO, and Global South countries represent a transformative shift in global trade and investment dynamics. By emphasizing regional and intercontinental collaboration, these alliances are reshaping the global economic order, advocating for more equitable financial models, and enabling a multipolar system that empowers developing economies. As these relationships mature, they will likely continue to foster economic growth, innovation, and resilience across vast and diverse regions, creating a robust alternative to traditional Western-led economic paradigms.

8.10 CONCLUSION

In 2024, intra-trade and investment trends among BRICS, the SCO, and the Global South reflect a marked rise, fueled by strategic efforts to achieve greater economic autonomy from Western financial systems. Initiatives highlighted at the BRICS summit underscore this ambition, with a strong focus on expanding local currency transactions to reduce dependency on the US dollar, bolstering the NDB to serve as an alternative funding source, and pursuing large-scale infrastructure projects, particularly under China's BRI. This approach is not only strengthening the intra-BRICS trade but is also enticing the SCO and Global South nations seeking diversified trade avenues and financial resilience.

Energy trade has seen substantial growth, especially in oil and gas, as countries like China and Russia strengthen ties in response to Western sanctions. India has similarly benefited by securing discounted Russian oil, a move that underscores the bloc's cohesive response to external pressures. This reallocation of energy resources bolsters economic resilience, cushioning BRICS nations against inflationary pressures and supporting internal energy security while reducing reliance on traditional Western markets.

Moreover, the BRICS+ initiative is paving the way for robust partnerships with ASEAN and SCO members, whose rapid industrial growth has spurred demand for cost-effective energy solutions and infrastructure investments. Joint ventures in digital infrastructure and renewable energy are increasing, reflecting the bloc's commitment to sustainable development and a more equitable global financial system. This approach not only supports shared prosperity and stability across these regions but also strengthens the global economic influence of BRICS and its partners in the Global South.

KEYWORDS

- **conference**
- **demilitarization**
- **economic**
- **investment**
- **organization**
- **resilience**
- **trade**

REFERENCES

Brasil, B. (2025, July 5). BRICS summit signs historic commitment in Rio for more inclusive and sustainable governance. https://brics.br/en/news/brics-summit-signs-historic-commitment-in-rio-for-more-inclusive-and-sustainable-governance.

Brics Today. (2025a, August 20). China-SCO trade reaches US$247.7 billion in first half of 2025. https://tvbrics.com/en/news/china-sco-trade-reaches-us-247-7-billion-in-first-half-of-2025/.

Brics Today. (2025b). BRICS economic partnership strategy 2025: Framework for sustainable growth. https://bricstoday.com/brics-economic-partnership-strategy-2025/.

EY. (2025, July 23). BRICS+ 2025 growth and trade promoting initiatives. www.ey.com/en_in/insights/tax/economy-watch/brics-2025-growth-and-trade-promoting-initiatives.

India Foundation. (2025, June 30). India–China trade paradox: Dependency and geopolitical rivalry. https://indiafoundation.in/articles-and-commentaries/india-china-trade-paradox-dependency-and-geopolitical-rivalry/.

India Today. (2025, August 10). Why 'Make in India' still depends so much on China-made products. https://www.indiatoday.in/business/story/make-in-india-made-in-china-manufacturing-economics-trade-deficit-report-pm-modi-geopolitical-2769387-2025-08-11.

Mepei.com. (2025, August 2). Overview of the outcomes of the 2025 SCO member states foreign ministers Tianjin meeting. https://mepei.com/overview-of-the-outcomes-of-the-2025-sco-member-states-foreign-ministers-tianjin-meeting/.

New Indian Express. (2025). Trade deficit with China swells to $100 bn in FY25. www.newindianexpress.com/business/2025/Apr/16/trade-deficit-with-china-swells-to-100-bn-in-fy25-2.

Reuters. (2025). India trade deficit with China widens to record $99.2 billion amid dumping concerns. www.reuters.com/markets/asia/india-trade-deficit-with-china-widens-record-992-bln-amid-dumping-concerns-2025-04-16/.

UNCTAD. (2023). BRICS investment report 2023. *United Nations Conference on Trade and Development*. https://unctad.org/system/files/official-document/diae2023d1_en.pdf.

CHAPTER 9

A Comparative Analysis of China and India's Development Since 1980

ABSTRACT

This chapter undertakes a rigorous comparative analysis of the developmental trajectories of China and India since 1980, with particular emphasis on their contrasting policy paradigms, institutional architectures, and resultant economic outcomes. Although both nations initiated liberalization and reform in the closing decades of the 20th century, China pursued a state-centric, export-driven growth model characterized by centralized planning and strategic industrial policy. In contrast, India adopted a more incremental and heterodox approach, shaped by democratic imperatives, structural pluralism, and federal constraints.

The analysis interrogates a spectrum of developmental indicators—including GDP growth, industrialization, poverty reduction, human capital formation, and technological advancement—within the broader political, societal, and geopolitical milieus that have shaped each country's evolution. It further examines the differential impacts of governance structures, foreign investment regimes, and global economic integration in sculpting the respective ascents of China and India on the world stage.

Despite China's accelerated economic transformation and infrastructure-driven modernization, persistent challenges—such as income inequality, ecological degradation, and regional imbalances—remain salient in both contexts. Drawing on empirical evidence and scholarly discourse, this chapter contends that while China has demonstrably outpaced India in quantitative terms of economic development, India's democratic resilience, institutional pluralism, and demographic dividend may confer distinct advantages for sustainable and inclusive long-term growth.

The BRICS Coalition and a New Global Order: Akhilesh Chandra Prabhakar (Author)
2026 Apple Academic Press, Inc. Co-published with CRC Press (Taylor & Francis)

DOI: 10.1201/9781779642936-9

Ultimately, the comparative experiences of these two Asian giants illuminate the intricate interplay between state capacity, institutional configuration, and developmental strategy in shaping the trajectories of emerging economies within the Global South.

9.1 INTRODUCTION

China and India, the two most populous nations globally, embarked on transformative economic trajectories during the late 20th century. Despite parallels in their histories of colonial subjugation and reliance on planned economic systems, the developmental paths they pursued post-1980 have diverged in fundamental ways (Prabhakar, 2025). Both nations have achieved extraordinary economic progress, yet the dynamics of their growth reveal profound contrasts in policy frameworks, institutional arrangements, and structural adaptations.

China's economic reform era, inaugurated in 1978 under Deng Xiaoping, was distinguished by a measured and pragmatic strategy of liberalization. The country leveraged initial agricultural reforms, export-led industrialization, and substantial foreign investment to transition from a predominantly agrarian economy into a global manufacturing giant. Conversely, India's liberalization initiatives, launched in 1991 as a response to a balance-of-payments crisis, catalyzed a services-driven growth model. This transformation, powered by the rapid expansion of its IT and telecommunications sectors, represented a slower but consistent shift away from its state-controlled economic framework.

Comparing these two economies illuminates the complex interplay between governance structures, economic strategies, and socio-political contexts. China's centralized governance model has enabled swift decision-making and efficient policy execution, while India's democratic and pluralistic system prioritizes inclusivity, often at the cost of slower reform implementation. These divergent approaches have yielded distinct outcomes, evident in metrics such as GDP growth rates, poverty alleviation, human capital enhancement, and integration into global economic networks.

By the 1980s, both nations shared a broadly comparable economic foundation. Yet, today, China's GDP is approximately five times larger than India's, illustrating a striking disparity in their economic achievements. This divergence is attributable to China's deliberate emphasis on infra-structure modernization, technological innovation, and an export-oriented economic paradigm, which has provided a robust platform for sustained growth and global competitiveness.

This study critically examines the comparative development of China and India since 1980, with a focus on the evolution of their economic policies, sectoral growth dynamics, and socio-economic progress. By evaluating their respective successes, challenges, and long-term trajectories, this research aims to derive insights with broader implications for other emerging economies striving to achieve transformative growth.

9.2 AIMS AND OBJECTIVES

9.2.1 AIM

The central aim of this study is to undertake a thorough comparative analysis of the economic development trajectories of China and India since 1980. This investigation seeks to uncover how the distinct paths these two nations have followed have been shaped by divergent policy frameworks, institutional contexts, governance models, and strategic priorities. By critically examining both the successes and challenges encountered by China and India, the study aspires to extract valuable lessons that may inform the development strategies of other emerging economies.

9.2.2 OBJECTIVES

1. To systematically compare and contrast the economic policies implemented by China and India from 1980 onward, with particular emphasis on the pivotal reform periods in both nations.
2. To analyze the influence of governance structures on the efficacy and success of economic reforms within each country.
3. To evaluate the role of sectoral development—manufacturing in China and services in India—in shaping the respective growth trajectories of both nations.
4. To assess the socio-economic outcomes of their growth models, particularly in terms of poverty reduction, human capital development, and income inequality.
5. To examine the challenges faced by China and India in sustaining their growth models, including demographic shifts, environmental

sustainability, and the need for innovation-driven economic transformation.

6. To draw broader insights from the comparative development of China and India that may offer valuable guidance for policymakers in other developing economies.

9.3 SIGNIFICANCE OF THE STUDY

This study holds significant value across several domains:

1. **Policy Insights:** It provides policymakers in developing countries with critical insights into the various approaches to economic growth and their long-term implications. By analyzing the strengths and limitations of China's export-led industrialization and India's services-oriented growth model, the study aids in the formulation of more effective strategies tailored to the unique contexts of other nations.
2. **Developmental Frameworks:** This research contributes to the academic discourse on development economics by offering a comparative perspective on two of the largest and most influential developing economies in the world. The analysis enhances the existing literature on economic transformation, providing a framework for understanding the roles of governance, policy, and global integration in shaping developmental outcomes.
3. **Lessons for Emerging Economies:** The experiences of China and India serve as critical lessons for other emerging economies, particularly in Asia, Africa, and Latin America, that are striving for rapid economic growth. By identifying key factors that have propelled or hindered development in both countries, the study provides practical insights for addressing challenges such as poverty, income inequality, and industrial stagnation.
4. **Global Economic Implications:** Through an examination of the global repercussions of China and India's rise, the study illuminates broader shifts in the global economic landscape, particularly concerning the redistribution of wealth, labor, and production. This has far-reaching implications for global trade, supply chains, and international economic diplomacy.

9.4 LIMITATIONS OF THE STUDY

Despite its comprehensive approach, this study is not without limitations:

1. **Scope of Time Period:** Although the study concentrates on the period since 1980, it is important to note that the long-term impact of more recent reforms and global developments may not be fully captured. The enduring effects of current policies, especially in areas like technological innovation, demographic shifts, and environmental sustainability, are still unfolding and could lead to significant changes in the near future.
2. **Data Limitations:** While the study draws on widely accessible economic data, there may be gaps or inconsistencies, particularly with respect to regional disparities, informal sectors, or social indicators. Differences in how China and India report data could introduce inaccuracies or disparities in the comparisons made.
3. **Causal Inference:** Establishing definitive causal relationships in a comparative study of this nature is inherently challenging. The complexities arising from the interaction of various factors, such as global economic trends, historical legacies, and external influences, complicate the attribution of outcomes directly to specific policies or reforms.
4. **Generalization:** While the study focuses on China and India, caution must be exercised when generalizing its findings to all emerging economies. Each country's development path is shaped by unique political, historical, cultural, and external factors, and as such, the insights derived from this comparative analysis may not be universally applicable to other contexts.
5. **Focus on Economic Factors:** Though the study addresses important social outcomes such as poverty reduction and human capital development, it is predominantly concerned with economic factors. The political, cultural, and geopolitical dimensions that may also influence the development trajectories of China and India are not explored in depth within the scope of this research.

Despite these limitations, the study provides a nuanced and comprehensive understanding of the comparative development of China and India, contributing both theoretical insights and practical recommendations to the broader discourse on development economics.

9.5 METHODOLOGY

This study adopts a multi-method comparative approach to systematically analyze the divergent economic development trajectories of China and India since 1980. The methodology amalgamates both qualitative and quantitative research methods to offer a thorough examination of the policy frameworks, governance structures, and developmental outcomes in these two nations. The research is organized around the following core components.

9.5.1 COMPARATIVE HISTORICAL ANALYSIS

At the heart of this study is a comparative historical analysis that investigates the economic policies and reforms introduced in China and India over the last four decades. This methodology involves an in-depth review of secondary sources, such as government reports, academic publications, and policy documents, to identify the pivotal phases of economic transformation in both countries.

1. **China:** The analysis begins with a focus on the reforms initiated in 1978 under Deng Xiaoping, including the de-collectivization of agriculture, the promotion of export-oriented industrialization, and the opening of the economy to foreign direct investment (FDI). The study further explores the subsequent liberalization initiatives of the 1990s, alongside China's ongoing emphasis on innovation and technological advancement in the 21st century.
2. **India:** This study examines the liberalization reforms that commenced in 1991, triggered by a balance of payments crisis. Key reforms, such as trade liberalization, the privatization of state-owned enterprises, and the rapid growth of the IT and services sectors, are explored in depth. Additionally, the challenges India faced in accelerating industrialization and diversifying its economic base are critically assessed.

9.5.2 *QUANTITATIVE ANALYSIS OF ECONOMIC INDICATORS*

Quantitative analysis is employed to contrast and compare key economic indicators across both countries. The metrics examined include:

1. **GDP Growth Rates:** The study assesses the growth trajectories of China and India by analyzing their respective GDP growth rates from 1980 onwards.
2. **Poverty Reduction:** Data on poverty rates, income distribution, and social development indicators are compared to evaluate the impact of each country's growth model on poverty alleviation.
3. **Human Capital Development:** Key indicators, such as literacy rates and life expectancy, are analyzed to gauge the role of human capital development in sustaining economic growth in both nations.
4. **Sectoral Contributions:** This component explores the evolution of the economic structures in China and India, focusing particularly on the rise of China's manufacturing sector and India's service-oriented growth model, using data on sectoral contributions to GDP and employment.
5. **Foreign Trade and Investment:** The study evaluates the extent to which each country has integrated into the global economy by examining trade volumes, FDI flows, and participation in global value chains.

9.5.3 *CASE STUDIES*

To enrich the analysis and provide a more granular understanding of the economic policies that have shaped the developmental paths of both nations, the study includes case studies focused on critical sectors and regions:

1. **China's Export-Oriented Growth:** A detailed case study on China's evolution into a global manufacturing hub through its export-led industrialization policies and their subsequent impact on global trade.
2. **India's IT and Services Revolution:** A case study examining the rapid expansion of India's IT sector, highlighting its role as a key driver of economic growth and its broader influence on global outsourcing.

3. **Rural Development and Urbanization:** A comparative case study exploring the rural–urban divide in both countries, focusing on the policies designed to promote urbanization, rural development, and their effects on economic inequality and poverty.

9.5.4 INTERVIEWS AND EXPERT OPINIONS

Where applicable, qualitative data will be gathered through interviews with development economists, policymakers, and industry experts who have either observed or participated in the economic transitions of China and India. These expert insights will provide a more nuanced understanding of the decision-making processes behind major reforms and their long-term ramifications.

9.5.5 COMPARATIVE POLICY ANALYSIS

A key dimension of the methodology involves a comparative analysis of the governance structures in China and India. This will center on:

1. **Governance Models:** A critical assessment of China's centralized, top-down governance model and India's decentralized, democratic structure. The analysis will explore how these differing governance frameworks have influenced the design, implementation, and success of economic policies.
2. **Institutional Frameworks:** The role of state institutions in driving economic growth will be examined, focusing on state-owned enterprises, regulatory bodies, and the relationship between public and private sectors in both countries.
3. **Policy Response to Globalization:** This aspect evaluates how each country has adapted to globalization, particularly through policies on foreign direct investment, trade liberalization, and technology transfer, and their integration into the global economy.

9.5.6 LIMITATIONS AND ASSUMPTIONS

This methodology assumes that the data used for comparison is largely accurate and comparable across both countries. However, limitations exist regarding the consistency and quality of data, particularly in relation to informal sectors, regional disparities, and social indicators. Additionally, the study acknowledges that secondary sources may carry inherent biases, reflecting national narratives or historical perspectives. Given the complexities involved in comparative research, causal inferences will be approached with caution, focusing primarily on identifying patterns and correlations rather than asserting definitive causal links.

By combining historical, quantitative, and qualitative data, this multi-method approach facilitates a comprehensive exploration of the divergent economic development paths of China and India. The study offers a nuanced comparison of their respective development trajectories, providing valuable insights into the broader implications for emerging economies worldwide. Through its rigorous methodology, this research aims to contribute significantly to the understanding of how distinct policy frameworks and governance models can shape the economic futures of nations.

9.6 REVIEW OF LITERATURE: COMPARATIVE DEVELOPMENT OF CHINA AND INDIA SINCE 1980

The economic trajectories of China and India since 1980 have been extensively studied, providing insights into their growth models, structural changes, and policy frameworks. While both countries have initiated market-oriented reforms in the late 20th century, their distinct approaches and outcomes have been a subject of scholarly comparison.

9.6.1 ECONOMIC REFORMS AND GROWTH PATTERNS

China's economic reforms, initiated in 1978 under Deng Xiaoping, focused on incremental liberalization, starting with agriculture and extending to industrial and financial sectors. By contrast, India adopted significant reforms in 1991, prompted by a balance-of-payments crisis, transitioning from a state-controlled to a market-oriented economy. According to Lin (2011), China's "dual-track approach," which combined state control with market liberalization, was instrumental in maintaining stability during reforms, while India's "big bang" reforms were more disruptive but necessary to open its economy (Lin, 2011).

9.6.2 SECTORAL CONTRIBUTIONS TO GROWTH

China's growth has been predominantly driven by manufacturing and export-oriented industrialization, while India has relied heavily on services. Felipe et al. (2013) observed that by 2010, manufacturing contributed nearly 30% to China's GDP, compared to less than 15% in India (Felipe, 2013). India's comparative advantage in IT and business process outsourcing (BPO) has made its growth more reliant on skilled labor-intensive sectors (Bosworth, 2008).

9.6.3 FOREIGN DIRECT INVESTMENT (FDI) AND TRADE

China's proactive policies in attracting FDI through special economic zones (SEZs) and robust infrastructure development have been pivotal in its integration into global value chains. India's FDI inflows, although growing, have been constrained by bureaucratic hurdles and slower infrastructure development. Huang and Khanna (2003) highlight that China's openness to foreign capital outpaced India's until the late 2000s, fostering rapid industrial and technological advancements (Huang and Khanna, 2003).

9.6.4 HUMAN CAPITAL AND POVERTY REDUCTION

China's investments in health and education during the pre-reform era provided a strong foundation for its subsequent economic growth. India, in comparison, struggled with disparities in literacy and health outcomes, which slowed poverty alleviation efforts. Ravallion and Chen found that while both countries achieved significant poverty reduction, China's progress was faster due to its high agricultural productivity and labor-intensive industrialization in the early reform years (Ravallion and Chen, 2007).

9.6.5 INSTITUTIONAL AND POLITICAL CONTEXTS

The centralized governance structure in China has facilitated swift decision-making and policy implementation, whereas India's democratic framework, though robust, has often led to slower consensus-building. Bardhan argues that China's authoritarian model allowed for focused economic reforms, while India's federal and pluralistic setup required balancing diverse political interests, impacting the pace of reform (Bardhan, 2010).

9.6.6 *CHALLENGES AND SUSTAINABILITY*

Both countries face challenges in sustaining their growth trajectories. China grapples with an aging population, rising inequality, and environmental degradation, while India contends with unemployment, infrastructural deficits, and income disparities. As per Eichengreen et al., both economies must transition from factor-driven to innovation-driven growth to avoid the "middle-income trap (Eichengreen et al., 2012)."

9.7 DEBATE/DISCUSSION

The comparative development of China and India since 1980 underscores the impact of divergent policy choices, institutional structures, and economic strategies. While China's manufacturing-led, export-oriented approach yielded rapid industrialization and poverty reduction, India's service-led growth has been slower but resilient. Understanding their respective paths offers valuable lessons for policymakers in other developing economies.

1. **Initial Context:** In 1980, China's GDP was $303 billion, marginally exceeding India's $186 billion. At the time, both nations were predominantly agrarian economies beset by widespread poverty, inadequate infrastructure, and nascent industrialization. However, their respective policy responses and strategic priorities over the subsequent decades led to dramatically divergent developmental trajectories.
2. **Economic Growth:** By 2024, China's GDP had catapulted to $18.5 trillion, reflecting an extraordinary 61-fold expansion, while India's GDP grew 21-fold to $3.93 trillion. This stark contrast highlights China's ability to sustain exceptionally high growth rates over an extended period, underpinned by its focused and cohesive economic policies.

China achieved an average annual GDP growth rate of nearly 9%, driven by extensive reforms, meticulous economic planning, and a thriving export-oriented strategy. Conversely, India's growth, though commendable at approximately 6% annually, was tempered by protracted structural reforms and a comparatively insular economic approach.

1. **Infrastructure and Industrialization:** China's steadfast prioritization of infrastructure development has been pivotal to its economic transformation. Massive investments in transportation networks, energy infrastructure, and urbanization projects have resulted in world-class logistical systems, exemplified by its high-speed railways and efficient port facilities. These advancements have not only facilitated trade but also significantly boosted industrial growth.

   India, by contrast, has struggled with persistent infrastructure deficits, characterized by chronic underinvestment and project delays. These shortcomings have curtailed industrial expansion and limited the country's ability to compete globally. Today, China's manufacturing sector contributes 28% to global output and employs 200 million people, dwarfing India's modest 4% contribution and 60 million workforces—a stark indicator of India's productivity and scalability challenges.

2. **Technology and Innovation:** China's relentless emphasis on technological advancement and innovation has established it as a global leader in high-tech industries. Through state-led initiatives in research and development (R&D) and robust support for emerging sectors, China has achieved dominance in areas such as electronics, renewable energy, and artificial intelligence (AI).

   India, while excelling in its IT and services sectors, has lagged significantly in manufacturing innovation and technology-driven industrial growth. This disparity reflects the divergent priorities of the two nations and their varying capacities to adapt to and leverage technological advancements.

3. **Trade and Exports:** China's export-driven growth model has been the cornerstone of its economic ascent. With annual exports valued at $3.5 trillion, China has emerged as the world's largest exporter, underpinned by a competitive labor force, seamlessly integrated supply chains, and advanced logistics capabilities.

   India's export performance, although showing steady improvement, remains modest by comparison. Fragmented supply chains, coupled with lower production efficiency, have hindered its global competitiveness. This disparity highlights the importance of cohesive trade policies and robust infrastructure in enhancing export potential.

4. **Per Capita Development:** On a per capita basis, China's GDP reached $25,015 in 2024, vastly eclipsing India's $10,123. This pronounced gap underscores China's success in rapidly urbanizing and lifting millions out of poverty through sustained economic expansion. While India has made considerable strides in poverty alleviation, its progress has been relatively gradual, mirroring its more measured economic transformation.

9.7.1 *FACTS/FINDINGS OF THIS STUDY*

9.7.1.1 *ECONOMIC GROWTH TRAJECTORIES*

1. **China:** China's meteoric economic ascent has been primarily driven by a state-directed, export-centric strategy, which facilitated its integration into the global manufacturing network. Since the late 1980s, the country has sustained an impressive annual GDP growth rate of approximately 9–10%, propelling it to become the world's second-largest economy in terms of nominal GDP.
2. **India:** India's economic trajectory has been notably more erratic, with a pronounced acceleration following the 1991 economic reforms. In contrast to China's heavy reliance on exports and manufacturing, India's growth has been predominantly powered by its services sector, particularly information technology (IT) and BPO. India's average annual growth rate has been more moderate, around 6–7%.

9.7.1.2 *POLICY AND ECONOMIC REFORMS*

1. **China:** In 1978, Deng Xiaoping introduced a suite of market-oriented reforms, ushering China away from central planning toward a more market-driven economy. These reforms included the establishment of SEZs, the liberalization of FDI, and rural restructuring, which triggered significant migration to urban centers.
2. **India:** India's economic overhaul commenced in 1991, characterized by liberalization, deregulation, privatization of state-owned enterprises, and tax reforms. Nevertheless, India's reform process was more gradual and less assertive than China's, with the services sector assuming a more dominant role in the country's economic growth relative to manufacturing.

9.7.1.3 INDUSTRIALIZATION AND URBANIZATION

1. **China:** China's industrial sector, particularly its manufacturing base, has been the cornerstone of its remarkable economic growth. The country has emerged as the "world's factory," producing a vast array of export goods. Urbanization in China has been rapid and transformative, with millions migrating from rural areas to burgeoning cities, thereby creating a substantial labor force for its industrial economy.
2. **India:** India's industrialization has been more protracted, with a considerable portion of its economy still anchored in agriculture and small-scale industries. While urbanization has intensified, it lags behind China in scale, and many regions continue to grapple with inadequate infrastructure and developmental disparities.

9.7.1.4 SOCIAL INDICATORS AND POVERTY REDUCTION

1. **China:** Over the past four decades, China has made extraordinary progress in alleviating poverty. According to the World Bank, the country has lifted over 850 million people out of poverty, a feat largely attributable to rapid urbanization, industrialization, and robust infrastructure development.
2. **India:** India, too, has made notable strides in poverty reduction, though at a slower pace. While the burgeoning services sector has generated millions of jobs, poverty rates remain stubbornly high, and income inequality has intensified in some regions. Rural areas, in particular, continue to face significant challenges concerning poverty, healthcare, and education.

9.7.1.5 INFRASTRUCTURE DEVELOPMENT

1. **China:** Infrastructure development has been a key pillar of China's economic ascent. The country has invested heavily in transportation (including high-speed rail and highways), energy, and urban development, positioning itself as a global leader in infrastructure innovation and implementation.
2. **India:** India's infrastructure development has lagged considerably behind China. While sectors such as IT and telecommunications

have flourished, other critical infrastructure—particularly in transportation, energy, and power generation—remains underdeveloped, contributing to inefficiencies and regional disparities.

9.7.1.6 *ENVIRONMENTAL IMPACT*

1. **China:** The rapid pace of industrialization and urbanization in China has come at a substantial environmental cost. Air and water pollution, deforestation, and escalating greenhouse gas emissions have been prominent issues. However, recent years have seen China taking substantial steps to mitigate these effects, with investments in renewable energy and a commitment to achieving carbon neutrality by 2060.
2. **India:** India faces a similarly daunting environmental challenge, marked by pervasive air pollution, deforestation, and significant water scarcity. Despite ambitious renewable energy targets, India's continued dependence on coal and other polluting industries remains a formidable obstacle to environmental sustainability.

9.7.1.7 *HUMAN CAPITAL DEVELOPMENT AND EDUCATION*

1. **China:** China's considerable investments in education and healthcare have been pivotal to its economic transformation. The country has developed a robust education system, particularly excelling in the fields of science, technology, engineering, and mathematics (STEM), which has been instrumental in fueling industrialization and technological advancement.
2. **India:** India, too, has made progress in education, particularly in higher education and technology. However, it continues to face significant challenges in providing quality education and healthcare to its vast population, especially in rural and underdeveloped regions, where access to these services remains inadequate.

9.7.1.8 *POLITICAL SYSTEMS AND GOVERNANCE*

1. **China:** China's centralized, one-party political system has afforded the country a unique advantage in implementing long-term economic policies and reforms with remarkable stability and efficiency.

However, this model has been criticized for its disregard for political freedoms, human rights abuses, and pervasive censorship.

2. **India:** India, as the world's largest democracy, operates under a multi-party system, which promotes political freedoms and public participation. Yet, this system often leads to policy gridlock and inefficiencies in governance, as political fragmentation and coalition politics impede rapid decision-making.

9.7.1.9 TECHNOLOGICAL ADVANCEMENTS

1. **China:** China has ascended to the forefront of global technological innovation, particularly in fields such as telecommunications (e.g., Huawei), e-commerce (e.g., Alibaba, Tencent), and AI. Its emphasis on fostering innovation, enforcing intellectual property rights, and heavily investing in research and development has positioned China as a technological juggernaut.
2. **India:** India has carved out a niche in IT services, with global titans like Infosys, TCS, and Wipro leading the charge. However, compared to China, India's technological ecosystem remains less advanced, with slower progress in sectors like high-tech manufacturing, innovation, and research and development.

9.7.1.10 GLOBAL INTEGRATION

1. **China:** China has been proactive in seeking deeper integration into the global economy. Its accession to the World Trade Organization (WTO) in 2001 and subsequent expansion of its global influence via initiatives such as the Belt and Road Initiative (BRI) have solidified its position as a formidable global economic and geopolitical power.
2. **India:** India has been more cautious in its approach to global integration, opting for a strategy that seeks to preserve domestic industries while incrementally opening up to foreign investment. Although India has established robust ties with Western nations, particularly in technology, defense, and trade, its global influence remains predominantly regional in contrast to China's more expansive reach.

China and India, the world's two most populous nations, are not only demographic giants but also pivotal engines of economic and geopolitical transformation within BRICS and the Global South (Ministry of External Affairs, 2025). As of July 2025, BRICS+ (including new members) comprises approximately 4.44 billion people, or 56% of the world population, with China and India together representing more than 64% of the bloc's demographic weight (EY, 2025).

- **China:** 1.41 billion (32% of BRICS+ population)
- **India:** 1.43 billion (32.2% of BRICS+ population)
- **Other BRICS+ countries:** 1.6 billion (36% of BRICS+ population)

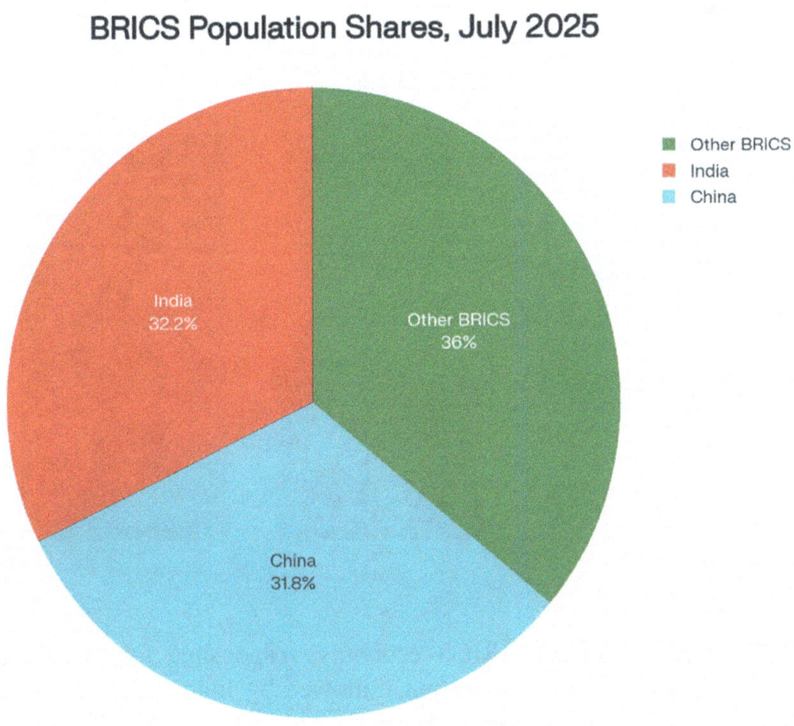

These demographics underpin vast consumer bases and labor pools, giving BRICS collective leverage in global supply chains, commodity pricing, and market demand (Policy Circle, 2025).

China and India contribute to BRICS (% in 2025)

- **China:** 42.3%
- **India:** 16.1%
- **Other BRICS countries:** 41.6%

Economic influence (PPP GDP Shares, 2025)

- **China:** 18.6% of global GDP (PPP)
- **India:** 7.1% of global GDP (PPP)
- **Other BRICS+ countries:** 18.3% (combined), with BRICS+ reaching 44% of global output, a figure surpassing the G7's 29% share.

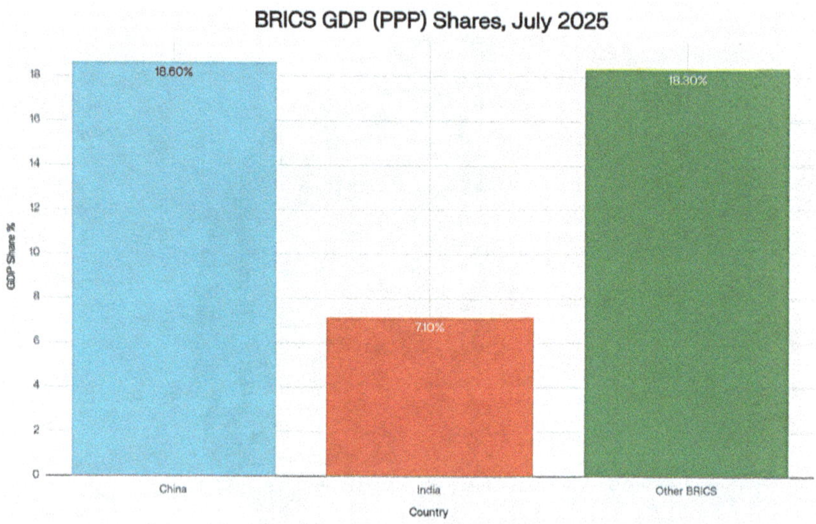

China is the largest BRICS economy, responsible for more than 40% of the bloc's economic output, followed by India with substantial and rising influence, especially through technology, digital innovation, and South–South initiatives (Brasil, 2025). These economic giants shape commodity markets, investment flows, and global developmental norms (New Indian Express, 2025a).

9.7.2 RESHAPING THE GLOBAL ORDER

Both China and India champion reforms to global governance—advocating for a multipolar world system, equitable representation in international institutions, and new frameworks for financial cooperation (Forum, 2025). Their combined weight drives BRICS proposals for United Nations reforms, de-dollarization, infrastructure financing, and the inclusion of more Global South countries into major governance forums (Geopolitical Economy, 2025).

Examples of impact:

- Expansion in international trade conducted in local currencies (Alert, 2025).
- Leadership in digital payments, fintech, and green technology exports.
- Advocacy for Global South issues in G20, BRICS, and climate discussions (Tradeimex, 2025).

These facts and their visualization illustrate the outsized contribution and transformative potential of China and India within BRICS and the Global South, positioning both as central to reshaping the future global order (Schipke, 2025).

9.7.3 INDIA-CHINA TRADE AND INVESTMENT TRENDS (2025)

Recent data through July 2025 reveals key trends:

Trade flows and deficit:

- **Total bilateral trade (FY24-25):** \$127.7 billion (India Today, 2025).
- **India's exports to China (FY24-25):** \$14.25 billion (↓14.5% YoY) (Express, Trade deficit with China swells to \$100 bn in FY25 , 2025).
- **India's imports from China (FY24-25):** \$113.5 billion (↑11.6% YoY).
- **Trade deficit (FY24-25):** \$99.2 billion, a record high.

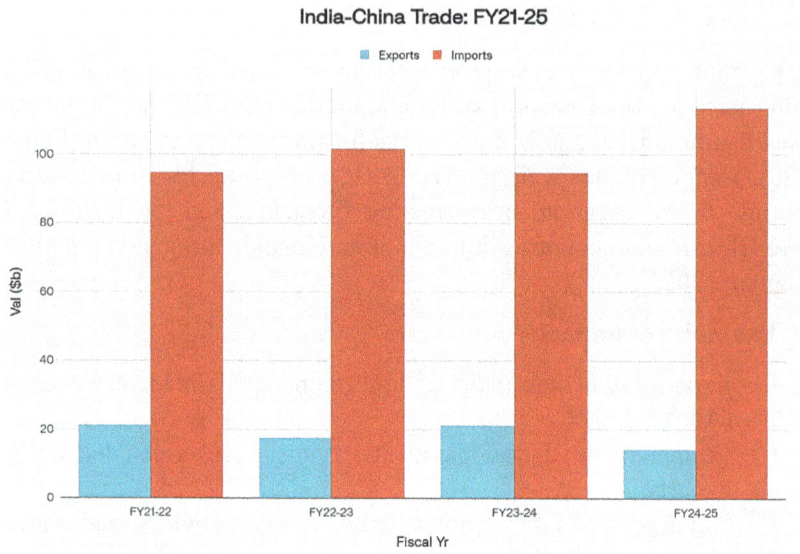

This bar chart illustrates the widening gap: India's exports to China have declined sharply since 2021-22, while imports, dominated by electronics, EV batteries, solar cells, and critical manufacturing inputs, have surged. China is now India's second-largest trading partner, after the United States.

Investment trends:

- **Cumulative Indian FDI into China (till March, 2025):** $2.5 billion (Beijing, 2019).
- **Chinese FDI in India (2023):** $42.05 million (↑324.4% YoY; Ministry of Commerce, China) (Briefing, 2025a).
- **India's total FDI inflows (FY24-25):** $50+ billion (↑13% YoY) (Briefing, 2025b).
- **Policy developments:** India is set to ease restrictions on Chinese investment in non-sensitive sectors to restore capital inflows and de-risk supply chains (Angel One, 2025).

Bilateral investments continue in renewable energy, consumer goods, and manufacturing, although curbs persist in sensitive segments, like telecom and digital infrastructure.

9.7.4 STRATEGIC IMPLICATIONS

India's heavy dependence on Chinese imports exposes domestic manufacturers to supply chain vulnerabilities. PLI (Production Linked Incentive) schemes aiming to boost internal manufacturing often rely on imported Chinese components. Indian exports to China remain concentrated in basic commodities, while high-value goods and services make up a small share. Structural reforms and investment treaties (BITs) are underway to address these imbalances and promote balanced growth.

- Reuters. ((2025, April 16)). India's trade deficit with China widens to record $99.2 billion. https://www.reuters.com/markets/asia/india-trade-deficit-with-china-widens-record-992-bln-amid-dumping-concerns-2025-04-16/reuters
- New Indian Express. (2025b, April 15). Trade deficit with China swells to $100 bn in FY25. https://www.newindianexpress.com/business/2025/Apr/16/trade-deficit-with-china-swells-to-100-bn-in-fy25-2newindianexpress
- India Today. (2025, August 10). Why "Make in India" still depends so much on China-made goods. https://www.indiatoday.in/business/story/make-in-india-made-in-china-manufacturing-economics-trade-deficit-report-pm-modi-geopolitical-2769387-2025-08-11indiatoday
- Angel One. (2025, August 17). India May Ease Curbs on Chinese Investments to Boost FDI and Trade. https://www.angelone.in/news/economy/india-may-ease-curbs-on-chinese-investments-to-boost-fdi-and-tradeangelone
- CEIC Data. (2025, March 25). India Total Exports to China. https://www.ceicdata.com/en/indicator/india/total-exports-to-chinaceicdata
- CEIC Data. (2025, March 18). India Trade Balance. https://www.ceicdata.com/en/indicator/india/trade-balanceceicdata
- China Briefing. (2025, June 19). China-India Economic Ties: Trade, Investment, and Opportunities. https://www.china-briefing.com/news/china-india-economic-ties-trade-investment-and-opportunities/china-briefing

- India Briefing. (2025, July 6). India FDI Tracker 2025. https://www.india-briefing.com/news/india-fdi-tracker-2025-38140.html/india-briefing
- EOI Beijing. (2019, November 28). Trade and Economic Relations. https://eoibeijing.gov.in/eoibejing_pages/MjQ,eoibeijing

This synthesis demonstrates the contrasting trends and underlying dynamics in India-China trade and investment: deepening engagement, structural imbalances, and ongoing policy recalibration.

9.8 CONCLUSION

In conclusion, the divergent developmental trajectories of China and India since 1980 underscore the pivotal influence of governance frameworks, policy decisions, and strategic investments in shaping national prosperity. China's state-driven model, underpinned by an unwavering focus on industrialization, infrastructure development, and export-led growth, has transformed the nation into a global economic powerhouse, elevating millions from poverty. In stark contrast, India has pursued a more market-oriented strategy, emphasizing the service sector and advancing gradual reforms, resulting in steady, though comparatively slower, economic progress. While both nations have achieved remarkable milestones in development, their contrasting models highlight the inherent complexity of attaining sustainable growth.

The comparative analysis of these two nations provides invaluable lessons, offering profound insights into the multifaceted nature of development and the varied pathways to enduring economic success. The experiences of China and India illustrate that prosperity is not a monolithic pursuit, but rather a product of customized strategies that account for a nation's distinct challenges, resources, and global positioning. Despite emerging from similar developmental starting points in the 1980s, China and India have followed profoundly different paths toward economic advancement. China's approach, marked by cohesive policy frameworks and strategic investments, has accelerated its transformation, while India's gradual market reforms, though impactful, have encountered significant challenges. The distinct developmental paths of these countries thus serve as a powerful reminder that economic success is shaped by the interplay of governance, policy, and strategy, with each nation carving its route to prosperity in accordance with its unique context.

KEYWORDS

- **artificial intelligence**
- **capital**
- **economy**
- **growth**
- **poverty**
- **research**
- **sustainability**
- **trade**

REFERENCES

Alert, D. (2025, July 31). Local currency trading gains momentum among BRICS nations. https://discoveryalert.com.au/news/local-currency-trading-brics-2025/.

Angel One. (2025, August 17). India may ease curbs on Chinese investments to boost FDI and trade. https://www.angelone.in/news/economy/india-may-ease-curbs-on-chinese-investments-to-boost-fdi-and-trade.

Bardhan, P. (2010). *Awakening giants, feet of clay: Assessing the economic rise of China and India*. Princeton University Press.

Beijing, E. (2019, November 28). Trade and economic relations. https://eoibeijing.gov.in/eoibejing_pages/MjQ.

Bosworth, B. A. (2008). Accounting for growth: Comparing China and India. *Journal of Economic Perspectives*, *22*(1), 45-66.

Brasil, B. (2025, May 1). BRICS GDP outperforms global average, accounts for 40% of world economy. https://brics.br/en/news/brics-gdp-outperforms-global-average-accounts-for-40-of-world-economy.

Briefing, C. (2025a, June 19). China-India economic ties: Trade, investment, and opportunities. https://www.china-briefing.com/news/china-india-economic-ties-trade-investment-and-opportunities/.

Briefing, I. (2025b, July 6). India FDI tracker 2025. https://www.india-briefing.com/news/india-fdi-tracker-2025-38140.html/.

Eichengreen, B. P. (2012). *Growth slowdowns redux: New evidence on the middle-income trap*. National Bureau of Economic Research.

EY. (2025, July 23). BRICS+ 2025 growth & trade promoting initiatives. https://www.ey.com/en_in/insights/tax/economy-watch/brics-2025-growth-and-trade-promoting-initiatives.

Felipe, J. M. (2013). *Manufacturing matters... But it's the jobs that count*. Asian Development Bank Economics Working Paper Series.

Forum, W. E. (2025, July 8). BRICS: Here's what to know about the international bloc. https://www.weforum.org/stories/2024/11/brics-summit-geopolitics-bloc-international/.

Geopolitical Economy. (2025, July 3). BRICS expands to 56% of world population, 44% of global GDP. https://geopoliticaleconomy.com/2025/07/04/brics-expansion-population-gdp-vietnam/.

Huang, Y., & Khanna, T. (2003). Can India overtake China? *Foreign Policy*, 137, 74-81.

India Today. (2025, August 10). Why 'Make in India' still depends so much on China-made goods. https://www.indiatoday.in/business/story/make-in-india-made-in-china-manufacturing-economics-trade-deficit-report-pm-modi-geopolitical-2769387-2025-08-11.

Lin, J. Y. (2011). *Demystifying the Chinese economy*. Cambridge University Press.

Ministry of External Affairs. (2025). BRICS-2025. https://www.mea.gov.in/Portal/ForeignRelation/BRICS-2025.pdf.

New Indian Express. (2025a, July 14). BRICS to buttress global south. https://www.newindianexpress.com/opinions/2025/Jul/15/brics-to-buttress-global-south.

New Indian Express. (2025b, April 15). Trade deficit with China swells to $100 bn in FY25. https://www.newindianexpress.com/business/2025/Apr/16/trade-deficit-with-china-swells-to-100-bn-in-fy25-2.

Policy Circle. (2025, June 28). BRICS summit to put local currencies at the heart of trade. https://www.policycircle.org/economy/brics-summit-de-dollarisation/.

Prabhakar, A. C. (2025, March 10). Divergent paths to prosperity: A comparative analysis of China and India's development since 1980. *Journal of International Cooperation and Development*, *8*(1), 15-28.

Ravallion, M., & Chen, S. (2007). China's (Uneven) progress against poverty. *Journal of Development Economics*, *82*(1), 1-42.

Schipke, A. A. (2025). Two giants: China and India shaping the global economy. https://research.nus.edu.sg/eai/wp-content/uploads/2025/03/EAIC-87-20250310.pdf.

Tradeimex. (2025, July 15). BRICS summit 2025: Global trade flows, tariff threats, agreements. https://www.tradeimex.in/blogs/brics-summit-2025-global-trade-flows-tariff-threats-agreements.

CHAPTER 10

BRICS and Sustainable Development: A New Vision for the Global South

ABSTRACT

This chapter interrogates the evolving role of BRICS as a transformative coalition in catalyzing sustainable development across the Global South. Amid enduring asymmetries in global governance and the systemic inadequacies of Western-centric development paradigms, BRICS has increasingly asserted itself as a counter-hegemonic bloc championing inclusive growth, ecological sustainability, and enhanced South–South cooperation. The analysis offers a critical appraisal of the consortium's collective vision, institutional mechanisms, and strategic undertakings—ranging from the establishment of the New Development Bank (NDB) to the construction of alternative financial architectures—designed to redress structural inequities, facilitate green transitions, and fortify developmental resilience among emerging economies.

Employing a comparative and interdisciplinary framework, the study examines the extent to which BRICS member states reconcile national developmental imperatives with global sustainability norms, while concurrently contending with heterogeneous political economies and institutional divergences. It contends that, notwithstanding persistent challenges of coherence, institutional capacity, and policy coordination, BRICS articulates a nascent yet compelling paradigm for reimagining sustainable development through a Global South lens—anchored in the principles of equity, multipolarity, and mutual empowerment. The findings contribute substantively to the broader discourse on post-Western development trajectories and the reconfiguration of the global geoeconomic order.

The BRICS Coalition and a New Global Order: Akhilesh Chandra Prabhakar (Author)
2026 Apple Academic Press, Inc. Co-published with CRC Press (Taylor & Francis)

DOI: 10.1201/9781779642936-10

10.1 INTRODUCTION

A defining feature of BRICS' diplomatic agenda is its emphasis on sustainable and inclusive economic development, which it views as crucial for addressing the pressing challenges confronted by the Global South. By championing equitable and inclusive growth, BRICS seeks to redefine development in a manner that prioritizes social, environmental, and financial sustainability, particularly for developing nations that have long been marginalized within global discourse.

The bloc's vision for sustainable development is grounded in the conviction that the global development model must be people-centric, adaptable, inclusive, and aligned with the unique needs and aspirations of developing countries. In stark contrast to the Western-driven paradigms of liberalization, privatization, and corporatization, which have often focused on economic growth at the expense of environmental and social well-being—along with the exploitation of natural resources and cheap labor by Western multinational corporations—BRICS advocates for a more holistic approach (Prabhakar, 2025). This approach emphasizes poverty alleviation, environmental stewardship, and social equity. This chapter explores BRICS' role in advancing sustainable development through initiatives such as the New Development Bank (NDB) and its support for the United Nations' Sustainable Development Goals (SDGs).

At the core of BRICS' commitment to sustainable development, lies its vision of a more just and balanced global order (Prabhakar, 2016).—one where the Global South plays an active role in shaping development policies and practices. By harnessing its collective economic strength and promoting cooperation among developing nations, BRICS aims to construct an alternative development framework better suited to the diverse needs of the Global South (Prabhakar, 2020). In this regard, the bloc's strategies for sustainable development present a bold and inclusive vision, one that seeks to redress the systemic inequalities that have long influenced the trajectory of global development.

BRICS' commitment to sustainable development constitutes a fundamental pillar of its broader vision for global cooperation and the establishment of a more equitable international order (Prabhakar, 2019). Central to this commitment is the bloc's proactive endorsement of the United Nations' Sustainable Development Goals (SDGs), which provide a comprehensive framework for addressing pressing global challenges such as poverty, inequality, and environmental degradation (Chaturvedi, 2020). This chapter examines how the BRICS nations have collectively advanced the SDGs, with a particular emphasis on poverty eradication, environmental sustainability, and social inclusion, thereby addressing the distinct developmental challenges faced by the Global South.

One of the primary mechanisms through which BRICS contributes to the SDGs is the strategic allocation of resources toward large-scale infrastructure development. Such projects are indispensable for the economic progress of developing nations, as they lay the essential foundations for sustainable growth—ranging from transportation and energy infrastructure to healthcare and educational systems. The New Development Bank (NDB), established by BRICS, plays a pivotal role in financing these initiatives, with a strong focus on projects that align with the SDGs, including those centered on renewable energy, sustainable urban development, and affordable housing. By investing in these critical sectors, BRICS seeks to bridge the infrastructural gaps that often hinder the development prospects of many countries in the Global South.

Beyond infrastructure, BRICS has placed a significant emphasis on environmental sustainability as a core element of its development strategy. The bloc advocates for a paradigm shift toward green, low-carbon economies, recognizing that environmental degradation disproportionately impacts poorer nations and exacerbates global inequalities. Through initiatives such as funding for renewable energy projects and supporting sustainable energy solutions, BRICS aims to both mitigate carbon emissions and stimulate economic growth. Moreover, the bloc's commitment to environmental sustainability extends to efforts aimed at protecting biodiversity, combating deforestation, and supporting climate adaptation strategies for vulnerable regions.

Social inclusion represents another critical dimension of BRICS' alignment with the SDGs. The bloc's focus on poverty reduction and equitable economic growth seeks to address the structural inequalities that hinder development in many countries within the Global South. BRICS advocates for inclusive policies designed to ensure that marginalized communities—such as women, youth, and rural populations—can access the benefits of economic growth. By promoting initiatives in education, healthcare, and gender equality, BRICS strives to ensure that no one is left behind in the pursuit of sustainable development.

BRICS' approach to the SDGs epitomizes its broader vision of fostering long-term inclusive growth that addresses the unique developmental challenges of the Global South. Through coordinated efforts in infrastructure development, renewable energy investment, and social inclusion programs, BRICS seeks to establish a sustainable and equitable future for all. These efforts also contribute to the global agenda outlined by the United Nations. As a whole, the bloc's strategies represent a pioneering model for how emerging economies can collaborate to promote sustainable development both within their borders and across the global landscape.

10.1.1 GREEN ECONOMY AND RENEWABLE ENERGY COOPERATION

At the heart of BRICS' sustainability agenda, lies a commitment to fostering a green economy and facilitating the global transition to renewable energy. As the world confronts the simultaneous challenges of economic growth and environmental degradation, BRICS has positioned itself as a leader in reconciling these issues by advocating for clean energy solutions and sustainable development. This chapter delves into the bloc's collaborative efforts to advance renewable energy, disseminate best practices in sustainable development, and set ambitious carbon reduction targets, all of which are integral to achieving long-term environmental and economic resilience.

BRICS' approach to promoting a green economy is rooted in the understanding that economic development and environmental sustainability are not mutually exclusive, but can, in fact, be mutually reinforcing. In response to the increasing urgency of climate change, the bloc has made substantial progress in fostering cooperation across renewable energy sectors, such as solar, wind, and hydropower. Its commitment to transitioning away from fossil fuels is evident in its collective efforts to invest in clean energy infrastructure, thereby reducing dependence on non-renewable energy sources (Dasgupta, 2019). These initiatives not only align with the global push for a low carbon economy but are also pivotal in meeting international climate targets, particularly those outlined in the Paris Agreement.

Among the most significant examples of BRICS' collaborative initiatives in renewable energy is its concerted focus on solar energy. Countries like China and India, with their rapidly expanding solar industries, have led the charge in creating large-scale, affordable solar power infrastructure. These projects not only bolster energy security within BRICS nations but also serve as a model for other developing economies, demonstrating that renewable energy can be a viable and sustainable alternative to traditional power generation methods.

In addition to solar energy, BRICS is deeply involved in the promotion of wind and hydropower energy. Brazil, with its long-standing expertise in hydropower generation, has been instrumental in sharing its knowledge and experience with fellow BRICS members, facilitating the development of large-scale hydropower projects across the bloc. Concurrently, Russia and South Africa are increasingly focusing on expanding their wind energy capacity, further diversifying the bloc's renewable energy portfolio. Through this exchange of knowledge and collaborative investment, BRICS is collectively constructing a green energy infrastructure that supports economic growth while safeguarding environmental integrity.

BRICS' efforts extend beyond the mere development of renewable energy sources; the bloc has also set ambitious targets for carbon emission reductions and energy efficiency. Committed to the goals of the Paris Agreement, BRICS encourages its member states to adopt national carbon reduction strategies that align with their specific economic and environmental contexts. This includes efforts to enhance energy efficiency, foster the adoption of cleaner technologies, and incentivize green investments. By establishing concrete targets and holding its members accountable, BRICS is championing a comprehensive transition toward a low-carbon economy that aligns with global climate objectives.

Moreover, BRICS has actively worked to create an enabling environment for the green economy by facilitating the sharing of best practices and promoting knowledge transfer among its members. Through a series of dialogues, workshops, and conferences on sustainable development, BRICS has created platforms where member states can exchange experiences related to the implementation of renewable energy projects, the development of climate policy, and the adoption of green technologies. This cooperative approach is essential for building capacity in the energy sector and fostering a more inclusive, collaborative global approach to sustainable development.

In conclusion, BRICS' focus on the green economy and renewable energy cooperation represents a crucial pillar of its broader sustainability agenda. Through joint initiatives in solar, wind, and hydropower energy, along with its commitment to ambitious carbon reduction targets, the bloc demonstrates that economic growth and environmental sustainability are not only compatible but inherently complementary. By working collectively to advance clean energy solutions and share best practices, BRICS is positioning itself as a global leader in the transition to a sustainable, low carbon future.

10.1.2 SOCIAL DEVELOPMENT AND INCLUSIVITY

A cornerstone of BRICS' vision for sustainable development is its unwavering commitment to promoting social development that prioritizes inclusivity and equitable growth, and good global governance (BRICS, 2022). Recognizing that genuine economic progress cannot be transformative unless it benefits all strata of society, BRICS has focused its efforts on addressing critical social challenges, including education, healthcare, gender equality, and the empowerment of marginalized communities. This chapter delves into the bloc's comprehensive social development initiatives, highlighting its dedication to creating a more just and inclusive society where vulnerable populations are afforded the opportunities and resources to flourish.

At the heart of BRICS' social development agenda, lies the conviction that inclusive growth is fundamental to the long-term prosperity of its member nations and the Global South as a whole. To achieve this, BRICS has introduced targeted programs designed to reduce inequality and empower historically marginalized groups. Education and healthcare have emerged as central focal points in this endeavor, as both are essential for enhancing the quality of life and providing equal opportunities to all. By investing in infrastructure and expanding access to vital social services, BRICS seeks to close the gaps that often prevent disadvantaged communities from realizing their full potential.

Education stands as a pivotal element in BRICS' social development strategy. By prioritizing access to quality education, the bloc aims to equip future generations with the skills and knowledge necessary to break free from the cycle of poverty. BRICS has backed initiatives designed to broaden educational access, particularly for girls and marginalized groups, through scholarships, vocational training programs, and strategic partnerships with international organizations. These efforts are geared toward empowering individuals, enabling them to engage more fully in the global economy and thus contributing to the overarching social and economic development goals of the bloc.

Healthcare constitutes another key area in which BRICS has made remarkable progress. With a shared understanding that access to healthcare is an intrinsic human right, BRICS member countries have committed to improving the healthcare systems within their nations. This includes increasing access to primary healthcare services, advocating for preventative care, and strengthening healthcare infrastructure. Initiatives such as the BRICS Health Ministers' meetings have facilitated cross-border collaboration and knowledge-sharing on healthcare policies, thereby enhancing the bloc's capacity to tackle public health challenges, particularly in rural and underserved areas.

Gender equality forms a foundational pillar within BRICS' social development framework. The bloc has made substantial efforts to advance the rights of women and girls, recognizing that gender equality is not only a matter of social justice but a crucial driver of economic growth. BRICS nations have implemented policies aimed at eliminating gender-based violence, encouraging greater female participation in the workforce, and ensuring equal access to education and healthcare for women. Additionally, BRICS has been an advocate for the increased representation of women in leadership roles and political decision-making processes, believing that empowering women is essential for achieving both sustainable development and social cohesion.

Empowering marginalized communities lies at the core of BRICS' inclusivity agenda. The bloc has focused on creating opportunities for historically excluded groups—such as indigenous peoples, ethnic minorities, rural populations, and people with disabilities. Through inclusive development policies and affirmative action programs, BRICS aims to ensure that all citizens, irrespective of their socio-economic status, have the opportunity to contribute to and benefit from economic development. By providing marginalized communities with greater access to education, healthcare, financial services, and political representation, BRICS works to reduce systemic inequalities and foster social integration.

In conclusion, BRICS' emphasis on social development and inclusivity underscores its commitment to creating a more equitable and just global order. By addressing critical issues such as education, healthcare, gender equality, and the empowerment of marginalized communities, BRICS seeks to reduce inequality and ensure that the benefits of economic growth are shared by all. Through its targeted programs and collaborative partnerships, the bloc sets a powerful example of how emerging economies can lead the way in fostering inclusive social development, ensuring that no one is left behind in the pursuit of sustainable and equitable growth.

10.1.3 BRICS AND THE QUEST FOR A NEW GLOBAL ORDER

The ascent of BRICS heralds a momentous shift in the global power landscape, marking the advent of an alternative global order that directly challenges the longstanding hegemony of Western powers. Comprising Brazil, Russia, India, China, and South Africa, BRICS represents a coalition of emerging economies united by a shared vision: to reshape the global system in a manner that is more inclusive, equitable, and reflective of the diverse aspirations of the Global South (Amin, 1990). The bloc's emergence signifies a pivotal turning point in the redefinition of global governance, offering an alternative paradigm for economic, political, and social cooperation—one designed to rectify historical imbalances and unlock new opportunities for developing nations.

At the core of BRICS' mission, lies the firm conviction that the prevailing global order, primarily shaped by Western institutions and values, no longer meets the evolving needs of a rapidly changing world. For decades, international organizations such as the United Nations (UN), the World Bank, and the International Monetary Fund (IMF) have been critiqued for their insufficient representation and for perpetuating systems that disproportionately benefit developed nations, often at the expense of the Global South. In response, BRICS has positioned itself as a steadfast advocate for the reform of these institutions, striving to foster a more democratic, multipolar world where the voices of emerging economies are not merely acknowledged but also wield tangible influence in decision-making processes.

A central tenet of BRICS' vision for a new global order is the promotion of a more balanced and just economic system. The bloc calls for a radical transformation in the way international financial institutions operate, pressing for a more equitable distribution of power and resources. Initiatives such as the New Development Bank (NDB) and the Contingent Reserve Arrangement (CRA) exemplify BRICS' efforts to offer alternative mechanisms that provide financing for development projects, reduce dependence on Western-dominated financial systems, and promote sustainable economic growth within the Global South. These initiatives reflect BRICS' broader objectives of nurturing economic self-reliance, minimizing the influence of Western-controlled financial institutions, and providing a platform for developing nations to thrive without the conditionalities that have historically accompanied aid and loans from traditional global powers.

Beyond economic reform, BRICS is committed to addressing pressing global challenges through sustainable development and environmental stewardship. The bloc's active support for the United Nations' Sustainable Development Goals (SDGs) and its emphasis on green energy underscores its dedication to the global transition toward sustainability. Through initiatives focused on renewable energy, poverty alleviation, and social equity, BRICS envisions a new global order that prioritizes environmental and social justice, with a strong emphasis on inclusivity, mutual prosperity, and the reduction of global inequalities.

Diplomatically, BRICS seeks to cultivate a global environment of peaceful cooperation based on mutual respect and non-interference in the domestic affairs of sovereign states. This commitment to multilateralism and dialogue is a direct challenge to the unilateralism and power politics that have long been associated with Western dominance. Through its regular summits, diplomatic initiatives, and strategic partnerships with other emerging economies, BRICS is positioning itself as a critical player in global diplomacy, advocating for the peaceful resolution of conflicts, the strengthening of international law, and the reinforcement of regional security arrangements. By doing so, BRICS offers a model for international cooperation that is rooted in fairness, equality, and respect for the sovereignty of all nations.

However, the quest for a new global order is fraught with challenges. The diverse political systems, economic priorities, and regional interests of BRICS member states present ongoing obstacles to achieving cohesion and coordinated action. Moreover, resistance from entrenched global powers and the complex dynamics of international diplomacy complicate BRICS' efforts to transform the global system (Unit, 2019). Nevertheless, despite these hurdles, BRICS continues to gain prominence and influence, with its initiatives serving as a beacon for other emerging economies that seek a more equitable role in global governance.

10.2 CONCLUSION

BRICS stands as a formidable force in the reconfiguration of global power structures. Through its resolute commitment to reforming international institutions, advancing sustainable development, and fostering peaceful cooperation, BRICS represents a key factor in the quest for a more inclusive and just global order. As the world continues to evolve, the future success of BRICS will depend on its ability to navigate internal differences, expand its influence, and build strategic alliances that promote its core principles of equity, sovereignty, and mutual respect.

KEYWORDS

- **affordable housing**
- **environmental sustainability**
- **global inequalities**
- **mutual prosperity**
- **power politics**
- **poverty eradication**
- **social inclusion**

REFERENCES

Amin, S. (1990). *Delinking: Towards a polycentric world.* Zed Books.

BRICS. (2022). *BRICS social development forum 2022: Policy documents and proceedings*. BRICS Portal.

Chaturvedi, S. T. (2020). The BRICS and the UN sustainable development goals: A partnership for global development. In *The BRICS and the future of global order*. Springer.

Prabhakar, A. C. (2016). BRICS: A new world economic order. In *The current global recession: A theoretical and empirical investigation into developed and BRICS economies*. Emerald Publishing Group.

Prabhakar, A. C. (2020). Trade and economic integration in BRICS: Towards multi-polarity. In *Foreign direct investments: Concepts, methodologies, tools, and applications*. USA: IGI Global.

Prabhakar, A. C. (2025). *Sustainable and inclusive economic development: A global perspective*. Apple Academic Press (CRC Press) Taylor & Francis Group. https://www.appleacademicpress.com/-sustainable-and-inclusive-economic-development-/1746.

Prabhakar, A. K. (2019). *Regional trade and development strategies in the era of globalization*. IGI Global.

Unit, I. S. (2019). Challenges to cohesion in BRICS: Divergent political systems, economic priorities, and international diplomacy. *Institute for Strategic Development Reports, 2019*(4).

CHAPTER 11

Global Power in Transition: Geoeconomic Drivers of a Tripolar World Order

ABSTRACT

The global geopolitical and economic landscape is undergoing a profound transformation marked by the twin forces of de-dollarization and deglobalization. As traditional Western dominance faces increasing resistance, emerging powers, such as China, Russia, and a coalition of Global South nations are challenging the unipolar order led by the United States. This chapter explores the dynamics of a shifting world order, where the concentration of power is giving way to a tripolar structure anchored by the United States, China, and a resurgent Eurasian bloc. Through an analysis of currency diversification, trade realignments, and strategic decoupling, the study highlights how economic sovereignty and regionalism are redefining global influence. This chapter also assesses the implications of this transition for global governance, supply chains, and security frameworks. Ultimately, it argues that understanding these geoeconomic forces is critical to navigating an era of strategic rebalancing and increasing multipolar complexity.

11.1 INTRODUCTION

The post-Cold War era, long defined by the predominance of a unipolar world order under U.S. leadership, is undergoing a profound transformation toward a more intricate and fragmented global system. This shift is propelled by two deeply interwoven forces: de-dollarization—the

The BRICS Coalition and a New Global Order: Akhilesh Chandra Prabhakar (Author)
2026 Apple Academic Press, Inc. Co-published with CRC Press (Taylor & Francis)

DOI: 10.1201/9781779642936-11

progressive diminution of the U.S. dollar's supremacy in international finance—and deglobalization—the strategic retreat from hyper-globalized interdependence in favor of regionally oriented, resilient, and politically congruent economic frameworks. Together, these dynamics are fundamentally reconfiguring the architecture of international relations and giving rise to an emerging tripolar world, with influence increasingly concentrated in three principal spheres: the United States, China, and a loosely consolidated Eurasian bloc led by Russia and bolstered by states across the Global South.

In an era marked by resurgent protectionism, intensifying technological bifurcation, and heightening geopolitical volatility, nation-states are reclaiming agency over their economic destinies. They are diversifying away from dollar-centric financial systems, fortifying domestic industrial capacities, and reconfiguring trade alignments along strategic and ideological lines. This evolving geoeconomic landscape is not merely reactive to episodic disruptions, such as the COVID-19 pandemic or the Russo-Ukrainian conflict, but indicative of a more profound and enduring structural recalibration—one rooted in shifting strategic imperatives, sovereignty-driven policymaking, and the erosion of Western-centric globalization.

As of June 2025, global trade has soared to an unprecedented $33 trillion. Yet, despite this colossal volume, approximately 54% of cross-border transactions continue to be settled in U.S. dollars—an enduring legacy of post–World War II financial hegemony. This longstanding dominance, however, is increasingly being contested by rising economic coalitions, most notably BRICS (comprising Brazil, Russia, India, China, South Africa, and newly inducted member states), which are actively redefining the contours of global economic power.

With over 180 nations now engaging with BRICS in various capacities, the bloc is rapidly emerging as a formidable counterweight to traditional Western-dominated institutions. On a Purchasing Power Parity (PPP) basis, BRICS nations presently contribute 50% of global GDP—more than double the 21% share commanded by the G7. Projections indicate this figure may ascend to 55% by 2030, bolstered by the ongoing expansion and integration of member economies.

This tectonic shift is acutely reflected in evolving trade dynamics. In the first half of 2025 alone, China—the principal engine of BRICS growth—conducted bilateral trade worth 6.11 trillion yuan (approximately

$855 billion) with fellow BRICS members. This represents a year-on-year increase of 3.9% in trade volume among member and partner countries. Significantly, BRICS and its affiliates now account for nearly 28% of China's total foreign trade during this period.

China's trade portfolio with BRICS partners encompasses a strategic spectrum of goods, including chemicals, metallurgical products, advanced electronics, and key raw materials for the pharmaceutical, defense, and industrial sectors. Noteworthy expansions have also occurred in the export of petrochemical equipment, metalworking machinery, and agricultural technologies—particularly cotton harvesters and combine harvesters—underscoring the diversification of trade offerings.

In a move emblematic of de-dollarization efforts, China is also spearheading the development of a new digital trading infrastructure in collaboration with Shanghai Cooperation Organisation (SCO) countries. Simultaneously, deepening logistics cooperation with Africa and Latin America signals a broader ambition to construct parallel trade architectures that circumvent the dollar-centric global financial order.

The ascent of BRICS, coupled with a reconfiguration of trade flows and payment systems, marks a pivotal moment in the evolution of global commerce. The Global South is no longer a passive recipient within a Western-devised framework but is now proactively engineering an alternative economic paradigm. In doing so, it is challenging centuries-old hierarchies and propelling the international system toward a genuinely multipolar future.

This chapter seeks to unpack the core drivers of this global power rebalancing, critically examining the mechanisms through which de-dollarization and deglobalization are accelerating the crystallization of a tripolar order. It further analyzes the strategic calculus of principal actors, evaluates the broader ramifications for global governance and economic stability, and contemplates whether this emergent paradigm heralds a more balanced multipolar world—or a more unstable and fractured international system.

11.2 THEORETICAL FOUNDATIONS OF GEOECONOMICS AND POWER TRANSITION

The concept of geoeconomics—coined by Edward Luttwak (1990)—has evolved into a vital analytical lens for understanding how states use economic tools to achieve geopolitical objectives. Luttwak's assertion that "logic of conflict is now expressed in the grammar of commerce" underscores the transition from military to economic means of competition (Luttwak, 1990). Similarly, Blackwill and Harris (2016) expand on this by identifying sanctions, investment flows, and trade agreements as key instruments of geoeconomic statecraft (Blackwill and Harris, 2016). Power Transition Theory (PTT), as articulated by Organski (1958) and later refined by Tammen (2000), frames the geopolitical tensions that emerge when a rising power challenges an incumbent hegemon. Scholars, such as Kupchan argue that the erosion of U.S. primacy and the assertiveness of China and Russia are not anomalies but natural outcomes of systemic rebalancing (Kupchan C. A., No one's world: The West, the rising rest, and the coming global turn , 2012).

11.2.1 DE-DOLLARIZATION AND THE DECLINE OF U.S. MONETARY HEGEMONY

De-dollarization refers to the gradual reduction of reliance on the U.S. dollar in global trade, finance, and reserves, signaling a pivotal shift in monetary hegemony and financial sovereignty among emerging and established economies. Eichengreen (2011) provides a foundational historical account of dollar dominance, emphasizing the structural advantages which positioned the dollar as the primary global reserve currency post-World War II. However, Subacchi (2020) underscores the vulnerabilities and geopolitical risks inherent in the current dollar-centric global financial system. Contemporary analyses by Yilmaz and Gokmen (2022) reveal how China's proactive promotion of the yuan and Russia's strategic pivot to non-dollar trade are actively challenging the entrenched currency hierarchy. Furthermore, innovations such as central bank digital currencies, notably China's digital yuan, are posited as transformative instruments that could potentially accelerate the erosion of dollar primacy in global settlements.

The scholarly literature on de-dollarization critically examines the multifaceted mechanisms through which global actors endeavor to reduce dependency on the U.S. dollar as the dominant reserve and settlement currency. Eichengreen (2011) provides a foundational historical account of the dollar's ascendancy, contextualizing its pivotal role within the post-World War II international monetary system and highlighting the structural advantages conferred by the so-called "exorbitant privilege" (Eichengreen, 2011). Building upon this foundation, Subacchi (2020) articulates the inherent vulnerabilities embedded within the current dollar-centric global financial architecture, emphasizing the systemic risks posed by political volatility and economic imbalances (Subacchi, 2020a, b).

More contemporaneously, Yilmaz and Gokmen (2022) assess the reconfiguration of the global currency hierarchy as China's active promotion of the yuan (renminbi) and Russia's strategic pivot toward non-dollar trade practices gain momentum, representing substantive challenges to dollar hegemony (Yilmaz, 2022b). Parallel to these geopolitical maneuvers, the advent of central bank digital currencies (CBDCs)—notably China's digital yuan—is identified by scholars, such as Auer R. E. (n. d.) and Prasad (2021) as a potential inflection point with considerable implications for the erosion of the U.S. dollar's centrality in international payment systems Auer R. C. (n. d.).

Collectively, this body of scholarship affirms that de-dollarization involves a complex interplay of geopolitical strategy, technological innovation, and financial policy evolution, marking an epochal transformation in global economic governance.

11.2.2 DEGLOBALIZATION AND REGIONAL ECONOMIC BLOCS

Deglobalization refers to the reversal or slowing down of globalization processes, characterized by reshoring of production, increased protectionism, and regionalism (Baldwin, 2016). Since the 2008 global financial crisis, the interconnectedness of international trade and investment has been challenged by geopolitical tensions, technological changes, and policy shifts prioritizing economic resilience and national security (Rodrik, 2011). Events such as the U.S.-China trade war, Brexit, and the COVID-19 pandemic have exposed vulnerabilities in global supply chains, prompting nations to increasingly focus on securing domestic industries and regional partnerships (SP Global, 2024).

Regional economic blocs like the Belt and Road Initiative (BRI), Eurasian Economic Union (EAEU), and Regional Comprehensive Economic Partnership (RCEP) emerge as geopolitical instruments reflecting alternative visions of global governance. These blocs facilitate trade, infrastructure development, and political cooperation to counterbalance Western-led institutions, particularly through China and Russia's strategies for expanding influence within the Global South (Acharya, 2017a, b).

This trend toward regionalism coupled with slower global trade growth—sometimes termed "slowbalization"—signals a restructuring of the global economic order, privileging strategic autonomy and resilience over hyperglobalized integration.

11.3 EMERGENCE OF A TRIPOLAR ORDER

The emergence of a tripolar world signifies a transformative shift in the global power structure characterized by the coexistence and competition of three dominant poles: the United States, China, and the European Union (EU). This evolving multipolarity challenges the unipolar dominance that followed the Cold War, reflecting the redistribution of economic, military, and diplomatic influence among these major actors.

The United States remains a principal global power with unparalleled military capabilities and significant soft power, but its relative dominance is contested by China's rapid economic growth, technological advancements, and assertive geopolitical strategies, particularly within the Indo-Pacific region. Concurrently, the European Union, despite internal challenges, wields substantial economic weight and normative influence through its regulatory frameworks and multilateral diplomacy.

This tripolar configuration embodies complex interdependencies and rivalries. Unlike the Cold War bipolarity, the relationships among these poles are not strictly adversarial; they involve strategic cooperation in areas, such as climate change, trade, and security, combined with fierce competition in technology, influence, and governance models. The tripolar system heightens the importance of diplomacy, alliance management, and institutional adaptability as each pole seeks to shape global norms and institutions to its advantage.

The notion of tripolarity—though less explored compared to bipolarity or multipolarity—has been gaining scholarly traction. Khanna (2008) was among the first to posit a "Second World" caught between three major poles: the United States, China, and Europe (Khanna, 2008). However, recent works by Allison and Lukin suggest that a Eurasian bloc, with Sino-Russian alignment at its core, may emerge as a distinct third pole, displacing the European Union as a coherent geopolitical actor (Lukin, 2022a, b).

Mearsheimer (2019) examine the structural forces undermining liberal internationalism (Mearsheimer, 2019), and Cox analyze a fragmented, interest-driven global system where regional hegemons exert localized dominance (Cox, 2012a, b).This aligns with Buzan and Wæver's (2003) Regional Security Complex Theory (RSCT), which underscores the relevance of spatial geographies in shaping global order (Buzan and Wæver 2003).

11.4 THEORETICAL AND CONCEPTUAL FRAMEWORKS

This study is firmly grounded in the theoretical paradigms of neorealism and multipolarity, both of which collectively offer a sophisticated analytical framework for examining the evolving role of BRICS within the contemporary international system. Neorealism, as articulated by *Waltz*, posits that the anarchic structure of the international order compels states to prioritize the accumulation of power as a means of ensuring their survival, thereby engendering enduring balance-of-power dynamics (Waltz, 1979). Within this framework, the strategic ascendance of BRICS can be interpreted as a calculated, coordinated response by pivotal emerging economies to contest entrenched Western dominance and to promote a more equitable and inclusive global order (Ikenberry, 2003).

This study is situated at the confluence of geoeconomics, international political economy, and strategic studies, drawing upon a constellation of theoretical paradigms to elucidate the redistribution of global power in the 21st century. The conceptual edifice of this research is anchored in four interrelated frameworks: Geoeconomic Theory, PTT, Tripolarity Theory, and the RSCT. Together, these frameworks provide a nuanced and multidimensional lens through which the deployment of economic instruments, institutional realignments, and strategic recalibrations can be analyzed within the evolving global order.

Complementing this neorealist lens is the theory of multipolarity, which asserts that the international system is undergoing a paradigmatic transition from a historically unipolar or bipolar structure toward a more diffuse and pluralistic configuration, characterized by the proliferation of influential actors across diverse geopolitical regions (Kupchan, 2012). The growing economic dynamism and assertive geopolitical engagement of BRICS nations mark a potential inflection point in the reconfiguration of global power, directly challenging the authority of traditional Western-led institutions, such as the International Monetary Fund and the World Bank (Stuenkel, 2015, 2016).

In addition, Dependency Theory—as formulated by Prebisch (1950) and subsequently advanced by *Cardoso and Faletto*—provides a critical interpretive lens through which to interrogate the enduring structural asymmetries embedded in the global economic system (Cardoso and Faletto, 1979). These systemic inequities, which disproportionately favor the Global North, are precisely what BRICS seeks to confront. By promoting South–South cooperation and establishing alternative financial institutions, notably the New Development Bank, BRICS endeavors to reduce dependency on advanced industrial economies and to construct more autonomous and sustainable pathways to development.

11.5 GEOECONOMIC THEORY

At its core, this inquiry is rooted in the principles of geoeconomics, a field that reconceptualizes economic instruments as strategic tools of geopolitical agency. Edward Luttwak (1990) notably captured this paradigm shift by asserting that the "logic of conflict" had begun to manifest through the "grammar of commerce." Geoeconomics fundamentally disrupts the traditional bifurcation of economics and geopolitics, positing that trade regimes, investment flows, financial coercion, and sanctions are increasingly wielded to achieve national strategic objectives without recourse to military engagement.

In this framework, the study critically examines mechanisms, such as de-dollarization, digital currency ecosystems, trade reorientation, and geostrategic infrastructure initiatives (e.g., the BRI) as tools of economic statecraft within an increasingly polarized international system. This approach facilitates a deeper understanding of how global influence is being recalibrated, not merely through conventional military superiority but via the deliberate orchestration of economic power.

11.6 POWER TRANSITION THEORY (PTT)

Originally articulated by Organski (1958) and subsequently expanded by Tammen (2000), PTT contends that the international system is most prone to conflict when a rising power approaches parity with, or threatens to surpass, the incumbent hegemon. PTT provides a compelling explanatory model for the escalating strategic rivalry between the United States and China, alongside the resurgence of Russia as a revisionist actor.

Through the lens of PTT, this study interrogates the behavior of great powers undergoing systemic transition—particularly how the United States endeavors to retain its hegemonic status, while China and the Eurasian bloc actively construct alternative institutional and normative frameworks. This theoretical construct further illuminates patterns of systemic volatility, hegemonic resilience, and opportunistic alliances within an increasingly multipolar and competitive global environment.

11.7 TRIPOLARITY THEORY

While traditional analyses of global order have primarily revolved around unipolar or bipolar paradigms, this study advances the concept of tripolarity as a defining characteristic of the contemporary international system. Tripolarity is conceptualized as the coalescence of three relatively autonomous and strategically assertive power centers: the United States, China, and a revitalized Eurasian bloc—anchored by Russia and augmented by actors, such as Iran, India, and Central Asian republics.

This framework allows for a reconceptualization of the global order not as a binary confrontation, but as a complex matrix of asymmetrical alignments, intersecting spheres of influence, and divergent governance ideologies. It illuminates the prevalence of strategic ambiguity, balancing behavior, and functional multipolarity, thereby offering a more granular understanding of the emerging tripartite configuration of global power.

11.8 REGIONAL SECURITY COMPLEX THEORY (RSCT)

Regional Security Council Theory posits that security interdependence is most acute within distinct geographical regions, wherein regional actors—rather than global hegemonic powers—become the primary architects of security regimes and economic integration when global governance structures prove inadequate.

Taken together, these theoretical perspectives—neorealism, multipolarity, and Dependency Theory—illuminate the complex interplay between structural constraints, collective agency, and transformative aspirations that underpin BRICS' efforts to recalibrate the architecture of global governance.

The conceptual framework underpinning this inquiry positions BRICS at the nexus of three mutually reinforcing and analytically significant dimensions:

Complex challenges: This dimension encompasses a broad spectrum of structural impediments that constrain BRICS' cohesion and geopolitical effectiveness. These include:

1. Heightened tensions between Russia and Western powers;
2. Intrinsic economic and political asymmetries among BRICS member states;
3. External pressures from dominant global actors (Wilson, 2015).

These systemic challenges are theorized not merely as operational difficulties but as structural conditions that test the internal coherence and strategic unity of the BRICS coalition.

Latent potential: Latent potential refers to the vast, though under-exploited, economic, technological, and demographic assets of BRICS nations. Together, these countries represent over 55% of the global population and command a significant share of the world's natural resource reserves.

Harnessing this latent potential necessitates enhanced intra-BRICS collaboration in:

1. Science, technology, and innovation;
2. Infrastructure development;
3. Human capital investment.

Realizing this potential is pivotal to articulating new paradigms for inclusive and sustainable development.

Strategic opportunities: This dimension captures the proactive capacity of BRICS to shape global governance through:

1. Institutional innovation (e.g., expanding and consolidating the New Development Bank);

2. Influencing agenda—setting processes within key multilateral platforms, such as the G20 and United Nations;
3. Advocating for a multipolar and representative world order (Hopewell, n.d.).

Such strategic opportunities highlight the coalition's potential not only as a reactive bloc but as a normative and institutional entrepreneur in the international arena.

Crucially, these three dimensions are interdependent. BRICS' ability to confront and navigate complex systemic challenges determines its success in mobilizing latent capabilities, which in turn shapes the extent to which it can leverage strategic opportunities. Together, they underscore BRICS' transformative potential in influencing the trajectory of a reimagined, post-Westphalian global order.

Within this analytical framework, the study explores the ascendancy of regionally anchored institutions—such as the Shanghai Cooperation Organisation (SCO), the Eurasian Economic Union (EAEU), and the Regional Comprehensive Economic Partnership (RCEP)—as endogenous responses to the perceived erosion of the liberal international order. It also facilitates an examination of intra-regional alignments, geostrategic buffer zones, and contested influence corridors, particularly across the Eurasian and Indo-Pacific theaters.

11.9 SYNTHESIS OF FRAMEWORKS

1. Collectively, these four frameworks coalesce into a comprehensive analytical matrix that enables a multidimensional exploration of the geoeconomic reconfiguration of global power;
2. Geoeconomic Theory explicates the strategic deployment of economic instruments;
3. PTT elucidates the systemic catalysts of geopolitical contention;
4. Tripolarity Theory conceptualizes the emergent balance of global influence;
5. RSCT contextualizes the rise of localized power constellations amid global fragmentation.
6. This synthesis furnishes a robust intellectual foundation for interrogating the structural, institutional, and strategic transformations underpinning the emergence of a tripolar world order in the 21st century.

11.10 FINDINGS AND RESULTS

The global economy may soon be divided into three major trading blocs, led respectively by the United States, China, and the European Union. In fact, European Commission President, Ursula von der Leyen remarked in April that *"The West as we knew it no longer exists."*

This trend toward deglobalization finds its roots in the intensifying geopolitical and economic rivalry between the United States and China. Recent developments surrounding the BRICS summit have further intensified discussions about reshaping the current global economic order, which has long been dominated by the United States in partnership with the European Union. As a result, the notion of the EU pursuing an independent geopolitical and economic trajectory is no longer implausible.

In this emerging tripolar world:

1. The U.S.-led bloc is projected to encompass most of the Western Hemisphere, along with its traditional allies in Asia and the Middle East.
2. The China-led bloc would likely include Russia, much of East and Central Asia, major African economies, and select nations in Latin America and the Middle East.
3. The EU bloc, though smaller, would consist of the European Union, the United Kingdom, Iceland, Norway, Switzerland, Turkey, and Ukraine—though there are concerns that Ukraine could face devastation akin to that of the former Yugoslavia.

According to a report by *Fortune*, this economic fragmentation could cost the global economy approximately \$3.8 trillion, owing to escalating global conflicts, a looming U.S. recession, geopolitical frictions, and an intensifying trade and tariff war.

A Wells Fargo analysis of data from 100 countries—which collectively represent 97% of global GDP and 93% of global exports—categorized these economies into the three proposed blocs. According to this breakdown, the U.S. bloc accounted for roughly 50% of global GDP in 2023, while the China and EU blocs each represented approximately 25%.

In a scenario where these three blocs each impose a 15% universal tariff on imports from the other two, Wells Fargo—using the Oxford Global Economic Model—estimated that global real GDP would grow only 9.1% between 2025 and 2029, compared to 11% under a baseline of largely unrestricted trade. This shortfall equates to a $3.8 trillion loss in global output over that five-year span—roughly $1800 per household of four.

Crucially, the model indicates that while the most severe growth-suppressing effects of these tariffs are experienced in the first two years, the global economy never fully rebounds to its baseline trajectory, suggesting that the consequences of economic division could be both immediate and enduring.

11.11 THE 2025 SUMMIT OF BRICS IN BRAZIL

BRICS is dedicated to reshaping global governance, increasing South–South cooperation, climate finance, cooperation on artificial intelligence, and new health programs to address inequalities in emerging countries. Trade settlement in local currencies is another major agenda, with the purpose of making the bloc less dependent on the U.S. dollar—a clear message to Washington that BRICS wants greater financial sovereignty.

Recently, it has expanded to include more countries like Egypt, Iran, Ethiopia, and the UAE, reflecting its growing ambitions.

The group represents:

1. Over 55% of the world's population;
2. About 40% of global GDP;
3. Significant reserves of natural resources and expanding technological capacity.

11.11.1 BRICS: ECONOMIC WEIGHT

As of 2025, the BRICS consortium—comprising Brazil, Russia, India, China, South Africa, alongside newly inducted members, such as Egypt, Iran, Ethiopia, and the UAE—accounts for approximately 35% of global GDP in nominal terms and exceeds 40% when measured at purchasing power parity (PPP), according to IMF estimates (2025). Collectively, these nations encompass nearly 55% of the world's population, underscoring their substantial demographic and economic heft.

11.11.2 BRICS: TRADE AND INVESTMENT

Intra-BRICS trade surpassed an impressive $900 billion in 2024, a testament to the bloc's burgeoning regional economic integration. Within the grouping, China retains its status as the preeminent economic powerhouse and principal trade partner; however, India has distinguished itself with the fastest GDP growth rate, registering an estimated 6.8% in 2024 (World Bank).

11.11.3 BRICS: ENERGY AND RESOURCES

Although BRICS nations indeed possess substantial reserves of both rare earth elements and fossil fuels, the oft-cited percentages necessitate careful scrutiny. In the wake of its 2024 expansion, the BRICS consortium collectively commands approximately 72% of the world's rare earth element reserves and around 42% of global oil and gas reserves. While the assertion that BRICS controls over 60% of the world's rare earth resources is broadly consistent with the revised estimate, the actual figure signifies a marked strategic leverage in critical supply chains. These rare earth elements—integral to high-technology industries, including electronics, renewable energy systems, and advanced defense technologies—are predominantly mined and processed by China, thereby amplifying international apprehensions surrounding supply chain fragility and the potential geostrategic instrumentalization of these resources (India Today, 2024). With respect to hydrocarbon reserves, the claim that BRICS nations hold 40% of the world's proven oil reserves slightly underrepresents the post-expansion figure, which now stands at approximately 42% (Info BRICS, 2024). Nonetheless, this proportion must be appraised in the broader context of global energy dynamics. The Organization of the Petroleum Exporting Countries (OPEC) continues to exert a dominant influence, maintaining control over an estimated 79.5% of the world's proven oil reserves as of 2023 (OPEC, 2023). This contrast between BRICS and OPEC underscores the imperative of employing precise and contemporaneous data when analyzing global energy geopolitics and resource-based power asymmetries.

BRICS nations collectively command over 60% of the world's rare earth element reserves, approximately 40% of proven global oil reserves (OPEC, 2023), and substantial deposits of critical minerals essential for the transition to green technologies, positioning the bloc as a pivotal actor in future energy and resource security landscapes.

11.11.4 BRICS: ALTERNATIVE FINANCIAL SYSTEMS

The New Development Bank (NDB) has cumulatively approved loans exceeding $40 billion since its inception, while recent initiatives to facilitate trade settlements in local currencies seek to curtail dependency on the U.S. dollar. Nonetheless, widespread adoption remains impeded by pronounced currency volatility and investor apprehensions.

11.11.5 BRICS: SOFT POWER AND DIPLOMACY

BRICS has increasingly emerged as a salient advocate for the Global South, amplifying the voices of developing economies on the international stage. However, the bloc continues to lack the diplomatic coherence and strategic alignment exhibited by forums, such as the G7, a deficiency laid bare during crises, like the Russia-Ukraine conflict, which exposed internal rifts.

11.11.6 BRICS: TECHNOLOGY AND INNOVATION GAP

While China demonstrably leads the grouping in critical domains, including artificial intelligence, semiconductors, and green technologies, pronounced disparities persist among other members. India exhibits considerable promise in information technology and space exploration, yet Brazil, Russia, and South Africa continue to trail in establishing robust digital infrastructures.

11.11.7 BRICS: INSTITUTIONAL EVOLUTION AND STRATEGIC RELEVANCE

Since its establishment of the New Development Bank (NDB) in 2015, BRICS has emerged as a credible institutional force in the global development landscape. The NDB has sanctioned over USD 39 billion in loans for infrastructure and sustainable development initiatives across member and non-member countries alike. Complementing this financial apparatus is the Contingent Reserve Arrangement (CRA)—a USD 100 billion pooled reserve fund designed to provide liquidity support to member states facing balance of payments crises, particularly in scenarios of speculative currency volatility.

In response to the increasing weaponization of the global financial system, BRICS has initiated efforts to construct alternative cross-border payment mechanisms aimed at reducing dependency on Western-dominated systems, such as SWIFT. These initiatives are partly geared toward mitigating the impact of unilateral sanctions, most notably those imposed on Russia by the United States and its allies. Furthermore, BRICS has progressively evolved into a multidimensional platform for policy coordination in areas, such as global public health, climate change mitigation, and food security—roles that gained increased salience following the U.S. withdrawal from the Paris Climate Accord.

11.12 INDIA'S ROLE IN BRICS

Since 2014, India's participation in BRICS under a right-leaning, market-oriented administration has been characterized by a calibrated diplomatic approach—one that avoids overt anti-Western posturing while actively shaping the bloc's strategic agenda. The Modi administration has emphasized thematic priorities within BRICS that include counterterrorism, balanced multipolarity, equitable global trade frameworks, and the advancement of the Sustainable Development Goals (SDGs).

India has played a prominent role in steering the operational ethos of the NDB, particularly in ensuring inclusive financial governance that amplifies the voices of smaller and developing economies. While maintaining strategic ties with the United States and European Union, India's continued engagement with BRICS reflects its desire to sustain a diversified foreign policy orientation and enhance its influence within non-Western multilateral groupings.

11.13 STRATEGIC OUTLOOK AND CHALLENGES

The Rio de Janeiro Summit arrives at a critical inflection point: U.S.-China tensions have intensified, protectionist rhetoric—particularly from U.S. President Trump—has resurfaced, and the Middle East remains engulfed in geopolitical instability. Concurrently, a large cohort of developing nations is grappling with sovereign debt distress, climate vulnerability, and constrained access to concessional finance.

In this volatile global context, BRICS' capacity to navigate internal strategic divergences—notably the complex bilateral relationship between China and India—will be instrumental in determining its future coherence and relevance. The bloc's potential to advocate substantive reforms within the United Nations, World Trade Organization (WTO), and World Bank remains a litmus test for its credibility as a viable counterweight to Western-dominated institutions, such as the G7.

With an expanding membership base, increasing normative assertiveness, and a pronounced emphasis on financial sovereignty, BRICS is signaling that the Global South demands a recalibrated role in global governance. The imperative is not merely symbolic inclusion, but a structural reordering of decision-making power to reflect the complex realities of the 21st century.

11.14 BRICS AND THE EMERGING GEOECONOMIC ORDER: DE-DOLLARIZATION, FINANCIAL SOVEREIGNTY, AND GLOBAL TRADE DYNAMICS

11.14.1 DE-DOLLARIZATION EFFORTS

BRICS member states have increasingly articulated their intention to reduce dependency on the U.S. dollar in international trade and finance. These efforts encompass a variety of measures:

1. Facilitating bilateral trade in local currencies, thereby minimizing exposure to dollar volatility and U.S. monetary policy.
2. Developing alternative payment infrastructures outside the SWIFT system—such as Russia's SPFS and China's CIPS—to insulate their economies from Western sanctions and surveillance.

The broader objective underpinning these initiatives is the construction of a multipolar currency ecosystem, designed to enhance financial sovereignty and mitigate systemic vulnerabilities induced by dollar-centric global finance.

11.15 THE NEW DEVELOPMENT BANK (NDB)

Established in 2014, NDB serves as a cornerstone of BRICS' institutional architecture. It operates with the following strategic imperatives:

1. Financing infrastructure and sustainable development projects in emerging and developing economies.
2. Offering a viable alternative to Bretton Woods institutions, like the International Monetary Fund (IMF) and the World Bank, which are often perceived as instruments of Western conditionality.
3. Issuing loans in local currencies, thereby reducing foreign exchange risk and enhancing borrower autonomy.

The NDB symbolizes the bloc's commitment to reforming the global development finance landscape from the periphery.

11.16 TOWARD A COMMON SETTLEMENT CURRENCY

Some BRICS leaders have proposed the creation of a common settlement currency, aimed at facilitating intra-BRICS trade without supplanting national currencies. If actualized, such a currency could:

1. Realign global trade patterns by offering a non-dollar-denominated transaction mechanism.
2. Serve as a geoeconomic buffer against Western financial instruments of control.

However, implementation faces formidable challenges—including macroeconomic asymmetries, geopolitical tensions, and institutional trust deficits—which must be addressed through sustained multilateral engagement.

11.17 GOLD AND COMMODITY-BACKED FINANCIAL INSTRUMENTS

There is growing interest within BRICS in designing commodity-backed financial architectures, particularly those anchored in gold reserves:

1. Russia and China have discussed mechanisms for gold-backed settlement systems that could potentially challenge the dominance of fiat currencies.
2. If successfully implemented with high levels of transparency and accountability, such systems could restore investor confidence and lend greater stability to cross-border finance.

11.18 DIGITAL FINANCE LEADERSHIP

BRICS nations are increasingly at the forefront of financial innovation:

1. China's digital yuan pilot projects underscore its ambition to lead the digital currency revolution and bypass legacy banking structures.
2. India's Unified Payments Interface (UPI) stands as a global benchmark in real-time digital payment infrastructure.
3. By pooling expertise, BRICS has the potential to accelerate cross-border Central Bank Digital Currency (CBDC) interoperability, advancing financial inclusion and regulatory sovereignty.

11.19 SHIFTING INVESTMENT FLOWS AND FINANCIAL SAFETY NETS

Instruments like the Contingent Reserve Arrangement (CRA) provide member states with a financial cushion in times of liquidity crises, reducing reliance on the IMF's conditional assistance. These mechanisms:

1. Enhance financial resilience among emerging economies.
2. Encourage a gradual South–South reallocation of capital and investment flows.
3. Reduce systemic dependence on volatile North Atlantic capital markets.

11.20 CHALLENGES TO THE BRICS FINANCIAL VISION

Despite the group's expanding ambition, several internal and external impediments persist:

1. Internal political and economic divergences: Vastly differing governance models, ranging from liberal democracies to authoritarian regimes, complicate the formulation of cohesive policies.
2. Geopolitical frictions: India-China territorial disputes and Russia's estrangement from the West create diplomatic fissures within the bloc.
3. Economic volatility: Recurrent recessions, political instability, and high unemployment in member states, such as Brazil and South Africa constrain collective growth trajectories.

4. Institutional immaturity: The NDB and CRA remain nascent compared to the financial firepower and influence of the IMF and World Bank.
5. Perception and legitimacy: Disparate foreign policy orientations and developmental priorities undermine BRICS' ability to present a united global front.
6. Currency vulnerability: BRICS currencies are often exposed to speculative attacks and external shocks, with no shared monetary or fiscal framework in place.

11.21 STRATEGIC OPPORTUNITIES FOR BRICS

Despite its constraints, BRICS holds immense transformative potential in the global economic order:

1. Economic growth and trade diversification:
   (a) The bloc enables members to reduce dependency on Western financial systems and expands access to new markets through initiatives, like the NDB and local currency trade settlements.
2. Enhanced global influence:
   (a) Representing 55% of the world's population and 40% of global GDP, BRICS offers its members enhanced negotiating capacity within international institutions, such as the UN, G20, and WTO.
3. South–South cooperation:
   (a) BRICS facilitates developmental knowledge-sharing, technology transfer, and collaborative poverty alleviation strategies across the Global South.
4. Infrastructure and development finance:
   (a) The NDB offers non-conditional, infrastructure-focused finance that better aligns with member states' domestic needs than traditional Western loans.
5. Technological and scientific collaboration:
   (a) Opportunities abound for joint research and development in AI, renewable energy, space technology, and digitalization.

6. Advancing de-dollarization:
   (a) Efforts to settle trade in national currencies and reduce exposure to USD fluctuations bolster financial autonomy and shield economies from extraterritorial sanctions.

11.22 THE ROAD AHEAD

BRICS has undeniably repositioned itself as a vital platform in the evolving global financial architecture. While its vision of a multipolar economic system faces considerable hurdles—ranging from intra-bloc rivalries to institutional limitations—its collective economic heft, expanding membership, and normative push for equity and autonomy provide significant momentum.

By fostering financial innovation, advocating reform in global governance structures, and championing the developmental interests of the Global South, BRICS is not merely challenging the status quo but redefining the contours of 21st-century global economic diplomacy.

Whether the bloc can translate its potential into structural influence will ultimately depend on its ability to overcome internal divergences and institutionalize robust mechanisms for cooperation. Nevertheless, BRICS' trajectory signals an irreversible shift toward a more diversified and decentralized global order—one where emerging powers no longer remain peripheral stakeholders but central architects.

11.23 CONCLUSION

This chapter has rigorously interrogated the evolving configurations of global power in the 21st century, foregrounding the pivotal role of geoeconomic dynamics in engendering a tripolar world order centered around the United States, China, and a revitalized Eurasian bloc. Anchored in the theoretical scaffolding of PTT, geoeconomics, RSCT, and tripolarity, the study reveals that economic statecraft, strategic decoupling, de-dollarization, and emergent regionalism are collectively hastening the erosion of the unipolar hegemonic paradigm.

The findings illuminate that this reconfiguration of power is neither abrupt nor linear; rather, it is governed by a constellation of interdependent structural transformations—including technological revolutions, demographic realignments, resource redistributions, and institutional recalibrations. Furthermore, the weaponization of interdependence and the strategic reordering of global trade and financial architectures are reshaping the very norms and instruments of international engagement.

Although the emergent tripolar configuration ostensibly promises a more balanced and pluralistic global structure, it simultaneously engenders considerable risks: the fragmentation of global governance, intensification of zero-sum strategic rivalries, and the proliferation of regional security dilemmas. The long-term viability of this order will largely depend on how principal actors navigate geoeconomic asymmetries, manage geopolitical anxieties, and reconcile normative divergences.

Amidst the profound realignment of global power structures and the erosion of long-standing alliances, it is imperative that India proactively recalibrates its foreign policy by deepening diplomatic, economic, and strategic engagements with pivotal states, such as China, Russia, Iran, North Korea, South Africa, Brazil, and Venezuela. As the international order transitions toward multipolarity, cultivating robust partnerships with these nations would not only reinforce India's strategic autonomy but also facilitate enhanced cooperation in critical domains, such as energy security, defence modernization, and technological exchange. Furthermore, such calibrated outreach would significantly strengthen South–South solidarity, positioning India as a central architect of an emerging, pluralistic global governance framework. In embracing this pragmatic realignment, India can more effectively mitigate external uncertainties while asserting a more consequential and sovereign role on the world stage.

11.24 RECOMMENDATIONS

Recalibrate multilateral institutions for geoeconomic equilibrium: There is an urgent imperative to reengineer international institutions so they more accurately reflect the emergent tripolar distribution of power. This entails expanding global representation, dismantling entrenched Western-centric institutional biases, and embedding enforceable mechanisms to counteract geoeconomic coercion and monetary hegemony.

Institutionalize strategic regionalism as a stabilizing mechanism: Regional organizations, such as ASEAN, the African Union, and BRICS+ must be strategically fortified to function as autonomous nodes of stability and integration within the tripolar constellation. Their capacity for economic convergence and political coordination should be enhanced to reduce structural dependencies on legacy Western frameworks.

Cultivate robust and adaptive economic sovereignty: States must prioritize investment in resilient economic architectures—particularly in the domains of digital infrastructure, critical supply chains, and energy security—to shield themselves from geoeconomic shocks and coercive dependencies. Strategic autonomy must be pursued with nuance, avoiding counterproductive isolationism while reinforcing national self-reliance.

Advance a normative pluralism in global governance: For the tripolar order to be sustainable, it must be undergirded by a pluralistic normative framework that accommodates ideological diversity without compromising on foundational principles, such as transparency, reciprocity, and the peaceful resolution of disputes.

Amplify South–South cooperation and collective agency: The Global South must be re-positioned from passive recipient to active architect within the tripolar order. Deepening intra-South collaboration in trade, technological innovation, and development finance is critical to correcting entrenched structural asymmetries and fostering a more equitable global order.

Embed scenario-based strategic foresight in policy formulation: Governments, multilateral institutions, and academic communities must institutionalize foresight-driven methodologies that enable anticipatory governance. Strategic scenario planning will be indispensable in navigating the volatility and uncertainty inherent in the ongoing geoeconomic transformation.

KEYWORDS

- **de-dollarization**
- **deglobalization**
- **multipolarity**
- **power transition theory**
- **regional security complex theory**
- **South–South cooperation**
- **tripolar world**

REFERENCES

Acharya, A. (2017a). *The end of American world order*. Polity Press.

Acharya, A. (2017b). *The making of global international relations: Origins and evolution of IR at its centenary*. Cambridge University Press.

Auer, R. C. (n. d.). *Rise of the central bank digital currencies: Drivers, approaches, and technologies*. BIS Working Papers.

Auer, R. E. (n. d.). Central bank digital currencies: motives, economic implications, and the research frontier. *Annual Review of Economics*, *13*(2021), 597–620.

Baldwin, R. (2016). *The great convergence: Information technology and the new globalization*. Harvard University Press.

Blackwill, R. D., & Harris, J. M. (2016). *War by other means: Geoeconomics and statecraft*. Harvard University Press.

Buzan, B., & Wæver, O. (2003). *Regions and powers: The structure of international security*. Cambridge University Press.

Cardoso, F. H., & Faletto, E. (1979). *Dependency and development in Latin America*. University of California Press.

Cox, M. (2012a). Global governance and liberal internationalism under stress: The state and emergence of regional powers. In: T. Dunne & B. Schmidt (Eds.,), *Contemporary security studies*. Oxford University Press.

Cox, M. (2012b). Power shifts, economic change and the decline of the west? *International Relations*, *26*(4), 369–388.

Eichengreen, B. (2011). *Exorbitant privilege: The rise and fall of the dollar and the future of the international monetary system*. Oxford University Press.

Ikenberry, G. J. (2003). *International relations theory and the Asia-pacific*. Columbia University Press.

India Today. (2024, March 15). Why China's dominance in rare earths poses a strategic risk. https://www.indiatoday.in.

Info BRICS. (2024). BRICS expansion boosts share in global resource reserves. https://infobrics.org.

Khanna, P. (2008). *The second world: Empires and influence in the new global order*. Random House.

Kupchan, C. A. (2012). *No one's world: The West, the rising rest, and the coming global turn*. Oxford University Press.

Lukin, A. (2022a). *China and Russia: The new rapprochement*. Polity Press.

Lukin, A. (2022b). The Eurasian pivot: Sino-Russian strategic alignment and the tripolar world. *Journal of Eurasian Studies*, *13*(1), 45–62.

Luttwak, E. N. (1990). From geopolitics to geoeconomics: Logic of conflict, grammar of commerce. *The National Interest*, *20*, 17–23.

Mearsheimer, J. J. (2019). The great delusion: Liberal dreams and international realities. Yale University Press.

OPEC. (2023). Annual statistical bulletin 2023. Organization of the Petroleum Exporting Countries: https://www.opec.org.

Organski, A. (1958). World Politics. Alfred A. Knopf.

Prasad, E. (2021). *The future of money: How the digital revolution is transforming currencies and finance*. Harvard University Press.

Prebisch, R. (1950). *The economic development of Latin America and its principal problems*. United Nations.

Rodrik, D. (2011). *The globalization paradox: Democracy and the future of the world economy*. W.W. Norton & Company.

SP Global. (2024, August 15). The evolution of deglobalization. https://www.spglobal.com/en/research-insights/market-insights/geopolitical-risk/evolution-of-deglobalization.

Stuenkel, O. (2015). *The BRICS and the future of global order*. Lexington Books.

Stuenkel, O. (2016). *Post-western world: How emerging powers are remaking global order*. Polity Press.

Subacchi, P. (2020a). *The cost of free money: How unfettered capital threatens our economic future*. Yale University Press.

Subacchi, P. (2020b). *The people's money: How China is building a global currency*. Columbia University Press.

Tammen, R. L. (2000). *Power transitions: Strategies for the 21st century*. Chatham House.

Waltz, K. N. (1979). *Theory of international politics*. McGraw-Hill.

Wilson, D. (2015). *The BRICS dream: New grouping or new hegemony*? Foreign Affairs.

Yilmaz, B. A. (2022a). The rise of the multipolar currency world. *Geopolitics*, *27*(1), 50–75.

Yilmaz, H. A. (2022b). The global currency reconfiguration: The rise of the renminbi and the decline of the US dollar? *Journal of International Economics*, *128*, 103447.

Index